THE BEST OF

SEXOLOGY

The
ILLUSTRATED MAGAZINE
of
SEX SCIENCE

Dedicated to Bettie Page

Bettie Page inspires in me much thinking about the subject of sexology. Here Bettie is seen between photographic modeling sessions at the Irving Klaw studio, reading a *Sexology* circa 1950s.

THE BEST OF
SEXOLOGY
The ILLUSTRATED MAGAZINE of SEX SCIENCE

Edited by Craig Yoe

RUNNING PRESS
PHILADELPHIA · LONDON

Special Thanks to Clizia Gussoni, Jayne Antipow,
Mike Hill, Luke McDonnell, Priya Rajdev, Warren Bernard,
Jon Anderson, and Jennifer Kasius. This book was fun to
put together thanks to their efforts between the covers.

Other books by the author:

Secret Identity: The Fetish Art of Superman's
Co-creator Joe Shuster (Abrams)

Clean Cartoonists' Dirty Drawings (Last Gasp)

9 8 7 6 5 4 3 2 1
Digit on the right indicates the number of this printing

Library of Congress Control Number: 2008928067

ISBN 978-0-7624-3323-0

Cover design by YOE®! Studio
Interior design by YOE®! Studio
Edited by Jennifer Kasius

Running Press Book Publishers
2300 Chestnut Street
Philadelphia, PA 19103-4371

Visit us on the web!
www.runningpress.com

INTRODUCTION

Hugo Gernsback

Born Hugo Gernsbacher, Hugo Gernsback (1884-1967), the man who put the "Oh, gee!" in *Sexology*, had three wives, so he must have known a little about sex. (The wives were serial, not simultaneous, so don't get TOO excited.) With these spouses Gernsback did his part to further the species. But Gernsback fathered more than human children: he's known famously as the "father of science fiction," having started the first magazine in that genre. You now hold in your hands (or hand, depending on how stimulating you find this material) Hugo's other brainchild, the pioneering sex magazine, *Sexology*. Gernsback rounded up scientists, doctors, and science fiction artists, and used his unusual crew to tell us about America's favorite pastime from their sometimes courageous, often kinky, always kooky viewpoint.

A worker at his father's winery ignited Hugo's lifetime-long interest in science when he showed him how to hook up wires, a battery, and a bell to make a ringer. In addition to the sound, Gernsback was fascinated by the "wonderful green sparks" the device emitted. When just 10 years old, Gernsback discovered an edition of Percival Lowell's book *Mars as the Abode of Life*. It's said the book's idea of life on Mars drove young Gernsback "into a two-day delirium, during which he babbled incessantly about Martians."

Gernsback learned English at a boarding school in Luxemburg, and there he discovered Mark Twain, which sparked an interest in America. After boarding school came the study of electrical engineering, during which he spent much of his time concocting a portable radio transmitter and a battery he dreamed would make him a wealthy man.

After his studies, Gernsback moved to Hoboken, New Jersey, and, with his battery, secured patent No. 842,950 in 1907. This and other inventions (Gernsback eventually had 80 patents) had varied success. Hugo invented the "Telimco Wireless Telegraph," which he marketed for $8.50 a piece. This device, according to ads Hugo wrote, promised to "keep your boy at home." It brought Gernsback wealth and got him out of the house to the finest theaters and restaurants in New York City, donning expensive clothes and a monocle for effect.

Hugo's electrical devices became a crusade for which he started his first of over 50 magazines. *Modern Electrics* launched in December of 1909 and sold an electrifying number of 10-cent copies with Gernsback publishing, editing, writing, doing the layouts, and selling the ads. In 1911 Gernsback spent a night writing a futuristic story set in 2660 to fill some empty space in the periodical. The space was filled before the tale was finished, so he made it a cliffhanger. His readers were intrigued with the adventure and eagerly wanted to know what transpired. The story continued

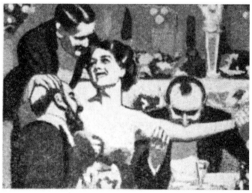

for 11 more installments and was eventually published as a book. Thus, Gernsback became associated with science fiction, a term that first appeared in one of his later magazines, *Science and Invention*. Gernsback had an all-fiction issue of *Science and Invention*, to which readers responded enthusiastically. Hugo was in turn inspired to start *Amazing Stories*, the first science fiction pulp. Speaking of amazing stories, teenagers Jerry Siegel and Joe Shuster saw a flying man on the cover of a 1928 issue, which provided much of the inspiration for the creation of Superman.

In recognition of Gernsback's seminal contributions, the prestigious Hugo Award, named after him, is science fiction fandom's highest honor.

Gernsback was always trying new magazines to expand his horizons and to fill his coffers. In an article in the January 1955 issue of *Sexology*, the origins of this ground-breaking magazine of Gernsback's were recalled: "The young publisher noted frequently during the twenties

Front cover of the first issue of Sexology, Summer, 1933.

that professional medical magazines paid scant attention to sexological topics. The general public knew little about sex, its functions, and its hygiene. It was a taboo subject, something 'nice' people never read about openly in the press or magazines." Gernsback asked himself, "Why keep one of man's greatest urges, the sex drive, and its many ramifications in perpetual darkness and human beings in prehistoric ignorance?"

Publishing *Sexology* in 1933, when America was belatedly stuck in, if not pre-historic times, Victorian times, was a bold move. The motivation was surely an equal part of evangelism and profiteering. Americans weren't supposed to read about sex, but maybe could under the guise of education. And what things Gernsback chose to educate our virgin-eyed and -eared grandparents on: vampire sex and homosexual chickens!

In spite of *Sexoloy*'s titillating approach to coitus, the sparks didn't exactly fly at first. *Sexology: The Illustrated Magazine of Sex Science* had a bit of "foreplay" to get beyond. For 15 years it just scraped by, and that was with Gernsback's notorious and disdained low rates for his publications' artists and writers. Gernsback consoled himself that he was ahead of his time and "kept up its publication, grinning, despite many handicaps and publishing problems." One of the problems during the first years of the magazine was that charges were filed against it for obscenity law violations. But in all cases the charges were eventually dismissed, a sign of America beginning to openly awaken to its populace's sexual side.

The first cover was pretty racy and must have caught the eyes of both the man and woman on the street and legislators alike. Future issues succumbed to a more *Readers Digest* all-type cover design, which possibly

"There are fetishists who derive sexual gratification from wet clothes, either on themselves or their sexual partner. Some get satisfaction from standing in a shower fully dressed."
— from Sexology, June, 1954

made the magazine a bit more respectable, able to get more prominent display at newstands (and, for sure, kept the art expenditures down).

One famous science fiction artist, who was a mainstay for *Sexology*'s first decades, was Frank R. Paul. Maybe not an artistic virtuoso, Paul did handily create brightly colored, pulpish futuristic cities, machines, and aliens for Gernback's *Amazing Stories* science fiction covers. His prolific output and perfunctory skills served well for *Sexology*'s many cutaway views of sex organs, illustrations of sex devices, and the great illustration you'll see in these pages of man's sex organs if they were a machine.

A more imaginative artist, who signed her name simply "Tina," started doing her thing between the covers of *Sexology* in the 1950s. Tina's one-name appellation was probably to keep her identity under wraps, rather than to facilitate recognition à la Cher or Madonna. Like Paul, her artistic skills were somewhat less than stellar, but there was no lack of imagination in her delineations. And Tina's work fit perfectly as the magazine moved into the swinging '60s. Her art had an almost LSD-fueled surrealism which I love. (Does anybody know Tina's whereabouts? I'd love to get in touch.)

The '60s and '70s were probably the beginning of the decline of *Sexology*. The long, hard-fought crusade for over-the-counter magazines to talk about sex eventually paved the way for *Playboy, Penthouse, Cosmopolitan, Playgirl,* and the thousands of men's and women's magazines that proliferated the nation's newsstands. The glossy colors and large format, the revealing photos, the fold-out pinup girls with staples in their navels, the cartoons, the pipe-puffing, robe-wearing, swinging editors of these publications made *Sexology* look old-fashioned in comparison. Gernsback's achievement of his goal to get America reading about sex was ironically the cause of *Sexology*'s demise, as his competitors went "full frontal" into the subject. *Sexology* gave it a last few moments of passion as the magazine began to talk about drugs, swinging, hippy-style free love, and sex organ worship, but the sex(ology) act reached a conclusion, if not a climax. Now all we have is the afterglow of the sparks.

Gernsback has to be given a lot of credit. He's a Sex Saint. While many of *Sexology*'s articles are unintentionally hilarious in retrospect, you might be surprised that, for the most part, you won't be laughing at puritanical denunciations of masturbation, homosexuality, or pre-marital sex. Rather, Gernsback and his writers were usually quite progressive and enlightened in those matters.

What is now most enjoyable and laugh-producing is how Gernsback's writers tried to keep the discussion lively, in recognition that talking about sex is never as fun as doing it. There are astonishing features on breast-feeding fathers, women with extra breasts, Hitler's sex life, rubber fetishism, discussions debating twin beds vs. singles, spotlights on notorious husband poisoners and, every couple of months, a feature about Eskimo sex.

The articles often tackle ludicrous subjects and the art is so bad it's good. While the magazine was actually pretty progressive, some of it reads as politically incorrect by today's nit-picking standards. But, as wacky, ill-conceived, ribald, silly, exotic, stimulating, funny, messy, strange, embarrassing, bizarre as sex always is, the sex is good.

The Ten Commandments
For a Happy Marital Life

1. Thou Shalt not covet another mate, while thou art wedded to thy present one.

2. Thou Shalt lead an intelligent sex life, neither making too great nor insufficient demands upon thy mate. Unsatisfactory sex life is a main cause of divorce.

3. Thou Shalt be patient and sympathetic in ALL thy intimate marital relations. Above all, strive for that perfect goal where thy mate's gratification is ALWAYS placed above thine own—the solid foundation of a lasting marriage.

4. Thou Shalt keep thy body clean, and thou shalt not hesitate to speak up when, unbeknownst to thy mate, an offensive body odor develops.

5. Thou Shalt court and caress thy mate frequently, as on thy honeymoon; thou shalt not let down in thine appearance either by day or by night, lest thy mate tire of thee and thy slovenliness.

6. Thou Shalt cultivate a healthy body, conceal minor ills, and *never* speak of them to thy mate. Stoicism in bearing discomfort and pain brings admiration; hypochondriasis evokes contempt.

7. Thou Shalt not leave on display evidence of minor body defects: false teeth, false hair, hearing aids, trusses, falsies or artificial eyes. When not worn, they distress thy mate.

8. Thou Shalt not foist thine in-laws or other relatives upon thy mate over lengthy periods, either in thy home or business—this practice destroys many marriages.

9. Thou Shalt not discuss money matters before thy mate leaves for work, during meals, and before bedtime. Adopt the inviolable rule of one-minute-money-discussions—*and watch the clock.* Quarrels about money are another great cause of divorce.

10. Thou Shalt not find fault, nor shalt thou nag, or use sarcasm unceasingly—lest thy mate leave thee for more pleasant company. Smiles and laughs are the best marital insurance.

SEXOLOGY, the pioneer sex education magazine, founded in 1933, has received over 97,000 letters from readers in all parts of the world since its inception.

Through the years, SEXOLOGY has collected a wealth of data on every imaginable sexological subject. Outstanding among the charted and tabulated information are facts about the Marital Status. Thus the magazine has obtained an excellent index as to what makes satisfactory marriages or unsatisfactory ones, and what are the main causes of divorce.

SEXOLOGY presents to those who embark on matrimony, and to the married, a short and vital set of rules of marital behavior.

CAN HUMANS

Man has ever speculated about the possibility of crossbreeding human beings and animals. The ancient myths constantly refer to the results of such interbreeding. Carnivals and side-shows today present apparent part-human-part-animal "specimens." A noted physician analyzes the possibility of this biological phenomenon from a scientific point of view in a penetrating article.

Gorilla and Woman, by Frémiet, noted French sculptor, exhibited at the Jardin des Plantes Museum in Paris. This figure expresses the age-old fears of bestiality and crossbreeding between apes and humans.—Brown Bros. Photo.

by D. O. Cauldwell, M.D., Sc.D.

WHAT are the difficulties of cross-breeding human beings and animals? Dr. Alfred C. Kinsey, America's foremost sexologist, in a special communication to SEXOLOGY on this subject, says:

A number of factors prevent interspecific crossing. Sometimes there are physiologic differences in the constitution of the egg and the sperm which make it impossible for the sperm to enter the egg. There may, of course, be differences in the gross anatomy of the two animals which will prevent successful copulation. The most important single factor is the number and the arrangement of the chromosomes in the egg and the sperm. During cell divisions, whether in the very early stages of embryonic growth, or in later stages of development, the chromosomes received from the mother and father parents arrange themselves so that the contributions from the two parents match in number and in chemical affinity, or else have an equivalence which may allow a chromosome from one parent to take a position opposite two or more chromosomes of the other parent. The mechanisms of chromosomal arrangements in cell division are described in any modern elementary text in Zoology or Botany, and especially in Genetics and Cytology texts.[1]

The two epoch-making studies by Dr. Kinsey on the sexual behavior of men and women offer

and ANIMALS CROSSBREED ?

The Lion in Love by Georges Gardet, celebrated French sculptor. This figure illustrates the tender loving care of a woman taming the "King of the Beasts."

indisputable evidence of the frequency of mating relations between human beings and animals today.

On the problem of crossbreeding, Dr. S. W. Britton, University of Virginia physiologist, has asserted:

"Anyone who says it can't be done needs to study up his theory. Men and apes are not far apart physiologically compared with other animals. We have already successfully cross-bred by artificial insemination. In the last ten years this method of breeding has taken such great strides that theoretically anything is now possible. The ideal plan would be to inseminate a female gorilla with semen from a man. . . ."[2]

On the other hand, most scientists agree that there have been no scientific proofs of any offspring resulting from matings between humans and animals. When there is indisputable evidence that such crossbreeding has taken place, SEXOLOGY, ever on the alert in such matters, will publish the facts. Until then, readers are here presented with the current established scientific opinion that *different species cannot interbreed.*

The ancients believed that humans and animals could mate and produce offspring. They also believed in the existence of mythical human-animal creatures whose ori-

A Zonkey—the result of cross-breeding a zebra and a donkey —shown standing beside its mother.— *Wide World photo.*

gin was attributed to the gods.

Reader's Letter

The following letter f r o m a reader gives a modern version of this ancient fantasy:

Editor, SEXOLOGY:

I do not agree with the findings of SEXOLOGY on some subjects. In your September issue, Mr. D. R., of New York (Question and Answer No. 3806), asked whether cross-breeding between humans and animals is possible. Your answer was that it is impossible.

I happen to be the owner of a specimen half-human-half-calf. This I have had on exhibition for a number of years on the carnival midway and at State Fairs. The specimen was born on a farm in Alabama several years ago.

Why is it a penitentiary offense for a man to be caught riding a sheep train? It is because the genitals of the female sheep are more like those of a human female than are the genitals of any other animal.

Only yesterday a woman who visited my show told me that she had seen another specimen that had a baby face and ears. Recently another fellow told me that he knew of a case of an army officer returning home on leave who found his wife about to give birth. When birth took place, the result was puppy dogs. Not long ago the same thing happened to a doctor's wife in a Texas city.

Science doesn't know everything. Scientists only surmise and have an opinion with little evidence supporting whatever they are working on.

Every week people tell me of cases of people they know who have given birth to puppy dogs. And by the way how about the *Rabbit Woman* who gave birth to 16 rabbits? Who is the father of the *Wolf Boy?* Could it not have been a wolf?

You had better do some checking from some of your readers and find out truth and facts.

Our reader, unfortunately, is guilty of numerous oversights. He says that "scientists only surmise w i t h little evidence supporting what they're working on." Yet he, himself, offers only *hearsay* stories instead of evidence, and no facts! The question constantly arises:

Since human-animal sexual contacts frequently take place, why cannot offspring result? Biologists and geneticists, for the most part, indicate that *no one knows why crossbreeding is impossible*. However, with m o d e r n biological knowledge, one can speculate about a number of reasons for the absence of fertilization and conception in animal-human mating.

Uterine and Vaginal Animals

Animal husbandrymen, upon initiating their first efforts to artificially inseminate animals, encountered undreamed of problems. In time they learned they must use different p r o c e d u r e s on *uterine types* of animals and *vaginal types*.

Humans, sheep, rabbits and cows are *vaginal* types. *Uterine* types are represented by dogs, horses and pigs. The periods of gestation in these animals are:

Uterine Types
Dog (bitch)	**Nine weeks**
Horse (mare)	**11 months**
Pig (sow)	**16 weeks**

Vaginal Types
Human (woman)	**Nine months**
Sheep (ewe)	**Five months**
Rabbits (doe)	**30 days**
Cows	**Nine months**

In *vaginal* types, semen for impregnation is deposited artificially directly into the vagina. Semen falling on the outer lips may find its way into the vagina and travel upward through the uterus into the fallopian tubes where, if a mature egg is waiting, fertilization may take place. *Vaginal* types require a much smaller quantity of semen than *uterine* types.

In *uterine* types the semen must be deposited directly i n t o the uterus. In the mare, for example, the uterus lies deeply within the abdominal cavity. It is for this reason that the stallion must have a genital organ of such immense length as compared with other species.

Barriers to Crossbreeding

When we consider the sheep (so often mentioned in folk-tales), our first question of compatibility in an

The Liger—the result of crossbreeding a lion (father) and a tiger (mother). "Shasta" measures 4 feet long and 30 inches tall. Her shoulders show father's influence, while otherwise she is marked pretty much like her mother.—*Wide World photo.*

attempt at cross-breeding with a human being suggests a primary obstacle—there is a *wide divergence in the periods of gestation.*

When we consider the dog and the human, even if artificial insemination is attempted so that the semen may be deposited in the animal's uterus, the period of gestation in either direction defeats us. It cannot be expected that the semen of the dog could impregnate a human female. His fertility is timed by Nature to that of a female who bears in nine weeks—not nine months!

Pursuing this a step further, we find another element of incompatibility. The *spermatozoa* (fertilizing agents) swim in the seminal fluid. It is this fluid that protects them against the greater heat of the female genital tract. The quantity of seminal fluid in proportion to the number of spermatozoa varies greatly in innumerable animals, including man.

In mythology the ancients, who so often believed in the impossible, conceived the idea that the Greek god Zeus was enamored of the beautiful Leda. But in the ancient Greek religion it would have been improper for a god to have consorted with a mortal. Zeus, therefore, changed himself into a beautiful swan and thus cohabited with Leda.

Man has been known to have sexual contact with certain fowls. Tales of cross-breeding between man and fowl (except among the ancients) seem to be missing. Yet, in a theoretical sense, were the sperm and egg all that are required for breeding, such cross-breeding might be as reasonable to suppose as other types.

But—consider the bat! The bat is a mammal capable of flight. *Estrus* (heat) and mating occur in the fall. The sperm remains alive inside the body of the female, who does not ovulate (mature eggs) until the following spring. The comparatively short-lived sperm of the human male would quickly die, were cross-breeding between these two mammals attempted.

Two other important factors now come in for consideration. One involves the eggs of numerous animals including man and the other a certain substance in the seminal fluid. The egg, whether human or animal, is enclosed in a tough outer coating. Hence there must be enough of a substance known as *hyaluronidase* in the seminal fluid to soften this outer covering to permit penetration of the spermatozoon. *Evidently there are vast ranges of difference between the resistance of eggs in various female animals (including women) and in the same individual at different times.* Likewise the hyaluronidase content of semen varies in different animals and in the same animal at different times. The general range of incompatibility is extremely great. The chemical content of the semen of any given male (human or animal) may be so scant as to be ineffective; although it may also be so powerful as to disintegrate the egg (ovum).

A striking phenomenon occurs in various rodents, but has been particularly observed in the rat. After copulation a part of the semen coagulates and forms a mu-

Actaeon, ancient mythological creature—half man, half stag —is being attacked by dogs. —New York Public Library.

cous plug w h i c h prevents any possibility of the escape of semen. This is another example of contrast between the reactions of the semen of various animals.

Interbreeding of Man and Ape

Let us c o n s i d e r man's nearest relatives, the apes. The gorilla, the largest of the man-like apes, once had a worse reputation for ferocity than he has today. An account was given in 1698 by an Englishman named Andrew Bartell, who was a prisoner of the Portuguese at A n g o l a. He described male apes as abducting women.[3] If we consider the account true, it would be reasonable to believe that were interbreeding between humans and apes possible, such would have resulted and the civilized world would have had accounts of the fact.

The chimpanzee, much smaller than the gorilla, appears to be more comparable to man in many ways than the great apes—the gorillas. Sexual contacts between human males and various animals were given statistical study by Kinsey and his associates. It was learned that such contacts were more frequent than had been supposed. No report has been made of cross-breeding as a result.

Because of these reasons, our conclusion is that so far humans and animals cannot interbreed.

So much is possible in science that it would be unreasonable to assert that the day will never come when humans and animals may interbreed.

Through vast study, research and application, man may some day find the secret of cross-breeding between humans and the higher animals. Today all the evidence indicates this is biologically impossible.

References

1—Dr. Alfred C. Kinsey, in a special letter addressed to SEXOLOGY magazine. Nov., 1954.

2—"Leda and the Swan," Hugo Gernsback; SEXOLOGY; Vol. XVIII, August, 1951.

3—"Wild Life the World Over," Wm. H. Wise & Co., Inc.; 1947.

Poverty is not a crime; but poverty, especially in a crowded city, is the cause of a great deal of abnormal sex living, especially among young men and women.

Poverty and Sex Immorality

By JACOB HUBLER, M.D.

THERE was a time, in pioneer America, when there was a great deal of hardship but not much actual poverty, so far as the real necessities of life were concerned. But, for the last five years, there has been actual poverty, in addition to the ordinary, everyday hardships of life that seem to be the common lot of almost everyone.

The present depression has played the most important part in shaping the sex life of our nation today. There are many ways in which the sexual trends and habits of the very poor differ from those of the comfortable or rich; and, the more millions of newly poor

people in a nation which has been accustomed to the better things in life, the more these differences are being felt.

The depression has driven our young people back to the schoolroom, and away from the life of marriage. Night schools, short college, post-graduate courses are filled with young persons of both sexes who feel that, while living cheaply, they can increase their education. Lacking employment, they keep on going to school. But there is, at the same time, no change in their sex emotions and their sex urges; these remain the same, and they must have some expression. SEXOLOGY is receiving many letters from these youths, all telling the same story: "I am in love; I would like to marry; BUT I cannot afford it. Perhaps, in a few years, my income will increase, and then I can live in a different manner. In the meantime, my fiancée and I are trying to be as happy as we can. Are we right in doing so?"

In a recent survey of over two hundred college graduates, who had finally married, over half stated that they had had frequent sexual relations, before marriage, with the person whom they finally married. It is evident that premarital sexual experience is one of the results of the depression; and that it is growing to be as frequent among the educated, as it has been among those of lower intelligence.

Hard times always cause an increase in clandestine prostitution. The professional "joy-seller" does nothing else; but thousands of girls who work for a living have had so much unemployment, such short hours and such limited incomes, that they have been driven into occupations which favor occasional prostitution. The dancer in the "taxi" dance hall, who receives a few cents for every dance—the "hostess" in the night club or cheap restaurant whose salary is dependent on the amount of liquor bought by the patrons for themselves, or for her—are women who find it almost necessary to become prostitutes to hold their positions and make a living wage. And, with the depression, many positions formerly held by women have been taken by men; thus increasing the unemployment of women and the necessity of addition to their income through sexual means.

In greater poverty, there is not only an increase in the sexual activity of the married but there is also an increase in the number of pregnancies. The refinements of contraception (birth control) are costly, and the poor married woman is unable to care for her "sexual hygiene" as perfectly as her rich sister. These pregnancies happen to women who feel that they are absolutely unable to finance the cost of childbirth and another infant; and so, the number of abortions is also increasing, with a pronounced lowering of the birth rate. Illegal abortion is a dangerous process, attended by loss of working time, invalidism and, often, death—and these things are only a part of the price society is paying for the present financial depression.

With poverty, come improper housing conditions. Houses, apartments and rooms are for rent; while two and even three families are living where one family lived in the prosperous period following the war. The two-car garage, promised to every family by grandiose politicians, has turned into the two-family home. This means crowding of individuals, and the resulting loss of that privacy which is one of the necessities of decency and morals. When over half a dozen persons, young and old, occupy the same bedroom, and over 40 persons use the same toilet facilities, immorality, corruption of the young and spread of venereal disease are bound to occur. For example, the ideal of family life is to have a separate bedroom for each growing child, as well as for each adult and married couple. Put these groups all together in one bedroom, and there at once comes a breaking down of moral standards.

With this crowding there comes a disappearance of the home and family life. The child is driven to the street for entertainment; the young people cannot stay at home because they have no privacy—perhaps not even a place to sit down. They leave the home, such as it is; often leave it for good, and become vagabonds. The average American read with sorrow a few years ago of the bands of adolescents roaming through Russia; but now they can read of thousands of their own young people, boys and girls, who are traveling cheaply and aimlessly around the country.

With poverty comes leisure—an abundance of idle time. Idleness without occupation, without financial means to purchase hobbies or entertainment. The man without a cent cannot even go to the cheapest movie; the destitute cannot rear tropical goldfish or collect postage stamps; these are the pastimes of the well-to-do. An unemployed man with a slight reserve can go to a baseball game; but the man with ten cents in his pocket has to spend it for food or a night's lodging.

Sex life, however, is cheap. Not the life of the married or of the man who spends a day's wages on prostitutes—but, for even the poorest, there are forms of sexual diversion which have no cost. Every adult tramp can secure the services of a boy tramp in return for protection, education in tramp life and an occasional meal. Poverty in this class means simply homosexuality, and this is far more common than is thought. And, since "misery loves company," many a man and woman, who are both poor, indulge in sexual life simply as a mutual method of passing the time and for the momentary relief from the dullness of life. And, when everything else is lacking or impossible, there always remains the satisfaction of the sexual urge by masturbation, which can be had by the poorest beggar.

Economic students of the past spoke of the gulf between the rich and the poor; for a while, it was thought that there was no such gulf in America, but we know now that there is. Poverty and destitution has become common experience. The great menace of the present is not so much in unemployment and financial troubles, as in the sexual trends which are the result of these conditions. Everybody has been helped, in almost every way, but there still remain, almost unrecognized, the dangers resulting from the smashing of our former sexual codes and the lowering of our standards of morals, which have come through poverty. There can be no real return of prosperity to America till something is done to counteract the warped sexual life and habits which have been forced on millions of our citizens by the intense poverty of the depression.

CURIOSITIES

A South Sea Island father with a charm representing the human embryo in his nose. This was supposed to facilitate the birth of the child, which he thereby acknowledged as his own.

An unusual example of tattoo art in Japan. Many peoples have attributed sexual significance to tattooing.—*Photo from European.*

← An interesting place-name. Intercourse is a small Amish country town in Pennsylvania.

Different peoples often develop different ideals of beauty and of what constitutes sexual attraction. To the right is a case of steatopygia, or enlarged buttocks, considered very desirable by some African tribes. →

Sex
Life
On
a

SOUTH SEA ISLAND

*While the sex life among the natives
of some South Sea Islands is far
different from the popular conception,
there are many phases which prove
extremely interesting to students of the
subject. The sex customs on the various
islands and island groups vary considerably; infidelity is strongly tabooed in
some tribes, while others may not
consider it a crime.*

by H. Winfield

T HE sex life of the South Sea
Islands is always interesting
to those who have only
dreamed about them. The daily
life of the natives on one of these
tropical isles—*Raroia*—is charm-
ingly described in a new book,
*"Raroia—Happy Island of the
South Seas,"* by Bengt Danielsson,
who spent considerable time there.
The author is an anthropologist
whose descriptions of the family
and sex life of the Raroian natives
are authoritative and intensely interesting.

Mr. Danielsson and his wife as-
sisted in childbirths and treated the
natives for various ailments. The
natives' childbirth methods are rudimentary and unsanitary. In accordance with native custom, the
newborn child is wrapped in old
rags or towels. One old custom
was to bathe all newborn babies
in the waters of a nearby lagoon.
The use of hot water and modern
antiseptic techniques were unknown to the natives and seemed
superfluous to the native women.
One cause of the many infant
deaths on the island is the great
number of premature births.

Sex life on Raroia is open and
candid, says Mr. Danielsson, and
the natives experience no sexual
difficulties or repressions. In the
old days sex life was unrestricted
and one had no trouble in finding
a sex partner. Marital fidelity was
not a rule to go by, but actually a
breach of the sex life code of rules.
Public sex games were indulged in,

Tahiti and neighboring island people usually have strong Melanese characteristics. The above photo is of a young Fiji Islander with a white-race admixture.

tion by not contacting visiting sailors and tourists. As most of the natives have had syphilis, many from birth, they make the dangerous mistake of not fearing this disease. Gonorrhea and other venereal diseases should command some respect.

Young people may have children in several trial marriages, the offspring being assigned to relatives to raise. If a couple cohabits for an appreciable length of time and has a number of children, they may consider going through a marriage ceremony. The principal elements of a wedding in Polynesia are the wedding feast and the Church ceremony. Raroians have

trial marriages resulting. Apparently the natives believed that in this "free and open" sex life the young people would have a better opportunity to find a suitable sex partner with whom to settle down and eventually marry. This "trial and error" sexual experience is apparently often pursued to this day.

Sexual experience is sampled at an early age on Raroia, young people having such sex contacts at an age of 12 to 13 years. Young girls become pregnant easily and often, as modern contraceptive techniques are unknown. Girls of 12 have become mothers and when they reach 15 years of age they are considered mature.

Venereal disease is known to the natives; they try to avoid infec-

Women of the South Sea Islands like to adorn their hair or person with flowers. This picture shows Tahitian women with Red Mango Blossoms, as painted by Paul Gauguin. Dressed simply in colorful loincloths they echo the vividness of the tropical foliage which grows in Tahiti.

little regard for the *legal* formality of marriage, as it involves too many complicating economic problems.

People often change marital partners on Raroia. One man, about fifty years old, could not remember how many wives he had had. He had never been legally (or ecclesiastically) married. He could not remember how many children had resulted from his numerous liasions.

Sometimes young people on this ideal tropical island tire of life there and go to Papeete or some other spot. Young women who, perchance, go to Papeete do not have to worry if they have no money or relatives there to support them. With their youth and beauty they will experience no difficulty in locating a man to "keep" them. They may, on the other hand, decide to become prostitutes. Such is life on one of the fairest and most salubrious isles of the South Pacific.

Bared breasts are a commonplace sight among native women of Tahiti and other South Sea islands like Raroia. Photo shows three beauties of the famed Tahiti.

● ● ●

Imaginary Sexual Partner

AN important study on "visual masturbatory fantasies" appeared last year in *Archives of General Psychiatry* (Oct. 1960). According to the author of the study, Dr. N. Lukianowicz, it is the first full-length paper in the Western literature on the subject of the fantasies which may accompany masturbation in youngsters and adults.

Dr. Lukianowicz studied 188 male and female patients, all of whom had different neurotic complaints, which they at least partially attributed to their persistent masturbation.

Among his findings and conclusions are the following:

● In children, adolescents and adults who are temporarily deprived of heterosexual outlet, masturbation may be regarded as a normal way of gratifying the sexual drive. It becomes abnormal "if it replaces the usual desire for the only biologically important heterosexual act."

● Masturbation is often accompanied by vivid visual imagery of erotic content. There is nothing abnormal or undesirable about this.

● There seems to be no causal relationship between masturbation, visual masturbatory fantasies, and psychiatric illness. Mental illness does not produce masturbation or the accompanying visual imagery, nor does indulgence in masturbation contribute to psychiatric disorder.

● It is not advisable for a physician to try to interfere with the practice of masturbation. Treatment should be limited to treatment of any abnormal accompanying psychological conditions.

WHY WOMEN BECOME
PROSTITUTES

by
Elio
Telarico, M.D.

An analysis of the psychological reasons which impel women to sell their sexual services.

VERY frequently it is maintained that progress and civilization—because of their many artificial restrictions on the free play of the instincts—may at

Dr. Telarico, a journalist of note as well as a tuberculosis specialist in Rome, Italy, has recently written a series of articles on prostitution for the Italian press.

the same time also promote the causes of prostitution. Some authors try to prove this by asserting that among those societies where sexual life is still uninhibited and free (such as among many primitive tribes) there is no prostitution. Thus, they claim prostitution must necessarily be the fruit of modern civilized life.

Such assertions are easily disproved by facts. First of all, prostitution is as old as mankind. Secondly, there is no society on earth that can be considered to be truly free of prostitution.

In the dark interior of the African continent, to give an instance, there are still many nomadic tribes living in tents under most primitive conditions of civilization. It often occurs that these small groups live in considerable isolation so that a few hundred persons, nearly all of them related to each other to some extent, have virtually no contact with neighboring groups. However, even in these very small human settlements, in addition to the family women, there are always three, four or five women who engage in prostitution.

Thus the causes must be due to some other factor than civilization.

At this point it is easy to jump to those false conclusions that were quite prevalent during the last century. At that time, the belief in the hereditary origin of prostitution was vigorously held by many students of this problem, by Italian sociologists in particular.

Modern concepts have changed these opinions to a very considerable extent. It is now known that delinquency is made easier, but not determined by any particular environmental or psychological factor.

According to modern anthropology, prostitution is the commonest and most widespread form of female delinquency. Two types of prostitutes may be differentiated: the woman that is drawn to the trade by an irresistible urge and the occasional prostitute who is forced into this occupation by economic and social reasons.

Quite recently, a theory has been gaining ground which attempts to merge the two concepts by admitting the possibility of existence of social delinquency and of medical delinquency.

Since the problem could not be resolved or even discussed from an organic or constitutional viewpoint (the presence of a crime-causing brain center has not been proved), this problem has so far been approached mainly within a framework of sociologic theories.

The influence of various factors has been evaluated, including poverty, unemployment, inadequate housing conditions, lack of hygiene, sexual promiscuity, lack of religious values, the war with all of its tragic consequences, social upheavals and political ideologies.

But all of these adverse influences, as we shall see, are only auxiliary factors. Extensive psychological studies have provided abundant evidence that the mental and emotional functioning of prostitutes shows undoubted signs of developmental arrest and of regression.

It has been clearly established that in many prostitutes mental development has somehow remained at the childhood level with its particularly strong tendency toward mythomania (a morbid tendency to lie or to exaggerate).

When one studies prostitutes between thirty and forty years of age, it is immediately quite apparent that their psychologic age has remained arrested at a level far behind their actual chronological age. These women seem actually very immature and behave quite unpredictably. They follow rather blindly any urges they may feel at the moment, with all the deviations arising from this type of emotional in-

Streetwalkers in a Japanese city.—Photo J. P. Clébert.

fantilism. It would certainly be erroneous, however, to impute this defect to any supposedly "hereditary condition." This has now been amply demonstrated by clinical experience.

We take as our definition of a prostitute "any woman who habitually has more or less ephemeral sexual relations with men in exchange for sums of money or other mercenary gain." Thus, we refer only to streetwalkers and "call girls." We are not discussing ladies of high society (who may on occasion prostitute themselves because of boredom or simply out of curiosity), intellectuals (who justify their desire for wide sexual experience with the need for evasion), or the few women who give up their honor

to some famous man (most frequently a politician with dictatorial tendencies).

The relationship between neurosis or psychosis and prostitution is particularly close. It is very easy to show that women plying the "jolly trade" are afflicted with an acute sense of inferiority, lack of sufficient confidence in themselves, a morbid craving for prestige, strong tendencies toward irresponsibility and a curious preference for elaborate psychological stratagems and artifices.

The artifice of being able to transform the sexual act into a precise monetary equivalent actually constitutes the essence of prostitution. The ability to do this again and again gives these women an illusory sensation of power, making them feel that they have all men at their feet.

It must be kept in mind that the primary element nearly always can be traced to the psychological situation in the girl's family. She feels hemmed in from all sides. She concludes more or less subconsciously that the only way open to her to assert her personality is stubborn opposition, and for this reason she assumes a rebellious attitude.

This personal reaction is further strengthened by social influences—the girl somehow perceives that women are held in a very subordinate position in comparison with men who have so many rights.

She therefore rebels against this minor rôle assigned her, becoming a suitable candidate for the "opposition neurosis" from which she can become ransomed in a symbolic and sad fashion by the choice of prostitution and the continuous depersonalization arising from multiple sexual relationships.

Not without its own deep significance is also the fact that many of these women try, often repeatedly, to take their own life by suicide, for their profession is actually also only a different way of punishing and destroying themselves.

In this same connection we can also consider for a moment those

Prostitutes who infested London and other large cities have now been driven off the street, but not out of existence, by punitive legislation.—
Photo J. P. Clébert.

An old drawing by Garnerey depicting a scene among ancient Greek courtesans.

very infrequent cases where previously normal family women suddenly become prostitutes after a severe psychologic shock (such as loss of a son, dramatic death by accident of the man they love, etc.).

To the persons who had known them before the event, the change seems quite incomprehensible, but in a way it is clearly understandable. These unfortunate persons suddenly lose all confidence in themselves; feeling so acutely the severe blow of destiny, their only apparent escape seems to be an attempt to free themselves of an impossible way of life. The persons revert to an infantile pattern of behavior, reacting in an incongruous manner.

There are some people who define as a prostitute any woman who has extramarital relations or who lives a relatively free sexual life, even when she does not make any attempt to turn her activities to financial or other personal advantage and seeks only pleasure in them.

General adoption of this definition would imply unjust condemnation of many women who do not belong in the category of prostitute at all. At the same time, this supports the contention that womanly honor and an independent sexual life are mutually incompatible. In our view, this contention is not only quite erroneous, but also harmful to society, since it actually extends and promotes the spread of prostitution.

The falsity of such contentions is confirmed by a number of facts. For instance, it is known that the problem of prostitution is much milder in those countries where independent sexual life in a woman is not regarded as connoting lack of honor.

We must guard against trying to create an artificial world in which there are only two types of women: the prostitutes on one side, and the ideal women on the other. Actually, such a division is impossible.

Arbitrary attempts to imply its existence are a powerful factor in promoting, in girls of a low intellectual level, the actual descent into prostitution with the consequences that derive therefrom: the desire to avenge themselves over their rivals, the honest women; and the morbid feeling of need for prestige in relation to men that makes these women so avid for money.

In this way, instead of the great and multiple privileges and responsibilities of matrimony they demand a comparable compensation for their services, thus trying to make up for the lack of affection and of respect for which they feel such an insatiable need.

In the *Magnificent Cuckold* by Crommelynk, a jealous husband sends his wife to prostitute herself with the whole village in order to ransom and purify herself from a supposed extramarital escapade. This is quite comparable to the manner in which these lost women behave when they try in this way to become idealized in order to acquire veneration on the part of men and thus a practical desexualization.

In a number of countries of northern Europe, "mercenary" love is gradually becoming displaced by "sexual comradeship" and premarital relations, which are not only widespread among young people of various social classes, but also quite matter-of-factly accepted by public opinion. It is precisely in these countries that prostitution is in the process of gradually becoming extinct.

At the same time another convention is disappearing: the habit of making absurdly sharp distinctions between ideal women to be exalted and those to be despised. This latter development has definite advantages for public morality—it implies the cracking of a dangerous barrier which was not the least cause of this ancient social ill of prostitution that still haunts the countries of the world.

● ● ●

The Chiriguanos of Southern Bolivia, in South America, house their young girls at puberty in a hammock suspended from the roof, where she must remain for a full month. During all this time no male may even look at her.

PHANTOM PREGNANCY

by Eugene B. Mozes, M.D.

Why do some women develop all the characteristic signs of pregnancy without actually being pregnant? Many cases have been reported of women who have literally "thought" themselves into spurious pregnancy.

PHANTOM or *spurious* pregnancy, sometimes called *feigned* or *hysterical* pregnancy, is one of the greatest medical curiosities. Known scientifically as *pseudocyesis,* it is a condition in which the woman firmly believes that she is pregnant, and develops the usual characteristic and distinguishing signs of pregnancy without being pregnant at all. She misses her periods, or they become extremely scanty; her abdomen swells gradually, as it would in ordinary pregnancy.

The signs sometimes deceive even a physician on superficial examination, as her abdomen may appear as large as that of a woman 8 or 9 months pregnant. One of the most striking symptoms is that the breasts usually become enlarged and sensitive, the area

A gynecologist in private practice, Dr. Mozes is Coroner of Stark County, Ohio, and a noted author.

around the nipples assuming a dark color like that during normal pregnancy, and milk of a thin consistency may be present. Almost every one of these women actually "feels" the movements of the baby, and some of them actually go through labor pains.

One of the most interesting of such cases was recently reported from Israel. The woman missed her menstrual period only twice, yet, insisting she was having labor pains, she presented herself at the maternity ward of a hospital. The obstetrician, after thorough examination, found that she was not pregnant at all and tried to convince her that her pregnancy was entirely imaginary. The woman could not be persuaded to leave the hospital. She was afraid she would lose the baby on the way home.

Other extreme cases of fancied labor pains have been noted in

←————————

A symbolic illustration by Tina of a false pregnancy. The woman, seriously disturbed emotionally, imagines herself pregnant so strongly that she actually develops the physical symptoms of pregnancy.

other hospitals. In one of these, the attending physician, in order to convince the woman that she was not pregnant, scraped her womb and showed her the tissues he obtained from it. He not only failed to convince her, but she was ready to sue the doctor for destroying her pregnancy.

The condition is far from purely imaginary. Many characteristic signs accompany it. Hippocrates, the "father of medicine," some 2,300 years ago described 12 cases he had observed. One of the most interesting cases having historical implication concerned the imaginary pregnancy of Queen Draga, the wife of the last king of the Obrenovitch dynasty of Serbia. Desiring to have an heir, the Queen's expectation was so strong that she finally persuaded herself she was pregnant. The famous Professor Snygirov, who was summoned from Russia, had great difficulty in convincing the Queen that she was a victim of pseudocyesis.

Up to the present time, 465 cases of pseudocyesis have been described in medical literature. The largest series observed so far was 27 patients in the Endocrine and Obstetric and Gynecologic Clinics of Jefferson Medical College Hospital, from July, 1946 to January, 1949. Drs. P. H. Fried, A. E. Rakoff and R. R. Schopbach made an extensive study which helped to clarify many interesting points involved in such pregnancies. These and previous studies firmly established the modern idea of pseudocyesis as the result of the interplay of psychological disturbances and an upset hormonal balance.

Psychological Factors

The basic psychological factor is an intense desire of the woman to become pregnant. Significantly, only one of these 27 women had a living child, although 16 of them had been pregnant previously, all but one losing their babies in the early or later part of pregnancy. Moreover, 24 of these had unsuccessfully tried, from 2 to 17 years, to become pregnant. Three other couples had made plans for early pregnancy because the husbands were elderly.

It was found that the underlying cause of this heightened desire to become pregnant was based on various factors. Some women became victims of imaginary pregnancy in their desire to secure a husband's wavering affection and to bolster a faltering marriage. Others were trying to prove that they were capable of becoming pregnant. Still others tried to compete with fertile women. And curiously, in some of these there was a strong guilt feeling, with actual fear of pregnancy, in which case the imaginary pregnancy must be regarded as a form of self-punishment.

Recently, an interesting case of pseudocyesis was reported from China, in which a deep-rooted desire for a child, together with great ignorance of sexual matters, resulted in false pregnancy. A 24-year-old Chinese woman, who had been married 5 years, came to the Obstetrical Service of the Kweilin Provincial Hospital. She was having regular labor pains that were, according to her calculation, more

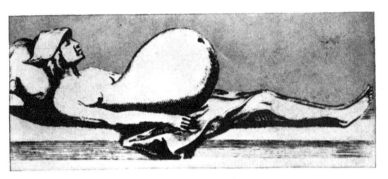

Large ovarian cyst which simulated pregnancy in a patient.—After drawing by Dr. Job van Meeckren, 1682.

than a month overdue. When she had missed her periods, being completely ignorant of such matters, the only explanation that occurred to her was that she was pregnant. During the first three months she had frequent nausea and vomiting, with typical "morning sickness." Five months later she "felt" movement, and her abdomen gradually became larger. She even had some swelling of the ankles

When she was examined at the hospital her nipples were found to be dark, as in normal pregnancy, the size of the breasts was increased and her abdomen was as large as in pregnancy of 7 to 8 months. She even had those stripes on the abdominal wall called *striae of pregnancy*. However, on internal examination, it was found that her womb was of normal size. After it was explained to her that her pregnancy was wholly imaginary, she accepted it without further argument although, interestingly, her abdomen remained large for a long time afterward. This easy acceptance is rather unusual, for the simple explanation that it is a false pregnancy is not sufficient in most cases.

An exactly opposite reaction in a similar case was recently described. It also illustrates the rôle that changed sexual satisfaction plays by arousing false hopes. After 7 years of childless marriage, during which both parties were intensely eager for a child, the husband was hospitalized as the result of an accident. When he came back from the hospital, a remarkable change came over the wife. Sexual relations became far more gratifying to her. As she herself expressed it: "It was marvelous. Felt different. More response to intercourse."

This heightened gratification led the woman to believe that now a child would be conceived. She developed sensitiveness of the breast and had morning sickness. Her abdomen became larger. After missing her periods for eight months, she had two successive pregnancy tests which were negative. Yet, even after this she was utterly unconvinced, questioning the accuracy of the tests. A week later

Queen Mary I of England had the delusion that she was pregnant and deceived not only herself but also the people of her kingdom.—*The Bettmann Archive.*

she experienced abdominal pains which she interpreted as labor pains. When the pains stopped, she exclaimed: "I felt the baby start and now it's finished. Something passed away."

Hormonal Disturbances

How do these signs of false pregnancy arise? The first clue was furnished some years ago by animal experiments. It was found that by stimulating the cervix of rats with a glass rod, the animals developed the exact counterpart of human false pregnancy. It was, furthermore, shown that the condition was due to the so-called "yellow body" (*corpus luteum*) in the ovary remaining present for an undue length of time because of an upset in hormonal balance.

The same thing happens in humans. The normal activity of the ovary depends on the hormones secreted by the pituitary gland. Great emotional upset is capable of influencing the function of the pituitary. One result of such upset is that the pituitary sends to the ovary an excessive amount of a hormone which causes the "yellow body" to be retained just as in normal pregnancy. A further effect is that the pituitary secretes a special hormone which activates the breast, thus causing secretion of milk. Furthermore, such hormonal unbalance leads to excessive fat deposit in the abdominal wall.

Women who imagine themselves to be pregnant are likely to be less active and to have an increased appetite. Thus they may gain as much as 25 to 50 pounds, further reinforcing their belief that they are pregnant. The increased appetite may be just as perverse as in real pregnancy, one such woman developing a craving for crab meat and ice cream. Many such women spend most of the time in bed, causing gas accumulation, which they misinterpret as fetal movements. Some claim they can feel a quickening as early as the first month, while others do not experience it until the eighth month. Intense preoccupation then can easily lead to imaginary labor pains.

While the intense desire for conception accounts for false pregnancy in susceptible married women, the psychological mechanism in unmarried girls is entirely different. Here, illicit intercourse may arouse a sense of guilt which, in turn, brings on great emotional disturbance, arousing the fear of

38

pregnancy. Imagined pregnancy leads to a further increase in guilt feeling, involving the entire body to such an extent that all the symptoms of false pregnancy appear. Psychological influences may be so strong that they are able to affect an ovary which either is not yet in a functional stage or has passed it by several years.

There have been cases of pseudocyesis described occurring in a girl 7 years old and, on the other extreme, in a woman past 79. A 53-year-old woman, well past change-of-life, developed all the symptoms of a false pregnancy because of her intense fear of losing her lover of many years.

Treatment

Although all the symptoms are wholly imaginary, it would be a great mistake to think that these women feign or simulate pregnancy consciously. Pregnancy to such a woman is real and actual. Bluntly telling the woman that she is not pregnant is useless and may be dangerous. One woman, after being informed of her true condition, threatened to commit suicide. A few of these women had as many as three or four similar episodes, obviously unwilling to accept the falseness of their pregnancies even after repeated experiences. A great ignorance is sometimes shown: some of these women "carry" the baby as long as two to four years, and even longer.

Effective treatment requires exploring the nature of the inner conflict which led to these false notions. Women who gain insight accept the condition much more readily. The value of psychotherapy was clearly evident in one woman. She had experienced three successive phantom pregnancies in the course of three years, despite the fact that she was informed that these episodes were actually false. However, after psychiatric treatment, allowing her to solve her inner problem, her cure had lasted more than three years at the time the report was made.

Recent researches showing the rôle of hormonal unbalance introduced an entirely new kind of treatment. By several injections,

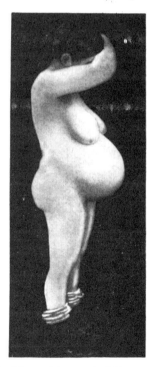

Pendulous abdomen simulating pregnancy in a woman suffering from rachitis (inflammatory disease of the vertebral column.)—Photo after Hirst.

the hormonal balance is completely restored and the woman again begins to menstruate regularly, which is usually sufficient to convince her that she was mistaken.

Eight of these patients who were sterile were treated by the new method of hormonal injection, plus psychotherapy. Not only did the periods return in a normal pattern, but four of the women really became pregnant.

The condition is much more frequent than is supposed. Consequently, it is important that a woman should never attempt to diagnose her own pregnancy; neither should she delay seeking medical advice if menstruation ceases for two or three weeks. In all such cases nowadays, a pregnancy test can readily prove the real nature of the pregnancy.

References

"Pseudocyesis: A Psychosomatic Study in Gynecology," by Paul H. Fried, M.D., et al. *Journal of the American Medical Association,* April 28, 1951, Vol. 145, pp. 1329-1335.

"Imaginary Pregnancy," by Maria Anaronova, M.D. *Medical Womans Journal,* 58:28-29. Sept.-Oct., 1951.

"Pseudocyesis: A Clinical Endocrine Study," by Drs. Paul Fried and A. E. Rakoff. *Archives of Neurology and Psychiatry,* 65:120-123. January, 1951.

"Pseudocyesis," by David D. Kulcsar, M.D. *Canadian Medical Association Journal,* 64:305-308, April, 1951.

"A Case of Pseudocyesis," by Desmond O'Neill, M.D. *British Medical Journal,* 245, July 23, 1955.

● ● ●

WOMEN'S SEX ACTIVITY

Sudden spurts of physical energy which wives whip up for no apparent reason invariably puzzle their more stable spouses.

DR. EDMOND J. FARRIS of Wistar Institute, Philadelphia, was not surprised at this. He now has discovered how married couples who want children can determine within a few hours the best time for conception.

Studying the sex activity of captive female rats, he found that the rats which were mated during periods of greatest physical activity became pregnant 97 per cent of the time. During such periods of physical activity there is, he believes, an increased activity of the animals' endocrine glands.

Testing the daily activity of women, he found that an increased output of sex hormones coincided with their greater physical energy.

Many couples who want children are childless because they miscalculate the period in which the wife is most likely to conceive. The testing methods of Dr. Farris offer hope to such couples. His methods have brought about prompt conception in difficult cases.

Sexology, January, 1947

● ● ●

In Every Male

"THERE is a tendency in every male to be something of a peeping tom. It is perhaps better this way (the striptease show) than to have people peep into your bedrooms at night."

—Dr. W. Holmes, Acting Head of Town Council, Ipoh, Malaya, issuing permit for striptease show.

YOUR SEX QUESTIONS ANSWERED

● **Breast Size (5585)**
Sexology, August, 1961

Sir:

My wife is 16 years of age. One of her breasts, the right one, is slightly smaller than her other one. Is there any method by which the smaller breast can be developed to the size of the other breast? Would exercise or massage help it to develop?

Mr. V. J., Indiana

▼

It is not at all unusual for the breasts of a woman to differ in size. As a matter of fact, it is more apt to be true than it is for the breasts to both be exactly the same in size. It is not advisable to attempt to do anything to change the size unless the difference is so great—we judge from your letter that this is not so—as to be what one might call actually disfiguring.

—Editor

● ● ●

● **Oversexed Husband (5426)**
Sexology, May, 1960

Sir:

Is there any medical help for an oversexed man? My husband and I have been married for nine years and are very much in love. But he is highly over-sexed and I cannot satisfy his needs because of sensitivity of the genital regions. He is a fine man, quiet and introverted with high moral standards.

Mrs. B. W., Nevada

Your husband is not necessarily "oversexed." Different individuals have varying sex needs and abilities and it is not always an easy matter for husband and wife to coordinate their desires.

Occasionally there are possible physical causes for such frequent sex urges. If so this should be established by medical examination. Sometimes there are psychiatric causes.

There are certain drugs or sedatives which can be administered by a physician, if he feels it necessary or advisable. These drugs however may too greatly cut down on sexual desire.

It may be necessary for you and your husband to realize that each of you must compromise in order to achieve as happy a sexual partnership as possible.

—Editor

● ● ●

● **Increasing Height (6184)**
Sexology, August, 1963

Dear Doctor: I am twenty years old and the mother of one child. I look about sixteen because I am only 4' 11". I hate being this short. My thirteen-year-old sister is as tall as I am. Do you know of any stretching exercises I could do, or anything else that would make me taller?

Mrs. W. C., New York

Answer: Since you are 20 years of age, you have probably reached the age at which further growth will probably not take place no matter what is done. At an earlier age it might have been possible by the administration of certain hormones to have increased your height slightly.

You still might consult an endocrinologist and see if anything could be done, although it would be doubtful that any real result could take place. An X-ray picture should be taken of your wrist to determine whether your bones have fused. If so, no further growth is possible.

There are no stretching exercises or anything of that kind that can be done that would help.

—Editor

41

A psychiatrist discusses the psychological disorder in which the sex drive is misdirected to an object or a part of the body.

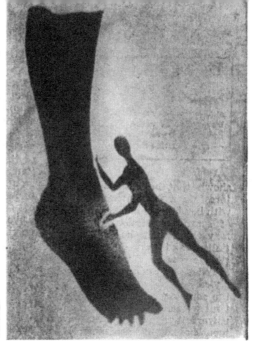

Lucy

Strange Sex Fixations

by Frank S. Caprio, M.D.

■ Fetishism refers to a type of sexual deviation wherein an individual is erotically attracted by a thing or a garment (such as underwear, or shoes) or by a certain part of a woman's body. This phenomenon occurs almost exclusively in men. The so-called *sexual fixation* may involve such parts of the female anatomy as the breasts, buttocks, thighs, legs, ankles, feet or hands.

Such an obsession with a *part* of the woman's body is sometimes

Dr. Caprio, a well-known Washington psychiatrist, is the author of "Helping Yourself with Psychiatry" and co-author of "Sexual Deviations."

called *partialism.* However, preoccupation is not always regarded as necessarily abnormal. It can exist as part of a man's *natural* sex interest.

Dr. Benjamin Karpman, author of *The Sexual Offender And His Offenses,* states:

"Almost every individual has certain anatomical preferences, and traces of partialism may be found in nearly everyone. A man who has a pronounced and overdeveloped interest in women's breasts, but who nevertheless engages in normal sexual intercourse, does not exemplify partialism. Before we may apply that term in such a case, it must be shown that he has no other interest in a woman; that contact with her breasts is his sole avenue of sexual expression. Only then may we say that he exhibits partialism and that he is a *paraphiliac* (sexual deviate)."

Today we see evidence in the styles and fashions emphasizing the semi-exposed bosoms of beautiful women. Men find themselves powerfully attracted to the prominent bosoms of such movie stars as Jayne Mansfield. One newspaper columnist sincerely believes that the country has gone bosom-minded!

Another actress became famous for her "million-dollar legs." This predilection for legs or breasts is common, and according to Dr. Karpman may be considered a *natural* component of the male sex drive.

However, there is a type of fetishism that comes to the attention of the psychiatrist. Deviates suffering from an abnormal type of partialism quite often get into difficulty with the law. The writer has had numerous occasions to examine sex offenders for the courts. One such offender admitted that he had a special attraction for women's buttocks.

When partialism produces impotence or a lack of desire for coitus, or leads to excessive self-gratification in preference to coitus or in some cases is accompanied by *sadistic* or *masochistic* gratification, then the condition can be definitely regarded as abnormal. (*Sadistic* refers to sexual pleasure gained through *inflicting* pain; *masochistic* to such pleasure received by *suffering* pain.)

According to psychoanalysts, partialism is caused by a fixation of the *libido* (sexual drive) in an immature stage of sexual development. Hence the condition is described by psychiatrists as a form of sexual immaturity. The sex drive becomes completely centered on the breasts or the buttocks, as the case may be, and intercourse becomes secondary.

A man whom I treated several years ago admitted that he had a breast fixation to the exclusion of regular marital intercourse. His wife, because of being deprived of sexual satisfaction, reported her husband's sexual problem to her physician, who in turn recommended psychiatric treatment.

The man related that during childhood he became fascinated by the sight of his mother's breasts; she made no effort to conceal them as she nursed his younger brothers and sisters. As a growing boy he was constantly preoccupied with mental pictures of women's breasts. Women with large bosoms attracted him; and he claimed that his wife had many physical features that reminded him of his mother.

This precocious interest among boys in their mother's breasts is not too uncommon. It does not always lead to fetishism. There are other factors that contribute to the development of this particular deviation, such as fear of impotence, fear of sex relations with women or a mother-fixation.

In another instance, a young married woman in the course of psychiatric treatment related how

her sexually deviated husband had an extreme erotic fixation on her buttocks. He was impotent. He showed very little interest in her breasts, had no particular desire for conventional coitus and was sexually stimulated only by her buttocks. His wife once asked him why he was so interested in that part of her body. He informed her that when he was eight years old he played a game with his sister involving the buttocks.

Another patient consulted the author because his wife had threatened to divorce him. She wanted to become pregnant and complained that her husband had never completed the sexual act. His exclusive interest in sex consisted of admiring her thighs and legs. Whenever he attempted intercourse, he experienced ejaculation before penetration.

Before marriage he had collected numerous pictures of women with well-shaped legs and resorted to sexual fantasies of women's legs. This fixation of his sex drive was traced to early adolescence. At the age of twelve he apparently became sexually stimulated as he watched his older sister putting on her stockings while dressing to go to work.

Even though he had been married three years, his wife was still a virgin. He availed himself of psychiatric treatment, in the course of which the insight he gained into the psychological cause of his condition enabled him to develop sufficient sexual maturity to achieve sex satisfaction for himself and his wife.

This partialism is closely allied to the more well-known kind of fetishism in which the deviate is attracted to feminine wearing apparel such as women's shoes, hair, gloves, handkerchiefs or undergarments.

In most cases, the patients are able to recall associations in childhood of an early sexual arousal with specific experiences that brought into sexual focus a particular part of the female anatomy. This played an important rôle in the shaping of their deviated adult patterns of sexuality.

As a rule, deviates who have a special preference for certain portions of the female anatomy are not dangerous. Like exhibitionists, they usually do not inflict any physical harm on women. They differ from rapists in this respect. Neither are they over-sexed. On the contrary, many of them suffer from impotence.

Uprooting the original experience of the episode that channeled their sex interests does not by itself lead to the cure. If the condition has persisted for a long time, it may require intensive psychotherapy and re-education.

THE PLANT FETISHER — By Tina

The Syngamophiliac derives sexual gratification in bringing about and observing fertilization in plants and animals. Our surrealist artist has here portrayed the aberrant (abnormal) syngamophiliac (who in this instance is a plant fetisher) watching with gratifying fascination the pollination of two orchids . . . (symbolized by the sprinkling of pollen by the tendril-like hand emerging from the upper orchid into the one extending from the lower orchid). The syngamophiliac often chooses the beautiful and exotic orchid in preference to all other flowers for pollination.

PREGNANT MEN

◆◆

One of the most extraordinary growths of the human body are parts of another human body. These parts may be an incomplete twin, or may be generated in some other obscure manner, not fully understood as yet by medical science. This most authoritative article gives full information on the unusual subject.

◆◆

by Maxwell Vidaver, M.D.

THE announcement, some years ago, by Dr. Russell Sweetser Ferguson of Manhattan Memorial Hospital, of a positive means of detecting a *teratoma* of the male testicle brings up a most interesting subject. A teratoma might be called a montrous* pregnancy in a man!

We are all aware that a man cannot bear children normally; but it is a well-known established fact that a teratoma, which is a "dermoid cyst," as explained below, may contain portions of the human structure—such as skin, hair, cartilage, bone, and even organs that are found in the developing foetus (unborn child). While this condition is rare in men, its counterpart occurs with relative frequency in the female ovary,

which is analogous to the male testicle. Cystic growths, as a general rule, are benign (mild and relatively harmless) tumors, never returning if completely extirpated. They should, however, be removed if detected, to avoid the danger of their suddenly assuming a malignant character. This rule is applicable, not alone to a cyst, but to any tumor wherever located.

Dr. Ferguson obtained the clue for his teratoma detector from the experiments of Dr. Bernhard Zondek of Germany. Dr. Zondek and his colleague Dr. Ascheim found that the pituitary gland (inside the skull, at the base of the brain) in the female enlarges during pregnancy, and produces two sex hormones (chemical substances) which are excreted in the urine. A urine analysis reveals the presence of these two hormones, and has proven an infallible test of pregnancy. Dr. Ferguson concluded that, if these hormones appeared in the urine in cases of normal pregnancy, they might appear in

---

*"Monsters" (Greek, Terata) are abnormal births, irrespective of size. Parts of the body may be either completely lacking, or duplicated—as with the organs of sex, in recorded cases, or the limbs, or vital organs, heart, head, chest. In the absence of the latter, of course, the monster cannot live. The word "monster" originally meant, only something shown as a curiosity—like the Siamese Twins, probably the world's most famous monsters.

the early stages of a developing teratoma. His reasoning proved correct. If the test is made during

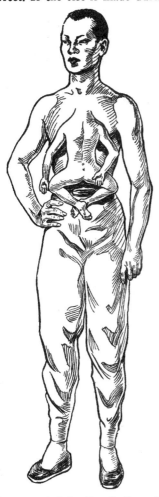

the early development of the foetal parts, (those like an unborn child's) the hormone reaction is strong and positive. In advanced cases of long standing, where the foetal parts have ceased to develop, the reaction is extremely weak, or even negative.

Dr. Zondek calls attention to a very interesting experiment in which a sexually immature mouse was injected with a concentrated solution of the urine of a pregnant female. Ovulation (this is the production of eggs) occurred in three or four days, just as if she were sexually fully developed. Dr. Zondek does not attempt to account for the strange action, merely recording the occurrence. He further states that if a male mouse is similarly injected, it causes a considerable enlargement of the seminal vesicles (attached to the testicles).

A teratoma is a dermoid cyst of the testicle. There are a great variety of cysts; and, while they are all classified as cystic tumors and in conformation resemble a *dermoid cyst,* ther contents are strikingly dissimilar.

The most interesting and extraordinary of this class of growth, is the dermoid cyst. It possesses all the earmarks of a pregnancy, and consists of a sac or bag comparable to the membranes in which the human foetus develops. It contains fluid, amniotic (amnion, the sac or "bag of waters" surrounding the child in the womb) in character, and has been known to harbor a completely formed foetus; though its most usual contents are foetal parts, such as hair, skin, cartilage, bones, and other portions of the infant structure.

The most frequent locations of

these extraordinary growths are the ovary in the female and the testicle in the male. The close relationship, structurally, between the ovary and the testicle accounts for its appearance in these two localities. In the testicle it is called a teratoma, but it is still just a plain dermoid cyst, masquerading under an alias. It may hide itself in an obscure corner, but it cannot alter its identity.

No adequate reason has yet been advanced, accounting logically for the existence of such a cyst. Innumerable theories have been suggested, and rejected as untenable. There is but one theory that seems to account for this anomalous growth. It is the sole theory that has successfully resisted the destructive test of time; and, while it has not been confirmed or proven, it is rational and seems to explain the existence of this odd condition.

We believe it should be identified as the *Embryonic** Theory of Cystic Formations.* The human ovum (egg) and all other ova, after impregnation (entrance of spermatozoa, or male cells) has occurred, undergo certain uniform alterations. We shall enter into an account of these embryological transformations, that follow in regular order, so far as their relationship to the formation of

these unusual cysts is concerned.

The ovum, after fertilization, divides into a vast number of cells, and is then known as the *blastoderm;* after further division, a differentiation occurs in the cell structure. Three distinct layers are

This tumor (teratoma) weighed 31 pounds before being removed. This Chinaman can't sit on a chair.

now discernible, the *ectoderm,* the *mesoderm* and the *entoderm.* (*Ecto*-outer; *meso*-middle; *ento,* inner; *derma,* skin). From these three groups of cells the various tissues, bones and organs ,of the human body are developed.

From the ectoderm are developed the central nervous system and the cutaneous (skin) structures; from the mesoderm are derived the muscular, circulatory

_____

**The "embryo" (from a Greek word meaning "to swell within") is any fertilized egg cell, human or otherwise, in its early stages of "germination". ("Germs" meant originally, the reproductive cells of higher organizations; bacteria are the "germs of disease" only figuratively, and not in the biological sense.) The human "ovum" or egg in its stage of growth is considered to be an "embryo" for about five weeks after fertilization; after which it is called the "foetus", up to the time of delivery.

portions of the body, the reproductive organs, and the connective tissue or framework of the various other organs; while the entoderm gives rise to the digestive tract (mouth, stomach, bowels, etc.) and the organs which are more or less intimately associated with it. The accepted theory of the formation of a dermoid cyst is that a few of these primitive cells remain dormant (inactive) in isolated localities of the body, yet are capable of development under

This bag contains the man's unborn twin —or at least a part.

favorable condition. Their predilection for the ovary and the testicle has never been satisfactorily explained. The presence of these embryonic cells in any particular individual is not evident, and can be determined only if development occurs. It requires some exciting incentive, such as an injury or an inflammatory condition, to cause these cells to start growth and development resulting in the formation of various parts of the human structure. We then have a condition resembling the early development of the ovum, and simulating an actual pregnancy. It is evident that the embryonic theory plausibly accounts for the formation of cystic tumors. It is an interesting subject, mysterious and strange, illustrating the extraordinary phenomenon that the embryonic cells possess the miraculous power of development, not alone to produce a definite complete creature, but to form only a few diversified parts of the body.

Dermoid cysts may appear in any portion of the body. Dr. H. Purdy called attention to a dermoid cyst, about the size of an apple, located just above the left eye, on the orbital ridge (bone under the eyebrow). Vision was completely shut off by the size of this tumor. Dermoid cysts in this locality are not unusual; but the statement by Dr. Purdy that, on opening the cyst, he found a foetus in the fourth week of embryological development (even though he reports that certain physical parts were missing) is a unique and startling announcement. An exhaustive literary search on the subject has failed to reveal a similar case.

It is true that ovarian (in the ovaries) dermoid cysts in women have been reported, in which a fully developed foetus was found; but these cases, we are more inclined to believe were aborted (arrested) ovarian pregnancies, which later took on a cystic character.

There is no record of a teratoma containing a partially-developed foetus, though portions of every conceivable part of the body have been found. The finding of teeth, however, seems to challenge belief. Dentition (formation of teeth) is not an embryological development, and therefore their presence must be regarded as questionable, if we accept the embryonic origin of dermoid cysts! (*Note.* See end of this article— *Editor.*)

Another theory of the internal teratoma is that it represents a double or twin birth, like those of fused, or inseparably connected twins. In those cases pregnancy starts as a normal twinning, but parts of the two bodies fuse and, as a result, individuals, such as the Siamese Twins, are produced. Any attempt, surgically, to separate such twins has always ended disastrously, for neither of the fused bodies has had all of the physical functionary organs.

A still more interesting instance of fusion is the growth of a partial body attached to the body of an otherwise normal human being. This condition is technically called an external teratoma. The *Encyclopaedia Britannica* cites the case of a Genoese, a well-built boy or man, who had such a growth attached to the lower end of his breast-bone. It was a well-formed child except for the lack of one leg; it breathed and slept, but had not digestive organs of its own. Geoffrey St. Hilaire describes a Chinaman who bore a rather ill-formed foetus in front of his abdomen; such freaks are frequently on exhibition in many countries.

The explanation which occurred to uneducated and uncivilized people was that such monstrosities were the result of sexual union between men and female animals, or between male animals and women. Strange as it may seem, the same idea prevails among the uninformed of our present social strata. By the Middle Ages, with a very intensive, though fantastic theory of a material group of devils, *Succubi* (female) and *Incubi* (male), the explanation evolved, wherever a child was born of an unusual shape, that it was the result of sexual union between a woman and an unearthly but amorous fiend of the air.

At the height of the miraculous, or at least it must have seemed so to the medieval mind, stand the cases of the true *Foetus* in *Foetu* (child within a child). These beings are formed by the actual enfolding beneath the abdominal (belly) skin, or even under the abdominal wall, of one foetus by another. The fully-developed and the inclosed child are really twins; where one has surrounded the other. The stronger embryo grows and is finally born; but the second twin, while continuing to live in the other abdominal cavity, remains stationary in size. When such a specimen was born, died at birth and was autopsied (dissected) the physician found, to his surprise, a fairly well developed foetus growing in the abdominal cavity of a male child. An excellent specimen of this type of abnormality was dissected and is preserved in the Hunterian Museum.

But occasionally the male child is born, apparently normal, yet, bearing in his abdominal cavity the little twin which he had absorbed during his foetal career. Such cases live on, apparently normal in health, till adolescence brings with it a rapid and intensive growth. The change is caused by the increased amount of the internal secretion of the testes (male sex glands). The miniature hidden foetus, which has been feeding all the time on the blood supply of its big brother, receives its share of the testicular secretion. It also responds by intensive growth, and soon an abdominal tumor is diagnosed. An operation reveals it to be peritoneal (within the belly) foetus, the highest type of teratoma; not always a complete human body, but clearly recognizable as a separate being. There does not seem to be any case of record where such an operation resulted in the surgical birth of a living child.

An extraordinary case of teratoma came under the care of Dr. R. J. Brines, of the Yencheng Sanitarium Hospital, in Honan, China. A young man of 24 had carried, since birth, a large tumor, which grew until it reached the size shown in the photographs. After much debate, it was removed; and the young man made a good recovery.

It was found that there was a small, but definitely formed, hand in the tumor. It was a teratoma!

At least ten thousand Chinese, says Dr. Brines, came to see "the baby" to which a man had given birth—and were highly disappointed at finding that it was only a hand.

Another case of an extraordinary teratoma was reported in Sept. 1946 in a dispatch to the *New York Herald Tribune,* from Tokyo:

Operating to remove an obstruction below the right eye of a nineteen-year-old girl, a surgeon at the Osaka Higher Medical School discovered a set of ten teeth there, the newspaper "Mainichi" reported.

The teeth, eight molars and two incisors, were found in a sac the size of a duck's egg. The case is unique in Japanese medical history. The discovery of atrophied parts of a human body, in addition to the teeth, led surgeons to believe the sac was actually a twin which never developed.

● ● ●

WE MUST PROTECT OUR ELDERS!

YOUTH may well view with alarm the conduct of its elders, judging from a report to the California Federation of Women's Clubs recently by Mrs. Grace Y. Hudson of Los Angeles. She made a survey of salacious magazine sales and reported: "We found 26 unfit to be read, and most of them are purchased by women over 40."

—*United Press dispatch from San Francisco, Calif.*

America's free-love experiment:

the Oneida Society

by Irving Mark, Ph.D., LL.B.

THE unique ideas of sex put into practice by the Oneida Community in New York State over one hundred years ago have always fascinated sexologists and social scientists. Nurtured in the New England soil of Putney, Vermont, in 1836, "Bible communism," as it was called, was transplanted to Oneida in 1848, the very year of the Communist Manifesto.

Disavowing private ownership of property and "property in women" vested through marriage, these social reformers took root there and continued to thrive on the practices of "complex marriage," *coitus reservatus* (intercourse without ejaculation) and eugenics until 1879.

John Humphrey Noyes, the founder of the Oneida Community, was born in Brattleboro, Vermont, on September 3, 1811. His father was a Dartmouth gradu-

---

Attorney, educator and historian, Dr. Mark is author of "Agrarian Conflicts in Colonial New York," and co-editor of "The Faith of Our Fathers."

ate with agnostic views, a businessman and Congressman. His mother, Polly Hayes, an aunt of President Rutherford B. Hayes, was known for her strong character. His sister married Larkin Mead, whose sons were to become eminent sculptors and architects.

Graduating from Dartmouth at the top of his class, he headed for law. But after a "religious awakening," he wound up at the theological seminary at Andover. From there he went to Divinity School at New Haven, where he established a "free church" based upon Perfectionist freedom from sense of guilt, free love, and spiritual marriage.

He became a seeker and preacher of Perfectionism. The trail led through Skid Row in lower Manhattan, to New Haven, where he launched *The Perfectionist,* and elsewhere in New England. Scandals arising from "bundling" by over-zealous Perfectionist converts drove him back to Putney. Here, he founded in 1836 a society of his followers known as "Bible Communists" who shared his

John Humphrey Noyes

Leader of the experiment
was a preacher
who instituted a system of
community love and exiled
those couples who practiced
sexual fidelity to each other.

views on community property and "complex marriage." In 1838 he proposed such marriage to Harriet Holton, a wealthy granddaughter of a former lieutenant-governor of Vermont.

His unique letter of proposal read: *"We can enter into no engagements with each other which shall limit the range of our affections as they are limited . . . by the fashions of this world. I desire and expect my yoke-fellow will love all who love God, whether man or woman . . . as freely as if she stood in no particular connection with me."*

When Harriet accepted the reciprocal freedom reserved under this marriage bond, Noyes wrote, in order that "there may be no mistake between us, that so far from regarding the act of sexual enjoyment as in itself unholy, I am sure that there is no sacrifice except that of the heart, that is more acceptable to God."

Around these views, Noyes and his wife gathered a Putney group including five others. By 1843, it had grown to 288 adults and nine children, all housed in three Perfectionist homes and, two years later, incorporated as the Putney Corporation of Perfectionists.

Although some of Noyes' ideas were in practice, it was not yet a community with common property ownership. The women were freed from the three-meals-a-day schedule, which was reduced to one. Moreover, Noyes set out to free women from "the tyranny of child bearing" which he regarded as a "relentless and mutilating trap" shackling man to his mate.

Noyes preached male "self-control" (i.e. *coitus reservatus*) as fully elaborated in his *Male Continence or Self-Control in Sexual Intercourse.*

Extolling its virtues, he declared: "My enjoyment was increased; my wife's experience was very satisfactory, as it had never been before. That we had escaped the horrors and fear of involuntary procreation was a great deliverance. It made a happy household."

"If it is beautiful and noble for the betrothed lover to respect the law of marriage in the midst of the glories of courtship," he added, "it may be even more noble and beautiful for the wedded lover to respect the laws of health and happiness in the midst of the ecstasies of sexual union."

On October 26, 1847, the inevitable storm broke over Putney. Noyes was arrested and charged with adultery. Released on bond, he was persuaded to flee to Massachusetts upon receiving news of warrants for two other members.

"I shall go," said Noyes, "not in cowardly flight from the law but to prevent the barbarians of Putney from lynching our innocent people."

Noyes sought and found a new haven on Oneida Creek, Madison County, New York, where his disciple Jonathon Burt had already hewn a saw-mill and cabins from the forest. To this bleak wilderness in February 1848, twenty-two adults and children fled from Putney, lashed by assaults, sheriff's attachments, and threats of prosecution.

By hard work, they built the foundations of the Oneida Community, sustaining themselves with farming, fruit-raising, and the sale of chairs and tables skillfully fashioned by them. More disciples came. By the end of the year the Community grew to 87 souls; by 1851 to over 200.

A branch community was even set up at Wallingford, Connecticut, where young persons with persistent "special, idolatrous attachments" were sent in exile.

The applicants were screened carefully. But two misfits got through. One was an old lecher, William Mills, who after expulsion sued the Community and had to be bought off with $2250. The other was the mentally unbalanced assassin of President James A. Garfield, Charles Guiteau, who unsuccessfully sought $9000 in blackmail.

But the Community had little financial success until it began manufacturing steel traps invented by Sewall Newhouse. This was

As a result of the practice of "complex marriage," children of the Oneida Community were raised as members of one common family. When monogamous marriage was restored in 1879, it was no easy matter to "match up" the families.—Culver.

soon followed by steel chains to be used with the traps; the canning of vegetables was begun in 1854, sewing and embroidering silk in 1866. In 1857 its inventoried evaluation was $67,000.

With the physical foundations firmly laid, Noyes returned to the elaboration of his ideas. Rejecting promiscuity as leading to anarchy, Noyes developed his theory of complex marriage more fully.

"Our Communities," he said, "are *families* as distinctly bounded and separated from promiscuous society as ordinary households. The tie that binds us together is as permanent and sacred, to say the least, as that of common marriage, for it is our religion. We receive no new members (except by deception and mistake) who do not give heart and hand to the family interest for life and for ever.

"Community of property extends just as far as freedom of love. Every man's care and every dollar of the common property are pledged for the maintenance and protection of the women and the education of the children of the Community."

He boldly separated sexual pleasure from reproduction. He argued forcefully against monogamous marriage, claiming that it was "not an institution of the Kingdom of Heaven."

"The abolishment of exclusiveness is involved in the love-relation required between all believers by the express injunction of Christ and the apostles, and by the whole tenor of the New Testament. The new commandment is, that we love one another, and that, not by pairs, as in the world, but *en masse*," he thundered.

"All experience testifies (the theory of the novels to the contrary notwithstanding), that sexual love is not naturally restricted to pairs. . . . On the contrary, the secret history of the human heart will bear out the assertion that it is capable of loving any number of times and any number of persons, and that the more it loves the more it can love."

Deploring the tendency of young and inexperienced lovers to seek each other out in "exclusive, idolatrous bonds," he thought it was better for older women to initiate young men into sex and older men, young women.

Influenced by Darwin and Galton, Noyes also put into practice his ideas on human eugenics, or stirpiculture" (selective breeding). He argued that as much scientific attention should be given to the physical improvement of human beings as was given to that of domestic animals.

Accordingly, in 1869 he announced that a committee on "stirpiculture" would shortly "select the parents of Community chil-

dren." Whereupon, three young Community women pledged:

"1. That we do not belong to ourselves in any respect, but that we do belong first to God, and second to Mr. Noyes as God's true representative.

"2. That we have no rights or personal feelings in respect to childbearing which shall . . . oppose . . . him in his choice of scientific combinations.

"3. That we will put aside all envy, childishness and self-seeking, and rejoice with those who are chosen candidates; that we will, if necessary, become martyrs of science, and cheerfully resign all desire to become mothers if for any reason Mr. Noyes deems us unfit for propagation. . . ."

Dutifully, thirty-eight young men pledged to offer themselves "to be used in forming any combinations that may seem to be desirable . . . [since] we are Mr. Noyes' true soldiers."

In the ten years that followed, 1869-79, one hundred carefully selected mothers and fathers reared 58 children, ten of whom claimed Mr. Noyes as father, who was 59 when the experiment began. The health, intelligence, and subsequent careers of many of these Community children in the "world outside" lent some weight to the value of Noyes' experiment, which he zealously supported in his "Scientific Propagation" (c. 1873).

The Community also practiced certain peculiarities of dress and diet. The women wore short dresses and pantalets and wore their hair short. Vegetables and fruits were exclusively eaten; meat, tea and coffee, only occasionally. Tobacco, intoxicants, profanity and obscenity were strictly prohibited. Under Noyes' supervision, "mutual criticism" became the principal means of discipline and government.

Their high reputation for industry, temperance, and freedom from profanity and crime, shielded the Community against serious disturbance. When a bill of indictment for immorality was brought against Noyes in 1850 it was quashed by the grand jury, when many witnesses were ready to attest that he and his group were "persons of good moral character."

But from 1873 to 1879, active measures against the Community were taken by several ecclesiastical bodies of New York, and by its archenemy Professor John M. Mears, culminating in a denunciatory resolution at a conference held at Syracuse University on February 14, 1879. Even from within the Community, a rival, James Towner, had insinuated that the Community was in mortal danger should some dissident charge Noyes with sexual irregularities.

Accordingly, on June 20, 1879, Noyes placed himself beyond the jurisdiction of New York by fleeing to Canada. From here on August 20, he urged his followers to give up complex marriage "not as renouncing belief in the principles and prospective finality of that institution, but in deference to public sentiment."

His proposition was accepted by the whole community on August 26, 1879. But it was no easy matter to "match up" the families. Most pairs arranged to be married under the laws of New York.

The renunciation of complex marriage was followed on January 1, 1881 by the transformation of the Oneida Community into the Oneida Community, Ltd., a cooperative joint stock company. Each adult member received an equal share of privately owned stock in the $600,000 issue.

The departure of the crusading spirit did not prevent the corporation from continuing to prosper. It has prospered even more in the twentieth century under the vigorous leadership of young men who had been born in the Community.

The Oneida experiment is a fascinating chapter in history. To the sexologist, the Community practice of *coitus reservatus,* with no apparent ill effects, is a challenging source of study. Eugenicists will continue to be interested in its large-scale experiment in human breeding, or stirpiculture." To the social scientist, the Oneida Community will always be significant as an experiment in Bible communism and complex marriage.

References

Orrmont, Arthur. *Love Cults and Faith Healers.* Ballantine, 1961.
Noyes, J. H. *History of American Socialism.* Philadelphia, 1870.
Noyes, Pierrepont B. *A Goodly Heritage.* Rinehart and Co., 1958.
"Oneida Community," *The Encyclopedia Britannica,* 13th edition, London, 1926.

• • •

so they say . . .

Reason for Sex Differences

"I REFUSE to adopt the all-too-often accepted neuro-physico-chemical reasons held responsible in our society for the differences in sexual response between male and female. I hold that two factors are chiefly responsible. One is the obvious anatomic arrangement that readily permits only the male to easily recognize sexual excitement and to achieve its culmination and satiation. The other is a result of generations of teachings and taboos that have relegated sexual relationships to a hush-hush area—for the female only. The latter has been promoted, partly at least, by the greater penalty and/or responsibility of pregnancy imposed on the female and partly by our economic order."

—*Dr. Ralph V. August in Fertility and Sterility.*

•

Infertile Couples

"SURVEYS indicate that for every 85 couples who have one or more children there are 15 unable to conceive any. However 35% to 40% of these infertile couples eventually can become parents if they seek medical help."

—*James C. Spaulding in the Milwaukee, Wis., Journal.*

•

Girls in Gangs

"OUR study revealed that the girls will do anything to please members of the gangs they are affiliated with. . . . They are promiscuous, truant and violent. They participate in petty theft, have out-of-wedlock pregnancies and use alcohol and narcotics excessively."

—*Arthur J. Rogers, Assistant to Commissioner of Youth Services in New York, as quoted in the N. Y. Times.*

For many years Adolf Hitler was the hated symbol of tyranny and lust for world conquest. Not until recently, however, have we had a close-up of the dictator's twisted and deviated sexual nature. In his frustrated sex life may be found much of the source of his terrific drive for political domination.

ADOLF HITLER'S
SECRET SEX LIFE

by Isadore Rubin, B.A., M.S. in Ed.

ADOLF HITLER'S lust for political power and for world conquest probably resulted in greater misery, destruction and death than have been caused by any single individual in history. The overwhelmingly cruel ambition of this would-be dictator of the world, we are now told, may have been in large part due to an effort to compensate for the fact that in the sexual sphere Hitler was completely frustrated and unable to complete the sex act with a single one of the many women with whom his name was linked.

Mr. Rubin, a writer and editor of long experience, is Assistant Publisher of SEXOLOGY and LUZ magazines.

Strong evidence for this belief is given in a recent book, *Unheard Witness,* written by one who for many years was closely connected with Hitler in the upper echelons of the Nazi leadership. Written by Harvard - educated Ernst (Putzi) Hanfstaengl, the book gives us a close-up of the dictator's twisted and deviated sex life.

According to Hanfstaengl, Hitler "was a case of a man who was neither fish, flesh nor fowl, neither fully homosexual nor fully heterosexual," a man who probably never had orthodox sex relations with any woman.

Completely impotent, Hitler was in turn sadistic and masochistic, finding these means to release his tremendous nervous energy, which could never find release in consummation of the sex act. (Sadism is deriving sexual gratification from mistreating or hurting one's partner, while masochism is deriving such gratification from being mistreated.)

Add to this the fact that he had hated his father, a stupid and brutal customs inspector, and adored his mother (in *Mein Kampf* he described himself as a *"Muttersöhnchen,"* a Mama's Boy) — and we begin to get the picture of the distorted sexual nature of the man.

Hitler's old army comrades had frequently told the story that his genital organs were almost freakishly underdeveloped and that he had shown considerable shame about disrobing himself in the intimate army situations. This was also possibly part of the underlying complex that he compensated for by his terrific drive for political domination.

According to those who knew him intimately, his demagogic gift of oratory was largely motivated by sexual reasons. The excitement of the frenzied crowds represented a substitute for the sexual response he could not evoke from a female partner, and his reaction to the audience was the counterpart of the sexual act. The last few minutes of his speeches have been described by his biographer as an "orgasm of words."

As is well known, Hitler was intimately connected with many women. There was the actress Leni Riefenstahl, who was more than willing to exchange her favors for privileges she obtained from Hitler for her film activities. There was also the long affair with Eva Braun, whom he married shortly before enacting their death pact.

Many women enjoyed his deviated intimacies and he was completely prepared to indulge in certain physical preliminaries. He would often make passionate advances to a number of women, including the wife of the author of *Unheard Witness*. Despite all this, he apparently could not carry these affairs to completion. He was always conscious of the fact that he could not have normal relations and felt insanely jealous of those who could.

Probably his deepest sexual attachment was to Geli Raubal, the daughter of his half-sister. This half incestuous affair, shrouded in mystery and touched with overtones of every kind of sex deviation, ended when Geli committed suicide in Hitler's apartment in the fall of 1931.

There were many mysterious details connected with her death. There were reports that the bridge of her nose had been broken and that her body showed other signs of maltreatment, but the affair was hushed up and never investigated.

Some time before her death, the girl was said to have called Hitler a "monster," remarking, "You would never believe the things he makes me do." Hitler at this period used to affect a heavy dog-whip and there are indications that he used it to make Geli submit to flagellation, or whipping, to bend her to his deviations.

It is known that he induced her to model for a series of pornographic sketches. He had drawn her with every anatomical detail, the kind of drawing that only an obsessed *voyeur*, or Peeping Tom, would put down on paper.

These sketches came to light when the Nazi party treasurer revealed that he was forced to buy them back from a man who had managed to obtain them and was trying to blackmail Hitler.

His voyeurism was also revealed by his taste for watching female cabaret artists and music hall acrobats—the less clothing they wore the better Hitler was said to have liked it. One of them, who had more intimate dealings with Hitler, later remarked that Hitler was

"just an old *voyeur*."

This compulsion may also explain why Hitler's favorite work of art was Corregio's "Leda and the Swan." This subject—one of the frankest sexual themes in the history of art—became almost an obsession with him. Any artist who submitted a painting with this as his subject was sure to be awarded a gold medal at any of the Nazi exhibitions.

It is more than interesting to note that one of Hitler's favorite films was "King Kong"—the story of a gargantuan ape who fell in love with a beautiful young girl and then went berserk. The film held Hitler absolutely spell-bound and he insisted that it be shown again and again. Perhaps to the impotent Hitler this story represented in fantasy the symbol of tremendous sexual power.

It has always been a matter for comment that from the beginning Hitler surrounded himself with homosexuals among the party faithful. This may have been due not only to his sexual inclinations. Hitler was also conscious of the fact that married men with children would not be his most

Hitler's favorite theme in art was that of Leda and the Swan—one of the frankest sexual themes in the history of art. Taken from ancient mythology, the story described how Jupiter, king of the gods, had assumed the guise of a swan in order to seduce Leda. Painting shown here is by the celebrated Leonardo da Vinci.—From the Spiridon Collection, Rome, Italy.

Hitler was held spell-bound by the American film "King Kong," story of a gigantic ape which fell in love with a beautiful young girl. Perhaps to the impotent Hitler the story represented the symbol of tremendous sexual power which he could achieve only in fantasy.

enthusiastic followers or reckless participants in the street-fighting his party used as one of the means of coming into power.

Of course it would be a great over-simplification to exaggerate the rôle played by one individual in changing the course of world history. It is also easy to over-emphasize the sexual motivations of Hitler's political ambitions. But there is little doubt that a distorted and frustrated sex life played its share in creating Hitler's megalomania and in throwing the world into a period of utmost turmoil and misery for well over a decade and a half.

● ● ●

SEX AMONG BIRDS

SEXUAL wooing among birds varies widely, according to the *National Geographic Society*. If the male *owl* sees a female he likes, he hoots at her in his most loving manner. Later, both the male and the female owls hoot. If the female owl is receptive to the male's attentions, she must change the tone of her hoot. After this salutation the male and female owls fly off together.

The male *penguin* courts the female by walking with her along the beach. If he is interested in wooing her further, he offers her a small stone or pebble. If the female accepts the pebble in her bill, the male then knows that he can pursue his courting.

Many birds offer gifts of some kind when they become suitors. The male *tern* may hold a fish cross-wise in his beak. Twigs are offered as a present by the *night heron;* they are a hint to the female that she should set up a nest.

CHASTISING THRILLS

by G. Mason Williams

"**O**H, Mother!" (whack!) "Please don't spank me!" (whack!) "I'll be good!" That conversation, heard in an adjoining room, would indicate that a small boy or girl was being punished by an irate parent for some fault of omission or commission, and was pleading for a mitigation of the penalty.

It might, also, with the same words, but something of a difference of pitch in the voice, indicate that a middle-aged or elderly man was seeking a thrill which was eminently satisfying to him, although physically painful. Every now and then the police of a large city interrupt such a rendezvous, and its description in the newspapers causes a certain degree of wonderment.

The patron described above is what is called a *masochist;* he may vary in his desires from a liberal spanking to a whipping which draws the blood from bare flesh. Years ago, in European papers, advertisements were not uncommon for customers of this kind; they offered "massage" or "English lessons"—the latter a phrase to be explained later—or other apparently legitimate services.

Not all spankings and beatings are pure punishment. Behind most corporal punishment lurks quite a different sensation, often masked to the spanker himself. The present article, by an authority in his field, makes this clear.

To explain this curious aberration, which is of a sexual nature, sometimes added to and supplementing n o r m a l instincts, and sometimes fully replacing them, would seem more difficult than to account for the apparently opposite tendency to inflict pain, which is called *sadism* and which also finds professional caterers. Almost anyone likes at times to give a certain amount of pain or annoyance to others, whether in anger or in jest. But a careful observation of the type of illustrations and reading matter intended for those who have special interest in this subject shows that the *masochist* takes an interest in the garb and the bosom, especially, of his corrector. We may follow the clew and say that, in his subjection to a domineering woman, of superior vigor, if possible, and stately presence, we have a return to the infantile mind. The mature, perhaps senile, man is imagining himself a child again with no worries and troubles, except the immediate one of physical punishment. Letters of *masochists* indicate, in many cases, that as children they were frequently beaten, whether systematically or capriciously, by their mothers. In this case, undoubtedly, we have the "mother complex" of which the psychoanalysts are warning us as a subconscious feature of most adult male mentality. The insistence on the breasts indicates a very early stage of juvenility—one in which this is the most conspicuous maternal feature.

More rarely, but undoubtedly, the *masochist* sometimes seeks to undergo punishment from a per-

The old Romans found a frenzied mass delight in watching the lions fall upon and devour the heinous criminals—among whom they classed all Christians—exposed for punishment in the arena. Incidentally, the picture is wrong; v i c t i m s were naked, for the lions' convenience.

son of his own sex. A famous historical incident is that of a British general, Sir Eyre Coote, who after his return from victories in India became involved in a peculiar scandal. He visited his old school, where he had frequently been punished as a lad; talked matters over with the boys, and paid some of them to take a few strokes with the birch; and then presented himself, in schoolboy fashion, for a whipping on the bare flesh. At this point, the school authorities detected the affair and called for the constable. But here, again, we see the attempt to be a boy again, at the cost of suffering the pains and penalties of that condition.

(The phrase, "English lessons," alluded to the method of punishment with the birch rod, retained in English schools long after its abandonment elsewhere, and until the present year a statutory method of dealing with boy delinquents. It is now reserved solely for pupils at a few very aristocratic schools where the sons of the wealthy are educated to become the Empire's future leading public officials. A century or so ago, a boy was hardly considered to have really become a member of his school till he had been flogged, publicly; and former students of Eton College, headed by a peer of the realm, one night stole out of the school precincts the "block" on which all had knelt to be whipped, to form the principal decoration of a club which commemorated their school experiences, of which this was the most typical.)

All *masochists,* however, do not carry their passion to this extent. We have all heard the phrase, "He's a glutton for punishment," applied to someone who seems to court defeats and humiliations. The condition of *masochism,* which is fundamentally linked with the sexual nature, accepts ill-treatment, contempt, humiliation as a *substitute* for blows, no less than in addition to them. The *masochist* nature enjoys a scolding— being put in one's place. In some rather barbaric countries, we are told, a woman whose husband did not beat her felt disappointed, because it was a sign that he had lost interest in her; a whip was

an appropriate wedding gift. It has been suggested by the modern psychologist that the very ill-treatment of a wife may cause her to be drawn more and more to a husband, when all the world wonders why she does not leave him and sue for a divorce.

Then, too, there has long been a feeling that suffering in this world is a means of acquiring virtue. The Hindu fakirs who repose on a bed of spikes feel that, for every discomfort (and, undoubtedly, they get used to it, like the Westerners who used to wear an undershirt of hair-cloth for the same reason), they will be rewarded with interest in the hereafter.

The *masochists* have existed at least since ancient days, as the Greek and Roman classics tell us; they were found among the American Indians, the Africans, the South Sea Islanders, who inflicted pain and mutilations on themselves to prove their manhood and assure themselves of their places in the tribe. The rite of circumcision, performed among such people at puberty, the knocking out of teeth, cutting and beating were part of the initiation of boys into manhood; and the youths under test had to bear them with apparent unconcern. Among even so civilized a people as the Greeks, boys were whipped before the shrine of Diana, as an offering to the goddess, and those who endured best were honored like the victors in athletics.

This aberration, though of very ancient date, found a name only in the nineteenth century, from an Austrian novelist. Sacher-Masoch, whose writings dwelt on the felicity of being a slave to a cruel and capricious mistress, a *Domina* (Latin for "Head-female-of-the-house"). Yet, except in this odd particular, the *masochist* male may not seem effeminate; nor is it necessary that the *sadistic* woman appear especially masculine, though the type is commonly represented as such.

To differentiate the *sadist* from the normal is harder; there is no definite line. The customs of the human race have been, in many particulars, *sadistic* since the memory of man can recall. Our own ancestors t o o k something more than a purely judicial delight in witnessing the execution, or corporal punishment, in public of both male and female offenders. To them this was not a rare event, particularly if they lived in a city; it was almost as readily available as a moving-picture show is now. They took their children to witness the performance as a moral lesson; and the latter might be encouraged to pelt criminals fastened in the stocks, as their elders hurled stones and cats at the more heinous offenders who were set in the pillory. Setting dogs on a bull or a bear was a favorite amusement, and the sour-visaged Puritans who objected to it were regarded as enemies of all joy of life. The husband beat his wife, and both beat the children when they had escaped from the inflictions of the schoolmaster. Yet all writers then praised the growing humanity of the age, as compared to Roman days, when the heads of the state sent hundreds of men and animals

into the arena to kill and be killed as a public amusement, and the householder could crucify his slave in the backyard if the unfortunate committed a trivial fault.

With all this racial inheritance, it is not to be wondered at that occasional acts of cruelty appear among ourselves. The "sex crimes" which make the headlines are, usually murders—sometimes deliberate, sometimes performed to silence

"The Domina"—an old sketch of "wish-fulfillment" type, showing the trend of the artist's mind.

a victim. But when a stepmother, annoyed at her husband, beats his child cruelly (as is frequently reported), that too is a sexual offense even though the offender, as frequently is the case, is quite unconscious of this fact. And, in many cases, the "laying on of hands" between husband and wife is a sexual act which takes the place of, and gives some of the emotional satisfaction, of the normal marital act. The neighbors may wonder why a pair are "fighting all the time," yet remain together. It may well be that the very fighting is what puts variety into an otherwise monotonous married life and makes it tolerable in spite of all the discouragements. It is to some extent a departure from the normal, but, if it suits the peculiar temperaments of the wedded pair —the neighbors had better not waste too much sympathy on them.

Recognizing, a hundred years or more ago, that some educators treated their young charges with wanton severity, legislators have increasingly cut down on the authority of the schools to administer punishment. Courts have lately sent parents to jail for beating their offspring; in the days of the American Revolution, hardly anything short of actual death of the victim could have brought the matter before the authorities. At the present time, spanking is probably the exception in most intelligent families. A Canadian physician, Dr. Griffin, speaking on the subject of discipline, recently observed: "To spank or not to spank is relatively unimportant; the important thing to keep in mind is the kind of end-product we desire." He pointed out by examples how many parents are unable to discipline their children by frequent beatings; others brought up model offspring without laying a hand on them. Three hundred years ago, in "the good old days" of the unspared rod, Rev. Thomas Fuller wrote "The Good Schoolmaster," maintaining the point that some boys would learn without being whipped, and should be allowed to do so; and that others would learn only under the rod, which should be vigorously applied, whatever their mothers thought (father was, of course, in favor of the discipline he had himself undergone at their age). The only thing that can be said is that the reactions of children, like those of their elders, differ; and, the more introspective and reflective a child, the more likely is severity in youth to produce abnormality in maturity.

And, if you take pleasure—even a glow of righteous satisfaction— in giving a youthful offender "what he has coming to him" (or her), remember that, while it is an emotion you share with a great many of your fellow-creatures, it is what the psychologists call *sadism*— which is a high-priced word for an undesirable thing. It expresses an urge you may not suspect.

● ● ●

HOW PROSTITUTES ARE MADE

MORE than half the girls who become prostitutes grew up in broken homes, according to Mazie F. Rappaport, Baltimore welfare official.

"Most who come to our attention never learned how to live with themselves, or adjust to society because of their unstable childhood environment," said Miss Rappaport, who termed prostitutes "the loneliest girls in the world."

Family life needs to be strengthened if we are to gain control over venereal disease, promiscuity, delinquency, she said.

—Pathfinder

A DOCTOR LOOKS AT
SELF-RELIEF

Aside from methods which may sometimes cause injury, there need be no concern about a natural and beneficial means of obtaining sexual release.

by Le Mon Clark, A.B., M.S., M.D.

THE young lady who was shown into my office glanced at me with an embarrassed smile. When the nurse closed the door, she said ruefully, "I don't suppose there is any delicate way of telling this."

After a short pause during which I, of course, jumped to the conclusion that she was pregnant when she knew she should not be, she went on, "I put a pencil up my urethra and it got away from me and I could not get it out again."

When quite patently I was not horribly shocked by the admission, she visibly relaxed. To my questions she was honest enough to admit that she had used it for

Dr. Clark, author of "Sex and You," is an ordained minister as well as a doctor of medicine. He taught Social Science at Cornell and Economics at Colgate University, was Clinical Assistant in Obstetrics and Gynecology at the University of Illinois College of Medicine, and now works in the field of sex education.

purposes of sexual stimulation, or autoerotism. She then volunteered the observation that relieving sexual tension, herself, seemed to be the best way to her. Intercourse carried the very real danger of extra-marital pregnancy.

At nineteen, she had indulged in heavy petting enough to know the danger of being swept further than she wanted to go if she let the tension become too great.

Examination revealed an intact hymen or maidenhead. The opening in it was just large enough to admit one examining finger. But that was sufficient to palpate or feel the urethra beneath the anterior wall of the vagina, and the pencil was not there. That meant it was up in the bladder. Checked by X-ray, the film showed the pencil as it was.

Fortunately, it was not a lead pencil with a sharpened end, but an eraser pencil, the kind that can be peeled down as it wears away.

The girl was sent to a hospital and a urologist called in. He found it possible to remove the eraser pencil with an instrument called the *cystoscope,* so that no operation involving cutting through tissue was necessary.

Instances such as this are not uncommon. Every gynecologist and urologist of any considerable experience has seen similar cases. Havelock Ellis reports, in his *Studies in the Psychology of Sex,* that in 1862, a German surgeon was called upon to treat cases of this kind so frequently that he invented special instruments for extracting hairpins from the female bladder.

The well-known British medical journal *Lancet* reported a most curious case some years back. A 78-year-old woman had been sewing in bed. She used the empty case of a clinical thermometer to hold some bodkins (British for large needles). In getting out of bed, she reported, she was conscious that something had entered her body. A month later, she was X-rayed and the thermometer case shown to be in her bladder. In her case, it was necessary to cut into the bladder to remove the case.

The report goes on to say, "Considering the difficulty so often found in introducing a catheter, this accident must be very rare." One wonders whether the writer had his tongue in his cheek when that comment was made. I should be inclined to say it was not only very rare, but simply impossible.

The really interesting thing about this case is that a 78-year-old woman would still have sufficient sexual drive to use the smooth thermometer case for sexual stimulation. She had probably lost it or had it drawn into the bladder through the action of the pelvic muscles at the moment of orgasm.

The female urethra is scarcely one-fourth as long as that of the male. It is a straight tube leading from the vulva, along the anterior wall of the vagina directly

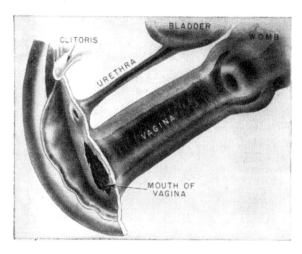

Stimulation of the urethra has often been used as a method of female self-gratification because of its close relationship to the walls of the vagina. However, to introduce any foreign object into the urethra is to invite serious trouble, as shown by the X-ray on the opposite page.

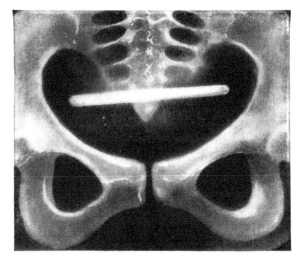

Actual X-ray photo of a pencil which had worked its way up into a woman's bladder after having been inserted in the urethra.—Courtesy, Dr. Le Mon Clark.

into the bladder. It lacks the sensitive prostatic urethral portion present in the male. It is surrounded by a network of nerves, all of which are highly sensitive.

Gentle stimulation of the anterior vaginal wall in all normal cases is gratifying, except where the individual is convinced, through tragic childhood training, that all things connected with sex are dirty, vile and sinful.

Gentle stimulation of the urethra in the female, either by the actual insertion of something into it or by something touching it or caressing it through the anterior wall of the vagina, has therefore served as a rather common method of self-gratification. *It is, as has been noted, a method of vaginal stimulation.*

Of course, to introduce any foreign object into the urethra may invite trouble by carrying infection into it or even up into the bladder. Or the objects may cause injury by

being drawn into the bladder, as in the cases just described.

The vagina, on the other hand, is a hardy place. It is protected by the lactic acid produced by a bacillus which acts as an antiseptic. Any reasonably clean, that is soap and water clean, object, will have very, very small possibilities of carrying infection into it.

Dr. Kinsey and his associates, in their volumes on sexual behavior in the human male and female, belittle the significance of vaginal stimulation as a source of gratification to the female. This will be discussed in a later article.

But history and archeology combine to demonstrate that instruments were used by women for intravaginal stimulation. In the excavations at Pompeii and Herculaneum definite phallus-like, "penis substitute" instruments were found. Frequently, they were made just the size and shape of the adult male organ in tumescence.

The older writers upon the subject of sex, almost without exception, accepted and furthered the attitude that every form of auto-eroticism was harmful, whether it involved the female or the male.

It was not until Dr. W. F. Robie began writing in this country, his first works being published in 1916, that we began to get the truth. Robie characterized self-relief as a harmless method of obtaining release from sexual tension in a civilization that did everything to beget such tension and left no safe route open for its release.

With the coming of modern psychiatry, it was realized that the harm caused by self-gratification was the conflict within the mind of the individual, the eternal struggle between his natural desires, and the moral preachments of his time.

The late Lawrence Gould in his book, *The Common Sense of Psychoanalysis,* tells the tragic story of the haggard-looking individual who stated that he had been "a physical and mental wreck all his life" as a result of self-relief. Gould quite naturally asked him how much he had indulged in the practice. "Three times that I remember," the man said. "What do you mean?" Gould asked. "Three times a day?"

"Three times altogether," the man replied!

The great Dr. Walter C. Alvarez, emeritus consultant in Internal Medicine at the Mayo Clinic, says in *The Neuroses:*

"Young men by the thousands are still much upset and worried over nocturnal emissions and masturbation, and then their future health depends on their getting quickly into the hands of a sensible physician who will tell them that emissions are signs only of good health, an actively functioning prostate gland and continence.

"He will tell them that the desire to masturbate is a sign of health and normalcy and nothing to worry about. The boy who never attempted to masturbate must have something wrong with his body or his mind. He should be told that Kinsey has found that almost all boys masturbate at some time to get rid of the great nervous tension that builds up because of continence. . . . It may help the religiously trained boy to have pointed out to him that the Bible has nothing to say about masturbation."

Marcus Aurelius, nearly two thousand years ago, said, "Moderation is a gift from Heaven." That is all one needs as a guide.

Where self-relief in the male or the female brings release from tension, promotes repose and helps attain relaxation and sleep, it is not only harmless, but definitely beneficial. Aside from what slight recognition one should give to the problems of over-indulgence and methods which may cause injury, there need be no concern whatever about this natural practice, which goes back far into prehistoric time.

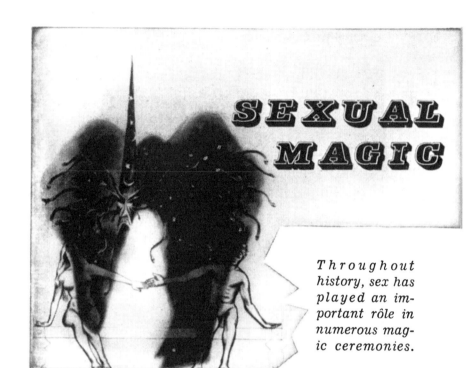

SEXUAL MAGIC

Throughout history, sex has played an important rôle in numerous magic ceremonies.

by Robert E. L. Masters

THE whole vast range of occult, or magic, theories and practices, from antiquity through the present day, is thoroughly permeated with curious sexual beliefs and rituals.

A knowledge of these theories enables us to understand not only the culture of other eras, but also the basis of many superstitious beliefs still existing in many parts of the world.

Mr. Masters is a technical writer specializing in the field of psychology.

In general, two types of sex magic were found in systems of occultism. One theory held that one had to abstain from sex acts in order to be effective magically. This thinking was based on the beliefs that there was a magical force to be found in sexual energy. This force, normally wasted in intercourse between the sexes, could be changed and used for magical purposes by the person versed in magic.

In direct contrast, other systems of magic attempted to generate a magical force or "current" by the

Drawing by H. H. Oelrich, first prize winner in Sexology art contest.

←

commission of sexual acts. This thinking was prevalent both in the rituals of primitive tribes and in the medieval practices of Satanism and witchcraft.

The more innocuous of the magical practices of pagan and primitive peoples—and certainly the best known—are the fertility rites. Here the male and female organs of copulation, particularly the male, were endowed with some of the powers of the overall generative principle of nature. Often the sex organs were worshipped in symbolic form: phallic stones, trees, obelisks, etc.

Such rites were often accompanied by promiscuous sexual activity, supposedly pleasing to the gods, or capable, on the principle of sympathetic magic (like produces like), of making seeds germinate and crops flourish.

Apart from these well-known fertility rites, however, there have been other beliefs among primitive peoples in the magical efficacy of specific sexual acts—some of them ordinarily regarded as taboo — which are interesting and worthy of mention.

Although some authorities have described incest as universally prohibited by all peoples, anthropologist Robert Briffault points out that some primitive tribes believed that incestuous unions could have beneficial as well as unfortunate magical results.

In Celebes such incestuous unions were believed to produce failure of the crops. The Galelarese regarded them as the cause of earthquakes and volcanic eruptions, and in Mindanao they were supposed to cause floods.

On the other hand, the Kalangs of Java believed that incestuous unions between mother and son were blessed with success and prosperity. The peasants of Archangel believed that marriages between blood relatives were "blessed with a rapid increase of children."

Among the tribes of British Central Africa there was a curious notion that a man who committed incest with his sister or his mother was thereby rendered bulletproof.

The Kiwai Papuans of New Guinea were an example of those primitive peoples who practiced promiscuous sexual activity aimed at producing positive results. This tribe staged large-scale, ritualistic sexual orgies for the purpose of collecting quantities of seminal fluid. They used this fluid in magical rites designed to stimulate the propagation of plant, animal and human life.

The belief in the magical efficacy of semen, usually that of the human male, though sometimes that of various animals such as the goat, bull and other animals popularly associated with great virility, has been particularly widespread, and not at all exclusively in primitive societies.

Sperm have been used in numerous magic ceremonies, in "love potions" and in attempts to restore virility. One of the strangest of all these uses was suggested by that hero of occult legend known as

Paracelsus, a Renaissance physician who is also, and more creditably, known as the father of chemotherapy and a forerunner of modern psychiatry.

Paracelsus' formula for the creation of the "homunculus" — an artificially made human being generated from the sperm without the assistance of the female ovum— went as follows:

"If the sperm, enclosed in a hermetically sealed glass, is buried in horse manure for about 40 days and properly 'magnetized,' it begins to live and move. After such a time it bears the form and resemblance of a human being, but it will be transparent and without a corpus. If it is now fed with the elixir of human blood until it is about 40 weeks old, and if allowed to remain during that time in the horse manure, in a continually even temperature, it will grow into a human child, with all its members developed like any other child . . . only it will be much smaller. We call such a being a homunculus, and he may be raised and educated like any other child, until he grows older and obtains reason and intellect, and is able to take care of himself. . . ."

In the medieval lore of Satanism an equally peculiar use of the male sperm is mentioned—though no magical power is attributed to the semen itself — this time by demons, who were believed to transport it for the purpose of impregnating women.

Henry T. F. Rhodes, in his valuable book on "The Satanic Mass," remarks that "It seemed quite natural, for example, to Guazzo, a distinguished scholar and Ambrosian brother of the late 16th Century, to discuss quite seriously the fertility of demons. Quoting numerous classical authorities, he comes to the conclusion that having no natural bodies, demons cannot impregnate human women. But since he accepts it as proved that pregnancy can result from intercourse with them, he advances an explanation of the fact.

"It would appear that demons were the first discoverers of the

One of the most ancient types of sex magic is found in the worship of the sex organs, exemplified by these symbols of the phallus, or male organ, gathered from many parts of the world. Though they take various forms, all of them unmistakably reveal the phallus-like origin. By worship of these objects, it was believed that fertility could be procured not only for the individual, but for the crops and animals which served for food.

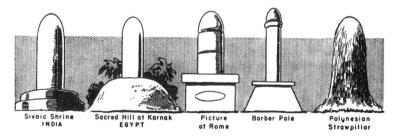

| Sivaic Shrine INDIA | Sacred Hill of Karnak EGYPT | Picture at Rome | Barber Pole | Polynesian Strawpillar |

process of artificial insemination since they are able to transport human semen over great distances and in such a way that it retains its potency. By some method, unknown or unexplained, they were able to inject it so that pregnancy resulted. This then remarkable feat ensured that Satanic characteristics would be imparted to offspring."

There is a vast and diverse literature relating accounts of human sexual relations with demons and other supernatural entities, and even with the devil himself. A sizeable portion of this literature was amassed during and just subsequent to the various historical witch hunts and witchcraft trials.

Much of the testimony by those who allegedly participated in the acts was obtained under torture or threat of torture, but one must agree with that authority on such matters, the late Rev. Montague Summers, that the testimony, wherever it cropped up, showed a surprising consistency.

For example, testimony from many times and places is to the effect that at the witches' Sabbath, a midnight gathering supposed in medieval times to have been held annually for the purpose of demonic orgies, the participants kissed the phallus or the posterior of the devil,

his representative or his image.

Some of the "witches" who claimed to have had sexual relations with the devil described not merely the act, but the devil's genital apparatus.

Apart from their belief that the devil and other demons attended the witches' Sabbaths and other ceremonies, the practitioners of magic believed—and believe today in those not too rare places where witchcraft is still practiced—that a potent magical force could be generated by sexual intercourse of large numbers of individuals *en masse*.

This belief is also common to some voodoo sects, and, following preliminary rituals, promiscuous sexual relations are indulged in by large numbers of persons for the purpose of generating magical currents.

It has been suggested by some authorities that this "sexual magic" was the most secret ritual of the original Knights Templars, suppressed at the beginning of the 14th Century for alleged homosexual and other sexual practices. More certainly, it was the "great secret" of the Order of The Templars of The East, founded in 1902 by the Austrian occult scholar Karl Kellner.

Irish Round Tower   Gilt Stone CUZCO   Potreqn Menhir INDIA   Mexican Shrine   POLYNESIA

"Witches Preparing for the Sabbath," painting by Hans Baldung Grün in the Frankfort Museum.

This order was later taken over by the late Aleister Crowley, who openly recommended and practiced sexual magic, and founded an abbey—Thelema—at Cefalu in Sicily, where disciples were indoctrinated in the sexual rites and what are usually described as orgies were standard procedure in the development of one's occult powers.

Included among magic sex rites were acts of bestiality—usually the union of a woman and a goat—for purposes of predicting the future. This is a particularly ancient form of sex magic, practiced, according to Herodotus, by the Persian conqueror Xerxes and by the Roman emperor Julius Caesar.

The ancient Roman naturalist Pliny, always a mine of old wives' tales, cited a number of magical causes of impotence and sterility.

Impotence resulted, he said, from drinking the ashes of a brya plant mixed with the urine of either a eunuch or an ox. Sterility resulted if one urinated on the same spot where a dog had urinated earlier.

Entertaining magical practices for determining the sex of one's offspring are found all over the world. For example, in the Tyrol, if a boy is desired, the man keeps his boots on during intercourse. Among the Slav peasantry, he wears his hat.

An ancient Hindu recipe has it that, for a boy, the penis should be anointed with the blood of a hare; for a girl, with goose fat.

Albertus Magnus, another great in the annals of the occult, prescribed, for a boy, that the woman should drink a potion made of the powdered entrails and womb of a rabbit mixed with wine. For a girl, both parents should concoct and drink a beverage composed of the pulverized liver and testes of a young pig mixed with wine and honey (note the principles of sympathetic magic at work here).

It is clear that all of these beliefs and practices fly directly in the face of logic, reason and all scientific knowledge currently regarded as valid. In many instances, they would seem to be the products of diseased minds and to belong, therefore, to the realm of sexual and psychological pathology.

This is not at all to say that all of the individuals who participated in the practices described above, or who accepted the theories, were mentally ill. We well know that many things seem to work if we expect them to work.

And doubtless many people are genuinely deceived as the result of certain occult "techniques" which have as their very purpose — although the individual who engages in them may not be aware of that fact—a derangement of the senses, the development of hallucinations, peculiar states of consciousness, etc.

In the case of the witches of the Middle Ages, the so-called witches' ointment with which they anointed themselves in preparation for their flight to the Sabbath appears to provide a clue.

These ointments, as we know from old records, contained opiates and belladonna in large quantities. Absorbed by the skin, these drugs—quite capable of producing hallucinations—were doubtless responsible for many of the strange events the witches sincerely believed themselves (in some instances) to have experienced.

Similar rational explanations may usually be offered wherever other occult sexual practices appear to have been "successful."

Hindu goddess with the *ankh*, Egyptian symbol of life, covering her pubic region, and a serpent, male sex symbol, on her arm.

By HUGO G. BEIGEL, Ph.D.

■ "Should a woman initiate sex relations with her husband?" In one form or another, this question has been put to me many times.

"My husband does not seem to care for sex relations any more," said one woman. "What can I do about it?"

"Very often I feel like making love," said another. "But I'm too embarrassed to make the advances to my husband. If I do, I'm afraid he'll lose respect for me."

A third wife complained: "I notice very often that my husband is playing with himself. I want to cry out, 'What are you doing that for? Here I am.' But it's too embarrassing. So I pretend to be asleep."

Myra, a good-looking woman of about forty, was the first to put the question directly. But hers was a very special case, where she had married a man ten years her senior and both had agreed to live on terms of friendship rather than as husband and wife. After a short period of sexless marriage, she began to regret her part of the bargain. But she did not know what to do to make her husband realize her willingness.

All of these cases illustrate the fact that women, though distressed about sexual neglect, rarely try to put matters right on their own initiative.

Dr. Beigel, formerly professor in the Dept. of Psychology, Long Island University, is consultant in personal and sex problems, author of SEX FROM A TO Z, *editor of* THE JOURNAL OF SEX RESEARCH, *and Secretary of the Society for the Scientific Study of Sex.*

WIVES SHOULD MAKE

Some men need wives who will initiate sex relations

Some women evidently consider it unnatural to initiate sex relations, even with their own husbands. Others fear that the expression of sexual desire would mark them as wanton and thus unladylike. Some are prevented by pride or genuine shyness. Behind it lurks the dread of being rejected.

And, of course, rejection is not always an impossibility. There are men whose pride in their masculinity is greater than their security about it. They resent what to them is a taking over of the male prerogative: the right to make the advances. With these men, chances of successful female advances probably are no better than fifty-fifty at best. And they are worse if alienation in a marriage has grown into aversion.

If the man's withdrawal is due to homosexual leanings, or to fear of ultimate failure because he over-rates an uninhibited woman's sexual appetite, he may reject her. Sexual advances by a woman are particularly not likely to succeed if the husband has grounds to suspect that his wife is competitive and tries to control him.

But in general, there usually are less ominous reasons for a man's unexplained sexual abstention. A man may be beset by worries, tiredness, misunderstandings, fear of his

the aggressor without a considerable loss of pleasure. In some marriages of this kind, it is the wife who must take the lead.

A man may sulk because once or twice his advances were refused, or because the wife complained about the manner in which he made them. Now his confidence is shaken and he is too proud to "bother her again." It is then definitely up to the wife to make the next move, all

SEX ADVANCES

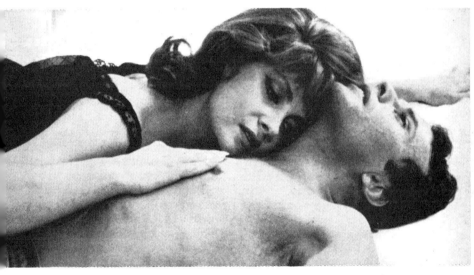

wife's pregnancy, sulkiness, and even fleeting sexual interest elsewhere.

In these and similar situations, the female's demonstration of her desire may be just the medicine the man needs. Certain male personalities, in fact, long for active sexual behavior on the part of their wives. Passive by nature, they cannot be

the more so if she knows that her sexual apathy has caused the rift.

In other instances, the man's frustration may stem from his wife denying him special sex activities. The best the wife can do is to indicate her desire to seek variety in sex activity and to try to work out a mutually agreeable way to satisfy his wishes. Men appreciate their mate's cooperation in sex play. They interpret suggestions for novelty and experiments as tokens of love and as confirmation of their own sex ability.

How, then, should a woman go about making sexual advances?

In all instances of sex initiation, the senses must be engaged. For some, sight is important; for others, it is touch that is crucial. A young woman may succeed in initiating sexual activity by parading her body in a transparent negligee. But such a technique may be of small value for a considerably older woman whose flesh may not look as good as it feels.

However, this should be no reason to give up. Marital seduction does not begin in bed, but at the breakfast table. That is to say, the woman who wants to lure her husband into her arms has to show all the consideration and attention she is capable of. She might do well to take stock of her behavior.

She should consider, for example, which of her actions or omissions disappoint, frustrate, or annoy her husband. Has she been too critical? Is she a nag? Does she complain too much, make too many demands, try to control him?

While the woman must, in some respects, remember that she is a wife, in others she should forget it and behave as if she were still a lover. She once made herself attractive for him; she now often runs around the house looking her sloppiest.

Loving gestures are a splendid means of communication, too. Fingertips stroking his hand, a hand resting warmly on his arm, nuzzling against his shoulder, all are signals of devotion that are easily noted.

And then there is talk. Let it be loving talk, but let it be frank too, especially regarding the sex relationship. A man's faulty, inconsiderate attitude may well have provoked a woman's. If misunderstandings can be cleared up and sensitivities smoothed, there no longer is reason to restrain one's wishes.

Often, the man will now take the initiative and indicate "when." Unless he does so, there is nothing to prevent the wife from doing so. Light caresses serve as an invitation. Men have erogenous zones pretty much in the same parts of the body that women have them. They, too, enjoy physical stimulation and contact.

Timing is important; after a restful day, on a weekend, upon a return from an animated party, or a stimulating movie the atmosphere may be just right.

Some men naturally may not function sexually the way they used to. After a good night's sleep, however, with no rush ahead, many men wake up with desire. A woman can use this opportunity for her amorous advances.

In Myra's case, the initial difficulty was her ignorance of her husband's erotic ideas, tastes, and reservations. She started going on the assumption that he possibly had his own secret quirk and insisted, "If it's fun and does no harm. . . ."

She had been right. Slowly, step by step, her husband's preference for a particular activity he felt ashamed of came to the fore—first in words, then in bedroom action. She found it gratifying. She called up in the morning and said: "I feel more like a woman than ever."

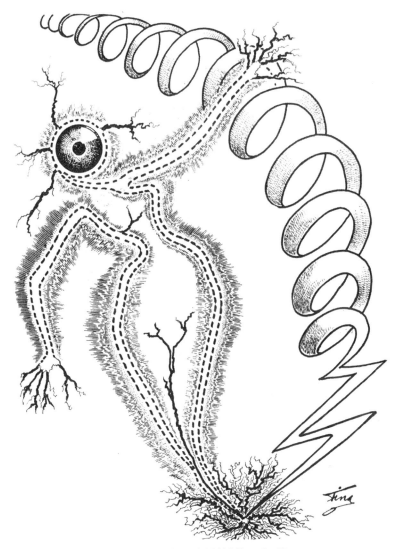

THE FEMALE CLIMAX — By Tina

The mechanics of the female climax—as seen by a surrealist artist—is vividly expressed in this highly imaginative illustration. In the dim past the prehistoric human female did not attain a climax—even today according to sexologists over 30% of our females still do not experience it during marital union. Those who do, know it as a tremendously electrifying sensation. It builds up with an ever increasing spiraling force that reaches its zenith in an all-consuming nervous explosion which permeates the entire being—as depicted so graphically in our illustration—both physically and mentally. In this it is unique and unmatched in all other human experiences.

CHASTITY BELTS

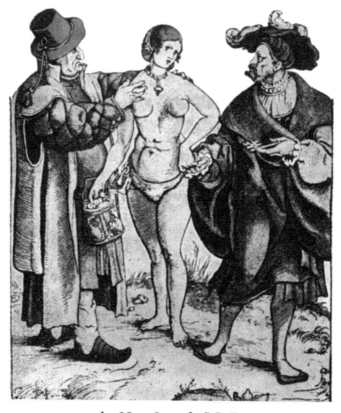

by Marc Lanval, S.Sc.D.

Husbands once compelled their wives to wear chastity belts. These locked iron girdles were supposed to assure a husband of his wife's fidelity during his absence from home.

WHO has not heard of that curious device known as the "chastity belt?" Basically, it is a piece of pierced metal

Dr. Lanval is a famous Belgian sociologist and sexologist, and author of The Intimate Lives of Women.

which is placed over the lower part of a woman's abdomen, coving the genital organs and kept in place by a strap, chain or belt passing around the waist to the back, where it is secured by a padlock. The key to the lock re-

XVI Century chastity belt. The edge of the elaborate metal belt is trimmed with velvet.—Photos by Rogers-Viollet, Paris.

mains in the possession of the woman's husband or someone to whom he has delegated authority.

This "girdle" was used widely in European countries. When and how did the use of the chastity belt develop? What is the social significance of this barbarous practice?

Male and Female

The first subdivision in any organized group of humans was based on sex differentiation—men and women. Because of the physiological difference between the sexes, each subdivision led a distinct and different kind of life, following different customs in most societies. The female subdivision was further divided: One group comprised eligible, unattached women (virgins, unmarried women and widows); the other, women who were no longer "free" (wives, concubines and slaves).

As our civilization emerged from the primitive stage, the male believed that *he* was the bearer of the spark of life which made women conceive. He reasoned that his must be the original sex, since the continuity of the group depended upon him. He falsely concluded that the male must be superior to the female. Thus he applied all his ingenuity to acquiring one of those females for his own exclusive use, both to gratify his sexual needs and to perpetuate his line through offspring.

There came into existence social institutions based on the idea of the legal right of a man to the exclusive possession of a woman and to the certainty that his children were authentically "legitimate." As a result, the female, far more than the male, from infancy on, was bound in a net of restrictions and taboos, ethical, social, political and religious. These were to better insure the male's exclusive rights and to preserve the female's value when she officially reached the stage of eligibility for marriage, purchase or slavery.

Women were forced to wear special and easily recognizable symbols indicating unmistakably whether the wearer was "eligible" (virgin) or whether she was "taken" (married).

Roman Girdle of Chastity

In ancient Rome an unmarried woman wore a white woolen girdle around her tunic, long or short, tied with a special kind of knot called a "Hercules knot" (in honor of Hercules, the god who symbolized the ideal husband). This detail of dress was not only an indication of the wearer's marital status (virgin or widow), but it served as a sort of shield to protect her from the advances of men who might attempt to assert their male superiority either by brute force or the charm of seduction.

This social technique operated smoothly because of the general acceptance by all men, whether married or not, of a convention whereby each man protected the exclusivity of all other men's rights so that they would respect his rights to his own woman.

The expression *zonam solvere*, used by Horace and Ovid, the Latin poets, means "to undo the girdle of her dress" (on the night of her wedding) or "to consummate a marriage." The white woolen girdle, therefore, was the symbol of chastity.

This protecting shield had two aspects. From the social point of view, it was a protection against the depredation of the males; from the psychological point of view, it was a tangible reminder to the girl of her duty to remain "pure," both morally and physically. In this connection, an ordinance was promulgated in 1420 by Charles VI, King of France, forbidding prostitutes to wear such belts, for fear that people might falsely suppose that the wearer was a girl or woman belonging to the nobility or the rich commercial class.

The white woolen girdle of Roman origin was a true *chastity* belt. It inspired reticence in the display of intimate thoughts and decency in conduct, and had a re-

straining effect on sexual relations. While this symbol of social restraint had the desired effect on girls, women who had ceased to be virgins were readily able to find the means to escape restraint. Actually, what is known today as a *chastity* belt could more aptly be called a *continence* belt. It was invented as a result of the decadence of morals after the ancient woolen girdle, which was purely symbolic, had lost its power to prevent infidelity.

Origin of the Belt

Breeders of pedigreed dogs sometimes used an apparatus called an "abstinence and prudence gate." Essentially this was a square of metal with slits which was attached to the hindquarters of valuable breeding females by an arrangement of leather straps. It prevented their being covered by an "unauthorized" male. It was a kind of birth control for pedigreed dogs. This suggested the idea of something similar to be worn by women whose husbands were obliged by circumstances to be away from home for long periods of time.

Chastity belts first appeared in northern Italy, which was famous for the artistic workmanship of its jewelers. The first belts were fashioned of ivory, gold and silver. Voltaire states that the use of chastity belts was common in Rome and in Venice during the Middle Ages.

The Crusades

Unquestionably one of the times when men had to leave their homes for a prolonged period of time occurred during the Crusades in the sixth and the eighth centuries. Military expeditions set out from Northern Italy and Western Europe to fight in Asia Minor. The nobles were at the head of these armed troops. Upon departing they locked their wives into these devices, specimens of which we still have today.

It was not a general custom for the legitimate wife to wear this apparatus. It was a matter of the husband's individual choice. It appears that Henry II, King of France, made his wife, Catherine de Medici, wear a chastity belt. The Prince of Modena did the same with his wife, Charlotte Aglae of Orleans.

In the evolution of moral standards, women's emancipation made progress. Slowly but surely she acquired human rights and respect. Proof of this lies in the creation of Courts of Love, dedicated to

Chastity Belts of the XVI Century. Note the ornately engraved pictures on the girdles.

romantic love, ladies' knights, pages, etc. — a social innovation that contributed to the coming of the Renaissance. Beginning with the fifteenth century the Occidental world rediscovered the beauties of the ancient Greek and Roman cultures and freedom for women made greater strides than before.

As a result the social structure of society, on the level of the family and of the country as a whole, became more orderly and the rules became more inflexible. Social classes became more strictly defined. There had come into being a class of men who had become rich through commerce, industry or navigation. They arrogated to themselves certain privileges which, until then, had belonged exclusively to the "high born." While marriage remained

..a stable, monogamous institution, the morality of the day tended more and more to be favorable to the erotic fancies of rich men. Thus the reign of the "kept woman," the "favorite," the official "mistress" began, creating in effect an extra-legal additional home for the man on the style of the famous Greek courtesan system. Co-existing with the legitimate hearth were the wife's primary function to reproduce legitimate offspring.

Thus in this age we encounter the elite, the aristocrats of the oldest profession in the world (prostitution) being exercised as a "liberal profession" with young women deliberately hiring themselves to a single employer. We have remarkable examples of this in the favorites of the Kings of France. The novel and drama have given us countless heroines of this type: Laïs, Aspasia, Manon, Thaïs, Ninon de Lenclos, Cleo de Merode, etc.

Mistresses Wore Chastity Belts

Motivated as much by jealousy as the desire to get their money's worth, wealthy men who bought love compelled their mistresses of the moment, in exchange for support and gifts, to wear a chastity belt of which they kept the key. This was one of the risks and obligations of the profession of "kept women." The custom guaranteed the master's self-respect; he rewarded her by his generosity, but substituted the humiliation of a fee with the humiliation of her being kept under lock and key.

The classic example of this relationship is that of King Henry IV of France, who presented his beautiful mistress, Gabrielle d'Estrées, with a richly decorated chastity belt, relying only on his prestige as king to induce her to wear it during his absence at the battlefront. She, as proof of her love, handed him the key.

Francesco Carrara, the tyrant of Padua, forced his mistresses to wear chastity belts. P. C. Remondino, in his *History of Circumcision* (1801) relates that the women of the Sudanese harems wore chastity belts when they were obliged to leave the harem for any purpose. These belts were made of a bamboo peg which was inserted into the vagina, and a shield that covered the vulva.

Modern Use

In the centuries that followed there were no further spectacular examples of this kind, only rare and isolated cases.

In 1892, a Mr. Hufferte, a Paris candy manufacturer, forced a young worker in his factory, whom he had made his mistress, to wear a chastity belt. The girl complained to the police and had the man arrested. He was sentenced to two years in prison.

In 1910 a Paris druggist was accused of mistreating his wife. The police in making an investigation found the woman chained to the bedpost and wearing a kind of coat of mail locked with a key.

In 1930 a woman was taken to the hospital after a mental breakdown. She was wearing a chastity belt that had been purchased in a Paris shop.

Another case came to light in Paris in 1932. Henri Littière, of a jealous nature, visited the Cluny Museum and admired the chastity belts he saw on display there. He had one made by a manufacturer of surgical instruments and forced his wife to wear it. He was arrested and sentenced to prison for three months. Nevertheless, two years later he was brought into court on the same charge.

Something must be said about the mentality of women who submitted to the wearing of a chastity belt. Husbands in former days probably had little trouble in inducing their wives either by force or moral persuasion to wear an object which calmed their suspicions concerning their exclusive ownership of the women. But there are also women who are flattered when their husbands evidence jealousy concerning them. It satisfies their vanity and they feel that the humiliation involved is worth that price. This explains why lovers sometimes had little difficulty in inducing their mistresses to agree to the wearing of a chastity belt.

The above explains why, in spite of the fact that as a result of two world wars women have in many respects won equality

Close-up of chastity girdle shows Adam and Eve scene engraved directly on the belt.

with men as far as civil rights and ethics are concerned, there are still some women who accept such degrading servitude. Such cases do exist; but we consider them instances of sexual deviation or we relegate them to the domain of psychopathology. Chastity belts were a symbol of women's slavery and male superiority in bygone days when primitive ideas prevailed.

• • •

MARIHUANA AND SEX

THE majority of investigators believe that marihuana smoking is a causative factor in a large percentage of our major crimes and sexual offenses. In New York City, a committee empowered to make a study of marihuana usage found that marihuana has no specific stimulant effect in regard to sexual desires. Investigators frequented the haunts of marihuana smokers; these rooms are often decorated with pictures of nude subjects suggestive of perverted sexual practices.
—*Science Digest*

SEXOLOGY
An Authoritative Guide to Sex Education

THE KINSEY REPORT

A S this is being written, at the end of August 1953, a sexual paper cyclone has burst over the United States, the like of which has never occurred in history, anywhere. Thousands of newspapers and magazines have frenziedly discussed a new scientific volume: *"Sexual Behavior in the Human Female,"* by Dr. Alfred C. Kinsey and his associates. (See also page 208.)

Some of America's foremost writers, authors and editors have all dutifully written their 5,000-word stories about the new book. All would have written far more, but by special arrangement with Dr. Kinsey, all articles were limited to this length before the actual publication of the volume in mid-September.

These articles created an unprecedented nation-wide furore. Hundreds of churchmen, lawyers, judges, physicians, scientists and plain laymen immediately stepped into this vast limelight voicing their opinions either pro or con, learnedly or ignorantly—because when it comes to sex, *everybody* has his fixed and positive convictions.

Remarkable also was the phenomenon that none of the critics had ever laid eyes upon the actual book—which was not to be released till nearly a month later! Each self-appointed critic had read one or several of the pre-publication 5,000-word articles, and from these they judged the volume as if they had read the ponderous 842-page book!

The Kinsey survey, eight years in the making, is a highly statistical, scientific volume. It has many charts, graphs and tables, similar to Dr. Kinsey's first volume published in 1948, *"Sexual Behavior in the Human Male."* Kinsey reports the facts on sex only as he and his staff find them.

He rarely gives an opinion, but reports only the cold scientific facts as he sees them. These facts and figures are carefully checked and re-checked for accuracy and most of the world's sexologists, knowing Dr. Kinsey's high scientific standing, accept them as facts.

Nor is Kinsey interested in the moral aspects of his findings—he leaves that to the sociologists, and rightly so.

SEXOLOGY finds all this terrific hubbub over

THE KINSEY REPORT

Kinsey's book strange and bewildering. It is as if the whole country had suddenly discovered sex! For 20 years, SEXOLOGY—the world's pioneer sexological magazine, published uninterruptedly since 1933—has reported ALL the sexological facts. Dr. Kinsey would be the last to claim that his two volumes contain *new* sexological disclosures—only his *statistics* are new.

Yet SEXOLOGY, for 20 years, has published consistently everything that is known to sexological science. Indeed, SEXOLOGY was on the scene long before Dr. Kinsey started his epoch-marking work.

Like Kinsey, SEXOLOGY, too, for many years, has been under continuous fire for daring to reveal the truth of mankind's sexological behavior and mores.

Great authors and sexologists in profusion such as: Dr. Wilhelm Stekel; Judge René Guyon; Dr. Norman Haire; Dr. Edwin W. Hirsch; Dr. Ashley Montagu; Prof. Marc Lanval; Dr. P. Russo; Dr. Frank S. Caprio; Dr. Wilfrid D. Hambly; Dr. Harry Benjamin; Dr. Olivier Loras, and many others have constantly contributed to its pages in the interest of sex enlightenment.

Through the long pioneering years, many millions of copies of SEXOLOGY have brought consistent sex advancement to America and to dozens of foreign countries of the world.

To educate the public in practical sex information of every kind, SEXOLOGY originated a most comprehensive *Question and Answer* Department that was highly revolutionary during the thirties. It caused the banning of the magazine in many parts of the country—just as Dr. Kinsey's new volume is threatened to be banned in many places in the U. S.

SEXOLOGY, too, notes with satisfaction that Dr. Kinsey now confirms what this magazine has maintained to be a fact for twenty years, namely that sex disparity accentuates divorce after long years of married life. SEXOLOGY, in many editorials and articles, has continuously asserted that a large percentage of divorces are caused by sex disparity, usually due to poor sex technique by either husband or wife—or both. This is only one of a long list of examples of sex information published for years in SEXOLOGY and now confirmed in Dr. Kinsey's new volume.

Summing up, SEXOLOGY may be pardoned for asking: "Why all this belated sexual news-explosion? SEXOLOGY's millions of sex-enlightened readers will raise incredulous eyebrows at the present strange sex hullaballoo. It's all old hat to them!"

Von Muchow

WIFE SWAPPING
by Richard Stiller, B.A., M.A.

***Desire for sexual novelty is not unusual, but the
costs of organized adultery may run very high.***

A WEEKLY newspaper circulated in Canada and New England recently carried the following ad in its "Are You Lonesome?" column:

Massachusetts Couple

**Happily married, broadminded white
couple, mid-thirties, 5'2" and 5'6",**

wish to meet similar couples for modern activities. Artistically inclined. Please enclose photo. Mass.-Conn. area.

Persons who answered such ads, according to the Massachusetts State Pornography Squad, found that "modern activities" was a euphemism for wife swapping and that "broadminded" included an interest in voyeurism (peeping)

*Mr. Stiller is a free-lance writer
and former teacher of social studies.*

and the photographing of sexual activities.

Referring to ads such as the one cited above, Postal Inspector Joseph Moore of Springfield stated: "Sometimes people who are just looking for companionship—with no sex overtones—answer these ads. They think the advertisers really are photography buffs looking for pen pals or something."

The New England States, and Massachusetts in particular, seem to be a recurring scene of wife-swapping parties. Amesbury, for example, achieved brief notoriety some years ago as the locale of a version of sexual roulette known as "Keys." This special form of wife swapping spread throughout the country as far as Washington, D. C., and Tucson, Arizona.

In playing "Keys," a number of couples gather in one home, and after a few drinks the wives throw their house keys into the center of the living-room. The husbands then scramble for the keys, making sure that they avoid those to their own homes. The paired-off couples slip off, one by one, to the women's homes, leaving, finally, the hostess and the male who has picked up her keys. The rest of the night is spent in sexual experimentation with the random partner.

It was a series of such keys "games" and resultant sexual dissatisfaction and jealousy that resulted in the murder of electronic technician Melvin Clark, Jr., by his wife, Lorraine, in Amesbury in late 1954.

The game of switch has many variations. It can be played in public or in private; in light or in darkness; for one "engagement" or for an interval ranging from a night to an entire vacation period; and with such added fillips as spectators, musical accompaniment, or the recording of the entire proceeding in sound motion pictures.

Two factors must be present: the wife swapping must be for a specific, short-lived duration, after which the original marriage partners return to each other; and it must be mutually desired.

Nevertheless, despite the most careful planning and mutual observance of the "rules," wife swapping (or husband swapping, for that matter) eventually tends to break down into plain old-fashioned promiscuity characterized finally by explosions of jealousy, resentment, and possibly violence. The Clark murder is an obvious case in point. Thus what begins in a mood of light-hearted gaiety, as a mere game, may have a tragically destructive climax.

According to *Pageant* magazine (February, 1955): "In all the stories of wife-swapping activities there seem to be certain common denominators. Locale is one. Age-level of the players is another, plus income level. Invariably the gamesters live in a suburb, seldom a large city. The people are usually in their 30's or early 40's, their incomes are above average, their children, if any, are in their early teens and fairly self-sufficient."

Promiscuity, adultery, and marital infidelity are nothing new, of course. Men and women have been engaging in extra-marital sexual relations since the very inception of marriage and its restrictions on sexual activity.

What is new about wife swapping is the element of knowledge and consent. In this "game," mates know and approve of their spouse's sexual adventuring. What is more, they actively desire it, sometimes out of boredom laced with a touch of voyeurism, sometimes out of repressed feelings of guilt or sexual inadequacy; but most often from a desire for variety and excitement.

In such mutually agreed upon sexual exploring, husbands and wives seem to have divorced sexual intercourse from its romantic, affectionate, emotional base.

Sometimes, a rare permanence and stability arise out of a case of wife swapping. Such a situation was cited in a recent issue of SEXOLOGY (January, 1959), in which Dr. Edward Dengrove described two young college instructors who spent their summer vacations together in a rented cottage. During these vacations, the young couples exchanged partners, and each man spent the vacation with the wife of the other. At the end, the wives rejoined their original husbands for another academic year.

Occasionally one reads in the press of a case of permanent wife swapping, wherein couples exchange mates through mutual divorce and remarriage. Such, for example, occurred in 1957 in San Francisco when the Schwartzes and the Brookses traded mates, the children and the houses remaining with the women, and the two men simply changing their residences.

In some cultures, wife swapping has none of the "decadent" or "immoral" overtones it has in ours. Among the Eskimos, for example, it was once quite customary for a host to "lend" his wife to a weary traveller for a night's comfort and enjoyment. They also apparently had a custom which is an almost exact duplicate of the game of "keys."

Dr. Ira Reiss in his recent book, *Premarital Sexual Standards in America,* points out that "some of the Eskimos while away the bleak winter months by playing a game called 'putting out the lamps,' in which married and single couples put out the oil lamps and scramble for a new partner for the night."

But in our officially monogamous world, wife swapping deviates from what is considered the norm, and therefore labors under a burden of psychological damage. Dr. Dengrove describes a wife who tried to force her husband into a wife swapping arrangement, and when he refused, had sexual affairs of her own with other men. She found this increased her desire for her own husband. In another case, the editor of SEXOLOGY received a letter from a man who stated that his wife insisted that he have relations with a young woman, despite the fact that they had been married for some time, and were, presumably, well adjusted sexually.

"Ever since my wife started to loan me to this woman," he wrote, "she became more aggressive in our sex relations and more demanding." He went on to describe two couples of his acquaintance who claimed they derived greater sexual satisfaction from their wives after weekly wife-swaps.

The novelist Ernest Hemingway, in *To Have and Have Not,* describes a kind of voyeuristic one-way wife swapping. In this case, a wealthy middle-aged man married to a beautiful young woman achieves sexual gratification only by observing her in sexual intercourse with various lovers.

One of the earliest novels of Philip Wylie—*As They Revelled—*

These two couples from a small town in Wisconsin made news headlines in 1955 when they legally traded mates. They are shown here after a double wedding, following their divorce.—*Wide World.*

is based on the wife-swapping adventures of four couples. The action takes place in suburban Connecticut in the early 'thirties.

In the course of a summer, the eight individuals involved exchange sexual partners. There is a considerable amount of talking and theorizing about "love"—or as the author puts it—"modern, civilized, biochemical, endocrinological, adept, expert, unemotional, functional, promiscuous, unbigoted and enlightened love."

"The trouble with all of us," one character tells another, "is that we've tried for so many generations to live by the ridiculous precept of having only one woman in a lifetime—that we've ruined our natural feelings about everything. If the fact that you're faithful is what makes the difference in whether or not I love you— then my love is worth only as much as your adherence to one minor law. And it's a rotten law, too. Just a selfishness."

The novel makes the point that sexual adventuring for its own sake is self-defeating and psycho-

logically harmful. The climax finds the four couples engaged in a kind of blindman's buff version of "keys."

A ninth character is blindfolded and as bits of jewelry belonging to each of the eight are dangled before her she requires that the owner—presumably unknown to her—perform sexually with one of the other participants. Actually, by permitting her to see under the blindfold, the author contrives to have each of the individuals paired off with his or her illicit lover.

The result is a crisis of lust, jealousy, and hatred that leaves scars on all of the "players" and damages each marriage irreparably.

Near the end of the book, the author sums up as follows:

"If the truth about love—or about adultery—the truth about clandestine romance and affairs and stolen kisses and assignations could ever emerge from the heady realm where it is kept by popular taboos, then all men and women would know that more often than not the players are merely reading their lines and performing their business.

"Sex is, indeed, a primary biological demand. But a life of the libido outside a satisfactory marriage is at the least unessential and at best a spiced variant which palls on much tasting. So most such adventures that pass beyond normal imagining, which is a legitimate function of the mind, to the deed of clambering into other peoples' beds, are reluctant cohabitations, not love, not the indomitable expression of the need to procreate, but only accident and half-hearted curiosity, the foment of chivalry and gallantry, the unwillingness to be a spoil-sport, the misconstruction of the motives of the other partner, generosity, valor, amusement, casualness, a gross appetite for sweets, anything but what they seem—and over most such sins there should be little cause for jealousy, less for spleen, and none for murder. . . ."

Most psychiatrists and psychological consultants feel that monogamy is the healthiest state, and that therefore wife swapping or other forms of promiscuity are psychologically damaging.

According to Dr. Abraham N. Franzblau, "the assumption that the illicit is better and more satisfying than the licit is a characteristic of immaturity. It is given circulation only by those who have never known the joys of even a moderately happy marital relationship."

Dr. Fred Feldman, Professor of Psychology at the University of Southern California Medical School and consultant to numerous family agencies feels that: "Marriage sometimes is thought of as a restriction of sex, confining it to the limits of monogamy. But actually, marriage is the only way for real sex freedom to develop. . . . Free expression in sex demands complete trust, for the individual is fully revealed as a person. . . . The true sex freedom is achieved when one has sufficient trust in the partner to reveal himself (or herself) without inhibition. Such trust is possible only in marriage."

And psychiatrist Frederick W. Dershimer states: "It is in man's self-interest to be monogamous. Promiscuity is the artificial, self-defeating state. The people who are most promiscuous have probably never had a fully satisfactory sex relationship."

Yet Dr. Kinsey, who made no judgments and drew no "moral" conclusions, found that 75% of men and 25% of women desire extra-marital sexual experience. Under such circumstances—particularly in a culture as contradictory in its attitude toward sex as is the United States—we can expect sexual adventuring in all its forms—including wife swapping—to persist as aspects of the sexual scene.

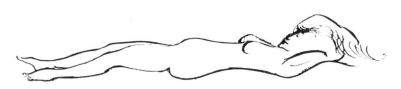

"Wayward" and Wandering Girls

By WINFIELD SCOTT PUGH, M.D.

AH, no, gentle reader, this is not an attempt to unravel an enigma. There is no mystery in ."why girls leave home"; on the contrary, it is a source of wonder that more young women do not make hurried exits from the parental residence. Such a view of the situation is not a prevalent one; but my honest conviction, that the blame for waywardness among young girls has long been placed on the wrong shoulders, recently led me to express frankly that opinion in the presence of a clergyman.

My visitor was visibly shocked by my temerity, and it was some time before he regained his poise. "You see, Doctor," said the reverend gentleman, "our association feels that it has a mission, and is interested in breaking up the pernicious traffic in souls — 'white slavery' to give it that exact, but perhaps vulgar title."

The visit of this eminent clergyman was opportune. Recently I had occasion to scan a report by Captain John H. Ayres, sixteen years in charge of the missing persons division of the New York City police. In the report there was this significant statement: "There has never been an authentic case of white slavery. Certainly some girls do run away to lead the gay life," the official writes, "but I never heard of one forced to do it." Certainly those responsible for issuing this statement are qualified to render such an opinion. How strikingly at variance it is with the popular conception.

"Of course," said one of our country's leading educators, in a discussion some time ago, "I don't believe, Doctor, you realize that many of these wayward girls, who forsake their loving parents to plunge into a sea of iniquity, are problem children." What an expression! An answer was not difficult to find: Whenever you locate a "problem child" it will not require the keen wit of a Monsieur Dupin or Sherlock Holmes to find one or both parents to be "problem" cases.

I will not attempt to quote statistics regarding runaway girls; let it suffice to say that there are many and the number is increasing all the time. Reader, you may ask why do not boys take wings in a similar way from the parental nest? Well, many do. Boys, you must admit, have it a little easier; most parents do not expect them to be plaster saints. Mothers always say, "Boys will be boys." However, if the male offspring were treated in the brutal way many of his sisters are, all but the "timid soul" variety would quickly vault the old rail fence and speedily vanish in a cloud of dust.

In many of our households the sex impulse is indulged begrudgingly; for too many would still have us believe it is a moral weakness, to be utilized only when offspring are desired. I need not describe in too great detail the old-school who denies himself all the good things of life, his wards are in for a hard session. The mother who has been denied a normal marital life is the counterpart of our jailer. The mere fact that a girl is being kept a prisoner might be tolerated; but it is the unnecessary watchfulness and constant spying

The mother's jealousy of the daughter (for that is what it is) breaks out in unwarranted suspicions of immorality and vituperative reproaches of an moralistic, but really indecent kind.

mothers who have been reared in a confused and stifling atmosphere, taught obedience and self-denial without end. They are thoroughly steeped in the ancient tradition that woman's place is in the home first, last, and always. (All this is quite in accord with the doctrine, *Kinder, Kirche und Küche,* of the former Kaiser and more recent Führer). When you have a jailer by the mother that finally shatters the daughter's nerves, unless she is made of iron.

When discussion of sex is forbidden in the home, and the young girl is constantly warned against the aggression of men, is there any wonder that the girl's curiosity is aroused? We are always fascinated by forbidden things. A certain amount of curiosity is the most normal thing in adolescence and, when that curiosity is met with suspicion and unjust accusations, deep tragedies occur. When a fanatical mother, in an outburst of hysterical frenzy for fear that her daughter will "go wrong," flies at the girl with mean and ungrounded accusations, the young girl answers the bewildering attack with defiance; she may express her defiance by running away from her home and her spying mother.

Let us halt here for a moment and analyze some of these mothers. I know you are going to say that the mother of that runaway girl is a fine and noble woman; she has never done a wicked thing in her life. Well, that all depends on what one may call wicked. Girls do not leave healthy homes of their own free will; it is quite contrary to feminine nature. However, when a mother is denied those very definite things that her nature demands, she must vent her spleen on someone permitted to have the things her mother is denied. Yes, the child may have all the food she desires, but the mother resents the thought that the impulses of sex may enter the picture. Such mothers are sex-starved and their system rebels, often with explosive violence. Remember that Byron said, "Man's love is of man's life a thing apart, 'tis woman's sole existence." These very rigid women who regard all sex as unclean are often in desperate conflict with their inner selves. One may say to herself, "This is wrong;" while the subconscious says, "You lie!" Such women present pathetic studies in frustration and are more in

need of mental treatment than their rebellious daughters.

Let us analyze a few cases at hand. Here is a very celebrated one to start with. Miss L., aged 17, was a very charming and well-educated girl who ran away from her small town home to a nearby city; not long after, the police found her asleep in an alley and turned her over to a welfare agency. Here was a girl who had been a veritable prisoner most of her life. Two brothers also had run away from home, several years previously. The father did not worry much, but the mother felt her offspring might be contaminated by the low boys in the street. This worked out all right for the sons, but not so well for the daughter. Since then she had not been allowed out of her mother's sight. When she went to the grocery, Mother always watched her from behind the lattice. If the storekeeper happened to be busy with another customer, the suggestion was made that the girl had been flirting with the sales clerk. Even the elderly grocer was a suspect. Mother was not the least backward in calling on Mrs. Grocer, who loved her husband, and many nasty words were bandied around the shop.

Now, Miss L. was approaching womanhood and had reached that stage where it seems girls go along with a rush, becoming sex-conscious and "boy-crazy." But the daughter in spite of her mother's ravings, had been most loyal to her. One evening a strawberry festival was given at the church, and Miss L. was going with some girl friends.

At the festival, she met a young man who appealed to her and they chatted until about 11:30 at night. Was mother awaiting the return? She was! And the greeting to the young man was, "Didn't you have enough money to pay for the room all night?"

A physician has well observed that "The first shock of a bullet is no more than a brisk punch. The wrecked body does not send its protest to the soul till ten or fifteen seconds later. Then come thirst, throbbing agony, and a ridiculous amount of screaming." So it was with Miss L. and, as she turned in her bed, she went through the tortures of a wounded creature.

Before long the village gossips began to discuss a new motion picture, said to have been based on the *Song of Songs* by Herman Sudermann, one of the world's most gifted writers. Mother slipped off under cover of night and satisfied her hungry soul. Daughter was forbidden to gaze upon the picture, as unfit for a young girl; nor was she permitted to know her mother had seen it. Somehow, somewhere, the girl obtained a copy of this immortal tale (which, incidentally, should be read by everyone) and suffered page by page with Lily Czepanek. Alas, things of beauty cannot always be a joy forever. So it was not long before mother, in rummaging through her daughter's belongings, came upon the hidden volume. "Aha!" she shrieked. "Haven't we enough of these hussies around America without learning about a foreign slut?" Poor little L. did not know what it was all about. "First thing you know,

the neighbors will be talking about us, and my house will be disgraced," continued the old termagant. The scene ends with Lily locked in her room, a prisoner at night, and forbidden to see any boys. The persecuted child fled at her first opportunity. She was more to be pitied than censured.

Another case: An attractive brunette, aged 19, was arrested on a charge of vagrancy. It appears evident that her mother and father were by no means in close harmony. Of recent years, in fact, it was noticed that her father had become a frequenter of the nearby saloon. Mother, it seems, spent most of her time in religious devotion. There had been no marital relation between the parents of this household for a long time. The husband was able to lose himself in the fumes of alcohol, while mother concentrated her efforts on saving the younger generation. That inane cry about "flaming youth" has been screamed aloud for centuries. I am not such a youngster myself, and I can remember when people talked about the wildness of my own generation. This same idea, my old schoolmate pass along to their little goslings.

The young heroine of our story, it appears, had developed a taste for silk stockings and other nice things. Why not? Such knickknacks are all dear to the feminine heart. The child managed to hide some dainty silks for a while, but when mother noticed a lipstick—*crescendo*—"Heaven help us!" she bleated, "Little did I realize this house was harbouring a loose woman. So," the fond parent continued in this vein of gloom, "with silk stockings and indecent clothes you think fine feathers make fine birds, but they don't." Little did she realize that the saying ,"Fine feathers do not make fine birds," is merely the poor man's excuse for his tawdry existence. This charming girl did not leave home because she wanted to, but a tyranny no longer bearable compelled it.

There is another type of mother who succeeds in a similar manner in chaining her daughter for life. You will see such women, at about forty-five, engaged in clerical positions. These mothers usually resent any visitors to the house, and a man is never tolerated. Only too frequently, a girl's mother will go to the boy friend telling him he is too good for her daughter. After dinner daughter must get her sewing box and stay home from the wicked world. If any visitors are permitted they are usually older than the girl, so that she may adopt their ways and thus become old before her time.

Feigning illness is a great stunt with these parents, and some are mighty clever actresses, knowing just the psychological moment to make their appeal. If the headache has been worked overtime, it is now an attack of dizziness incident to hard work all day long in the house while the daughter was having a good time at the office chewing gum and reading novels.

I know one of these old tyrants who has a daughter forty years of age. All possible men are driven away, and plainly told the girl is a hussy. Yet this girl has supported her mother ever since she was sixteen. When a possibility of marriage presents itself, the mother attempts to frustrate it. Her trick is to keep dinning the following into daughter's ears: "Why, you know the change of life is coming on within you, so what good can you be to any husband?" The only means of defence the daughter has is to stuff her ears with cotton. Keep telling people something, and they are sure to believe it; this is a good old advertising motto and holds in the home as well. Recently, the daughter wanted to go up state to see a friend, but the mother insisted she would die if the daughter went. I advised her to risk the death of her mother, and the old lady was alive and kicking very lustily when her daughter returned. Types such as we are now portraying are well depicted by Radclyffe Hall in her great story, "The Unlit Lamp," and in that strong novel of Samuel Butler, "The Way of All Flesh." Some of these mothers may be likened to the child who feels its parent is giving too much attention to a new baby, and finds it can make a slave of its mother by feigning illness.

Many a daughter would like to escape from home, but mother has so impressed her with tales of dreadful ogres who lie in wait for young girls that she loses courage. Many will never marry.

The solution of the problem of the "wayward girl" is found, not by going to the cities to which these girls have fled, but rather, by going to the homes from which they have fled.

HOW TO HAVE A SUCCESSFUL HONEYMOON

Ewing Galloway

by Marvin Sentnor, M.D. and Stephen Hult, M.A.

*Careful preparation for this important period
will pay high dividends in future happiness.*

SOME recent writings assume
that the ignorant young
couples are a thing of the remote, Victorian past; that nowadays all honeymooners are thoroughly familiar with the best sex-
manuals and know enough from
talk with friends and personal experimentation to take all the
anxiety and hazards out of the
situation.

Perhaps—but extensive discussions with contemporary practi-

*Dr. Sentnor is a specialist in
obstetrics and gynecology practicing
in New York.

A graduate in psychology, Mr.
Hult has done research for various
institutions on the sexual behavior
of various groups and is now working on a history of sexual knowledge.*

tioners, family doctors and gynecologists indicate that this is still
an area of enormous ignorance.
Joking and talking may be freer
and easier, but the important factual information is still lacking
for far too many newly-married
men and women.

Various factors in the setting
can still be of great advantage in
making the first intercourse a
good rather than a bad memory
for one or both. Privacy must be
highly assured—both in time and
place. That is, locking the room
or stateroom door gives privacy of
location, but it is equally important to be sure there is time
enough for an utterly unhurried
fulfillment.

If the wedding party lasted late,
and the travel schedule means

there are only a few hours before resuming the trip or making an early start, the husband may forestall tensions and uncertainties by confiding to his bride that lying in each other's arms will be bliss enough for these few hours. The consummation should come at the next stopping place when they have a long private time (day or night) for that purpose.

First intercourse for the bride brings with it the various problems connected with virginity and the hymen.

One thing should be clear to both husband and wife—neither pain nor profuse bleeding has to occur when the hymen is ruptured during the first sex act. Ignorance on this point has caused a great deal of needless anxiety, misunderstanding and suspicion.

The hymen is, in essence, a fragile membrane that more or less completely covers the entrance to the vagina in most female human beings who have not had sex relations. (Hymen, in fact, is the Greek word for membrane.)

Often it is thin and fragile and gives way readily to the male organ at the first attempt at intercourse. As might be expected, girls in this situation bleed very little and perhaps not at all in the process of losing their virginity.

It is also important to realize that many girls are born without a hymen or at most only a tiny trace of one; so that *the absence of the hymen is by no means positive proof that a girl has had sex relations.*

But there is a basis in fact for the exaggerations of the folk-lore beliefs. Some hymens are so strongly developed that they can-

not be torn without considerable pain to the girl and marked loss of blood. More rarely, the hymen is so sturdy that it does not yield to penetration.

Extreme cases are on record in which the doctor has had to use instruments to cut through the hymen to permit marital relations to be consummated. These cases, for all their rarity, are so dramatic that friends and relations repeat the story until the general population may get an entirely false notion of how often the hymen is a serious problem to newlyweds.

In recent times, when sexual matters began to be discussed more scientifically and more openly, the emotional aspects of virginity received considerable attention. Obviously, the bridal pair has many adjustments to make to their new situation. Is it necessary to add to the other tensions the hazard of making the loving husband the one who brought pain to his bride?

Gynecologists and marriage manuals began to advise that the bride should consult a physician before marriage. If he foresaw any problem because of the quality of the hymen, it was recommended that simple procedures be undertaken at once to incise the hymen or, preferably, to dilate it.

As a natural outgrowth of this approach it was often suggested that the doctor should complete the preparation for painless intercourse by dilating the vagina.

This recommendation was based on the fact that the hymen was not the only barrier to smooth consummation of the sex act. The vagina is an organ capable of remarkable contraction and dilatation. This is obvious when it is remembered that, during childbirth, the vagina must dilate enough to permit the passage of the baby.

The intricate system of muscles that manage the contraction and dilatation of the vagina are partly under voluntary control. But an instinctive reflex may work against the conscious intention of the woman. That is, when first penetration takes place, the pressure and pain signals may *involuntarily* cause all the vaginal muscles to contract in an effort to bar the intrusion and prevent further pain.

The advantages of dilatation by the physician are both physical and psychological. Since it is a purely professional situation, none of the pain is associated with love-making or the beloved. By using instruments of gradually increasing size, the vagina is gently, and with minimum pain at each stage, taught to yield to an object of the appropriate shape.

In this process the vaginal muscles come under better conscious control by the girl. She learns how to relax them to *accept*—instead of contracting them to *repel* the entering object.

Apart from the standard problem of controlling the vaginal muscles, other serious barriers may exist that need special gynecological treatment. It is far better to have such conditions treated in advance than to have them show up on the honeymoon where they can create a really serious situation.

When no medical problems exist, the newly married couple generally prefer to cope with the adjustments of their new relationship by themselves. Special in-

formation and guidance about the possible difficulties are still of great value. Folk-lore, superstition and remembered passages from erotic literature can create physical and emotional problems if blindly taken as scientific facts and useful hints.

The importance of loving tenderness is obvious. The long, unhurried approach and the deliberate prolongation of fore-play work on several levels. Under the excitement of caresses and sexual stimulation the vagina relaxes and dilates and the local moisture greatly increases, providing an excellent lubricant to help achieve an easier penetration.

Extensive observations by physicians during vaginal examinations have established the fact that a single finger inserted along the anterior wall (the top line of the vagina as the woman lies on her back) may cause a great deal of distress in a virgin. *But* during the same examination, *two* fingers may be inserted along the posterior wall (the bottom of the vagina in the same position) without any pain; and in fact without any difficulty *if the pressure is kept downward at all times.*

These regional differences of sensitivity to pain may be of crucial significance during the earliest intercourse. The husband and wife should start with this anatomical information clearly in mind. They may then adjust their positions and movements to avoid too much pressure on the urethra and the anterior wall of the vagina; at least until repeated intercourse has dilated it and pain is no longer a possible threat against the full pleasure of lovemaking.

In fact, the technical procedure

in medical examinations may be wisely adapted to his romantic purposes by the husband during the honeymoon.

Locker-room talk often stresses the idea that a man is doing the girl a favor if he is forceful and ruthless during the first penetration. The false reasoning is that a gradual advance prolongs the pain while a swift powerful act gets it over with and leaves the girl pleased with his virility and grateful for his decisiveness in settling the problem once and for all.

Such talk is seriously in error. Ruthlessness at this time can be a very severe shock to the bride, both physically and psychologically. The insistent, forceful penetration may tear and inflame the vaginal walls as well as do excessive damage to the hymen.

The pain and distress associated with the performance may easily give the wife a deep-seated dread of marital relations and cause her, unconsciously, to make the sex act unpleasant and difficult for both by exercising her vaginal muscles to complicate his penetration instead of relaxing them to facilitate it.

Serious attention must also be given to the husband's problems in the honeymoon situation. The necessity for keeping alert to his bride's hazards can act as an interference with the man's spontaneous desire. The emotional stimulation may be so great that he may experience a premature climax. This is a very common experience and should in no way discourage or dishearten either husband or wife.

Or the frequent need to check and discipline himself to the wis-

est pace of the consummation can put him off stride and make it impossible for him to be continuously ready for penetration over a long period. The signals to proceed may therefore come when he is momentarily not able to take advantage of them.

The best course is to recover his physical excitement by a change of pace that makes him ardent again. This may require imagination and reminding himself that now he can be demanding and self-centered. He can take security from the fact that the progress he has made by his gentle approach will not be lost.

Now while he uses talk, caresses or requires caresses from her, his bride will sympathetically understand the situation and eagerly help him restore his physical situation so they can have the consummation they both so eagerly desire.

A final word. The accumulated information on this point shows that first intercourse, even when it is achieved with minimum pain or difficulty, is seldom an overwhelming sexual experience to a woman. Too many new things are happening for it to be a complete erotic fulfillment.

Only under rare circumstances would a bride experience an orgasm during her first intercourse. Both man and wife should be aware of the fact that a lack of climax, and even the absence of the anticipated keen pleasure are not a sign that the wife may be cold or frigid.

If the early approaches are wise, understanding and patient, the satisfactions of marital fulfillment will probably be discovered before the marriage is much older.

Sex in Dreams

by Emilio Servadio, LL.D.

Sigmund Freud, the founder of psychoanalysis, conceived the idea that sexual symbols appeared in dreams. Although many psychiatrists today believe that this theory is far-fetched and invalid, psychoanalysts attempt to interpret the sexual content of dreams in their treatment of emotionally disturbed patients.

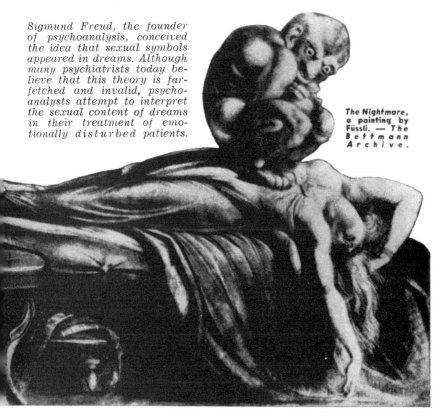

The Nightmare, a painting by Füssli. — The Bettmann Archive.

THE occasional "sexual" dreams of persons who admit having them usually contain very plain and obvious dream-scenes of love-making or coitus. The number of sexual dreams is far greater than most people imagine. They, in a broad sense, are a very common feature of the human mind.

The word "sex" has many more connotations than the expression "reproductive urge." A confusion between the two should be impossible nowadays, after Professor Freud's momentous discoveries on

Prof. Dr. Servadio is a distinguished Italian psychologist and author who was formerly vice-president of the Italian Psychoanalytic Society.

child-sexuality, and all we have learned about sexual activities which have no reproductive aim. We should bear in mind that many strange sex representations may be present in the dreams of the healthiest persons, in the form of *repressed* and *unconscious* phantasies. These phantasies can give rise to dreams whose sexual nature may escape attention—(1) because they do not seem sexual in a strict and outmoded sense, and (2) because they appear to the dreamer in a distorted form which makes them unrecognizable.

"Concealed Sex"

Here is an example of such "concealed" sexual dreams. A young girl dreams that a robber ("a very handsome man") enters her bedroom from the window and is about to steal her handbag which contains some valuable jewels. She is afraid and wakes up.

At first sight, one might say that such a dream does not contain anything sexual. Nevertheless, some acquaintance with the "dream language" is sufficient to explain that the "handsome robber" is a seducer, that the "room" and the "handbag with the jewels" represent the feminine sex organs, and that the whole scene is the expression of two opposite tendencies: (1) a desire to be sexually attacked by a man who wants and might obtain intercourse; (2) the fear that this might actually happen.

The "defense" of the dreamer in relation to her own sexual wishes is threefold: first, she "projects" her intentions on somebody else (the initiative is apparently taken by the "robber," while the dreamer situates herself simply as a passive onlooker and victim); secondly, she conceals the deed under the veil of symbols (the scene, after all, represents a theft, not a sexual attack); thirdly she gets no satisfaction from the dream, but simply fear. What could be more acceptable, according to the rules of one's own inner "censor"?

A young patient of mine dreamed that he was in the street on a rainy day; he opened his umbrella and invited a lady to take shelter under it with him. He remembered afterwards that the lady was an acquaintance of his mother, and he admitted having had amorous phantasies about her. Here again, we must rely on some knowledge of symbolism and dream distortion in order to grasp what the dream means, namely, a sexual "offer" accompanied by a display of the dreamer's virility (the "umbrella" may be considered a symbol of the male organ and its "opening" a representation of sexual arousal).

A sexual dream in disguise can only take place, it seems, if two factors are at work: the primary impulse or wish (which can be near consciousness or deep in the mind), and the inner "censor" which objects to a *direct* representation of the wish and compels the dreamer's mind to use hints, metaphors and symbols. The standards of the dream's "censor" may be quite different from those of the conscious moral code. It sometimes accepts very crude representations of the dreamer's phantasies,

Night Vision, a painting by Jacob Jordeans.—From
"Sexualspiegel" (Sexual Mirror), by Erich Wulffen.

while admitting other symbols, which one might expect to be unobjectionable, only under elaborate camouflage.

Sex Symbols

The interpretation of a dream—sexual or otherwise—can seldom take place through the simple "unveiling" of the symbols it contains. Nevertheless, a knowledge of dream symbolism is indispensable to anyone who is seriously engaged in psychoanalytic work—a work which inevitably involves dream analysis.

Many symbols have been interpreted by Professor Freud in his monumental work *The Interpretation of Dreams* and his statements on the subject have been advanced through the study of mythology, folklore, poetry, religion, primitive rituals and the close scrutiny of thousands of dreams. Here are a few examples of sexual symbolism in dreams.

Freud believed that "all elongated objects, sticks, tree-trunks, umbrellas ... all sharp and elongated weapons, knives, daggers, and pikes, represent the male member. ... Small boxes, chests, cubboards and ovens correspond to the female organ; also cavities, ships and all kinds of vessels. ... Steep inclines, ladders and stairs, and going up or down them, are symbolic representations of the sexual act. ... In the dreams of men one often finds the necktie as a symbol for the penis. ... Most of those animals which are used as genital symbols in mythology and folklore play this part also in dreams: the fish, the snail, the cat, the mouse.... But above all the snake, which is the most important symbol of the male member.... The genitals may be represented in dreams by other parts of the body: the male member by the hand or the foot, the female genital orifice by the mouth, the ear, or the eye...."

This list is incomplete. The things that can be symbolized are few, but the symbols which can represent them are numerous. Only wide experience gives the interpreter the ability to apply "the right symbol in the right place" and to use dream symbolism without neglecting several other aspects of dream interpretation.

Another patient of mine, a married man in his thirties, had several difficulties in his sex life, mainly because of his inferiority feelings towards his elder brother and his father, whose male assertiveness he still felt as something more than he could hope for in himself. He dreamed that he was in a hotel room with his friend Bill, and was asking Bill to lend him a purple tie. On second thought, the tie did not seem to suit him, and he was trying to select one of his own. In the meantime, Bill had gone in the adjoining room and had asked two ladies to have dinner with them. The dreamer was saying: "I am not ready yet."

As indicated by Freud, the "tie" is a symbol of the male member and more generally of maleness. The dreamer would like to "bor-row" a better one from somebody else (a brother figure), but quickly dismisses the thought. He also dismisses the idea of having dinner with Bill and two ladies (a hotel party whose possible implications and developments are only too obvious). His "unreadiness" is an indirect but clear expression of his sexual inhibitions (immaturity).

An Unusual Symbol

A lady of 26 had a very pretty dream in which a sexual idea was symbolized in a somewhat unusual fashion. She already had three children and did not like the idea of having more, although she had a very satisfactory sex life with her husband and was not prepared to stop marital relations. The two contradictory ideas (sexual desire, and the wish not to become pregnant again) were expresesd as follows: She dreamt that her husband was inviting her to sit down on a bench in a quiet and secluded park. She was quite willing to do so, but was giving her husband a half-serious, half-joking warning, "Beware of the paint!"

The day before, this lady had seen several loving couples sitting on the benches of a public park. In the dream, she would like to enact a similar situation with her husband and, obviously, to go far beyond the preliminary steps of love-making. Her fear of becoming pregnant, however, is represented, too, in her symbolical warning: she is afraid that the "paint" (the seminal fluid) might cause inconveniences (conception).

Among young or uneducated people, we still find dreams in

which sexual symbolism is practically the only disguise and where, therefore, it is only necessary to "translate" the symbols in order to understand their hidden significance. A woman whose husband was a policeman dreamed as follows: "... someone broke into the house and she anxiously called for a policeman. But he went peacefully with two tramps into a church, to which a great many steps led up; behind the church there was a mountain, on top of which there was a dense forest. The policeman was provided with a helmet, a molding plane and a cloak. The two vagrants, who went along with the policeman quite peacefully, had sacks like aprons tied round their loins. . . ."

This dream contains a whole series of sexual symbols. The "church" is the feminine organ; "climbing up a flight of steps" means sexual intercourse; the "mountain" is the *mons veneris* (female pubic region); the "forest" represents pubic hair; "helmet, molding plane and cloak" are symbols of malenes; the "two vagrants" with "sacks" are the testicles. The dream obviously represents a sexual act. The dreamer wishes the act to be performed by her husband, who would thus "save" her from a possible extramarital relation into which she might be tempted by some seducer (the intruder who "breaks into the house" has the same meaning as the "robber" in the dream of the young girl).

Due consideration of sex wishes and phantasies in dreams is extremely fruitful, as it helps us towards a better understanding of sexual problems and gives sexuality its proper place in the individual's personality structure and in human relations in the whole pattern of society in general.

● ● ●

TESTOSTERONE FOR FRANCE

MANY of the 500,000 French babies born annually during the occupation are believed to have been German-sired. Despite these contributions, the French birth rate, already low before the war, ran consistently behind the death rate. In six years (1936-42), France's population dropped 4,000,000. The return of 2,000,000 Frenchmen from German prison camps and slave labor battalions, now under way, will be a step in the right direction, but probably not enough of one. For many of these men have been so weakened by undernourishment and ill treatment that they have temporarily lost either the desire or the capacity for fatherhood.

From London came news of a French attempt to solve this national problem. The report (which the French Ministry of Health understandably denied): the French Government is buying £25,000,000 worth of that restorer of physical and sexual vigor, testosterone, the male hormone. Treatment, by injection, will be voluntary, secret and free to any man under Government medical care or returning from captivity.

—*Time Magazine*

by Edward Dengrove, M. D.

Priapism . . .

uncontrollable erection

Persistent erection of the male organ is a painful ailment which is usually unaccompanied by sexual desire. It requires immediate medical treatment.

The ailment *priapism* is named after the ancient Greek god Priapus, who was worshipped as a symbol of fertility. According to legend, Priapus was the son of Aphrodité and Dionysus. —Woodcut by Bouquet in "Les Plaisirs et les Fêtes," by Magré.

THE penis, the male organ of procreation, is usually relaxed and flaccid. In this state it is not prepared to fulfill its important rôle in human reproduction. If successful sexual union is to be effected, the male organ must become enlarged and rigid—only then is copulation possible.

Usually, erection is the natural result of sexual excitation. However, certain other causes, unrelated to the sexual function, may result in uncontrollable erection which may be persistent and painful—a condition known medically as *priapism*. In order to fully understand how this ailment is caused, some knowledge of the mechanism of erection is necessary.

The penis is composed of a tube, called the *urethra,* through which urine is discharged from the bladder and through which the semen also must pass. The urethra is surrounded by two hollow bodies (*corpora cavernosa*), one on each side, composed almost entirely of sponge-like tissue. Sexual excitation causes an increased flow of blood through the arteries into the corpora cavernosa and the spongy tissues. At the same time, there is a decrease in the blood flowing out from them. When they become engorged, or filled with blood, the penis becomes tense and rigid, much as a tire does when it is filled with air. The muscles which raise the organ then begin to work. When the excitation lessens, as after an ejaculation, the blood leaves the organ through the veins, the supply of blood to the penis decreases, and the organ becomes flaccid.

The sexual excitation necessary to prepare the male for intercourse is the result of stimuli—ideas and impressions received through the senses of sight, hearing, smell, taste or touch—which are sexually attractive. Close physical contact with the person one loves is an example of such a stimulus. These impressions are carried to the brain. The brain receives them and transmits their message through the spinal cord to the lower region of the cord, where centers of erection are located. From there the

Dr. Dengrove is a well known medical author and psychiatrist in private practice in New Jersey.

reaction is carried by nerves to the cavernous bodies of the penis, and that organ prepares for sexual union.

These nerves do not receive the message which stimulates them from the brain alone. Local stimulation and direct excitation of the genitals themselves also influence the nerves which regulate sexual activity. And they are affected by disease and injury, as is the case in *priapism.*

Priapus—God of Fertility

The word *priapism* is derived from the name *Priapus,* a mythological god of fertility, the son of Aphrodité, goddess of love and beauty, and Dionysus, the god of wine. Images of Priapus, represented as a faun-like creature with an enormous and erect sexual organ, were placed in gardens to assure women's fertility. They were also used as a charm to ward off the "evil eye." The first fruits of the harvest were offered to Priapus as a sacrifice, and he was reputed to bring good luck to those who worshipped him.

Case Histories

Priapism may last for only a few hours, or it may persist for several days, and, it is said, even years. Usually it is caused by a physical disturbance, although it was at one time falsely attributed to sexual excesses.

A case of such prolonged priapism is described in *Anomalies and Curiosities of Medicine.* The patient, a man of fifty-three, was suffering from a violent and painful erection which had lasted for five hours. The administration of a sedative afforded him some relief; but within a few hours the condition returned. Again it was relieved by medication, as were two other erections which occurred during that day. The man had been experiencing eight or ten erections a day for three years. No sexual yearnings accompanied these erections, although he had been having erotic dreams, sometimes three a night. After treatment which included diet, sponging, the application of ice and the administering of a drug, the man is said to have completely recovered.

Dr. Lowenfeld also tells of a form of painful priapism which occurs only at night in married men in their forties or fifties who, for various reasons, had to abstain from sexual relations. This condition might last, according to his observations, for years. Dr. Iwan Bloch attributed this type of erection to the effect of sexual stimuli originating from the genital organs, and revealing itself only during sleep, when it could not be consciously controlled.

In a case of priapism treated by the sexologist Dr. Magnus Hirschfeld, the erections also occurred only during the night. The patient had suffered from agonizing erections every night for fifteen years. They began almost as soon as he went to sleep and continued throughout the entire night, making sleep impossible. Thoughts of a sexual nature did not accompany them. The erections were painful, and the lack of sleep distressing. In an attempt to stop them, he had tried frequent urination. In-

stead, he had developed a desire to urinate which also occurred only during the night. None of the local remedies he had tried had relieved the priapism, which became worse.

The patient was found free from serious disease, although there had been some minor local changes in the prostate region which might have caused the priapism. It had been aggravated, however, by his constant concern about it. Some medication was prescribed; but all local treatments were discarded and psychotherapy instituted instead. After four weeks of treatment the patient was reported much improved. Within a few months he was able to sleep undisturbed.

Organic Causes

Most often priapism is *organic*. Many conditions may cause it. Sometimes it results from an inflammation of the nerves leading to the penis (*peripheral neuritis*), or from obstruction of the blood vessels that drain it. It may be caused by stones in the bladder, or inflammation of the urethra or prostate. Blood clots due to cancers, tumors, or inflammation of cellular tissue may cause priapism, as may injuries to the penis. It has been observed in epilepsy, tuberculosis, and inflammation of the kidneys. Local inflammation about the muscles which constrict the bulb of the penis are sometimes responsible. It is a symptom—relatively rare—of leukemia; and when that is the cause, radiation treatment often relieves it. Priapism sometimes appears after the use of

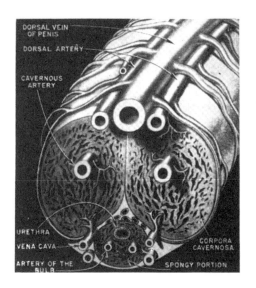

DORSAL VEIN OF PENIS

DORSAL ARTERY

CAVERNOUS ARTERY

URETHRA

VENA CAVA

ARTERY OF THE BULB

CORPORA CAVERNOSA

SPONGY PORTION

certain drugs. Excessive dosage of *testosterone propionate*, which is given to supply testicular hormone to men whose bodies are deficient in it, may result in priapism—a sign that the drug should be discontinued temporarily.

Infants and children up to one year of age often have erections that continue for long periods of time and are really a form of priapism. It has also been observed in persons who meet death by hanging.

Injury or disease of the spinal cord is a frequent cause of priapism. It is sometimes found in paraplegics (those who are paralyzed in the lower half of their bodies). Dislocations in the neck region between certain of the small bones or segments which comprise the spinal column — the *cervical vertebrae* — may severely damage the spinal cord, interfering with the transmission of the nerve messages which govern the centers of erection. A more or less permanent erection may then be the result. Sometimes it occurs spontaneously after an accident involving the spinal cord, due to an excitation of that portion of the spinal cord which is below the injury and cannot now receive regulating messages from the brain. Or it may not develop until some time after an injury; in such cases it is due to central irritation from seepage of blood into the substance of the spinal cord.

Rarely Gratifying

Priapism is rarely accompanied by any gratifying sexual sensations, although in cases where it is caused by excessive stimulation of the sexual centers, these may occur. Dr. Magnus Hirschfeld was consulted by a man of forty-five who suffered from prolonged erections and an increased sexual excitability which was disturbing him. Examination revealed that the man had a disorder of the spinal system.

Medical literature contains an account of a young man who was wounded by a rifle-ball. Five days after the injury, priapism set in. On the following day, the man had to be denied a female attendant, so sexually aroused was he. The priapism continued until a few minutes before his death, nine days later.

Intercourse usually affords no satisfaction, nor does it decrease the swelling of the sexual organ. Generally, it makes the condition worse. Cases have been reported of priapism occurring after sexual intercourse.

In a case of priapism, one must first determine the cause; on that the treatment depends. Local measures include protecting the organ with cotton padding, and arranging the bedclothes so as to avoid any painful contact. Lotions or ointments may be used to keep the skin soft. In painful priapism caused by an inflammation of the spinal cord, certain drugs can be administered which often give effective relief. Anesthesia also causes the organ to relax. However, in each individual case, the treatment must be prescribed by the attending physician on the basis of the cause of the ailment.

References

Anomalies and Curiosities of Medicine, by George M. Gould, M.D. and Walter L. Pyle, M.D.

The Sexual Life of Our Time, by Iwan Bloch, M.D.

Sexual Pathology, by Magnus Hirschfeld, M.D.

so they say . . .

Accolades, Not Censure

"THERE is a Protestant minister in the Northwest who has been punished for explaining sex to his teenagers. The punishment consisted of public humiliation, an apology to a board of education, and a promise not to mention the word to students again. I'm with the minister. Sex is a source of trouble only to those who do not understand it. . . . To my way of thinking, this holy man deserves accolades, not censure. He is trying to lift the veil of mystery from a subject that becomes evil only when it is suppressed.

"I would like to meet the ladies and gentlemen who form the Board of Education that degraded him. I would like to stare down into their beady eyes and ask one question: 'If it wasn't for sex, where would you be right now?' "

—Jim Bishop in his nationally syndicated column.

Explaining Elsa Maxwell

"I NEVER had a sexual experience nor did I ever want one. . . ."

—Elsa Maxwell to Jack Paar as quoted in Pageant magazine.

Descriptive Specialists

"WE see descriptive specialists in the texture and surface temperature of the body, ranging in the first case from marble to velvet; in the second, from hot to cool. There are body-geography and sexual-topology students—erotic spelunkers of a sort. Also, we have experts in the functional mechanics or general physics of sex relations. Many writers seem compelled to diagram precisely what is involved in sexual intercourse, either to instruct the reader or to reassure themselves that they know."

—Literary critic Edmund Fuller in Cosmopolitan.

WHAT IS YOUR

*SEX QUOTIENT

by Mark Tarail, B.A., M.S.

BY taking this test, you can measure your sex knowledge. Check whether the answer to each statement should be *Yes* or *No*. Compare your answers with the correct answers below. Give yourself 10 points for each correct answer and add the results. Your final score is your S.Q.

A score of 50 or less *indicates inadequate* knowledge; 50 to 60 equals *good;* 70 or 80 equals *excellent;* 90 or above equals *unusually superior.*

(YES) (NO)   1. Do Americans tend to marry today at a later age than 50 years ago?

(YES) (NO)   2. Should engagement be considered an irrevocable commitment to marriage?

(YES) (NO)   3. Do all persons have the same need for sexual expression?

(YES) (NO)   4. Should sexual activities be engaged in for procreation only?

(YES) (NO)   5. Are some parts of the body "untouchable" between husband and wife?

(YES) (NO)   6. Is it desirable for married lovers to be uninhibited in their marital relations?

(YES) (NO)   7. Is a pre-marital medical examination desirable?

(YES) (NO)   8. Will adhesions of the foreskin interfere with satisfying marital relations?

(YES) (NO)   9. Can a man who has once had gonorrhea or syphilis safely marry?

(YES) (NO) 10. Can a shocking first sexual experience influence future sexual reactions?

ANSWERS:

1. NO. The average age at marriage is younger today than in the past.

2. NO. The engagement period should be a time of exploration and experimentation on the basis of which final decisions are made by both parties.

3. NO. Sex drive and sex needs vary greatly from person to person.

4. NO. They also satisfy other physical and psychological needs in marriage. In satisfying marital relations between a healthy husband and wife, no part of the body is "taboo" or "verboten" in sexual play.

5. ON. In satisfying marital relations between a healthy husband and wife, no part of the body is "taboo" or "verboten" in sexual play.

6. YES. The free release of natural feelings is part of the fulfilling result of marital relations.

7. YES. It is highly desirable both for counseling, and to discover any genital or other problems that require correction.

8. YES. Such adhesions are not only the source of infections in the wife but also affect the husband's sex functioning.

9. YES. However, as a precaution he should be re-examined before marriage to make sure that he is completely cured.

10. YES. The first experience will often condition a person to fear or welcome marital relations.

INTENSE EXCITEMENT

AS

SEXUAL STIMULUS

by Justus Day Wilbur

*To achieve orgasm and satisfaction in
the sex act, some persons require a special
situation or circumstances. Appearing in
the following article are explanations
and classifying of such cases in groups.*

Sexual excitement is afforded by many tribal dances, the movements of the dancers
often having a sexual characteristic. Here African men are dancing (Fali villagers) to the music furnished by stringed instruments.—*Illus. "The London Sphere."*

WHILE we have long known or heard of masochists and sadists — deviated persons who seek sexual gratification through cruel methods — we are perhaps less familiar with some other sexual oddities. The *pyromaniac* who must see a house on fire or the sadistic demon who must kill and smell blood, before an orgasm is possible, are horrifying examples.

Astonishingly, there are persons who (with much outward show of indignation) need and desire, for maximum sexual satisfaction, discovery in the sexual act by onlookers. More numerous are those who can find satisfaction in sex only when it is surreptitious and secretly connived, at a rendezvous. The respectable, comfortable, leisurely marriage bed is to them an extinguisher of sexual desire. Excitement and thrill seekers appear to be the great modern inciters to adultery and divorce. There seems to be a need, for some, of the element of *illicit* love, dangerously carried on, with the constant excitement of fear that their intrigue will be discovered. Some persons develop very specific conditional requirements; as to time, place, amount of light, music, state of dress or furnishings, kind of bed, or any of a thousand obsessive specifications. We have heard frequently of one type of these persons, the fetishists who can experience climax only if milady's slipper or corselet or whatnot is first fondled, gazed at, or smelled. But there are many other variations of this same attitude, this divergence of orgiastic stimulus from its main target to side targets of various kinds. There are those who can experience an orgasm only during a thunderstorm, or with organ music, or only after a violent quarrel, or after a rough - and - tumble wrestling with her mate—these are a few of the examples which could be mentioned.

There are also other forms of high excitement which affect sexual zest and/or potency, particularly in men. I have heard of middle-aged men whose sexual cycle corresponded with the stock market. During a "bear market" or "panic" period they showed no interest in sex, but during a "soaring bull market" they were intensely sexual. There are similar tales of gamblers who were potent only when in a winning phase of their activities. Some business men also have been known to show little sexual interest in their wives in dull or business recession periods, but are more potent sexually when a "boom" or "sellers' market" is on. Alcoholics are also examples of the relation of temporary high excitement to the sexual impulse.

The main thing to note is not the strange nature of the particular requirement, but the fact that there is a general similarity in them all —*the factor of intense excitement.* Many women who appear to be frigid become very passionate if their particular special obsession is followed and humored. It seems that their sexual nature can be aroused only by some special *key.* These special keys fall into certain groups: (1) physical **violence,**

Intense excitement to arouse the sexual instincts is often noted among natives by erotic dances like the one shown. Here young women of the Belgian Congo are lined up for a village festival and about to start dancing to the weird music of the tom-toms.—*Reproduced from the book, "Toutes les Races."*

(2) emotional upheavals, (3) physical object fetishes, invoking an imaginative sex phantasy, (4) social situations of secrecy, discovery, danger, (5) guilt, fear, inferiority or other complexes which set up unconscious patterns of reaction, (6) exhibitionism, or symbolic affirmations of sexual power or desirability, (7) masochism or sadism in their more extreme forms, (8) abnormal sexual fantasy.

Every one of these, in all their manifold varieties of expression, is based upon the production of excitement and the artificial aid of specialized visualizations, in order to attain the orgasm which in the fully expressed person needs little more than simple intimacy.

I say *little* more, because the truth is that the human imagination is very complex, and practically all of us (if we searched it out) could find in our sexual relationship some tendency to desire excitement as a sexual whip. The sexual bite, the sexual tease, or romp, the posturing and coquetting, the jealousy, lover-quarrel, etc., are all mild excitements for sexual purposes. Recently a Greek girl and a West Coast girl were "kidnapped" by their lovers, resulting in the wavering girl's firm fixation of love—a form of sexual excitement, like the primitive marriage by capture. The savages' spring dance festivals are also excitement-makers, primarily.

In another category are the sharp-toothed metal bands worn by some male savages on their sexual organ, to lacerate their mates and thus create extra excitement through pain. White persons who have seen the wild, long-continued mating dances of savage tribes have noted their real purpose, which is to accomplish what ordinary intimacy does not, for them: the sexual awakening of these coarse, hardened humans, who need the enormous, long-continued excitement of tom-tom and night-long wild dancing to stir their sluggish impulses. Why are savages hard to arouse sexually? The answer appears to be that the savage *does not phantasy sex* as does the white man with his sin-taboos. The white man's brain is replete with a vast range of inhibitive, challenging, fantasy-creating, imaginative items of possible excitement which make him especially subject to a kind of excitement which is not physical but mental. How he manages these so as to give himself the fuller satisfactions which such a brain can provide, is the result of his social and individual life as a so-called *civilized* man. The savage must depend not so much on his cortex, his higher lobes of the brain, as upon his musculature—upon motion, sound, heat, rhythm and direct body activity. He is still more animal than human! By the same token, however, he is not subject to so many of the special abnormalities of the sexual instinct to which civilized humans are subject. Perhaps the savage is happier!

● ● ●

SHOULD SEX REMAIN A TABOO SUBJECT?

IF the physician will school himself to drop the cloak of embarrassment, a taboo carried over from childhood, and face the physiology of sexual activity in the same spirit as that of the cardiorespiratory or gastro-intestinal system, he will be surprised at what some of his patients wish to discuss and what questions they will ask. He need not, indeed must not, pry into private and intimate matters if the patient does not wish this done. At times, however, he need give the patient only half a chance to burst a dam of questions and complaints. A routine and perfectly proper question in the review of the patient's history under the heading of the genitourinary system may open the closet door for the patient to let in the light. In the unmarried, a simple "Do you have any sexual problem or worries?", in the married merely a "Do you and your husband (or wife) have a satisfactory sexual life?"—are questions of which there can be no criticism or to which the patient cannot object. The patient may answer with a "No" or a "Yes," and the matter may be dropped, or the patient may seize the opportunity to unload years of secret worries and unanswered questions. It is shocking to learn how often the patient adds, — "This is the first time a doctor has ever given me a chance to talk about this," or "I've tried to talk to my doctor about this but he has been too busy to listen," or "He did not want to listen," or "I am glad I've had a chance to talk about this. I've known my doctor so long I couldn't bring myself to talk this way." What an indictment of the medical profession!

—*Editorial: Journal Tennessee State Medical Association.*

Ben Franklin's advice to a young man

> Circulated secretly for over two hundred years, this letter has been described as "the most famous and wittiest essay Franklin ever wrote."

June 25, 1745.

MY Dear Friend—I know of no Medicine to diminish the violent nocturnal Inclinations you mention, and, if I did, I think I should not communicate it to you. Marriage is the proper remedy. It is the most natural State of Man, and therefore the State in which you will find solid Happiness. Your Reasons against entering into it at present appear to me to be not well founded. The circumstantial Advantages you have in View by postponing it are not only uncertain, but they are small in comparison with the Thing itself, the being married and settled. It is the Man and Woman united that makes the complete being. Separate, she wants his force of Body and Strength of Reason; he her Softness, Sensibility and acute Discernment. Together they are most likely to succeed in the World. A single Man has not nearly the Value he would have in that State of Union. He is an incomplete Animal. He resembles the odd half of a pair of Scissors. If you get a prudent, healthy Wife, your Industry in your profession with her good Economy will be a Fortune sufficient. But if you will not take this Counsel, and persist in thinking a Commerce with the Sex inevitable, then I repeat my former Advice, that in your Amours you should prefer old women to young ones. This you call a Paradox, and demand my Reasons. They are these:

1. Because as they have more Knowledge of the World, and their Minds are better stored with observations, their Conversation is more improving and more lastingly agreeable.

2. Because when Women cease to be handsome they study to be good. To maintain their Influence over Man they supply the Diminution of Beauty by augmentation of Utility. They learn to do a thousand services small and great, and are most tender and useful of all Friends when you are sick. Thus they continue amicable, and hence there is hardly such a thing as an old Woman who is not a good Woman.

3. Because there is no Hazard of Children, which, irregularly produced, may be attended with much inconvenience.

4. Because through more Experience they are more prudent and discreet in conducting an Intrigue to prevent suspicion. The Commerce with them is, therefore, with regard to your Reputation; and, with regard to theirs, if the affair should happen to be known, considerate people might be inclined to excuse an old Woman who would kindly take care of a young man, form his manners by her good Councils, and prevent his ruining his Health and Fortune among mercenary Prostitutes.

5. Because in every Animal that walks upright, the Deficiencies of the Fluids that fill the Muscles appear first in the highest Part. The face first grows lank and wrinkled, then the neck, then the Breast and Arms, the lower Parts continuing to the last as plump as ever; so that covering all above with a Basket, and regarding only what is below the Girdle, it is impossible of two Women to know an old from a young one. And, as in the Dark all Cats are Gray, the pleasure of Corporal Enjoyment with an old Woman is at least equal, and frequently superior, every knack being by Practice capable of improvement.

6. Because the Sin is less. The Debauching of a Virgin may be her ruin and make her life unhappy.

7. Because the compunction is less. The having made a young girl miserable may give you frequent bitter reflections, none of which can attend making an old Woman happy.

8th and lastly. They are so grateful. Thus much for my Paradox. But I still advise you to marry immediately, being sincerely, your affectionate Friend,

Benj. Franklin

●   ●   ●

WE ARE BOTH SEXES

PARADOXICAL as it may seem, everyone possesses both male and female organs. Their growth and development—the reason why one set of organs reaches maturity while the other set remains rudimentary—depend on the stimulation these organs receive from sex hormones. In the female, estrogens (such as ovarian secretion or theelin) predominate, while in the male, androgens (such as the secretion of the testicles, testosterone) predominate. These androgens thus stimulate the growth and development of the prostate gland. So far as is known, the prostate gland itself secretes no hormone.

—Progress Guide

HOMOSEXUAL CHICKENS

Unisexual mating has been observed by scientists in other animals besides man. This unusual sex behavior is described as it occurs among chickens.

by A. M. Guhl, Ph.D.

UNISEXUAL mating, such as males mounting males and females mounting females, occurs at times among chickens. Although such behavior is rare among hens, it is not unusual among cockerels. In fact, young cockerels in juvenile plumage may often try to mount any penmate resting on the floor. This activity may not be recognized as sexual behavior because neither pullets nor cockerels give the proper sexual responses but, instead, avoid these fowls which attempt to *tread* (mate with) them.

The psychological aspects of bird behavior are rather simple when compared with those of mammals. Nevertheless, our understand-

Dr. Guhl is Professor of Zoology at Kansas State College.

ing of unisexual mating behavior in chickens is still in the formative stage. At present some of the situations associated with this aberrant behavior are known.

Mating Stimuli

An adequate discussion would delve into the "heredity versus environment" controversy, and would become technical without throwing much light on an explanation. The essential factors in unisexual mating include a strong sexual drive and the circumstances which stimulate this urge.

The sexual drive has its pattern in arrangements of nerves which become triggered more sensitively under the influence of appropriate sex hormones. In cockerels, attempts to mount appear when the testicles enlarge and produce suf-

Wide World Photos

ficient *androgen* (male hormone). Injections of androgen into a male chick will encourage sexual behavior at an early age.

Much the same is true for the young female except that the sex hormone is an *estrogen* and *crouching* (female mating position) is the typical sexual response. This behavior appears at about the time the first egg is laid. There is evidence that the respective sexual drives may increase in intensity when the birds are deprived of the presence of the opposite sex. In a flock of laying hens, some individuals may crouch readily when startled by their caretaker.

No precise study has been made of all the stimuli which may produce sexual behavior in cocks or hens. A sexually active cock may *display* toward either males or females, particularly when the flock has been assembled recently and the individuals are not acquainted. The more common displays of the males are either an attempt to grasp the comb or hackle, or to *wingflutter* (a circuitous dance about another bird).

The strongest stimulus for mounting is the sight of a hen crouching or a bird resting on the ground in a position similar to the mating crouch. Dead birds may be trod repeatedly when the drive is at a high level. Some poultrymen believe that laying hens are inclined to crouch more often than nonlaying ones, but other factors are also involved.

The stimuli which evoke crouching are elusive. Hens in a laying flock, which have had no males present for some weeks, may crouch soon after a male is released in their pen. Under conditions of the sex ratio usually found in breeding flocks, crouchings are fewer and the element of "surprise" seems to be a key stimulus. A furtive approach by a male appears to be effective, whereas a sexually aggressive male is avoided. Rarely will a hen take the initiative by approaching a male and crouching.

Social Rank

Unisexual matings may be influenced by the positions of the birds in the social organization of the flock. Individual fowls can be ranked according to their aggressiveness or social dominance. The social ranks are determined by the number of individuals each dominates by pecking without being pecked in return. For example, in a flock of 42 birds, a hen with rank number one would peck all other birds in the flock, and number 42 would be pecked by all and peck none. The other members of the group would occupy various social levels between these two extremes. The cocks usually do not peck the hens but show passive domination over them. Thus a flock has two peck-orders, one for each sex.

Experiments have shown that the high-ranking male usually does most of the mating and sires the most chicks. The lowest-ranking cock may be psychologically castrated, in the sense that he may refrain completely from any sexual behavior as a result of social suppression. It has also been shown that high-ranking hens are very "bossy" and are not as disposed to submitting to the male as are low-ranking hens.

However, if several of the hens at the top of the peck-order are removed and penned together, thereby making a smaller flock with fewer hens to dominate, they may become less dominating and are as submissive to the male as their low-ranking sisters. One may conclude that the psychological influences linked with the habit of dominating facilitate reproductive behavior in the males but inhibit it in females.

Unisexual matings among cockerels on the summer range of our poultry farm are quite common. These males are reared apart from the pullets. The "bosses" in this large flock drive the least aggressive ones and tread them when they are caught. Many cockerels are killed because they have little opportunity to feed and drink, become weakened, then cannot withstand the stress of their unfortunate situation. Small groups of males confined indoors show similar behavior. Causes of this aberrant behavior are a strong sexual drive in the absence of females, and psychological suppression, debility, and fatigue which result from extreme social tension among the lowest ranks in the peck-order.

Homosexual Hens

Unisexual matings among hens are rare and unique because females usually do not take the initiative in normal reproductive behavior. The writer has records of about two hundred unisexual matings involving eleven different hens in which the social ranks of the birds were known. The observations include different strains and successive generations of *White Leghorns*.

Apparently heredity was not a major factor, as neither the parents nor the offspring of these aberrant birds showed unisexual behavior. In all but seven of these 200 matings the hens taking the male rôle ranked higher in the peck-order than the one trod. In most of these instances the mating behavior was, except for intensity, similar to that of normal males.

Of the 200 treadings, 124 were by one hen, showing that the frequency varied greatly among the hens. Although these hens mounted their social inferiors, the bossiest of the hens were not necessarily the most addicted to masculine behavior.

What stimulated these hens to mount other hens? In nearly all of the situations, the hen which was trod was either resting on the floor or *dusting* in the litter. These postures resemble a crouch, with some exceptions, such as, with wings folded rather than out-

The cock's dance or *wing flutter* is shown as he makes a sexual approach to (courts) a cornered hen.

The cock is performing the wing flutter while the hen is crouching receptively.

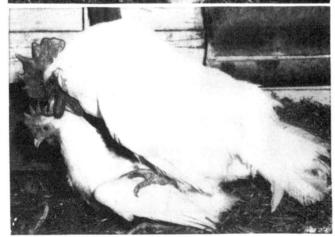

When *treading* (mating) a cock mounts a crouching hen, stands on her outstretched wings and holds her by the feathers on her head. —Photos courtesy of author.

stretched. Twenty - one treadings resulted from the following sequence of events: A hen threatened to peck one of its social inferiors which responded by crouching in the typical female fashion and subsequently was mounted. Three others were very unusual: The hen mounted another which had just been trod by a male, and had not yet gained her feet. In all of the observed treadings a prone position was the strongest stimulus.

Of particular interest is the fact that none of the hens appeared to exhibit their masculine traits. Furthermore, these unisexual matings among hens were performed by hens that were laying eggs, and when males were either present or absent. Four instances were noted in which a male trod a hen as soon as she had dismounted from treading another hen.

This article discusses some of the conditions under which homosexual matings may occur; however, although it explains such behavior among males, it does not suggest any causes underlying the initial treading among females.

One may postulate individual variations in the development of the nervous system. Marked developmental deviations have been found in structures such as reproductive organs in chickens. But, at present, there is no known method of tracing nerve pathways for such complicated acts.

In birds, such as chickens, whose sex is readily identified by the different outward appearances of males and females, it is unusual to find typical female behavior in males and male behavior in females. However, in such birds as pigeons, in which sexes cannot be distinguished externally, it is common to find both male and female behavior patterns in each sex.

If such a theory is acceptable, it would be necessary to know the stimulus situations under which male behavior in females could be evoked, because such anomalies probably would require a stronger stimulus than would be necessary in normal males to trigger the mating pattern. The act, having been consummated initially, could persist through learning and habit.

● ● ●

SHE BRED BABIES FOR COUPLE

A COUPLE who could have no children set her up in their home while she bore two children by the husband, Mrs. Ferida Hayat, 36, Parisian playwright, charged last June in a Hollywood, Cal., court.

She filed suit for support of the son and daughter which she claims she bore for Maurice Albequerque, 40, who owns jewelry stores in Hollywood and in Paris, and his wife, Cecilia, 48. The suit named Albequerque as the father.

Mrs. Hayat said she met Albequerque in Lisbon and came here with him.

Then, she said, he introduced her to his wife, moved her into their Santa Monica home and persuaded her to give them a family.

After the second baby was born, she said, the Albequerques left to set up their new home, deserting her and the children.

Men in Lingerie

ANONYMOUS

MAY I say at the outset that I do not generally approve of anonymity, but my official position in a somewhat conservative atmosphere prevents my signing this article. However, I should like to state that I am a professional man, not a reformer, an ex-convict, or a minister.

Men in lingerie? Impossible, I said as we wound our way out of the hot, sultry valley, around the cooler mountain side up to the state prison—a prison which lies in a sweltering sinkhole at the upper end of a hollow, enclosed by two mountain ranges covered with much burnt-over scrub oak, chestnut stumps and mountain laurel. Impossible, I said — and yet I changed my mind.

For years the things I am about to reveal in this article have been told as rumors throughout the section, and a part of our mission was to substantiate these rumors. As a background, it should be said that the strongest, usually the hardest, and perhaps the youngest, prisoners of the state are sent to this prison. Here they are employed as coal miners, working two 12-hour shifts. The weak and old cannot survive the hard life of digging and loading coal, as some of the veins leave a working of only three or four feet. There are a few old men in the prison, but they are trusties, or work in the laundry or dining room.

As state prisons often go, this one is overcrowded—men double in their cells, some without cells, housed en masse in barracks. Vermin infest the barracks; hospital and medical service are inadequate. Records show about 20% of the prisoners to be syphilitic, and the treatment of these is irregular and spasmodic; killings within the prison are common; guards are underpaid and, to increase their meager earnings, graft off the prisoners, who receive a small sum daily for digging coal. Then too, the guards are of a low grade of humanity, in very many instances.

It was during our routine inspection that we began to dig more into the situation of "men in lingerie." On a previous visit, guards, prisoners, and the warden had talked freely of the situation. Another investigator had discovered this; so it remained for us to substantiate as nearly as possible his discovery.

In this prison, the making of "men in lingerie" (or "gal boys," as the prisoners refer to them) is somewhat as follows. A young "rat" or "soft" prisoner is sent to the prison. The warden or his chief deputy lectures to the young prisoner on the general rules of prison life and conduct. He then assigns him to the task of digging coal in the mines. The warden, or the chief deputy, says: "You go with 'Spud,' and Spud will teach you to dig coal." it develops that Spud is a burly, hardened, many times syphilitic, sex-starved inmate. Spud accompanies the new prisoner into the mines, preceding him with only one thought in his mind—sex. The prisoner is taken to their room, where Spud initiates him into the art of "spooning the black diamond," as prisoners speak of digging coal.

teaching methods Spud may employ until the prisoner is completely broken in body and spirit. He would rather do anything than continue the grueling task.

As they sit across from each other in the dark, 8 x 10 foot room, 300 feet underground, with flickering carbide lamps revealing black-splotched faces, one weary, the other eager, disturbed only by

To "reform" the young offender, our states maintain schools of perversion.

As teacher, Spud dominates the scene, taking the utmost out of the new inmate. If the prisoner refuses to work, Spud uses a pick handle on him or threatens to use a dirk (a long dagger made in the mines from a file with pieces of leather or comb or aluminum serving as a handle), which almost every prisoner possesses. Such

a distant rumbling of coal cars in the main shafts of the mine, the moment is most propitious for Spud's proposal, and this he realizes. He tells his prisoner that, if he will become his "gal boy," he will not have to load coal (Spud will do this) and that he will not have to come down to the prison dining room for his meals. Spud will buy candies, fruits and food from the commissary and bring them to his cell, and there will be other freedom from toil. Spud's inducements, intertwined with arguments, are falling on receptive ears—anything for a change. They are accepted. Carbide lamps are turned low and Spud teaches another inmate his first lesson in the art of becoming a "gal boy"—a "man in lingerie"—or "his moll."

Thus there are gradually built bonds of affection between Spud and his "gal boy" to such an extent that he will kill another prisoner over "her," will spend his earnings on "her," may refuse to work if separated from "her." In one instance after release, the "gal boy," who was married, was taken from his legitimate wife.

In the meantime—what has happened to the "gal boy?" "She" invariably will lose "her" self respect and "her" standing among the bulk of prisoners. Sometimes "her" voice and "her" walk change. "She" invariably deteriorates mentally and morally. "She" paints "her" toe nails with finger nail polish, "she" buys lipstick, rouge, powder and silk underwear, in order to please "her" man. These supplies come from prisoners who keep them in locked boxes in their cells. "She" has little work to do, because Spud does it for her, and

she has the best food available in the commissary.

There are numerous retreats for the perverted practices—in the mines, in the hospital wards, in the old barracks, behind the cloth-covered doors of the cells where two to four men live, in the laundry, in the storage houses and, for the trusties, on the farm outside the walls.

To some prisoners the fear of being forced into homosexuality is maddening. As we were inspecting the prison a young boy, possibly 19, stopped the warden, and asked if he couldn't be transferred from the mines, where he had been assigned two days before. He related that, on the previous night, the convict with whom he had been working stuck a dirk against his ribs and commanded him to yield. To the harrowing experience which followed he had to submit. The warden kindly consented to shift him to the laundry where he would be better protected.

Prison officials do not approve of the practices we have here related. Prisoners are punished for homosexuality when, and if, they are caught, but the warden unhesitatingly declares that "men in lingerie," or "gal boys," and their "men" constitute the prison's greatest disciplinary problem.

● ● ●

How Marriages Could Be Saved

"AMONG the persons who come to me for a divorce, sex is usually one of the biggest problems. Of course, this never comes out in court.

"So many marriages could be saved if we had healthier and more realistic and understanding attitudes toward sex."

—*Harold Lee Giesler, noted divorce attorney, in the Los Angeles Times.*

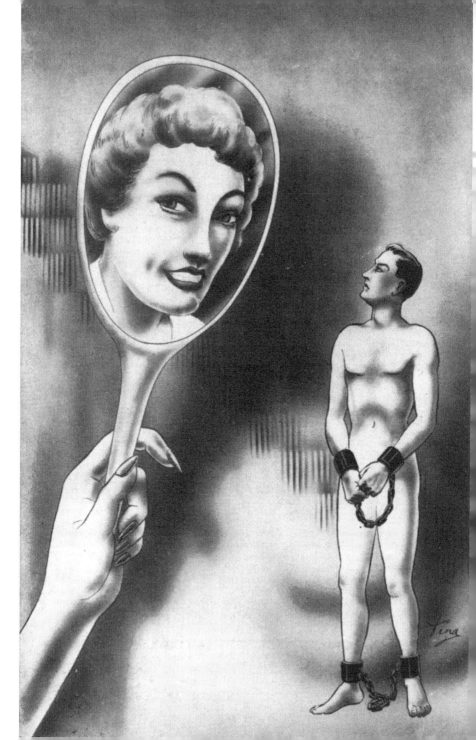

"VIRGIN" WIVES...

Some wives are unable to experience a sexual climax. Not having corrected their sexual maladjustment, some couples have never become sexually adjusted. Sexual incompatibility influences the divorce rate. A wife's frigidity may be due to the fact that her husband is sexually inadequate.

by Frank S. Caprio, M.D.

A VIRGIN - wife is one who forfeits her virginity on the honeymoon night, but never surrenders herself to her husband to the extent of accepting and finding satisfaction in the sexual act. She is forever preserving her "psychic chastity," as it were. She likely has been conditioned to restraints and generally fails to become an adequate sexual partner after marriage. Many of these *virgin-wives* believe that eventually, they will relax sexually and adopt a normal attitude toward fulfilling their marital obligations. But this doesn't always happen. They find they are unable to experience a sexual climax. In many instances it is because they do not know what to expect or feel. Many of them have never gotten over the pain of the first honeymoon sex experience.

The rupture of the hymen is sometimes accompanied by bleeding which frightens the bride and leaves her emotionally disturbed. Most virgin-wives get off to a bad start as a result of the pain and discomfort caused by the penetration of the hymen. Today many psychiatrists believe one way of overcoming the harmful psychological effects resulting from painful sex relations on the honeymoon is to have a physician cut the hymen (surgical defloration) and dilate the vagina just before the honeymoon (about two weeks before marriage). The hymen can be cut painlessly with a local anesthetic. After this anatomical preparation of the prospective bride for sex

---

NARCISSISTIC FRIGIDITY — By Tina

When an attractive woman is so enamored with her own image (narcissism) she is often apt to be sexually frigid in marriage. In this surrealist drawing by our artist, a woman's hand is seen holding a mirror in which is reflected the self-admiring face of the woman (symbolic of the narcissist-frigid wife). To the right is the figure of a man, chained hand and foot—representing the husband who is helpless to perform the marital act, because his wife's all-consuming love-of-self repels all efforts to approach her sexually.

relations, a psychiatrist can prepare both the bride and groom concerning proper sex-techniques and instruct them about impotence reactions, premature ejaculation and frigidity, advising them that if during the first six months of marriage they are not *compatible sexually,* they should seek professional psychiatric guidance.

This is far more intelligent than to endure years of incompatibility. *So many couples—during five, ten or more years of married life— never become sexually adjusted, simply because neither of them has taken the initiative to do something about their sexual maladjustment.* The first year of every marriage should be a probationary period—physically and psychologically. After that something should be done about incompatible relations, whether sexual or emotional.

Is Sex Instruction Necessary?

Some argue that if two persons love each other, they need not read books on sex. They say that the Indians never had sex instruction— that our grandmothers never read any books on sex. This is an irrational argument because it would be difficult to estimate the extent of sexual frustrations that existed among people living many years ago. The women apparently lacked the common sense that should have prompted them to complain about it. They were satisfied doing the cooking and raising the children. They did not consider a sexual climax important. They were more servile and restrained in those days. Today, women are more intelligent about these matters. They are able to recognize serious sexual disorders such as impotence and frigidity and can appreciate the inter-relationship between nervous disorders and sexual deprivation or frustration. Modern women understand the importance of being sexually gratified as well as being properly supported economically. At the same time it appears that there are more complaints about frigidity than ever before. That is because women are admitting that something is wrong sexually and want help and advice. Many women will not tolerate sexual incompatibility, which in turn influences the divorce rate.

A strikingly beautiful girl, married for the third time, was referred to me for a psychiatric appraisal of her health-complaints. She complained of severe headaches, fatigue and physical discomfort. When I questioned her about her sex life, she appeared quite embarrassed and was reluctant to discuss the matter with me. *Finally she told me she was still a virgin!* I asked what she meant. She said that none of the three husbands had succeeded in penetrating the hymen. Then she told me she had recently been dilated by her physician with an instrument, but she still complained of pain and would not permit marital relations. A gynecologist checked her physically and could not find any reason for her painful intercourse.

What happened was that the muscles of her vagina would go into a spasm, contract and make penetration practically impossible. She had been taught that sex was something ugly and dirty. She was afraid to be kissed by her first husband. Because of fear she could not relax and experience satisfac-

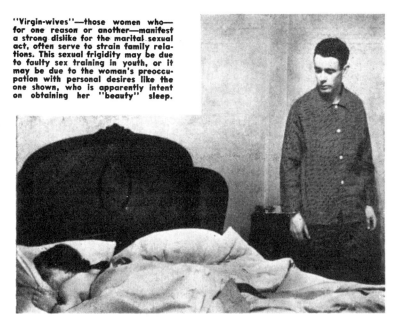

"Virgin-wives"—those women who—for one reason or another—manifest a strong dislike for the marital sexual act, often serve to strain family relations. This sexual frigidity may be due to faulty sex training in youth, or it may be due to the woman's preoccupation with personal desires like the one shown, who is apparently intent on obtaining her "beauty" sleep.

tion at the anticipation of sex relations. Her condition is technically known as "vaginismus" — a nervous spasm of the muscles of the vagina—rather a common complaint. These cases respond favorably to psychotherapy. Such a woman is taught how to relax—to eliminate fear and develop a desire for sex. One might say they are "frozen" emotionally and need to be "thawed out" sexually. There are many such cases of vaginismus due to the fact that the wife is suffering from a nervous disorder and is unable to surrender her "psychic virginity."

"Narcissistic Frigidity"

A more extreme kind of "virgin-wife" is the beautiful woman who regards sex as something sordid. She wishes there was no necessity of having to give herself to her husband. Menstruation is regarded by such a person as the "curse." Some beautiful women are frigid. *They are in love with themselves* (narcissism)—*in love with their face and body!* Many of them are unable to concentrate during the sexual act. Their mind is on other things.

I have interviewed several female patients whose income — as professional models — was quite high. Their husbands complained about their indifference to sex. Beautiful women who have been greatly flattered believe that all men are alike—they all have a "line." Being conditioned to constant flattery, beautiful women develop a fixation of their sex craving *at the narcissistic level.* They are unable to forget that they are beautiful. During sex relations they are more concerned about trying to keep their hair from being dishevelled than getting satisfaction out of the act itself.

One wife applied fingernail polish on her nails during marital relations. Her husband had known that his wife was sexually cold, but never thought that she was that indifferent to the act. Another husband told me that his wife continued to read a book while having marital relations.

One wife desired to have her baby delivered by a Caesarian operation rather than the natural way because she did not want her sex anatomy changed in any way. She did not want her vagina stretched because that might be construed as a renunciation of her femininity—a renouncing of her rôle as a woman—a desire to remain unchanged. There are other women who prefer to indulge in sexual deviations such as oral-genital contacts for the same psychological reasons, rather than submit to coitus. They are also classified as "virgin-wives."

"Penis Denial"

Then there are women who experience a sexual climax if they are fondled manually by their husbands, but who "freeze" as soon as their husbands attempt intromission. This is called the "denial of the penis" phenomenon—an unconscious refusal to be raped. Many women who are unable to find satisfaction in sex relations do not know the subconscious reason for it. They believe they are born frigid, and are resigned to their fate. They carry out their physical obligations in a mechanical, apathetic sort of way—as a duty rather than something really desired. Dr. Wilhelm Stekel calls this the "will to displeasure." The virgin-wife is actually saying in the language of her subconscious— "I must give myself to you as a dutiful wife, but you can't make me find satisfaction in it."

Virgin-wives, as a result of their frigidity, are generally *sadistic*. (Desire to inflict pain or distress in others.) Because of their inability to be gratified by sex relations they become hostile and nag and quarrel over trivialities. Almost all frigid women are highly nervous—neurotic personalities.

Husbands are partly to blame. Many of them are so inadequate that they are responsible for their wives turning against sex or not knowing how to be a good sexual partner. A wife must depend on her husband for instruction in all sex matters. But many husbands are poor teachers. They are too restrained themselves. A husband should make out of his wife the kind of sexual partner he desires. It is often impossible for the wife to be a satisfactory sexual partner if the husband is sexually inadequate. It is his duty to seek professional guidance if he is inexperienced and to insist that his wife investigate the cause of her frigidity by consulting a psychiatrist because sex-satisfaction is essential to a successful marriage. *Virgin-wives are in need of psychiatric treatment and should avail themselves of it if they wish to keep their marriage intact.*

● ● ●

MALE OPOSSUM CHANGED TO FEMALE

THE sex of a castrated male opossum was transformed to female by Dr. A. Bolliger, director of the Gordon Craig Research Laboratory of the University of Sydney, Australia, as reported by him in *The Australian Journal of Science*. The five-month-old opossum was given injections of female sex hormones (*estrogens*) for eight months, and thereafter began to molt, the usual coarse fur of the male being replaced by the characteristic soft fur of the female.

Extensive changes of the sex organs occurred, even though most of the estrogen was injected into the opossum during its adolescence and early maturity. These sexual changes were noticed to some extent in the living animal during and after estrogen injections and at post-mortem examination after the animal was killed at the age of two years. The scrotum was transformed into a permanent pouch about three months after the estrogen injections began. The penis had changed in shape and its shrinking continued until it had practically disappeared. A small body at the base of the urogenital canal was found to be divided by a deep groove into two parts, resembling the clitoris of a female. It contained no urethra.

Dr. Bolliger's opinion is that besides the great reduction in the size of the penis, a transformation of the male penis into a female clitoris had occurred— similar to the transformation of the male scrotum into a female pouch. This change of male into female sex organs, he believes, was due to estrogen treatment and castration. Dr. Bolliger states that male sheep, castrated at the age of two to four months and eating clover containing estrogen during adolescence, show marked changes in the secondary sex organs. These changes, though less extensive, are somewhat similar to the sex-organ transformation of the opossum.

Posed by a professional model

A psychological study of the motives and emotional life of the aristocrat of prostitutes.

The Call Girl

by Arthur Newman

WHAT makes a call girl—an expensive, independently operating prostitute—adopt her profession? To find the answer, Dr. Harold Greenwald, a practicing New York psychologist, interviewed 20 girls and psychoanalyzed 6.

The result is a unique study, *The Call Girl*,* that does far more than reveal the motivations and emotional life of this aristocrat

Mr. Newman is a free-lance writer on medical and psychological subjects.

among prostitutes. There is much material here that throws considerable light on the little-known inhabitants of the call girl's hidden world, and on many problems that concern the therapist—self-destruction drives, sadism, masochism and promiscuity.

Most of the girls interviewed by Dr. Greenwald had loveless childhoods. Rejected by the mother, often fatherless, they were overwhelmed by feelings of worthless-

*Greenwald, Harold, Ph.D.: *The Call Girl*, Ballantine Books, 246 pages, $4.50.

ness. They felt unwanted, unloved and unworthy of being wanted and loved. Three-fourths of the girls came from broken homes. None experienced the warmth, stability and permanence of normal family life.

It was inevitable that in these circumstances of deprivation and neglect many of the girls would have precocious sexual experiences. These were decisive in setting later behavior patterns because they helped fill the emotional void rejection had created.

By giving sexual gratification the girls found that they could get the affection and interest so completely lacking in their family life. They learned very early that sex was a commodity which they could trade not only for some measure of understanding and regard, but for candy and pennies — or something equally tangible.

Olive's case, cited in Greenwald's study, is typical. She never knew her father. She was rejected by her mother who never acknowledged her. Shuttled between grandmother and an aunt, she never got more than cold toleration from either. "Olive stated that when she was about six years old a cousin, who was then fifteen, got into bed with her one night and started caressing her. She found this quite exciting. He used to give her toys and bring home candy for her frequently. She loved candy, her aunt never gave her much, and this was one way of getting it."

And so the typical pattern develops: A broken family, rejection, precocious sexual experiences and early promiscuity. The call girl to be, as a member of a socially ostracized or constantly shifting family, never identifies with the community. Sometimes she is shunned because of her own deviant behavior. Friendless, she drifts to a large city and into the "gray world" of night clubs, bars and after-hours spots filled with people who have problems similar to hers.

Here she finds drug addicts, shady characters of all kinds, people who have lost attachment with normal society and have formed a society of their own. Here she makes her first contacts with call girls, pimps and madams; and it is here at the suggestion of the "pros" that she turns from unpaid promiscuity to paid prostitution. This step is important to her: *for the first time in her life she finds herself wholly accepted in a group.*

Interestingly, although many students of prostitution in the past have tried to explain the problem as a reaction to economic need, money factors were not most important as far as these girls were concerned. *Not one of the call girls interviewed explained her choice of profession in terms of desperate economic need.*

Once initiated in the profession, the call girl charges from $20 to $100 for each "sexual contact" and averages about $20,000 a year. Despite the relatively high income they enjoyed, the minks they wore, the expensive apartments they lived in and the high-priced cars they drove, all the girls felt anxious, worthless, insecure. To escape these feelings, they resorted to drink, drugs (15 used marijuana; 6 took heroin), and suicide (*all but 5 of the girls interviewed reported having made at least one suicide attempt*).

A whole series of less drastic ways were employed to dull or escape their feelings of guilt, isolation and worthlessness. One of these methods — described in psychiatry as *projection*—was to assert that all other women behaved in the same way they did. In other words, they projected their own feelings, attitudes and experiences onto others.

This is how Diane responded when asked about the attitude of respectable people to prostitution: "What do you mean so-called respectable members of society? They're the worst freaks of all. The more respectable they are, the freakier (perverted) they are. Take that professor, I've got to beat him with a whip, and get him a black fag (homosexual). It's the only way he can get his kicks. I'd love to see that society dame's face he's married to. . . . You know those respectable women give me a pain. They look down on us and yet they're the biggest whores of all. . . ."

Some of the girls submerged their guilt feelings by *denial*—they attempted to repress from consciousness those characteristics which are unwanted. Thus, some maintained that, to them, prostitution was like any other business.

Another type of defense frequently employed was one known as *reaction-formation*. Here, their behavior expressed in an exaggerated way the exact *opposite* of their original feelings or impulses.

Thus, fifteen of the girls admitted having had homosexual drives and relationships. These adopted an overly seductive manner and tried in their work and in their clothes to simulate an appearance of exaggerated heterosexuality.

Similarly: *"Half of the girls were totally frigid and in their relationships with customers, eighteen of the twenty were completely without sexual feeling. They denied this frigidity by feigning all the transports of uninhibited orgasms many times nightly."*

Again because of their early deprivation and their rage at it, the girls turned to self-abasement and self-degradation. By degrading

19-year-old Patricia Ward as she appeared in the vice trial of Minot Jelke, charged with having supplied call girls to men willing to pay the price.—*International News Photo*.

themselves, they revenged themselves on their mothers for failing them in childhood. This craving for love and attention, Dr. Greenwald believes, prevented the girls from maturing emotionally and becoming independent human beings. If they were to achieve maturity and independence, they felt unconsciously that they would then never receive the infantile love and attention they still yearned for.

Money for them became a symbol for the warmth and love denied them, but it was an unsatisfactory substitute to be squandered and used to attract the pimp. For the call girl, by the way, the pimp is a paid companion, a kept man who, unlike the procurer or the panderer, has no "sales function." On him the call girl showers gifts and money, and with him she has a physical relationship which is usually more satisfactory than those with clients, though it is rarely one of normal sex relations but is frequently limited to oral sex.

Why did these girls become call girls rather than street walkers? They are more attractive and therefore can command a higher fee. They are more intelligent and better educated. Three-fourths of the girls interviewed were above average intelligence, and nearly all had from ten to twelve years of schooling. One wrote songs, another designed hats, four painted, three wrote poetry, and two tried to write books.

Most important perhaps is the fact that most call girls come from middle- and upper-class families and can associate easily with clients from similar backgrounds, clients who frequently require varieties of sexual activity the ordinary prostitute would be less willing to provide. Speaking of prostitutes in general, Kinsey says: "There are a few who are better educated, with high school or even college background; and there are some who are physically energetic, mentally alert and intelligent. They more readily accept and provide the variety of techniques which the upper-level males find most satisfactory. . . ."

Of the six call girls Dr. Greenwald analyzed—all of whom came to him for relief from anxiety and depression, not for cure—five quit the racket. Some married and others entered legitimate businesses. He has little hope for a material reduction in prostitution as long as we jail instead of treat, and he calls for therapeutic institutional communities as a kind of compromise.

In this connection it is interesting to quote his remarks about the Soviet prophylacteria in an interview with Mike Wallace: "The League of Nations reported that the Russians had made great strides in the elimination of prostitution. They did it by setting up therapeutic communities in which the girls were trained for new occupations. They did it by making it socially undesirable for men to visit prostitutes. For example, they posted signs in a factory, if a man was found out, which said, 'Ivan Ivanovitch is a purchaser of human flesh.' They did it by never prosecuting the prostitute. They prosecuted the man instead."

Although Dr. Greenwald stresses the theme that the call girls he studied chose their profession as a result of personality factors, he does not absolve society from its responsibility:

"Even a girl showing all of the personality tendencies described above could not possibly become a call girl if our society did not make such an occupation possible."

• • •
so they say . . .

Present But Not Discussed

"IT is a curious fact that this most modern of civilizations still continues to regard sex as something which is present, but which is not discussed in polite circles. This, despite the fact that a lack of information or misinformation about sex is recognized as a contributing cause of some types of mental illness."
—*Edgar C. Cumings in article in Marriage and Family Living.*

Formula for Success

"THE only way to get a man is to be sexily attractive, and the only way to keep him is to be sexily satisfactory."
—*Author Somerset Maugham, replying to a woman's request for advice on how "to get and keep a man" (quoted in the NY Herald Tribune).*

Imbalance in Sex Appetite

"WHAT can be done to work out a mutually satisfactory sex relationship where the degrees of desire vary greatly?

"The first thing is to admit the situation exists. Husband and wife should be able to communicate with each other about the problem and discuss it frankly. They should realize that an imbalance in sexual appetites does not necessarily mean a lack of love and that a suitable adaptation can be achieved."
—*Dr. Abraham Stone in Pageant.*

Sophia Loren on Sex

"OVER here (America) you make such a fuss about sex, talk about it so much, write about it. Back home (Italy) it is a natural thing. My husband is always with me and we have other things to talk about."
—*Sophia Loren, Italian movie star, quoted in NY Herald Tribune.*

Sex Oddities

By HENRY SACKERMAN

IT may truly be said that there is no such thing as completely "normal" sex behavior; every human being has some particular preference of his own, and the sex act does not follow a rigid pattern. You may have wondered at times about certain extremely homely persons who apparently enjoyed a happy married life, or who were in love and engaged to be married. "What on earth can he see in her?" or "How can she bear even to look at him?" are commonly heard remarks. We see short, undersized, thin men falling in love with tall, heavy-set women twice their size, who return that love. We see t a l l, powerfully-built, handsome young men falling in love with and marrying short, dumpy, homely girls. Not even severe physical deformity seems to be a barrier against sex attraction; cripples and blind persons have attracted the love of healthy, normal individuals. The general impression that "like attracts like" is not well founded. Not even extreme differences in age serve to bar love. Girls of sixteen have fallen desperately in love with men of sixty, and it is not uncommon for a woman to fall in love with a man half her age.

Recently an example of the latter was brought to the author's attention. A 35-year-old woman school teacher in a Middle Western city high school, some years ago, became irresistibly attracted by one of her pupils—a handsome boy of 17. The teacher was definitely not good-looking; she was tall, quite stout, and not at all well-proportioned. The boy was slim and wiry.

For some time the teacher concealed her feeling for the boy, and fought against it, but little by little it overpowered her. She became more and more friendly to the lad, openly, and devised ways and means of inducing him to remain after class so they could be together alone.

To her astonishment and relief she found that the boy appeared to be definitely attracted by her—and it was more than merely appearance; the youth found himself infatuated with this woman who was more than twice his age. Both had strong moral ideas and, when they found they could no longer delay consummation, they eloped and were married.

The boy's actions came as a tremendous shock to his parents, when they learned of the marriage, and they took immediate steps to have the marriage annulled. The marriage was annulled, and the accompanying exposure cost the teacher her reputation and her chances of ever getting another teaching job. But she was still in love with her boy-husband, and he with her, and he swore that he would remarry her as soon as he had reached his majority—and this is exactly what happened. The strangely assorted pair are living together today as husband and wife, and seem content with one another.

When an old man marries a very young girl, it is generally conceded that the girl has merely married him for his money. But "case histories" afford proof that, as often as not, such marriages are based upon sex attraction. There are certain types of young girls who are irresistibly drawn to men old enough to be their fathers. The examples of odd mating could go on indefinitely, but it is more important for us to have some understanding of the causes of these

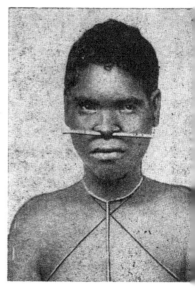

This is another decoration appealing to the fair sex, as a cute little natural moustache may with us. The rod is thrust through the cartilage of the nose.

strange and unpredictable alliances.

The sexual *fetish** is the foundation of such alliances. In its extremest form, the fetish may be fantastic. Here is a man whose sex instincts are aroused only by the sight of a certain type of woman's glove. The sight of the glove itself is sufficient to excite him and, to secure a complete emotional outlet, he has but to touch it.

Another man is incapable of physical relations with his wife, unless the latter will attire herself in black from head to foot; still another requires his sexual partner to be garbed in man's attire. A fourth demands that his partner

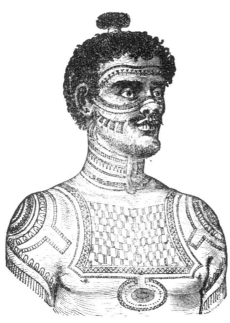

This Maori gentleman proves by his tattooing that he is neither a laggard in love nor a dastard in war.

*A "fetish" is something inanimate, or some feature of a person, which arouses sexual desire in a given individual.

Pretty, isn't it? This lady with her lip discs enjoys popularity that made the plastic operation worth while.

The perfume fetish is quite common. Men are attracted by a certain perfume, sometimes without even being aware of it. A rather amusing case is in my records: a girl complained that her lover had grown cold toward her. Her uncle, who happened to be a psychiatrist, noted she was no longer using the same perfume that she customarily did. He had a "hunch." He asked her when she had changed her perfume and, when she told him, he put two and two together and found that it was immediately after this change that her sweetheart had begun to grow distant to her. "Change back to your old perfume," said the psychiatrist, acting on his hunch. The girl, understanding nothing, followed his instructions and, to her amazed delight, her lover once more became ardent. The young man simply had a perfume fetish. The story is amusing, in one sense, but it has its tragic side as well. Fetishes of one sort or another have wrecked happiness as often as they have

wear a Louis Fourteenth costume, sparkling with jewels. The clothes fetish is so common that certain houses of resort in New York and Paris, and other metropolitan centers, provide wardrobes of costumes of all descriptions for their inmates to choose from, according to the patron's whim.

Although the clothes fetish seems more allied with the male than the female desires, women sometimes possess it too. Not long ago, a case was brought to my attention concerning a woman who refused to have union with her husband unless he wore full evening dress at the time.

This lady should be an electric lineman's wife; she carries enough wire with her. The more footage, the more style and beauty.

caused it to flourish and prosper.

Everyone has a sexual fetish of some sort; usually, it is of a mild, run-of-the-mill nature. A man who is attracted only by girls with blonde hair has a mild blonde-hair fetish. A girl who is attracted only to men who smoke cigars has a mild cigar fetish. There is nothing abnormal or wrong about having a fetish, if it is harmless.

What is the relation between the fetish and the odd matings that one sees from time to time? Does a little, undersized fellow fall in love with a big strapping woman twice his size because of a fetish? The answer would appear to be "Yes," and here is a sample of how it works:

A boy reaches maturity, and experiences his first physical stirrings. The first woman to come across his path at the time happens to be a large, stout blonde; she is the first who has ever aroused his natural impulse. It is at this point that a fetish may develop; the boy may thereafter, whenever he feels the physical urge, associate it in his mind with the large, fat blonde, and no other type of woman will interest him. He seeks constantly to re-experience the thrill of his first encounter with sex.

A girl loves her father deeply. She meets a man who is like her father, and her love transfers itself to him. In the man she loves she must find certain strong resemblances to her father and, if the fetish is strong enough she will find this only in a man of her father's age.

"She reminds me of my mother" is a commonly heard remark on the part of men who have fallen in love. The mother fetish is a common one; a boy, who loves his mother, seeks to continue and expand that love in the girl he marries. Consequently, the type of girl who attracts him physically is, in such cases, the type that most resembles his mother.

Thus it can be seen how the fetish may play a stronger part in mate selection than any other factor. The loveliest girl in the world may be completely lacking in sex appeal to a man whose particular fetish she does not complement. And a woman who is "as homely as a mud fence" may prove irresistible to a handsome, glamorous youth who could have his pick of the world's beauties, because she does happen to satisfy his fetish.

Most people who have fetishes in a mild form are not conscious of them. You are attracted to a certain individual, and have only a general idea concerning the reason. She or he is attractive, has a nice personality, etc. If there exists in your mind some fetish that has drawn you to that person, the chances are ten to one that you are not aware of it.

A man or a woman who is not physically beautiful need not worry about finding a mate; for the majority of marriages are not the result of the beauty of one or both of the parties. To find the right life partner is simply a matter of meeting enough persons of the opposite sex; if enough are encountered, sooner or later you will discover someone who attracts you strongly, and who is likewise powerfully attracted by yourself.

It is advisable for everyone to ascertain the nature of his or her own fetishes. What are yours? Do you prefer a certain type of individual? A certain quality of voice? A style of haircut? Whatever your individual preferences may be, consider them; then think back and see if you can locate the origin of the fetish. Does your fetish have any relation to your first sex experience? To your parents? To an emotional difficulty or tragedy? You will find this attempt interesting and illuminating; it is a worth-while endeavor for a student of sexology.

The supremely important result of knowing the truth about fetishes and their commonness, is to eliminate from one's mind the thought that one is necessarily queer or abnormal. Untold thousands of persons who have fetishes, and are aware of them, suffer because they think they are "different" and that, if the truth were known they would be scorned by society. This is far from the case: fetishes are common. In fact, everyone has a fetish of some sort, and it is not in any way a sign of abnormality. To be only a trifle "odd" sexually is to be 100% human and normal.

• • •
so they say . . .

Teen-Agers and Sex

"THE teenagers know much less about sex than they would like to!" An eleventh-grade boy philosophized thus—"my biggest problem is women; I can't figure them out."

> —*From a study on teenagers by Dr. H. H. Remmers of Purdue University and his associates, reported in* Newsweek.

Is the Clitoris Disappearing?

"THE question as to whether evolution is trying to do away with the clitoris was introduced by the frequent finding of this gland undeveloped and buried beneath an adherent prepuce. I investigated and found that because of the irritation caused by preputial adhesions, both girls and boys require circumcision in equal numbers. Imperfect cleavage in both sexes is apparently one of the stigmata of physical decline, rather than an evolutionary phenomenon. At some clinics today, the little surgical procedure for girls has become a matter of routine."

> —*Dr. Robert T. Morris, in his book "Fifty Years a Surgeon" (Dutton).*

Frequent Sex Demands

"TOO frequent demands on the part of the husband may sometimes be a manifestation not of real sexual desire, but of aggression or an attempt to escape from the functions of daily living. More often, however, a wife's complaint of too frequent advances is the result of her own inadequate sexual maturity, or else of the husband's failure to arouse her sufficiently to desire him more often."

> —*Dr. Abraham Stone, M.D.,* Ladies Home Journal.

NAPOLEON'S SEX CONQUESTS

Brown Bros.

The famous general won as many campaigns in the boudoir as on the battlefields of Europe.

by Richard Stiller, B.A., M.A.

HISTORY'S great rulers and world-shakers were often sexual extremists. Thus Attila the Hun perished of apoplexy in the excitement of his wedding night; Catherine the Great of Russia was a voracious nymphomaniac; and Napoleon Bonaparte won as many campaigns in the boudoir as on the battlefields of Europe.

Napoleon had many women, but he does not fit the rôle of the great Gallic lover who delights in amour for its own sake. As cold and ego-

Mr. Stiller is a free-lance writer and former teacher of social studies.

tistic in bed as in battle, he used his most important sexual partners as he used his soldiers: to advance his career and to secure his power. Mme. de Stael said of him: *"He neither hates nor loves. In his eyes he is the only one who counts. Everybody else is a mere cipher."*

His treatment of the actress Mlle. Duchesnois, related by Albert Guerard, is typical. He sent for her one night, and she arrived late; he had already become absorbed at his desk. His valet knocked and announced her.

"Tell her to wait."

An hour passed; the valet reappeared.

"Tell her to take off her clothes."
Mlle. Duchesnois was ushered into the Emperor's bedroom. She undressed and got into bed. Hours passed; dawn lit up the sky. The valet disturbed his master once more.

Without lifting his head, Bonaparte said: *"Tell her to go away."*

It is impossible to count all the women in the little Corsican's life. The prominent ones, however, are well known. Each was employed as a stepping stone to advance his career or to settle some pressing political question.

Through Félicité Turreau, wife of a general, he received command of the Paris garrison in 1795.

Through his first wife, Josephine de Beauhearnais, mistress of the revolutionary dictator of France, he was given command of the army in the crucial Italian campaign of 1799.

Through Désirée Clary, he was able to found a dynasty by placing her husband, Bernadotte, on the throne of Sweden.

Through Countess Marie Walewska, he ruled Poland and set the stage for his divorce from Josephine.

Through marriage with Marie-Louise of Hapsburg he allied Austria to France and achieved respectability and a male heir.

Nevertheless, Napoleon did not disdain sexual gratification. There is no doubt that he was fascinated by Josephine, whom he met in the decadent, luxury - loving days of the aftermath of the Reign of Terror.

Joséphine de Beauharnais, Martinique-born widow of a guillotined aristocrat, was six years older than the young artillery general, then barely thirty. The mis-

Mlle. George, a young actress and one of Napoleon's mistresses.—Portrait in the Victoria and Albert Museum, London, England.

tress of Barras, *roi des pourris* (king of the rotten ones), corrupt ruler of the Directory government, she was an exciting woman in a feverish milieu.

It was a time when women wore tunics of transparent gauze slit to the hips, with high waists that left their breasts bare. Napoleon was enchanted by this worldly, exotic, influential woman. *"She looked like a high priestess of pleasure and easy virtue."*

Bonaparte quickly fell in love with Joséphine, married her, and was rewarded with command of the army in Italy. Almost immediately he was in the field, leading his troops, tormented by his absence from his bride. He was nagged by doubts about her gaudy past and hints of a new lover she had taken after his departure.

From one post he wrote: "I go to bed without you. I sleep without you. I implore you, let me sleep." Further on into Italy, he sent his lieutenant back to France to bring her to him. "You will come, won't you? You will lie here beside me, on my heart, in my arms, your lips on mine! Oh, take wings, come!"

For a while Napoleon was quite heartbroken at her faithlessness. When his officers brought a statuesque Italian beauty to his tent, he ignored her. But he soon overcame his feelings and grew quite cynical about Joséphine. He began to have other love affairs.

He was abrupt and crude in his love making. He took a fancy, in Cairo, to the wife of a Lieutenant Foures. His men told him of her beauty and her easy virtue. He met her, asked her to sleep with him. He sent her presents. At first she delayed. Then Napoleon shipped her husband back to France on some military errand and invited Mme. Foures to dinner.

"He received her with dignified courtesy," wrote Elie Faure. "But suddenly, feigning awkwardness, he upset a pitcher of water on her dress. Whereupon he took her into his bedroom to repair the damage, and they both remained there so long that the dinner guests were left in no doubt as to the true situation."

Napoleon's affair with Mme. Foures continued as long as his stay in Egypt, and the voluptuous young woman became known to the French troops, with affection, as "Cleopatra." There was one amusing interruption when the English navy stopped the ship carrying Lieutenant Foures back to France. Napoleon's infatuation was well known to them; they landed Foures back on the Egyptian coast and wished him good luck. The poor husband rushed back to Cairo and found his wife in the arms of his commander-in-chief. The resourceful Napoleon merely "divorced" the Foures, reassigned the unfortunate husband, and continued with his Cleopatra.

There were many successors to Mme. Foures, despite his marriage. Napoleon had grown quite used to Joséphine's infidelity. By 1801 he had become Consul and was on his way to the imperial throne. He was now a conqueror, a maker of kings. He could have any woman in Europe. He was reaching his peak of power and prestige; Joséphine was growing older, already forty, losing her sexual attraction. Most of all he resented her inability to bear him an heir. Once, wrote Noël Gerson, he suggested a hunt at their country estate, Malmaison.

"'A hunt at this month!' cried Joséphine. 'You can't be thinking of such a thing, Bonaparte. All our animals are with young.'

"Bonaparte gave a bitter laugh. Turning to his guests he remarked crudely:

"'Well, we shall have to give it up. Everything is prolific on this place, except Madame.'"

In 1804, Napoleon saw Mlle.

Marriage of Napoleon and Marie Louise in the Palace of the Louvre, shown in a painting by G. Rouget in the Versailles National Museum.—*Bettmann Archive*.

George, a young actress, in *Iphigénie*. He sent his valet to summon her to his palace at Saint-Cloud. The young woman describes her experience:

"Little by little he helped me off with my clothes. And he made himself my *femme de chambre* (bedroom maid) with so much gaiety, so much grace and tact, that it was impossible not to be fascinated and drawn towards this man. He was no longer the Consul. He was a man in love perhaps, but it was a love without violence or abruptness.

"I left him at seven in the morning. But feeling ashamed of the charming disorder the night had caused, I said:

" 'Please let me tidy everything up.'

" 'Yes my dear Georgina, I will help you.'

"And he was kind enough to make a show of straightening out that couch with me, the scene of such abandon and affection.' "

Two years later the affair with Mlle. George ended, partly through her own foolish indiscretion. Napoleon suffered a fit one night in her bed in a secret upper room of the palace, and she screamed for help while still in the nude, bringing Joséphine and the palace attendants running to the scene. *L'affaire* George ended soon thereafter.

Napoleon remained married to Joséphine despite his lack of interest in her sexually. He had no one else in mind for a second wife, and as Emperor he did not want to appear frivolous. Besides, he was gnawed by doubts as to his ability to have children. Joséphine, in self-defense, had cleverly convinced him that perhaps he was the guilty party in their barren marriage. Joséphine had two chil-

Napoleon's first marriage—to the glamorous and exotic Joséphine de Beauharnais —led to his being given command of the army in a crucial campaign.—*Portrait in the Mansell Collection.*

dren by her first marriage. And, then, within a short space of time, Napoleon impregnated two women.

The first of these was a beautiful, amoral young woman named Éléonore de la Plaigne. Napoleon let her know that he liked her and she yielded immediately. She was perhaps the only woman in his life as callous in sexual matters as he was. She was interested only in material compensation.

"She herself," wrote Octave Aubrey, "told the story that, even in the Emperor's bedroom, she often took advantage of a momentary distraction on his part to push the hand of the clock forward a half hour. Always in a hurry, always keeping track of the time, Napoleon once satisfied would glance at the clock. 'So soon!' he would murmur. And back he would go to work, leaving Éléonore to dress and disappear, well pleased at having shortened the interview."

The second woman to bear Napoleon a child was Countess Marie Walewska. The Countess gave herself to him in the belief that he would liberate her native Poland from the Russians and the Austrians. She was sadly disappointed. Around Marie Walewska romantic writers have woven many tales of idyllic love. In actuality, Bonaparte's affair with her began as crudely and bluntly as all of his other sexual encounters. *"Talleyrand,"* he said brutally, speaking of his foreign minister, *"got her for me."*

Walewska's pregnancy was an important factor in Josephine's downfall. Napoleon now had proof that he could father children. Further, he was now at the peak of his power, Emperor of France and ruler of most of Europe. It was time to cement his ties to one of the great royal houses, and to found a legitimate dynasty. It was time to divorce Joséphine.

In 1810 Napoleon married Marie-Louise of Hapsburg, daughter of the Emperor of Austria. It was a brilliant political marriage, allying to France one of the oldest royal houses of Europe. Engineered by Prince Metternich, it was considered a triumph for Austria, as well. As for Napoleon, he had no illusions. "I am marrying a uterus," he said.

To his surprise, Napoleon found his young bride surprisingly interesting. She had a fresh, blond German youthfulness. "Marie-Louise, immature and innocent, turned out to be healthily sensual." On his wedding night, the Emperor drenched himself in cologne, and clad only in a bathrobe stormed his bride's bedchamber. The next

Mlle. Colombier was Napoleon's first love.

morning, while dressing, he said to an aide: *"Marry a German girl, my dear fellow! They are the best women in the world! They are sweet, they are good natured, they have everything to learn, and they are as fresh as roses!"*

Marie-Louise bore him a son, the King of Rome, but she is identified only with Napoleon's last chapter. His marriage to her parallels his downfall. Within five years Napoleon was defeated by the combined armies of Europe and imprisoned in Elba. In his final exile on St. Helena, the former Emperor, approaching fifty, was not even a shadow of his former arrogant self.

As Aubrey described him: "... the Emperor's virility was exhausted: he had lost all interest in sex . . . he had already begun to suffer from . . . disappearance

Countess Walewska bore Napoleon a child in the vain hope that he would liberate her native Poland.—From Bouchot, "Le Luxe Français—L'Empire."

Giuseppini Grassini, famous Italian opera singer, was one of Napoleon's mistresses. —From Aretz, "Napoleon and His Woman Friends."

of hair on the body, atrophy of the genital organs, and an extreme fineness of the skin. The result was total sexual frigidity."

He died, finally, on May 5, 1821.

References

Aubrey, Octave: *The Private Life of Napoleon.*
Guerard, Albert: *Napoleon 1.*
Saunders, Edith: *Napoleon and Mlle. George.*
Faure, Elie: *Napoleon.*
Gerson, Noël: *The Emperor's Ladies.*

● ● ●

THE WIFE WHO IS A MAN

ON trial in Brooklyn Court last April, Sergeant Reuben Anderson, 32 years old, was charged with giving false information to the personnel section of the War Department. He enlisted in the Army in 1942. In June, 1944, he married Lucy Hicks, 60 years of age. Anderson requested allotment checks for Lucy, as his wife. Lucy received nineteen $50 checks. Anderson, according to testimony, had known Lucy since 1934 and knew that Lucy was a man.

For twenty years Lucy, as a "madam," has operated a house of prostitution in Oxnard, California. A few months ago, cases of venereal disease were traced to that brothel. Its inmates, including Lucy, were compelled to undergo medical examination. *Here Lucy was found to be a man.*

Lucy appeared in court to testify—wearing feminine clothing: a short-sleeved dress, a veil hat, and a black wig. Lucy's voice sounds feminine. "Her" slender arms are feminine in appearance. Anderson, Lucy's husband, is a sergeant and an MP.

Lucy's parents wanted a baby girl. Lucy, the boy, was brought up as a girl, never wearing masculine clothes. Always posing as a woman, he has served as a cook, housemaid, and personal maid for wealthy women.

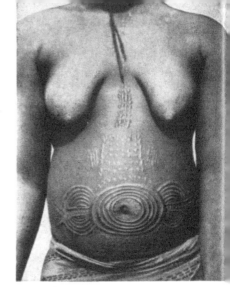

The tattooing of the human body has a sexual significance. This practice was common in ancient civilizations. It is still popular among contemporary primitive peoples and in American and European societies.

SEXUAL

Tattooing

by Robert Wood

THE practice of tattooing has behind it a long, curious and interesting history. Ivan Bloch, Ploss-Bartels and other investigators consider that it was, in common with painting and staining the body, a primitive form of clothing. As it was first intended to cover nakedness, it was natural that the less man clothed himself

Formerly Editor of the "Journal of Sex Education," London, Mr. Wood is a noted English sexologist, medical author and educator.

the more he tattooed his skin.

This situation is easy to understand if we realize that one of the primitive purposes of clothing was to protect the body against magical dangers. The use of clothing to conceal the body for reasons of modesty came much later in history. M. van Gennep called tattooing "a medico-magical mutilation." It is said that women in the Fiji Islands believe that tattoo marks will serve as a passport to the other world after death.

Briffault speaks of the practice of protecting the sexual organs by painting or tattooing. Sometimes these marks can hardly be seen, and are thus in no sense ornamental. In some cases the marks are made by means of incisions on the buttocks, into which lamp black is rubbed to make the markings permanent. If these marks are absent, sexual intercourse is thought to be ineffectual.

Native girls of the Caroline Islands are usually elaborately tattooed, the most complicated part of the design being in the region of the vulva. It is interesting to note that these girls had no objection to having the designs copied by the investigators. Exposing the genital regions in these circumstances did not matter, because the tattooings were regarded as protecting these vulnerable areas against evil spirits.

Sexual Indications

Although magical ideas may have been the original cause of the practice of tattooing, sexual purposes soon came to play a prominent part. Havelock Ellis speaks of the practice as a widespread attempt to beautify and call attention to the sexual organs. When curious travelers have asked primitive people why the males tattoo their bodies, the reply often given has been, "We do it to please the women." The magical charm became the means of allurement and sexual stimulation of the females.

Three examples of contemporary tattooing. Sexual scarification on the abdomen of a primitive West African woman. The Butterfly Woman, tattoo on the chest of a man. The Centaur and the Siren, tattoos on the arm of a French sailor.— African photograph from Chicago Natural History Museum; male tattoos from "Aesculape," French medical journal.

Among the peoples of the South Seas, in the Caroline Islands and in New Guinea, the girls in order to attract the men tattoo themselves exclusively in the genital region, and especially on the *mons veneris* (front pubic area). This serves to make this region conspicuous. Tattooing is also associated with phallic festivals, the onset of puberty and a girl's first menstruation.

Hanns Ebersten in his book *True Love and Pierced Hearts* sums up the history of tattooing. The practice is ancient. Tattoo marks have been found on Egyptian mummies 4000 years old, and tattooing was common in the ancient civilizations of Greece and Rome. It was banished from Britain by the early Christians, and rediscovered by Europeans through journeys to America and the East.

At first it was the vogue in funfairs, circuses, and side shows. In comparatively modern times it became a short-lived fashion in aristocratic circles. King Edward the 7th, King George the 5th, Don Juan of Spain and King Frederick of Denmark were all tattooed, and among famous living men Field Marshal Montgomery adopted the practice.

About 50 years ago tattooing degenerated and, with a few exceptions, became limited to the poorer classes and the underworld. In England, tattooing is now considered "not nice," or "vulgar," and men find it a handicap to success with better-educated girls. Unfortunately statistics as to its frequency are not available. It is nearly always limited to men, and in most cases tattooing is done before the age of 25.

Reasons for Tattooing Today

The motives which lead people to tattoo their bodies probably differ from person to person. Both Darwin and Westermarck considered that the main reasons were associated with the sexual impulse. This theory is confirmed by the character of much of the tattooing. Dr. Walter Bromberg in his recent book *Crime and the Mind* expresses the opinion that there are two main types of men who have their bodies tattooed. One is a very masculine exhibitionistic type, often a sailor. Such a man often increases the number of his tattoos until they cover most of his body.

The second group consists of younger men who bolster their feelings of inferiority and weakness by imitating their stronger and more virile companions. It should be noted that many of the heroes of the comic strips are tattooed. Tattooing thus becomes associated with muscular, bold and highly sexed men.

Sometimes this imitation is the outcome of a homosexual bond between two men. The whole procedure may have an erotic signicance for the homosexual. The penetration of the skin by a needle; the injection of fluid; the passive attitude of the subject—all these may be sexually colored. This homosexual component may, of course, be quite unconscious. If the tattooer is a woman, as is sometimes the case, the masochistic and the sexual factors are obvious. In prisons the inmates often tattoo one another with crude designs, ink and soot being used for coloring.

Lombroso was of the opinion that tattooing was most often found among criminals, and that it was due to their egocentricity. The impulse may be increased by their enforced sexual abstinence. Among those entering prisons, most tattoos were found on procurers and male prostitutes. In many cases the bodies of these men were extensively tattooed.

Sexual Designs

The sexual nature of much tattooing is clearly shown by the nature of the designs. Dr. A. Lacassagne examined the bodies of 378 soldiers, all of whom were tattooed. The total number of tattoo pictures was more than 1000, and 380 of these were overtly sexual.

Fischer and Dubois also traced tattooing to an erotic source, and pointed out the popularity of the practice during World War I. Soldiers had less opportunity to be tattooed than sailors. In the British and German navies the authors estimate that 20 per cent of the men had themselves tattooed.

Among young offenders admitted to reformatories, Robinsohn and Krauss found that 12 per cent were tattooed. Much of this tattooing was sexual in character and some dealt with various deviations. Homosexual tattoos, for instance, were found not only among male but also among female offenders. A frequent design on females was a mackerel sketched on the vulva.

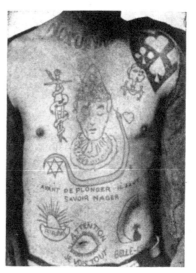

Tattoos on the torso of a man. Note the serpent, an ancient sexual symbol.—Photograph from "Aesculape."

Some time ago the French paper *Le Temps* published an account of a deserter from the army on whose body was found a complicated mass of tattooing. On his chest was a picture of two seductive women throwing kisses to a burly soldier. There were also pictures of music hall singers, men and women, on other parts of his body, and his back was covered with love scenes.

A famous tattooist in Hamburg advertised: "I have designs for everything a manly body should express, politics, erotics, athletics, religion, esthetics." The commonest designs are portraits of pin-up girls, and seductive and sensuous ladies in alluring poses.

One young man of 21 had the nude figure of a woman tattooed on his right thigh, and the faces of young girls on his right arm. His conflict over sex was expressed by the fact that on the opposite side of his body the word "mother" was tattooed, together with religious symbols.

Among other designs frequently found are snake ladies, voluptuous goddesses, knives with phallic-shaped handles, and slightly clad ladies reclining on couches. Occasionally an eye is tattooed on the buttocks, or a serpent is portrayed with its head pointing toward the genital region.

Pictures of women wrestling with snakes and cats chasing mice are also frequent. Occasionally a design is placed on a muscle, and the figures are made to wriggle, or a pair of lovers kiss whenever the biceps are flexed. According to Ebensten, one Berlin tattooist specialized in a complicated design called "The Rose of Jericho." This was made up of representations of the male sex organs intertwined with women's legs.

Tattooed Women

Although among civilized peoples tattooing is generally confined to the male, it is by no means unknown among females. About 60 or 70 years ago it had a considerable vogue among the rich society women of Paris, and a number of high-class tattooists opened fashionable establishments in the neighborhood of Montmartre. Sexual enticement of some kind seems to have been the chief motive in female tattooing. Often the design was placed upon the thigh or the shoulder. Sometimes it took the form of a butterfly, or a spider's web which threatened to entangle those who came too close.

Ivan Bloch refers to the number of cases of fashionable Parisian women who had themselves extensively tattooed. One great lady had had her body tattooed with obscene designs, chiefly of a sexual and satanic character. Two homosexual women had tattoos representing the bond which held them together as sexual partners. The two halves of a single design were engraved upon their bodies. Only when they stood side by side was the full meaning of the picture revealed.

One of the most remarkable pictures referred to by Bloch depicted a hunt in detail. The scenes wound around the body, the final goal being a fox tattooed in the genital region.

Recently in England there seems to have been a mild revival of female tattooing. A short time ago it was the fashion among adolescent boys to dress in Edwardian fashion. Most of these boys were of the working class, and some of them formed gangs of delinquents. They were known as *Teddy Boys*, and some of the tougher girls who associated with them had, usually on the arms, "home-made" tattoo designs.

On the whole it would seem that the ancient practice of tattooing is less popular now than in the past, when it was not uncommon for men and women to engrave their sexual desires, their dreams and their conflicts upon the skins of their bodies and limbs.

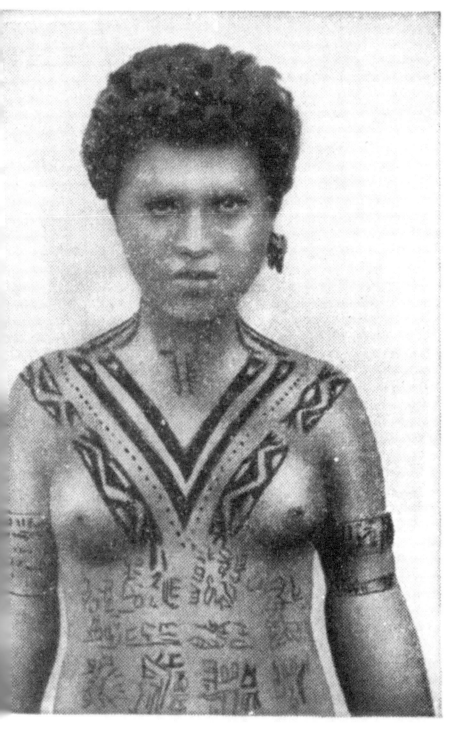

UNWED MOTHERS

...Society's Tragedy

Original painting by
L. Sterne Stevens

A realistic and humane program is offered to end the evils of criminal abortion and to salvage the wasted lives of untold thousands of unwed mothers and unwanted children.

by G. C. Hanna

SOCIETY says that you shall not be a mother unless you are married. Defy this edict and you are condemned for life. A menstrual period is missed, and a girl is panic stricken. For four weeks more she is in a state of anguish, hoping, praying that nothing is wrong — but fearing the worst.

Another period passes with no sign of the menses. Other symptoms of pregnancy appear. The girl's mental state now borders on hysteria in the fear of the fact and its detection. She is now a willing, perhaps eager, subject for the abortionist.

Mr. Hanna was Superintendent of the Institutions for Feeble Minded and Colony for Epileptics in Minnesota, and Superintendent of the Indiana Boys School. He is author of "The Juvenile Criminal," "The Menace of the Feeble Minded," "The Cost of Crime" and other writings in the field of sociology.

It is not so much a question of submitting to an illegal operation as of finding the operator. The abortionist when found may demand a fee that compounds the agony. Fear keeps the unhappy victim from confiding in her parents. She feels sure of their utter condemnation and in far too many cases it is forthcoming upon discovery of the daughter's condition. This highly unnatural lack of sympathy on the part of parents is also for the most part founded on fear, the fear that society will not be kind to them as the parents of a sinful daughter, a case of guilt by reflection. This fear may play as directly into the hands of the abortionist as that of the daughter, through the eagerness of the parents to avoid unfavorable publicity even at the risk of a loved one's life.

If death should result, it can be attributed to peritonitis or some other disease that accounts for polite deaths; thus they hope the sinful conduct of their daughter will be interred with her remains. They at least will be spared the social disapproval which attaches to the "illegitimate child."

Actually the word "illegitimate" is not properly applicable to a child. There can be illegitimate parenthood, but not illegitimate children—and a few enlightened states have stricken this term from the statute books.

Health authorities place the number of criminal abortions in the United States at from 700,000 to 3,000,000 each year, and the deaths resulting therefrom at from four to ten thousand. Such authorities agree that abortion accounts for perhaps one-quarter of all maternity deaths.

While many of these abortions and subsequent deaths occur among married women who for various reasons are unwilling to become mothers, a large proportion occurs among unmarried women. Untold numbers of these are girls between the ages of fourteen and twenty years.

In the light of such figures, is it not high time to scrap the hypocritical reasoning that has for so many centuries prevented recognition of simple biological and ethical truths? Cannot society offer a sane solution of this problem that confronts so many millions whose answer to a fundamental instinct is making them criminals, or the dupes and accessories of criminals?

The first step in a program to end the necessity for criminal abortion is the scrapping of outmoded social concepts. What is needed is a genuinely humanitarian approach based on the fundamental facts of biology.

While not encouraging looseness in sex morality, society could well afford to accord to a girl who becomes pregnant without benefit of a marriage ceremony the same consideration that it bestows on a wedded member.

So far as social expectancy is concerned, the offspring of the illegitimate mother is probably as likely to give a good account of itself as that of the legitimate—if given equal opportunity.

Reference is made here only to normal mothers. The offspring of the feeble-minded is in a different category, and the state has a moral, and in many states a legal, right to take such steps as will deny parenthood to the biologically unfit.

A realistic and humane program to end criminal abortion requires the establishment, under state authority and control, of proper institutions where unwed mothers (and also married ones whose situations have become desperate in pregnancy), may find retreat until such time as they can go forth to take places of usefulness without being required to wear forever the Scarlet Letter.

Babies born in these institutions would be wards of the state, their future status subject to the wishes and competence of the mothers. Many mothers would become so attached to the infants after some weeks with them under favorable conditions that they would not be willing to part with them.

These mothers, their former terror replaced by courage and a new outlook on life through the mental and physical rehabilitation afforded by the institution, would be ready and competent to assume full responsibility for the little ones upon leaving the institution.

Other mothers, for varying reasons, would wish to relinquish all claim on the children. These infants would be eligible for adoption. Here the demand is greater than the supply, giving rise to "baby farms" prospering on fees running into hundreds of dollars for each baby placed in a "home."

But baby farms and licensed maternity asylums handle only that small percentage of cases that comes to them instead of to the abortionists, and their methods may not be such as to stand the light of day. Scandals seem to follow many of them.

Adoptions made under state auspices from its institution would avoid the mercenary and unsavory factors of the baby farms, so that the babies placed in homes would have a chance to develop normally and share with the adopting parents the pleasures of family life.

The deplorable situation that is responsible for abortion has inspired a few philanthropically-minded individuals to found and endow homes to care for unwed mothers and to arrange for the properly safeguarded adoption of the offspring. These homes have rendered society a real service, their purposes being praiseworthy and their methods honorable.

However, they are unknown to the ordinary girl in need of their services and their facilities are so limited as to take care of only the merest fraction of cases needing their help. They are in no sense orphanages and are not equipped to retain, train, and educate those children whose mothers could not take them and those unsuitable for adoption for one reason or another.

A state institution combining the features of home, hospital, school, and workshop, whose population would consist of normal, healthy women voluntarily taking advantage of the shelter and advantages provided, could become practically self-supporting.

Childbirth ordinarily involves a brief period of incapacity so that, with a nursery as a unit of the institution, the mothers would be available for duties required by the institution for almost their entire stay there. The necessities of instutional life would furnish employment and training in a wide range of useful pursuits, training that would prove valuable in obtaining and holding jobs on leaving.

While cost is something that must be considered by every unit of government when the people are loaded down with taxes, as at present, the nominal cost of an institution capable of rendering society so great a service would represent a tiny fraction of the toll now being levied by the evil of illegal abortion.

While this plea is aimed at the protection of mothers and for the right of the unborn to see the light of day, it is believed that the national interest would be promoted by an additional million or more births a year, especially under auspices calculated to develop useful citizens out of the material salvaged from otherwise certain destruction.

And the babies would not constitute the only salvage. The thousands upon thousands of mothers — whose lives are lost or are wrecked annually by abortion and by the outright murder of babies born normally, as attested by the many little bodies left in whatever hiding places are available, and by abandonment of the living creatures on doorsteps, in railroad stations, and wherever it occurs to a distraught mother to leave them —could be saved to useful and perhaps happy lives by rational treatment of this whole question.

Many of these girls and women become prostitutes, thinking that all chance of acceptance is gone forever. Others are shamed for life and never dare to lift their heads in respectable society. Some marry worthless characters, far beneath them intellectually, morally, and in every other respect, and drag out their wasted lives.

Still others so brood over their disgrace and so suffer from the sting of social condemnation and ostracism that in their despair they sink into criminal ways; become alcoholics, drug addicts, or deviates of one kind and another; reach hospitals for the insane; or commit suicide.

All this is unnecessary, is economically wasteful, and constitutes a moral atrocity. What an advance in civilization will it be when a girl of normal intellect can know that — if she becomes pregnant while unmarried — she can find peace, comfort, respectability, and succor for herself and her unborn.

● ● ●

Bone in dog's penis. B—bone; E—erectile tissue; U—urethra. The human penis has no bone but this structure does occur in the genital organs of a number of animals, including the whale.

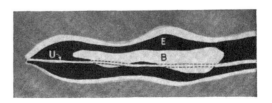

SEX ORGAN WORSHIP

How—and why—the phallic symbol was widely used in ancient art and religion.

E. Royston Pike

■ Carved on the hillside above the little village of Cerne Abbas in the south of England, is the gigantic figure of a man. He holds a club in his hand and is completely naked. But his most noticeable feature is an audaciously erect sexual organ.

Who cut the "giant" in the grass is not known, but it is generally supposed that the figure is a relic of prehistoric *phallic* (penis) worship. This belief would seem to be confirmed by the saying once current (if not still) among the villagers, when an unmarried girl had become pregnant, that "she has been sitting on the giant."

Such phallic representations have been found in most parts of the world; indeed, it has been claimed that phallic worship is one of the oldest and most wide-

Mr. Pike, a well-known British journalist and writer, is author of "Ethics of the Great Religions," *and* "Encyclopedia of Religion and Religions."

spread of the religious practices of mankind.

When it first arose, we have no means of knowing, but certainly it was long before history began. The word *phallic* is Greek, coming from *phallos,* penis. The subject was one which quite early received the attention of the ancient Greek writers.

But the cult existed ages before that. Stone pillars, such as are to be found in the Stone Age monuments of Europe and the Near East, and in parts of the American continents, are generally supposed to be phallic symbols. Such figures as the "Venus of Willendorf" and the male hunters painted on the walls of caves in France and Spain and on rocks in the African deserts, almost certainly have a sexual significance.

What is that significance? Why, in the perpetual darkness of the caverns that were their homes, did prehistoric artists paint pictures of men with penises of exaggerated length? Why did they carve big-

LEFT: PREHISTORIC PHALLIC STATUES found in Corsica by a team of French archeologists. This type of sexual symbol has appeared at almost every time and place in the known history of man.

breasted, big-buttocked female figures, with grossly enlarged genitals? The cave men were intensely practical people, faced with a practical problem. This was the problem of personal survival and the continued existence of the family and the tribe in an unkind world.

Children, plenty of children—that was the dominating necessity. Children who would become warriors and food-gatherers and guardians of the sacred flame that burned on the hearth of the home.

In the primitive health conditions that prevailed, infant mortality must have been tremendous. The only way to counteract it was for the women of the tribe to be almost continuously fertile. But how was this most desirable result to be secured?

It was known (though it had taken untold ages for it to be discovered) that sexual intercourse was a first step to childbirth. Yet it was obvious that not every act of intercourse, not by any manner of means, caused the woman to conceive. It was also believed that the phallus was the really effective instrument of generation. But how to reduce the number of "blanks?"

The answer was found in what readers of Sir J. G. Frazer's epoch-making book *The Golden Bough* will recognize as "sympathetic magic." The cave-man who painted animals of the chase on the rock face was convinced that he was thereby acquiring magical power over them. When the chase was resumed in the light of day above ground, the animals he had

portrayed, he hoped, would fall victim to his arrows and spear-thrusts.

In much the same way, images or models of the phallus were looked upon as magic charms which would add vigor and potency to the living organ in sexual intercourse.

In ancient Egypt large counterparts of the human phallus were carried in processions, and were supposed to represent the sex organ of Osiris, the god whom the Greeks identified with their Bacchus, god of wine. These festivals were imitated by the Greeks and introduced into Europe by them.

The Greeks also had a special god charged with the supervision of the genital organs. His name was Priapus, and his principal characteristic was a disproportionately large and erect penis. His statue, showing him with a human face and the ears of a goat, had a phallus carved prominently on its base.

Two thousand years later, Sir Richard Burton reported the existence of similar statues in West Africa. Very similar was the phallic worship which Sir H. H. Johnston found to be prevalent in the Lower Congo.

In the forests, he said, "it is not rare to come upon a little rustic temple, made of palm-fronds and poles, within which male and female figures, nearly or quite life-size, may be seen, with disproportionate genital organs, the figures being intended to represent the male and female principle. Around these carved and painted statues are many offerings of plates, knives, and cloth, and frequently also the phallic symbol may be seen dangling from the rafters."

Johnston made the point that there was not the slightest suspicion of obscenity in all this, and anyone terming this worship of the reproductive power as obscene must do so hastily and ignorantly.

"It is a solemn mystery to the Congo native, a force but dimly understood, and, like all mysterious natural manifestations, it is a power that must be propitiated and persuaded to his good."

Then there is a very illuminating account given by an English doctor who in 1861, on his way to the Far East, took the opportunity of visiting the great cave temple at Elephanta, near Bombay.

"In each of the monolithic chapels within the area of the main temple," he writes, "I observed a gigantic stone phallus projecting from the center of the floor.

"The emblem was wreathed with flowers, while the floor was strewed with the faded chaplets (wreaths) of the fair devotees, some of whom, at the time of my visit, fancying themselves unobserved, were invoking the subtle influence of the stony charm by rubbing their *pudenda* (genitals) against the unsympathetic surface, while muttering their prayers for conjugal love, or for maternal joy,

as the need might be."

Such practices recall those reported from certain towns of France not so long ago. These places had statues of a very obviously male saint, often called St. Foutin. Barren women, or those who feared to be so, went to the statue and either laid themselves upon it, if it were a horizontal one, or, more usually, scraped the phallus and mixed with water a "miraculous draught" which they drank in confident expectation. Sometimes (we are told) the stony organ was practically worn away or made unrecognizable by the devoted attentions of the worshippers.

But it is in India, past and present, that we find the most marked development of phallicism. Everywhere throughout the peninsula one may see the joined images of the male and female sex organs, the *lingam* (male) and the *yoni* (female.)

Although not quite so realistic in appearance as the phallus, perhaps, the lingam is a conventional representation of the penis, made of rounded blocks of stone or polished wood, and sometimes made more lifelike with veins painted on the surface. The yoni is also recognizable enough, a fairly lifelike representation of the female vulva, in the shape of a ring of brass or stone, in which the lingam is placed erect.

Thus we see that it is unwise to judge strange customs of distant people by our own morality. Phallic worship can be seen to have had a very serious and quite respectable purpose and origin. As the source of all private and public wealth, security, and happiness, the sex organs were quite logically objects of worship and veneration to early man.

Culver

A LINGAM, or phallic statue, in India.

YOUR SEX QUESTIONS ANSWERED

● **Mutual Masturbation (264)**
Sexology, January, 1935

Editor, SEXOLOGY:

I am nearly nineteen, and my boy friend two years younger, though he is mentally and physically built to appear older than he is. We are deeply in love, and consider the difference in age trifling. I have allowed him to use my body, to obtain sexual satisfaction, and find myself doing the same, when we are together. Is this dangerous, and how will it affect our lives in the future?

Miss R. G., New York

Answer:

In your question, whether your habit of mutual masturbation is dangerous and what effect it will have on your future lives, you do not state whether you want to know the physical or the mental result of your indulgence.

The chances are that you will never marry each other. Your life at this time is simply one of preparation for the more serious life of maturity. If you are both physically mature, your present form of love-making may do you very little physical harm (certainly not as much as solitary autoerotic practices would); but as a preparation for the broader and better part of adult life I think that it is very harmful. This boy is going to drift away from you; and then he will be followed by other boys and other men, and your entire viewpoint of adult relations will be in every way tinged and warped and twisted by your varied relations with men who have petted you in every way short of actual intercourse. You will become—in fact you are at present—

what the French call a demi-virgin.

We are not considering your relations from the standpoint of morals. In fact your behavior in the Islands of Samoa would be considered very usual and the proper thing. But the question of your future happiness and peace of mind as an adult woman has to be given due consideration. What you consider extremely wonderful now will be the cause of considerable regret when you grow older. You are both too young to see this with the eyes of an adult; but my opinion is that you are both children playing with dynamite. In this same mail there were two letters from children of your age who feared pregnancy, and wanted to know what to do about it. Their very serious position started with simple petting. If young people must have extreme sexual pleasure, they had better marry and have it legitimately. You and your boy friend had better say good-bye, and wait till you grow up.

—Editor

● ● ●

● **Superfluous Hair (2350)**
Sexology, December, 1946

Editor, SEXOLOGY:

I am a married woman 21 years of age and I am worried about the hair on my body. It is long, dark, and very much like that on a man. My breasts are small, and are covered with the hair.

Please give me some advice regarding this. I am much worried about it.

Mrs. W. L. T., North Carolina.

Answer:

Methods of treating excessive hairiness are unsatisfactory at present. Its causes are many. Some of the causes are ovarian

165

tumors, pituitary tumors, tumors or enlargements of the adrenal glands. In some families there appears to be an hereditary tendency to hirsutism (excessive hairiness).

In SEXOLOGY for April 1946, on Page 536 there is an excellent and comprehensive article on *Hirsutism in Females.* Conclusions were based upon a close study of 33 cases. In some of these cases the various glands mentioned above were diseased. On Page 75 September 1946 SEXOLOGY, there is a reference to a woman who became hairy and grew a beard. The hair disappeared when surgeons removed an ovarian tumor. Our February issue covered some interesting points on the subject of hirsutism in women. The article is to be found on Page 395 under the title of *Virilism in Women.* Another reference will be found on Page 101, September, 1945, SEXOLOGY. The title of the reference is *Hirsutism-Excessive Hair.* Back issues, when on hand, may be had for the price of the magazine (25c per issue) from the circulation department.

A thorough medical examination might be helpful in determining the cause. Even then, do not expect too much. The most reputable doctors are sometimes unable to determine obscure causes.

Don't spend your money on depilatories except for cosmetic appearance of the face and then be careful.

—Editor

Excessive superfluous hair—a glandular condition imperfectly understood particularly in females. Frequently this gives rise to facial hair in great abundance. Such an excessive case is shown in this illustration.

● **Fetish of Wife (3495)**
Sexology, February, 1953

Editor, SEXOLOGY:

My husband and I are both 26 years old. We love each other very much. I seldom if ever reach a climax during marital relations. My husband is a traveling salesman. During the days and nights that he is out of town, I wear baby rubber pants. Recently I made some larger ones which I wear when I go to bed alone and always experience a climax. I think that my husband suspects me of having this fetish. Should I tell him about my strange desires? He is very understanding and always wants to please me.

Mrs. H. S. W., California.

Answer:

Your fetish dates, as to origin, probably further back than you think. It *could* date back to infancy if you wore rubber pants in infancy. The pants and their odor are unconsciously (or subconsciously) associated with the satisfaction and stimulation you experienced through the natural act (in some form) of self-gratification. The wearing of the garment and its associated odor now stimulate the unconscious into action and you sense satisfaction.

When husbands and wives are close to each other, neither should be in the least inhibited toward or with the other. Both should feel that in their sex life everything between them is in common. Perhaps it would do no harm to explain your strange desires to your husband. At the same time this may engender greater confidence in you and he may surprise you by acquainting you with some deep secret of his own. Thus you both may be drawn closer and your sex relationship in marriage may be enhanced because you will both become willing to share everything pertaining to it in common.

In marriage, and particularly in the sex relationship in marriage, two persons can come about as near to being one as is possible. If there is any freedom we can claim entirely and defy the world to stop, it is freedom in our sex and love relations in marriage.

—Editor

Such things aren't supposed to exist but they do!

This is the first book to face these relationships frankly—and to offer an answer!

Fully, frankly, courageously it replies to such questions as:

> What are the dangers to an unmarried couple in arousing, but not fulfilling, physical desire?
> When does normal "sex play" approach the abnormal?
> What great problems face young couples who delay marriage for economic reasons?
> Is it physically dangerous for the young girl to permit the liberty of "necking" without "going any further?"
> Is a marriage in which there has been previous sexual intercourse more likely or is it less likely to go to smash?
> What is the surprising percentage of unmarried persons indulging in auto-erotic practices?
> What is the average normal periodicity of sex functioning in adults?
> On purely physiological grounds, is there any reason why temperate sex intercourse should be denied to the unmarried?
> etc., etc.

The
SEX LIFE
of the
UNMARRIED ADULT

320 Exciting Pages

EDITED BY DR. IRA S. WILE

The contributors include some of the most brilliant scientists of this nation, such as:

Robert L. Dickinson, M.D., Author of *Control of Conception, A Thousand Marriages, Human Sex Anatomy*, etc. Honorary Secretary of the National Committee on Maternal Health, an authority with over a half century of experience in gynecology, obstetrics and sex problems of women. **Morris L. Ernst, A. F., LL.D.** Co-author of *To The Pure; Censored.* Mr. Ernst's vigor and success in defending censorship suits has made him known as an arch-foe of "vice-hunters" in general. **Margaret Mead, B. A., Ph.D.,** Author of *Coming of Age in Samoa, Growing Up in New Guinea*, etc. Miss Mead has made an extensive research into the sex customs of adolescent men and women in primitive tribes. **N. W. Ingalls, M.D.** Widely known for his investigations in Early Human Development, both normal and abnormal. He is Professor of Anatomy at Western Reserve University, etc., etc.

Polymastia...
multiple breasts

Some women are born with more than two breasts. These extra mammary organs may be fully developed and found on any part of the body.

by Sarah R. Riedman, Ph.D.

The Goddess Diana, showing supernumerary breasts. In ancient times, multiple breasts symbolized fertility.

AMONG some ancient peoples, certain goddesses were portrayed as many-breasted, an attribute which symbolized fruitfulness and bounty. Thus the Greek goddess of grain and the harvest, *Ceres,* her Egyptian counterpart *Isis,* and *Hertha* of Scandinavia, worshipped for the plenty they were thought to bring

A noted physiologist, Dr. Riedman is author of Physiology of Work and Play, *co-author,* Story of Microbes.

to their people, were pictured with supernumerary (extra) breasts. But the single-breasted *Patinuru* of Brazil was feared because her milk was supposed to be poisonous. Undoubtedly actual multi-breasted women must have been observed among mortals, and the condition was surrounded with wonder, superstition, and ritualistic beliefs.

This abnormality — more than two breasts—is known as *polymastia.* The occurrence of extra nipples is called *polythelia*. Both conditions are seen in both sexes, the former, of course, in males with glandular abnormalities only. The occurrence of more than two breasts in humans has been estimated at approximately 1 per cent. A collection of cases recorded in medical history up to 1917 numbered 10,000.

While no longer associated with the supernatural, this condition evokes justifiable fears even in modern times; for the disfigurement constitutes not only a cosmetic problem with its accompanying psychological and emotional implications, but frequently these extra breasts may cause pain and discomfort and become the sources of benign and malignant growths.

Location

Extra breasts vary from small rudimentary nipples with practically no underlying breast tissue (often mistaken for pigmented moles), to fully functioning glands capable of secretion and of responding to hormone stimulation, becoming enlarged during pregnancy and the menstrual cycle, and producing milk during the lactation (nursing) period. If stimulated during this period by suckling or pumping, they may secrete milk in the same way as the normal mammary gland.

Extra breasts may occur singly, as a pair (one on each side), or they may be multiple. As many as *ten supernumerary nipples* have been reported in one woman, but rarely are there more *than one or two*. The most common location is in the armpit; such a structure may not actually be a separate breast, but may be connected with the normal breast on that side by means of a bridge of mammary tissue. Often the connecting tongue of tissue is lacking.

Another common location is along what is known as the *milk line*—on both sides of the trunk. They may appear on the chest, abdomen and groin, and resemble a double string of nipples similar to the mammary glands of a dog, cat or pig. In these animals (particularly the pig, in which the number of nipples varies from six to thirteen or even more) the multiple glands are normal and associated with the larger size of the litters. There is no evidence that

An unusual case of polymastia, or extra breasts. A case is known of a mother who nursed her children from all three breasts.—Von Muchow.

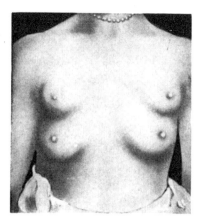

Woman with four breasts and nipples, photograph of a rare case.—*After Hirschfeld.*

the occurrence of extra breasts in humans is associated with the birth of twins, triplets, etc.

A human embryo (child in the earliest stages of its development in the womb) normally repeats some of the developmental features of the lower forms of life. For instance, the very early human embryo has little to distinguish it from the pig embryo. The development of the breasts is seen in the sixth week embryo in the form of a ridge of skin tissue along both sides of the body. At the end of the ninth week, when the human embryo is about an inch long, this milk ridge breaks down into a series of elevations, each with the embryonic tissue capable of forming mammary glands. Later, all except the two in the upper breast region disappear. The normal mammary glands develop from this remnant of the milk line. When supernumerary breasts do appear at birth, they are usually seen along the embryonic milk line.

Causes of Polymastia

Darwin explained polymastia as an *atavism* (throwback to an earlier evolutionary stage). However, this faulty development from a persistent milk ridge does not explain the occurrence of supernumerary breasts or nipples in several other places, such as the face, ear, neck, arms, thigh, buttocks, and even the labia majora of the vagina. Along with other physical abnormalities, these remain unexplained except as the results of faulty metabolism or accidental pressures brought to bear on the developing unborn child, thus causing mammary cells to be transplanted to distant parts. A full explanation of the causes of polymastia awaits further investigation of other abnormalities, such as misplaced teeth, hair, or eye fragments.

Also unexplained is the greater frequency of polymastia in some parts of the world than in others. For example, it occurs in 5 per cent of the females and 1½ per cent of the males of Japan, but in only 0.4 per cent of all English babies. Moreover, the locations of these extra breasts are different among different peoples: 88 per cent of the cases recorded in Japan appear *above* the normal breasts, while in Finland they are located almost exclusively *below* them.

The female breasts are modified skin glands which remain small until puberty; then, under the influence of ovarian hormones, they enlarge. The breast glands, before puberty, consist of rudimentary ducts extending a short distance below the flattened nipples. During puberty the ducts grow and the branching canals increase in number until at adolescence there is a complex network of tubes. Some milk-producing cells may develop with menstruation. With pregnancy, under the stimulation of one of the pituitary hormones, these cells *proliferate* (grow by multiplying new parts), filling the ducts with milk shortly after childbirth, when another hormone is introduced into the circulating blood of the mother by the pituitary gland.

Thus supernumerary breasts may be unnoticed if they are only rudimentary, without much connective or glandular tissue; or they may closely resemble the normal glands, with fully formed nipples, branching ducts, and glandular cells. As a rule, extra breasts near the center of the body are small and imperfectly developed, while those located near the side are well developed and capable of secretion.

When the mammary-stimulating hormones are circulating in the blood (dur-

ing menstruation, pregnancy and lactation), the extra breasts may swell and become painful. Until then unrecognized, they suddenly become troublesome, showing characteristic cyclic changes. Often they are mistaken for fatty tumors, until their response to hormones discloses them to be milk-secreting tissue and sometimes actual functioning breasts.

Surgical removal becomes necessary when the gland is located in a conspicuous place, causing cosmetic embarrassment, or when, even if not conspicuous, it may become susceptible to rapid and malignant growths. Whether the extra breasts are removed for cosmetic or medical reasons, surgical repair is a relatively simple procedure, and is usually advised by the physician in most cases.

A milk-giving supernumerary breast on the thigh of a nursing mother.—From an old engraving.

CHASTITY GIRDLES

...a study in Jealousy

Girdles of chastity were designed in the middle ages to prevent a wife from being unfaithful to her husband. However, the chastity girdles were not always as effective in this respect as the husband had anticipated. Love-relationship is spontaneous—it cannot be forced. The present authoritative article by our well-known British author and lecturer was compiled after arduous research from many European sources.

by Robert Wood

HUMAN possessiveness and jealousy have expressed themselves in many different ways, inflicting untold suffering and even death upon their victims. There are, however, few chapters in human history stranger or more grotesque than the story of the *girdle of chastity*—a story so improbable that it was at one time seriously doubted whether these girdles had ever actually been used.

The *girdle of chastity* is a mechanical device, fitted upon the female, and locked, its purpose being to make sexual intercourse impossible. The girdle consists of two parts—a band which encircles the body above the hips, and a part, made of metal, bone, or ivory, is hinged on to this flexible band in front. This second part is perforated, and is intended, when in place, to press firmly against the mons veneris (rounded elevation, covered with pubic hair, at the lower part of a woman's abdomen). It is locked into position, the lock often being placed on the encircling band.

Where Chastity Belt Originated

The origin and the date of the introduction of this practice into Europe are uncertain. The purpose of the girdle of chastity was the forcible prevention of the sexual act. The custom of fitting chastity belts was apparently unknown in the classical civilizations of Greece and Rome. The available evidence suggests that it arose in the East, perhaps in Africa. The most primitive form would seem to have been the fastening together of the *labia majora* by means of a ring or buckle, and in some cases by sewing them together. This is called *infibulation,* derived from the Latin word, *fibula,* meaning a clasp, or buckle. From these primitive and savage practices the girdle of

Medieval scene . . . Husband receiving key of chastity belt from wife sitting on edge of bed. After a copper engraving from the year 1706.

chastity described above seems to have developed. We know that the wearing of some kind of simple belt or girdle is fairly widespread among people, such as certain gipsy women in Spain, who attach great importance to chastity. Such a belt, however, is usually worn by the girl until her marriage, and is often cut by the bridegroom on the marriage night.

When was the girdle of chastity introduced into Europe? According to one account, it was invented by Francesco Carrara, the tyrant of Padua, who was put to death by the Venetians. This, however, is not supported by sufficient evidence. Havelock Ellis cites two different opinions as to the date of its introduction into Europe, one ascribing it to the 13th century, and the other to the Renaissance. Dr. E. J. Dingwall, writing 20 years later, regards the date of its introduction as still uncertain. Such girdles, he tells us, were known in the second half of the 12th century. The practice would thus seem to go back to mediaeval times in Europe, coming first probably to Venice from the Orient, at the time of the Crusades, and then to France and to other European countries.

Behind this practice there lay a whole philosophy of woman. In the early literature of chivalry she was idealized. She inspired veneration, and her chastity was taken

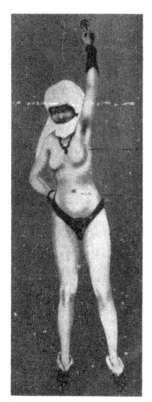

for granted. This view disappeared with the passing of the ideals of chivalry. In France the literature of chivalry was replaced by the Fabliaux. These were short tales in verse, and represented a completely different point of view. The deceived husband became a stock figure of derision. Woman was portrayed as lascivious, cunning and unscrupulous. These tales became very popular in the 12th and 13th centuries, and they contained what might be called the *new* view of woman. This view appears in the *Decameron of Boccaccio* in the 14th century, and in the writings of Rabelais, and Brantome in the 16th. In the Heptameron, which belongs to the same century, Marguerite de Valois presented, with courtly charm, the same view of woman. Her ladies are mostly as much inclined to dalliance as her men. The view of female human nature here propounded differs little from that contained in the famous anecdote of Rabelais. Panurge meets a man carrying two baby girls, aged about 2 or 3 years, in a double knapsack slung across his back. He asks if the little girls are *virgins,* and the man replies that he supposes that the one in front is still a virgin, but as for the one behind he would not offer an opinion. It was out of this philosophy of woman that the girdle of chastity arose. Woman, according to the German saying,

was chaste when no man was available, and true when only a single one was. Madame d'Epinay, the protectress of Jean Jacques Rousseau, once said that modesty was attached only with pins, and so chastity could be secured only by lock and key.

This fundamental distrust of woman, and disbelief in her honor and integrity was thus very widespread. The Italian writer, Poggio, in one of his facetious stories written at the beginning of the 15th century, tells of a jealous husband who castrates himself in order that if his wife becomes pregnant she

174

will not be able to deny her adultery. In 1608 Thomas Middleton, the English dramatist in his play *A Mad World My Masters* refers to the "gem" kept by the Italians under lock and key, and Shakespeare makes King Lear express himself about women as follows:

"*Down from the waist they are Centaurs*
Though women all above:
But to the girdle do the gods inherit
Beneath is all the friends."

"Love Laughs at Locksmiths"

This attitude led, as it was bound to do, to a battle of wits between men and women. The lover and the wife with the help of the locksmith pitted their wits against the husband. This situation furnished further opportunities for wit and satire. In the 16th century Sir David Lyndsay in Scotland wrote a satirical poem on the subject. It deals with a foolish and jealous old man who had married a young wife. He locks his wife's girdle up before going to sleep. She, however, steals the key from under his pillow, and is sexually intimate with her lover. The old man later wakes up and cannot find the key. His wife pretends to help him, and slips the key back. The poem closes with the old cuckold congratulating himself on the possession of the best wife in Fyffe. Similar situations were portrayed again and again. The importance of the locksmith increases, and it may even be that the familiar proverbial English phrase, "love laughs at locksmiths," arose

in connection with this situation. In illustrations of the period the husband is portrayed in the act of starting on a journey. His mind is set at rest by fitting a girdle upon his wife. The futility of such a procedure is usually suggested in some way, and in one 17th century German engraving the figure of the waiting lover is seen behind the curtains of the bed. It is interesting to note that the well-known erotic artist, Raphael Kirchner, who died in New York in 1917, drew a picture of an almost naked girl wearing a chastity-girdle, and triumphantly holding up the key. *See page* 155.

Chastity girdles of varying types are contained in various museums and collections throughout the world. There is the elaborate and beautiful girdle at the Ducal Palace at Venice. Another very fine one is in the possession of the museum at Kalmar. There are two in the Musée de Cluny at Paris, and others at Odenwald and Nürenberg and several in the museums of London. Dingwall tells us that the famous London waxworks exhibition of Madame Tussaud's possessed an example of one which the great German cultural historian, Eduard Fuchs, dated from the 16th century. This is no longer, unfortunately, on exhibition.

Although, unhappily, human jealousy remains to mar human happiness the girdle of chastity has almost completely disappeared. When practices of a similar kind occur, as from time to time they do, they represent not an institu-

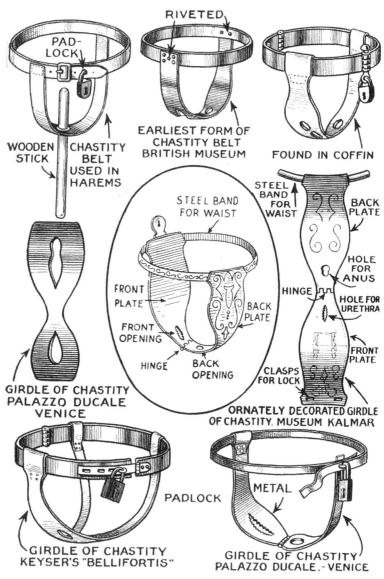

PAD-LOCK

WOODEN STICK

CHASTITY BELT USED IN HAREMS

RIVETED

EARLIEST FORM OF CHASTITY BELT BRITISH MUSEUM

FOUND IN COFFIN

STEEL BAND FOR WAIST

FRONT PLATE

FRONT OPENING

HINGE

BACK PLATE

BACK OPENING

GIRDLE OF CHASTITY PALAZZO DUCALE VENICE

STEEL BAND FOR WAIST

BACK PLATE

HOLE FOR ANUS

HINGE

HOLE FOR URETHRA

FRONT PLATE

CLASPS FOR LOCK

ORNATELY DECORATED GIRDLE OF CHASTITY. MUSEUM KALMAR

GIRDLE OF CHASTITY KEYSER'S "BELLIFORTIS"

PADLOCK

METAL

GIRDLE OF CHASTITY PALAZZO DUCALE.- VENICE

Above—Different types of Chastity Belts which have been exhibited at various European museums. These devices were often worn by medieval women when their warrior husbands went off to the wars. Husbands took the keys with them or else left them with individuals whom they thought they could trust. Belts were made mostly of metal and had holes for passage of body wastes.

tion but an aberration. Louis-Charles Royer, a French journalist, tells us of a Somali girl of about 11 whose sexual organs were sewn up. This, he tells us, is a pre-marriage custom in that district. In one of his stories he makes a jealous Frenchman behave in the same way to his mistress. This is by no means an isolated example, as girdles of chastity and various methods of infibulation have been treated several times in comparatively recent French literature.

When we turn from literature to real life we find occasional episodes which recall the past. In 1903, for instance, there appeared in Germany a patent locking device for "unfaithful married women." The inventor of this was a certain Frau Emilie Schafer. What demand there was for this device there is, unfortunately, no means of knowing. Dr. Dingwall cites a French case which occurred as late as 1910. This concerned a French pharmacist who lived in the Rue de Vaugirard, who was suspected by the police of cruelty to his wife. She was eventually discovered chained to the bed, and wearing under her clothes a kind of corset made of chain-mail and pad-

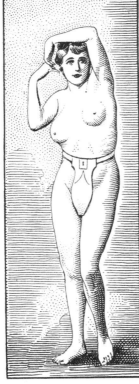

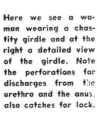

Here we see a woman wearing a chastity girdle and at the right a detailed view of the girdle. Note the perforations for discharges from the urethra and the anus, also catches for lock.

Steel Band for Waist

BACK PLATE

hole for anus

Hinge

hole for urethra

FRONT PLATE

Catches for the lock

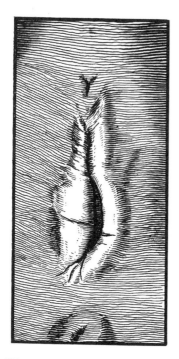

African natives and others have a chastity protector of their own . . . the art of sewing up the vaginal opening of young girls so that sexual congress is impossible. When the girl marries, her husband has to open the closed vaginal lips, or have this done by one of the tribal women trained for the purpose.

locked around the body. There is reason to suppose that such apparatus is still occasionally manufactured and used. Only rarely do such aberrations come to public notice.

The Danger of Jealousy

The subject of the girdle of chastity is not merely one of historical interest. The forms in which jealousy expresses itself change from age to age, but the passion itself remains with all its humiliating and painful consequences. The murder of Desdemona by Othello has been enacted time after time in all the countries of the world, and even today in spite of our greatly increased psychological knowledge, the *crime passionel* occupies a special place, and jealousy is still regarded as a proof of love.

Modern psychological research in no way endorses the traditional view that jealousy is in some way a noble passion, although its results are often unfortunate. Psychologists regard jealousy, at least in its more dangerous forms, as a defect in the capacity for loving. This defect is usually traced back to some childhood situation in which the feeling of inferiority or guilt was particularly intense. When such situations are never resolved or mastered the personality remains perpetually insecure, and emotional needs are incapable of being satisfied. The victim of jealousy becomes tyrannical, suspicious and parasitical. Psychologists tend to regard even the less extreme and more usual types of jealousy as stemming from personality defects, and although no one can hope to be entirely free from this passion the mature person should be able to control it.

As Havelock Ellis pointed out, jealousy is in reality a self-defeating passion, because it diminishes the lovability of the person manifesting it. It therefore tends unwittingly to bring about the very situation that it most desires to avoid. It implies a false view of human relationships, and a property-view of human beings. No person can possess another, and the love-relationship is both spontaneous and inward. It cannot be forced,

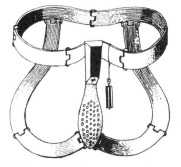

Chastity belt with sieve to pass urine and other discharges such as menstrual blood.

and a mere outward conformity (which is all that jealousy can ever exact) would not have any attraction for a mature and psychologically healthy person. La Rochefoucauld, with his usual fine insight, realized that jealousy was a manifestation, not of love, but of *self-love!* The person who is prone to jealousy can neither enjoy nor confer happiness, and when we read the story of the *girdle of chastity* we are inclined to agree with the man who said, "ten times rather an unfaithful than a jealous husband!"

Madame Juliette Litière, of Paris, exhibiting a chastity belt from which the court ordered her freed, two years ago. Mme. Litière admitted the implied compliment.

Twin Beds or Single?

By ARTHUR KAHN, Ph.T.

FOR a number of years it has been my privilege to be the recipient of the confidences and the unburdenings of the troubled souls of scores of men and women. From the material I have been able to gather from such confidential outpourings, it became impressively evident that the use of twin beds, or the single bed, as the case may be, by married people is responsible for much more domestic discord than is generally admitted.

Upon putting the question directly, most couples were definite in their viewpoint in this matter of beds. Those who prefer twin beds unreservedly condemned the single bed, and those who prefer the single bed were every bit as condemnatory of the twin beds.

Most topics of domestic discord are age-old but the question of twin-beds or the single bed is comparatively new. As a rule, it is never discussed in polite circles; for there is still a little prudery left in us with all our claims to modernism. The supporters of the single bed steadfastly claim twin beds are closely linked with the increasing rate of divorce, and point out that it is not mere coincidence that both appeared almost simultaneously. They also say that in those countries where twin beds have not yet come into popular use, divorce is noticeably less than in those countries where they are widely prevalent.

They decry the fact that no steps are taken to discourage the growing trend towards twin beds and claim they have good and sound reasons for their contentions. Some have gone as far as to denounce twin beds as the greatest boon to lawyers and, probably, the crafty creation of a shrewd lawyer in order to create more business for himself.

They go further, to say that to be unconcerned about this matter of beds is a preponderantly American trait. Let me cite verbatim what Mr. L. said: "We pride ourselves on this side of the ocean as the world's foremost leaders in modernism, open-minded and proud of our women's equality and the great part they play in the life of our wonderful country. Woman's emancipation has not only given her equal rights but independence which is gradually shaping a changed aspect of home life and the accepted standards of domesticity. She not only occupies a stronghold in the business world, professions and the arts, but runs her home along lines strange indeed to her mother and grandmother. These new standards have wrought revolutionary changes in the life of our country and our homes to a considerable extent; but the one least spoken of, yet most far-reaching in effect, is the twin bed."

"The twin bed is symbolic of the final word in feminine independence which is not proving to be all that was claimed for it. In a big percentage of cases it has taken away the last vestige of inequality between a man and his wife. From the first night she chooses to sleep in a separate bed she is no more the clinging mate that most real he-men want for a wife. She has overdone her emancipation and taken on an altered aspect in domesticity. That few inches of space between the beds grows into a vast expanse as big and wide as a barren desert. The next step is a separate bedroom."

Most of those in favor of the single bed were men, but it was a woman who said to me: "Most of the married folks I know who have twin beds are nothing more than hypocrites. I have observed that one bed is well worn while the other is practically unused."

Let us take an example of this viewpoint and see if the contentions of the single-bed advocates have any logic. Mrs. B. sued her husband for divorce. During the airing of their case in court, no mention was made of beds, although fundamentally that was the basic cause of their trouble. A friend of the husband's told me his version of the story outside of the courtroom. For the first two years of their married life, they were happy, contented and very much in love. The break in their wedded harmony came when the wife insisted on installing new furniture in their bedroom, which included twin beds in place of the former single bed. The wife claimed her husband's ardor cooled toward her for no apparent rea-

son. The husband denied such allegations and insisted his love was unchanged.

Many things were brought out at the trial which shocked and surprised them both. Infidelity was proven and a divorce granted. It evidently did not occur to either of them that the twin bed was the unmentioned culprit. Formerly, little spats and inconsequential disagreements were patched up each night and forgotten, but after the advent of the twin beds there was no patching up. Each little spat left unsettled and unforgotten, spread itself into the atmosphere of their home for days and nights; and succeeding ones accumulated on top of those until it appeared like last week's pile of unwashed dishes. All became jumbled into a hopeless mess of bitter antagonism and the pair drifted further apart until they reached a stage where they hated the very sight of each other.

And now let us take an example in favor of the twin beds. Mrs. K. was ordered by her doctor to sleep on a hard bed, in order to help her chronic back condition. She placed boards underneath her mattress and soon found this very efficacious in helping her to get a good night's sleep. After several nights, her husband, who had nothing wrong with his back and preferred a soft bed, began to voice his strenuous objections. She insisted that he ought to be glad to make such a sacrifice for her; while he stubbornly held out that his sacrifices might help her but would ruin him. The ensuing clash of wills soon led to a minor riot and was on the verge of causing a permanent separation. Their problem was easily solved by twin beds, which provided the wife with her hard mattress and the husband with his beloved soft one. Thus twin beds proved the means of saving an otherwise happy marriage from smashing on the rocks. Between these extremes there is an assortment of diverse reasons for and against twin beds.

The advocates of twin beds place a great deal of emphasis on the health angle. If the wife has a cold, there is every good reason of hygiene for the husband to avoid close proximity because of the danger of contagion. If the husband is a restless sleeper, inadvertently pulling the blankets over himself until he is virtually enfolded in them like a mummy, leaving his poor spouse exposed to the chilly night air—by all means twin beds is preferable.

Not all married couples can or do go to bed at the same time. Perhaps the husband comes home late from his lodge meeting and goes to bed long after his lady is asleep. He can undress in the bathroom and noiselessly slip into his twin bed without disturbing the wife. It may require a little practice, but I have the word of honor of a dozen men that they manage it regularly now after a little practice. And, when the wife has been to a late theater party, she can do likewise. There is no need to wake up dear little hubby who is so tired after a hard day's work and needs all the sleep he can get.

Another reason given is that all people do not fall asleep with equal facility. Some are fortunately endowed with the enviable ease with which they drop right off into a deep sleep, the moment the head is laid on the pillow. Others have to woo slumber with all their physical and emotional assistance before they can doze off into some sort of so-called repose. The quick sleeper will find the slow sleeper irksome and, invariably, the other's wakefulness is delaying the habitual rapidity of falling asleep. In fact, on numerous occasions the ready sleeper has been so disturbed by the other's slowness, kept awake by it beyond his accustomed time so often, that he loses what was formerly a good and healthy habit.

There is no greater envy than that of the poor sleeper lying in bed beside one who quickly falls off to sleep, while he remains staring into the blackness around him and wondering why he was cursed with insomnia. In the stillness of the night morbid thoughts seem to take on a reality beyond comparison to that of the daytime waking hours. The insomniac mulls over his troubles during those hours of wooing sleep and, often, cannot help but think that the sleeping spouse does not show sufficient concern over the family problems and cares, or she surely could not drop off to sleep so readily. Twin beds do not entirely overcome this type of case, but they help considerably.

The housewife who considers herself thoroughly modern, I also find very emphatically in favor of twin beds. With her it is entirely a matter of esthetics. She takes an extreme amount of pride in her home, its furnishings and her good taste. She has twin beds merely because they look nicer, fill the room so much better, present a more balanced effect and in every other respect give a more pleasing impression. Her bedroom is a showplace, not a secluded retreat to be used for the purpose of sleeping. To her, the matched bedspreads on the twin beds, in that particular shade of orchid that so cunningly harmonizes with the window drapes, are a most important thing. All else is relegated to a secondary place of consideration and of minor importance.

Those in favor of the single bed impressed me as being unconcerned with appearances, hygiene or such minor trivialities. Theirs is the solid, old-fashioned and time-tried viewpoint; they insist that a wife's place is *beside* her husband, not just figuratively, but in fact. They are the kind who are so full of tenderness and love until it is overflowing. The nearness of their mate means physical pronouncement of their seal of the bond of marriage. It is a form of outlet for their abundance of love for their spouse, as they not only like to think of their partner in marriage as close to them, but also like to sense it physically. They are like the collector of rare gems or antiques who is never satisfied with merely looking at his specimens, but finds himself touching them, fondling them and caressing them in his great fondness for his treasures. It gives such people an added feeling of oneness and that they are really married, not just living together under one roof. For such mates to be separated even in sleep is sacrilege and inviting danger. Their marriage is based on the clinging sense of unity that is innate within them and they can only be happy and contented with the single bed.

When both partners in marriage are the ideal complement to each other, this problem of beds does not usually arise. Their personalities are so well blended, that the likes and dislikes of one are the same as that of the other. It is only when there is a wide divergence of education, background, age, former environment and other such elevents that go into the making of the character of an individual, that there is likelihood of a clashing of the wills in this as in anything else pertaining to domestic tranquility. Adaptation is of course the only solution. One of the mates soon or later will have to allow the other to do all the dictating, while the weaker one must adapt his will accordingly—or sleep on the living room couch.

● ● ●

WIFE-SHARING IN TIBET

■ A man and his son can quite legally share the same wife—although she could not be the son's mother—according to the institution of polyandry in Tibet.

Polyandry, or wife-sharing, is a form of marriage in which one wife has a number of husbands. It is not unusual for a woman to marry a man and his son at the same time.

MUSICAL SEX SUBLIMATION — *By Tina*

The sexual urge may be sublimated in various ways. Some individuals find sexual gratification in listening to a moving musical passage. Our surrealist artist has given her interpretation of the conversion of a woman's sexual desires through music. The partly reclining female figure seen here represents the woman who sublimates her sexual desires. A spectre-like image emanates from her, symbolizing her psyche, and succumbs to the sensual stimulation of the melody.

sex fetishes

*A normal part of all love, fetishism sometimes
takes mysterious and unexplainable forms.*

by Kenneth Walker, M.D., F.A.R.C.

THE pattern made by sexual
desire takes many forms,
and it is difficult to draw
any sharp line between what can
be termed "normal" sexual desire and what has to be labelled
a "sexual deviation."

Fetishism is an example of one
of the many border-line expressions which sexuality may assume. By fetishism is meant a
shift of sexual emphasis from
the total personality of a person
who is loved to some isolated
physical feature, bodily function
or article of clothing.

Fetishism is rarely found in wo-

*Dr. Walker, a distinguished Brit-
ish surgeon, is author of "Marriage"
and "The Physiology of Sex," and
co-author of "Sex and Society" and
"Sexual Disorders in the Male."*

men, but it is comparatively common in men. Indeed, a certain element of fetishism can be considered to be a normal ingredient
in the love of a man for a woman.

**No man would be considered a
"sexual pervert" if he were to go
into raptures about his sweetheart's
lovely hair, her beautiful face, her
graceful figure and her attractive
voice. Nor would it be considered
eccentric or sentimental if he were
to treasure some belonging of hers,
such as a glove, a handkerchief or
a shoe.**

**Yet, in the focussing of the at-
tention on a single feature of his
loved one or on an article of clothing, he is displaying the characteristics of a fetishist.**

A woman's long hair often acts
as an erotic fetish and the attrac-

tion is sometimes combined with a desire on the part of the fetishist to ravish it. This explains certain incidents which otherwise would be unaccountable.

Reports of mysterious assaults on young women's hair frequently appear in the newspapers. A girl suddenly becomes aware that somebody is cutting off her pigtail and the thief then disappears into the crowd before she has had time to see him.

It is reported that a Hamburg student was prosecuted for this offense many times and that thirty-one pigtails, tied up and labelled with ribbons, were found in his room when it was visited by the police.

On being interviewed, he confessed that sexual intercourse had no attraction for him but that he was fascinated and erotically excited by long hair. He loved fondling it and smelling its fragrance and it was a joy to him to cut it off; a joy which, to his cost, had proved irresistible to him.

Fetishism may manifest itself in the homosexual as well as in the heterosexual male. A very striking example of fetishism was that of a young homosexual who was only attracted by young mo-

Attraction to rubber is a common form of fetishism.

Thefts of women's underclothes can sometimes be explained by fetishism.

Long hair has an irresistible attraction for some men.

tor mechanics, and then only when their faces were smeared with sweat and black grease. Another male fetishist showed an extreme partiality for cripples.

Conventional aesthetic standards make no appeal at all to the fetishist. He may be unmoved by a woman who is ravishingly beautiful and yet be strongly attracted to a very plain woman with dirty nails and soiled hands; or, as was the case with the famous philosopher Descartes, he may be attracted by a woman with a "delicious" squint.

The attraction exercised by an isolated feature or by an article of clothing belonging to the loved one may be so all-compelling and exclusive that when it is absent she ceases to have any charm for him. It would seem that the great German poet Goethe derived a great deal of pleasure from a

This old print portrays a fetishist who got erotic pleasure from viewing corsets.—From Dr. Magnus Hirschfeld's "Geschlechtskunde."

mild form of fetishism of this sort.

In a letter written at the age of 54 to the lady who afterwards became his wife he included the following request: "Send me, at the next opportunity, your latest dance slippers, that have been thoroughly 'broken in' and of which you wrote that they would be something belonging to you that I might press to my heart."

On receiving the said slippers, Goethe probably derived a considerable amount of erotic pleasure from doing what the lady, Christiana Walpens, had suggested that he should do.

Fortunately for Goethe, he was a remarkably well adjusted man who derived a great deal of pleasure from fondling his fiancée's dancing shoes without having to pay for it subsequently.

Had he been a less well-balanced person, he might have had to pay dearly for the element of fetishism in his nature, as the following case, recorded by Hammond, shows.

Hammond describes a young man, who from the age of seven onwards became sexually excited on seeing a woman's shoe. When he was old enough to make his own living, he got a job in a lady's shoe shop, where his obsession grew still stronger.

He had no desire at all for sexual intercourse with any woman and his erotic dreams all remained centered around shoes. Alarmed by his growing obsession with shoes he decided that it would be best for him to get married and thus rid himself of the obsessions. But as any psychologist might have told him had he consulted one, he proved to be completely impotent with his wife.

In the end, he did consult a

medical man who had the good sense to advise him to hang a shoe up over the bed which he shared with his wife. The shoe excited his desires so that he was able to have intercourse with his wife.

Eventually he was able to remove the fetish from over the bed and to derive his sexual stimulus directly from his wife. In other words he had undergone a cure by a slow process of sexual reconditioning.

Krafft-Ebing and Moll both regarded shoe fetishism as a latent form of masochism. For the masochist the shoe of the loved one may be the symbol of self-subjection and humiliation. The masochist desires to be trodden upon, and the shoe represents the means by which his act of degradation can be achieved.

While I agree that shoe fetishism is often linked with a certain element of masochism, I personally regard them as being different conditions.

Fetishism is usually due to an accidental conditioning of the fetishist. Kretschmer describes an interesting case in which a man was conditioned to respond erotically to female clothing through the accident of his mother's having put him into his sister's lace-trimmed nightdress. While wearing it in bed that night, the boy experienced, for the first time, libidinous excitement and pleasure.

This childhood experience was repeated and in time he was converted into a clothing fetishist. From puberty onwards he obtained erotic pleasure from wearing women's nightdresses in secret, and without their presence he was completely impotent.

I have had several impotent patients who responded erotically to

Culver

The world famous German poet Johann Wolfgang von Goethe probably had a mild form of shoe fetishism.

rubber sheeting. I recall one of them who was quite uninterested both in the sexual act and in women.

What really excited him and blotted out all else was the memory of a stern-faced hospital nurse approaching him dressed in a rubber apron. She was a nurse at the hospital to which he had been sent as a small boy and she had come into his room for the purpose of giving him an enema. Unfortunately her appearance had coincided with his private enjoyment of an early experience of sexual excitement and he had never forgotten her.

In another case, sexual pleasure had been experienced for the first time by the patient when he was lying on his nurse's knees being dried after his bath. His nurse was wearing a rubber apron and it was in this way that the link between rubber sheeting and sexual excitement had been made.

Childhood incidents of this kind sometimes explain what would

188

otherwise be very puzzling, namely the special requirements of certain husbands. Some men can only make love to their wives when the latter are partly or even completely clothed. Some are still more exacting than this and require that their partners should be wearing corsets or long black stockings.

In all probability some incident similar to those recorded above in the stories of the rubber sheeting addicts, is responsible for the peculiarity of these husbands.

It is likely that women also suffer from less obvious forms of fetishism but that because their rôle in love making is a less active one than that of the male, the peculiarities in their sexual pattern are not so apparent.

As reconditioning of the fetishist is usually a slow, difficult and occasionally unsuccessful treatment, it is best for the couple to accept the conditions which accident has imposed on their lovemaking.

Once the wife has realized that her husband is not responsible for his peculiarities and that they are not a sign of mental degeneration, she is not likely to resent having to cater to them.

After all, the great majority of an individual's personal idiosyncrasies are due to a conditioning process carried out earlier in life and they have to be accepted as characteristics of his personality.

● ● ●

NEW "ELIXIR OF YOUTH?"

AN extract made from cow embryos is now being used experimentally in therapy of the aged. The discovery of the reputed rejuvenating effects of this extract is credited to the French physiologists, Leon Binet and Colette Jeramec-Tcherna. They reported the results of their research to the French Academy of Science.

The report declared that in making the extract, the embryo is removed from the cow's uterus; then it is crushed and the pulp is converted into a fluid in a mixing machine. During this operation the embryonic substance is kept cold to preserve it. After an antiseptic is added to destroy any bacteria, the extract is ready for injection.

The reported effects, when the extract was injected in aged patients, were that their mind was enlivened, their muscular strength was improved, their healing properties were speeded up, etc. Apparently the extract helped such aged people to burn body fuel faster, thus providing more ready energy. The discoverers of this extract claimed that their experiments appeared to prove that the worn out human body benefits by the injection of the embryonic extract. It is obvious of course that many more tests are needed.

Sexology, April, 1958

● ● ●

"The Twist"

"THERE is sex implied in it—no doubt about that. But it is not a social sex urge. The sex image is confined to the individual; the partner might as well be a post.

"I don't believe the younger ones are aware of it as a sexual urge at all. The older ones, the better dancers, may have some stimulation from it, but I don't believe it often leads to consummation. They must be too tired."

—*Dr. Albert Ellis commenting on the new dance, "The Twist."*

Banish Fear
Prevent Disease
End Self Denial

Stop Worrying
Conquer Ignorance
Overcome Shame

The Mysteries of Sex Frankly Revealed!

AWAY with false modesty! At last a famous doctor has told *all* the secrets of sex in frank, daring language. No prudish beating about the bush, no veiled hints, but TRUTH, blazing through 576 pages of straightforward facts.

Love is the most *magnificent ecstasy* in the world... know how to hold your loved one ... don't glean half-truths from unreliable sources ... why not let Dr. H. H. Rubin tell you *what to do* and *how to do it!*

MORE THAN 100 VIVID PICTURES

The 106 illustrations leave nothing to the imagination... know how to overcome physical mismating... know what to do on your wedding night to avoid the torturing results of ignorance.

Everything pertaining to sex is discussed in daring language. All the things you have wanted to know

about your sex life, information about which other books only vaguely hint, is yours at last.

Some will be offended by the amazing frankness of this book and its vivid illustrations, but the world has no longer any use for prudery and false modesty.

Don't be a *slave* to ignorance and fear. Enjoy the rapturous delights of perfect physical love!

Lost love ... scandal ... divorce ... can often be prevented by knowledge. Only the ignorant pay the *awful penalties* of wrong sex practices.

ATTRACT THE OPPOSITE SEX!

Know *how to enjoy* the thrilling experiences that are your birthright .... know how to attract the opposite sex.

There is no longer any need to pay the *awful price* for one moment of bliss. Read the scientific pathological facts told so bravely by Dr. Rubin. The chapters on venereal disease are alone worth the price.

What Every Man Should Know

The Sexual Embrace
Secrets of the Honeymoon
Mistakes of Early Marriage
Homosexuality
Venereal Diseases
How to Regain Virility
Sexual Starvation
Glands and Sex Instinct
To Gain Greater Delight
The Truth About Abuse

576 DARING PAGES

What Every Woman Should Know

Joys of Perfect Mating
What to Allow a Lover to do
Intimate Feminine Hygiene
Prostitution
Birth Control Cost
How to Attract and Hold Men
Sexual Slavery of Women
Essentials of Happy Marriage
The Sex Organs

106 VIVID PICTURES

WHAT IS YOUR

*SEX QUOTIENT

by Mark Tarail, B.A., M.S.

BY taking this test, you can measure your sex knowledge. Check whether the answers to each statement should be *True* or *False*. Compare your answers with the correct answers below. Give yourself 10 points for each correct answer and add the results. Your final score is your S.Q.

A score of 50 or less indicates *inadequate knowledge;* 50 to 60 equals *good;* 70 or 80 equals *excellent;* 90 or above equals *unusually superior.*

(T) (F)   1. *It is physically possible for a fourteen-year-old boy to become a father.*

(T) (F)   2. *There are more female sex deviates than male.*

(T) (F)   3. *The honeymoon determines the success or failure of the marriage.*

(T) (F)   4. *Alcohol in large quantity is a cure for impotence in males.*

(T) (F)   5. *Persons with deviate sexual tendencies are often mentally ill.*

(T) (F)   6. *An induced abortion can produce sterility.*

(T) (F)   7. *Culture plays a large rôle in creating sex differences between males and females.*

(T) (F)   8. *Love alone is a sufficient basis for a successful marriage.*

(T) (F)   9. *Heredity plays little part in determining the direction of the sexual drive in humans.*

(T) (F) 10. *Everyone should undergo a medical examination before marriage.*

ANSWERS:

1. TRUE. Many fourteen-year-old boys have started to produce sperm.

2. FALSE. Far more males are found in almost every deviant category.

3. FALSE. The successful honeymoon is important but most marriages become successful as the result of later adjustments.

4. FALSE. Alcohol in large quantity causes impotence.

5. TRUE. Mental disorder may be a cause or a result of deviant practices.

6. TRUE. Sometimes, infection of the reproductive organs results and produces sterility.

7. TRUE. Many traits we think of as inborn result from different standards for boys and girls.

8. FALSE. Other factors are important, such as economic security, sexual satisfaction and mutual understanding.

9. TRUE. The expression of the sex drive is determined primarily by acquired experience after birth.

10. TRUE. A medical examination will often pick up hidden diseases and prevent future sexual and physical difficulties.

oday, many social scientists and other authorities have observed that adultery does not *always* damage a marriage. Indeed, they say that adultery can sometimes benefit a marriage. Recently, some quite respectable people have suggested that extramarital sex, especially when both marriage partners agree to it, is not a shameful moral lapse that must be kept secret but often a valuable and healthy part of certain people's lives.

Sex researcher Dr. Mary Calderone, for example, believes that extramarital sex can hurt *or* help a marriage: "I can conceive of situations in which it might be helpful in stabilizing a marriage," she says.

Dr. Alfred Kinsey wrote in *Sexual Behavior in the Human Male* that "there are some individuals among our histories whose sexual adjustments in marriage have undoubtedly been helped by extramarital experience. . . . Extramarital intercourse has had the effect of convincing some males that the relationships with their wives were more satisfactory than they had realized."

Even the British Council of Churches, in a recent report on sex and morality, refused to condemn adultery as necessarily immoral, saying that it "should not be seen as an automatic ground for divorce."

Despite the fact that countless marriages *are* wrecked by adultery with or without the mates' consent, a number of experts claim that a little adultery is less harmful to family stability than divorce.

The question is whether it is possible, knowing our tendencies to irrational jealousy, to have extramarital sex *and* a good marriage, too. If it is possible, if adultery can be openly acknowledged without creating intense jealousy or conflict, it might eliminate reasons for a number of divorces.

Many couples the world over are experimenting with adultery. Some are discovering that adultery is sometimes a valuable part of life, that its value as a sexual stimulant increases when it is *shared* with the marriage partner.

Though the statement may seem shocking to those who grew up with traditional Western values (as I have), my study of hundreds of openly adulterous couples (and correspondence with thousands more) over the past two decades has shown me that adultery with the consent of the mates often

A NEW KIND OF ADULTERY

BY EUGENE SCHEIMANN, M.D.

creates no marital rift. It creates no guilt because the behavior is considered legitimate by all participants; sometimes it brings the partners closer, sometimes it fails.

In the many interviews I have conducted for a study of adultery, I observed three types of adultery with consent that are most prevalent (precisely how prevalent no one will know so long as society continues to feel defensive about such behavior):

Condoned Adultery

A female patient recently came into my office wearing a new mink coat. "Your husband must have made a killing," I commented. "No, he has a new mistress. He's always especially good to me when he's having an affair."

This kind of adultery, implicitly condoned but usually not outwardly acknowledged, is especially popular in European circles and among the prominent and affluent. In the United States, it is often onesided: the husband has a mistress and keeps his wife "happy" with mink coats and other status-laden tokens.

In Europe, the wife is also likely to have a lover, and each partner conducts his affair with discretion and sophistication as a sort of "accessory" to marriage. In both countries, this kind of love affair, though condoned, is a separate life kept rigidly apart from marriage. Such marriages often suffer a lack

of intensity, warmth, and intimacy.

Acknowledged Adultery
Don and Elaine, an idealistic young couple I know, insisted on rewriting their marriage vows before getting married. They promised to love, honor, and cherish each other but refused to require eternal sexual fidelity. They do not believe that loving one's spouse automatically makes it impossible

or immoral to be sexually attracted to someone else, or to occasionally consummate that attraction.

Cooperative Adultery
Marge and Dick had frequently discussed the possibility of one or both of them having an affair. They finally agreed it would be unthreatening and perhaps even desirable. At the same time, they felt they couldn't do it without feeling disloyal.

Dr. Scheimann, a staff member of the American Hospital in Chicago, has published numerous papers in professional journals.

Thus, they agreed that sharing a sexual experience with another couple would meet their needs for new forms of excitement and also for total honesty. During a weekend at a resort with another couple, it happened. The couples ended up "swapping" for the evening.

In some ways, this form of adultery—"swapping" or "swinging"—is the most controversial. "Why not admit to each other what you want to do, forgive each other in advance, then go ahead and do it—together?" said one enthusiastic swapper. "If it doesn't work out, you simply discontinue it."

"My wife and I like to swing, but I'd be afraid to have a private love affair," said another mate-swapper. "The very secretiveness of such an affair would give it an inflated importance that might become uncontrollable and threaten the marriage," he explained. "Sharing the experience keeps it all in the right spirit."

Of course, such comments are not to be taken too seriously. *No form of adultery, in fact, is recommended for anyone.* If one enters this activity for revenge ("He cheated. Why can't I?") or need ("She doesn't understand me. I'll find someone who will."), it may well destroy the marriage.

But for those who for some reason feel that swearing fidelity in the marriage ceremony is unrealistic, and who feel that complete sexual possessiveness or jealousy is not necessary, adultery with consent may be the safest way to meet their needs.

Those who have a stable marriage with something lacking, who want to enjoy a new experience along with the comfort of an existing marriage, sometimes turn to adultery with the mate's consent.

I have seen adultery with consent add a rich, new dimension to the lives of couples who believe that sex with more than one person is enjoyable. As the years go by, these couples long to feel again the touch of a new body and the spark of a new personality, yet they nevertheless have a commitment to their marriage partner that makes them want to be totally honest with each other.

In any event, this new emphasis on honesty and sex sharing can be seen as part of the cultural revolution our society is now undergoing. Adultery with consent is most popular among the young, who no longer believe in the double standard and insist on "telling it like it is."

Many of these young people have been exposed to sensitivity training, "group encounters," and techniques in non-verbal communication. They feel comfortable with nudity and taboo words. Some have experienced communal living, and many believe in non-competitive sharing, including sex.

For most couples, of course, adultery with consent probably would not work. It violates a deeply ingrained morality or need for sexual privacy or both.

But, for many, adultery with consent seems to reflect the values of the age in which we live. Depending upon the personality and ethics of the individual, these values may be seen as "good" or "bad." In any case, there is no doubt that adultery—with or without consent—can destroy a marriage.

Adultery with consent (or, as it is sometimes called, co-marital sex or cooperative sex) may foretell a new form of marriage in the future. American men and women of the future may be less romantic than they are today. As Dr. Margaret Mead says, "The present marriage ideal is so high and the difficulties so many . . . that an examination is called for." Perhaps adultery with consent could be an extremely important part of that examination.

●　●　●

THE WAGES OF SIN

THE most luxurious bordello which the U. S. ever saw was Chicago's Everleigh Club, run by the Everleigh sisters, Minna and Ada, who insisted on being treated as gentlewomen at all times. Their profits amounted to more than a million dollars.

The Everleigh Club flourished from 1900 to 1911 in a 50-room mansion in Chicago. It boasted gold spittoons, silk drapes, thick rugs, expensive statuary and paintings, a gilded piano, and forty specially made brass and marble beds. Little fountains squirted perfume into its rooms at regular intervals. Its dinners sometimes cost $100 a plate and were served on gold-edged china. Champagne arrived in golden buckets.

The club's "young ladies" wore evening gowns and frowned at any mention of cash—checks were more refined. Customers who did not spend at least $50 a night—and the sisters considered $100 a nicer sum—were gently told not to return.

—*TIME*

ELECTRONIC MATING

Marriage today is still too much of a hit-and-miss affair. The scientific mating of men and women contemplating matrimony here described is a logical plan which must be adopted at an early date, if we are to curtail the constantly increasing divorce rate. Determining the couple's "sexual quotient" is just as important as the blood test now made as a matter of course before a màrriage is legally consummated. It is really surprising that we do not have more divorces than we do, when one stops to consider the haphazard manner in which men and women approach the state of matrimony. Scientific instruments are available right now which could, if used intelligently, help to allay much of the MIS-MATING *that now occurs.*

by Hugo Gernsback

MARRIAGE still remains man's greatest gamble. The world's divorce rate constantly accelerates at a dizzying rate. Clearly there is something seriously wrong with our customs and our approach to marriage—it cries out for radical reform.

Possibly the most curious and shocking shortcoming of civilized (?) man is his ignorance of sex. The function, without which the human race would disappear from the earth, is also the least understood by most people.

As a sexologist of over 30 years' standing, I am continuously amazed at the extraordinary ignorance on the subject by the average intelligent person.

There is still a widespread belief that certain foods are aphrodisiacs. People still believe that you can tell from a person's face, bodily build, or other "tell-tale" signs that this individual has certain sexual qualifications. Millions of men still think that merely by hearing a female's voice they can thereby obtain an accurate evaluation of her libido. Such men still feel, too, that the dimensions or configuration of a woman's bust is a true index of her love proclivities.

Of course all these ancient superstitions are pure nonsense—yet they persist, simply because people are deliberately misinformed by others who know nothing about the subject either. *It is a fact that when it comes to sex, the most fantastic untruths are accepted as gospel.*

People rarely speculate why so many of our most dazzling "sexy"

Before subject can marry, his or her Sex Quotient is ascertained by means of a number of mental and emotional tests. These are translated by several special recording instruments. The result is fed into an electronic computer which gives the S.Q. in percentages on punched index cards. A romantic film (rear projection) is shown in above test.

beauties of screen and theater shed husbands like a pair of gloves, and why other famous and exquisitely beautiful women, with the most alluring anatomies, never marry at all.

The simple truth is that worthwhile sex expression requires the affinity of *two* people. And if the couple are not sexually compatible, even Venus and Adonis would not be able to make a go of their marriage.

Frequently, too, nature plays ghastly pranks on humans. Thus many of history's — and the present's—irresistible, beautiful women heartbreakers can't tolerate mere males. *They prefer women*—homosexuals, like themselves.

The average individual — after aeons of hit-and-miss mating of his ancestors—still blithely persists in trusting the five senses when it comes to selecting a mate. The man looks at a pretty face and figure—*sight*. . . . He listens enraptured to her voice—*sound*. He feels her cheek—*touch*. . . . He inhales the fragrance of her skin or hair—*scent*. . . . He kisses her lips— *taste* . . . and promptly loses his head. The woman reacts similarly—and so they get married, *with a better than 80% chance that it won't last.* Our divorce courts prove it. So do statistics on unhappy marriages, where, because of children or for other reasons, the couples must live together—but not as man and wife.

Fortunately, this sort of antediluvian vegetation of the human race won't go on forever. Science *can* and *will* do something about

In the future, marriages will no longer be haphazard. The electronic brain (rear wall) and other instruments will tell prospective couples if it is safe for them to mate, or not.

it in the foreseeable future.

Time there was — just a few decades ago—when people married without regard to health, particularly venereal disease. There was a terrific public hubbub when some states first enacted blood (Wassermann) tests, against syphilis, before issuing a marriage license. Today such a test is taken for granted.

In many states and countries where laws prevail against cousin marriages, the public, highly antagonistic at first, now looks upon such eugenic laws as a matter of course.

But marriage itself still remains a stupid gamble—the planet's most outrageously costly and totally unnecessary lottery. Yet, we progress —exceedingly slow it is true—but we *do* inch ahead.

In all seriousness I propose an entirely new approach to solve the problem. I hasten to add that my plan—if adopted—will not eliminate all mismating, nor all divorce, but I sincerely believe that it will cut down a large proportion of unhappy marriages.

A Long Range Plan

There will be two stages to this plan. The first, to extend over a number of years, will concern itself mainly in accumulating a vast quantity of research material. Once this has been accomplished, we can then approach the second stage, that is, putting the plan into work.

Let us begin with stage one. A group of bright, young research scientists-psychologists should be organized under the tutelage of a brilliant, able leader such as Dr. Alfred C. Kinsey, author of "Sexual Behavior of the American Male."

The group of researchers then will interview 25,000 or more married couples. They will be armed with lengthy questionnaires as well as special test equipment. After a few years they will have ascertained which of the 25,000 marriages were successful and which were not. Like the original coded and self-proving Kinsey questionnaire, by eliminating any possible false answers, these marriage questionnaires will be as perfect as modern science and ingenuity can make them.

In due time—mind you, this is a long-term project—our scientists will have much vital scientific data and a long set of questions which all marriage candidates must answer routinely before a license can be issued to them.

The questionnaire and tests will go exhaustively into heredity, individual taste, sex habits, education, race, color and texture of skin, I.Q., general health, past illnesses, texture of hair, RH blood factor, odor preferences, physiological sensitivity over various parts of the body, musical sense, Rorschach test, artistic sense, speed of various perceptions, religious sense, color perception, physical contour, ethical sense — and perhaps a hundred other vital questions and tests.

This may all sound unnecessarily complicated and lengthy, but is not. It is far better that young people spend a few hours answering questions and undergoing a few tests than spend the greater portion of a lifetime in unhappy marriage.

When the research fact-finding period has been concluded, stage one of the plan has ended. We now reach stage two: Putting the plan into actual operation. This, of course will require the full cooperation of the States and Cities throughout the land. But I do not foresee much difficulty here, when so much is at stake, and where the resulting benefits to the country are so great.

Finding Your S.Q.

When stage two begins to function young people will also have to be tested for their S.Q.—the *Sexual Quotient*. This test will become as important as our present blood tests. No marriage certificates will be issued without a S.Q. test.

If the index cards of the marriage candidates reveal *complete* incompatibility, no marriage certificate will be issued by the state, till the condition has been remedied. This is, of course, a parallel to the Wassermann test, where candidates are not allowed to be married till the syphilitic condition has been cured.

In cases of total incompatibility, there is a chance of alleviation, either medically or psychiatrically (frigidity and other sexual disturbances).

How do we obtain a person's S.Q.? First, there must be a complete medical examination of the subject, which everybody of marriageable age *should* have, if much subsequent grief is to be avoided. This examination will quickly reveal obvious physical sexological defects or disturbances, many of which *can* be remedied. I will name only a few—there are scores of others in both sexes.

In the male: *Phimosis* (non-

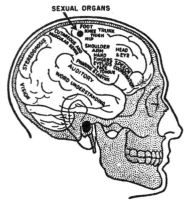

SEXUAL ORGANS

Man's sexual center is located at the top of the brain. This center directs and controls ALL sexual activities, man's libido, etc.

retractable foreskin); *cryptorchidism* (undescended testes); *hypospadias* (congenital urinary opening in the under part of the penis); *pseudohermaphroditism* (spuriously —that is, vestigially only—double-sexed); and sometimes *true hermaphroditism.*

In the female: *Infantile uterus* (undeveloped womb); *imperforate* (thick) hymen; *prolapsus uteri* (forward falling womb); *vaginitis* (inflammation of vagina); *menorrhagia* (excessive menstruation); *pseudohermaphroditism;* sometimes *hermaphroditism.*

After the physical tests, the sexual tests are evaluated. Let me debunk here the ages-old lie that sex is wholly physical. Nothing is further from the truth. Not even the most libidinous human couple can perform during fright or under other highly unpleasant conditions. This is because we have a

sexual center at the top of the brain (see cut). The sexual impulses travel from this center via the spinal nerves to the genitals. *Cut, or impair, this sexual communication line—either physically or psychically—and no sex performance results.*

Hence the *psychic* sexual tests are most important. Fortunately, we have today a number of excellent laboratory instruments which give us outstanding indices for such tests. Better instrumentation is being developed continuously.

The future tests will proceed somewhat as follows: The subject, male or female—it makes no difference which—is physically connected to a number of instruments, such as the following:

Electrocardiograph, which furnishes a most accurate tape record of the heart action, reliably portraying emotional stresses. The *Electropsychometer* (electronic lie detector), which also gives us a most reliable tape record of psychical highlights while the test proceeds. The *Electroencephalograph,* which gives a running curve of the brain function during the test.

To this is added a recording *Polygraph,* which gives other valuable clues and accurate indices of sexual emotion through the pulse action and rapidity of breathing, etc.

Now the person under test is given to read a specially prepared romantic short story. This is followed by a short motion-picture film made up from various well-known film productions, with the accent on "torrid" love scenes by famous film personalities.

Next we have a number of short sexological-educational, informative items printed on special cards. The text is culled from standard scientific works and the items are selected for the impact they make on the individual. (Many people are incredibly stupid when it comes to practical sex information. This particular, part of the test gives the laboratory people a good insight into the person's sex knowledge.)

There follows a final, lengthy Kinsey-type sex questionnaire into the intimate life of the individual with the double and triple checking technique. Such questions, if not answered truthfully, will trip up the subject when the question is put in another form later on.

Of course the various recording instruments perform a similar function in a different manner, insuring that the end result will be quite accurate.

The final computation of the subject's S.Q. is made by automatic machines, chiefly through the means of electronic calculators — the so-called electronic brain—and punched index cards. The rating is automatically printed on each card in percentages.

Each card will further note the percentages of important deviations from the accepted conventional, such as pseudohermaphroditism, homosexuality, bisexuality, sadism, masochism, transvestism, frigidity (in the female), impotence, whole or partial (in the male) and other vital information.

When the final S.Q. has been noted on the card, it becomes a comparatively routine matter for the psychologist in charge to "match" the male and female cards of the marriage applicants.

The answer will not be simply "compatible" or "noncompatible" but the machine rather will answer in percentages. Thus the electronic brain may say: 90%. Translated, this means that the marriage will be, in all likelihood, 90% satisfactory. The next two candidates may rate only 73%, and so forth.

The State Marriage Authority may refuse to issue a marriage license to applicants who rate 50% or less. That means that such candidates should find themselves more suitable partners.

It can be foreseen that with the present status of humanity, over 80% of the applicants will have to be coached for a number of weeks by the state. Faulty sexology must be unlearned and the subject must be re-educated to learn the actual practical facts of life if his coming marriage is to be even fairly successful.

And make no mistake—the male today lags frequently behind the female when it comes to matters of sex technique, according to most researchers. The male knows a terrific amount about sex—most of it long sexploded!

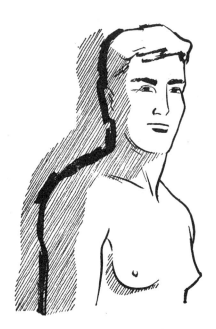

ENLARGED MALE BREASTS

by LeMon Clark, M.D.

More embarrassing than serious, this condition can be remedied without too great difficulty.

ROM time to time, letters from troubled readers are received, seeking assistance about a condition that causes considerable embarrassment—the enlargement of the male breasts.

The condition is known medically as *gynecomastia,* which comes from two Greek words meaning "woman" and "breast." It may occur at almost any age, though it develops usually during the early and middle adult years.

True gynecomastia is a persistent growth of glandular tissue in the male breast. It is usually bilateral, that is, both breasts are affected.

It must not be confused with a condition which is the result of

---

Dr. Clark, a practicing gynecologist, is Editor of SEXOLOGY's *Question and Answer Dept. He is author of* "Sex and You," "Emotional Adjustment in Marriage," *and other books.*

excessive deposits of fat over the pectoral muscles, the large muscles over the upper chest just beneath the breasts.

Such deposits of fat may develop in males where there is a defective state of the testicles, and occasionally are found just because of excessive weight gain.

Gynecomastia must also be differentiated from other enlargements of the breast. Trauma, or injury, which caused a temporary swelling, would not be gynecomastia. If the injury resulted in permanent change, and somehow brought about changes in the normal rudimentary glandular tissue, then true gynecomastia might result.

Temporary conditions are often observed in newborn infants and in young boys who are going through the stage of puberty.

A newborn boy baby may have enough breast stimulation from

the hormone *prolactin*—which circulates in the mother's blood just before the baby is delivered and stimulates her breasts to give milk—to cause his breasts to enlarge temporarily.

This stimulation may sometimes be great enough to bring about the actual production of some milk. This has been called "witches milk." It is a purely temporary thing which subsides quite naturally within a few days and requires no treatment. It is, of course, seen in newborn baby girls as well as in boys.

Sometimes when boys reach the stage of adolescence, they may also show evidence of breast gland stimulation. This, again, is usually a temporary thing. It should not excite too much concern, and nothing should be done about it for six or eight months.

What are some of the factors which may bring about unusual growth of glandular tissue in the breasts?

One such factor is disturbance of the glands which produce internal secretions, resulting in an endocrine imbalance.

The *Klinefelter syndrome,* a disease of the testicle which brings about degeneration of the sperm-producing tubules, and for which the cause is unknown, may result in gynecomastia. When it develops for any reason, it is a functional disorder involving the whole being of the individual, not merely a local change in the breasts.

Bodily infection, especially where glands are affected, may result in breast changes. Occasionally, mumps, or infectious parotitis, may affect the breasts, especially in the adult female who contracts the disease after the age of puberty. In the young adult male not only the breasts but the testicle may be seriously affected, resulting, in some cases, in irreversible sterility.

Hyperthyroidism, or abnormal function in the thyroid gland, may possibly cause breast stimulation and resulting gynecomastia.

Hepatitis, or inflammation of the liver, is thought to be another possible cause. The liver deactivates estrogen, female sex hormone. Males as well as females have some estrogen in their glandular output. Where the liver, because of inflammatory disease and consequent decrease in function, fails to deactivate the estrogen in the normal male, this hormone may stimulate the rudimentary gland tissue, resulting in true gynecomastia.

Interestingly enough, gynecomastia is not a result of emasculinization, or destruction of the testicles by injury, surgery or disease. It is not commonly encountered after removal of the testes.

True gynecomastia is not a malignant disease. While occasionally there are some symptoms causing discomfort—sharp, sticking pains in the breasts, or a sense of tightness or tension—actually these physical symptoms are rarely of real significance.

Why, then, is the condition of any significance? It is important primarily because of the psychic and emotional influence upon the individual.

The individual suffering from gynecomastia o f t e n develops doubts about his own masculinity. If it occurs in pre-adolescence it is not as emotionally disturbing as when it appears a few years later.

A pre-adolescent is not yet as keenly aware of its sexual significance. But once this awareness arises, the shame and embarrass-

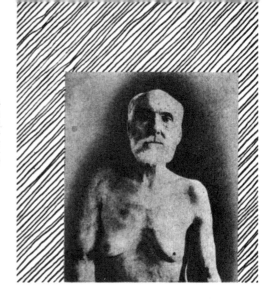

Examples of gynecomastia, or the enlarged male breast which have appeared in medical texts.—Photo on this page from "Geschlechtskunde," by Dr. Magnus Hirschfeld; center photo from "Office Endocrinology," by Dr. R. B. Greenblatt (C. C. Thomas).

ment can be extremely trying. A boy is subjected to the gibes of his fellows. "Wear a bra," "Join the other girls," "The little mother," are a few of the sneers which he must constantly face.

The distress he suffers may result in asocial behavior. On the one hand he may become completely withdrawn, refusing to mingle with his fellows or to take any part in sports. On the other hand, he may become obnoxiously aggressive and self assertive.

As has already been said, if some breast activity makes itself apparent just at the onset of puberty, nothing should be done. Several months should be allowed to go by, at least. Then, if the condition still persists or becomes more apparent, medical advice should certainly be obtained.

Treatment by the administration of male sex hormone, which would seem to be the natural treatment for the condition, has proved disappointing. It has commonly failed to reduce the size of the breasts.

Surgery, excision of the enlarged glandular tissue, is probably the method of choice.

The operation should be performed by a competent surgeon aware of the emotional factors involved. As little scarring as possible should result, and the nipples and the areola, the colored area surrounding them, should be left intact if at all possible.

In a fair proportion of all cases, it will be possible to make a semicircular incision around the edge of the areola. The glandular tissue is then removed, leaving the nipple intact. A frozen section can be done at once, during the operation, by a competent pathologist, and if there is no evidence of cancer, a few stitches will close the incision. After it is well healed, the incision will be almost completely inconspicuous.

If the hypertrophied breast was too large to be removed by an incision around the areola, a semicircular incision may be made somewhat lower down, where the arc of the circle would be larger.

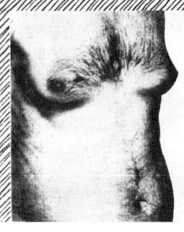
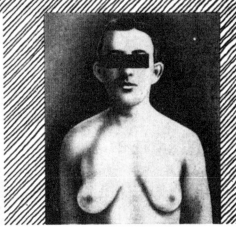

thus giving more operating room. But even such an incision, closed carefully, with care to preserve some of the subcutaneous fat, with removal only of the hypertrophied glandular tissue, may then be stitched so that it will leave a very inconspicuous scar in most cases.

Since shock to the emotional makeup and psyche of the individual may wreak havoc with his personality, where the individual suffers from gynecomastia, steps should be taken at once to correct the deformity. Adults should have no hesitancy whatever in consulting a competent surgeon.

Parents should be aware of the development in an adolescent boy and see that something is done about it. The child himself may be hesitant to speak about it, and may, in fact, avoid discussing it because of the emotional tension involved.

In such a situation the wise parent will take the initiative and see that the boy has competent medical and surgical advice and correct the deformity before serious damage is done to his emotional makeup.

● ● ●

BARNACLE'S SEX LIFE

THE sex life of the barnacle* is something of a mystery as most species are male and female combined. That's why the barnacle is invariably called it. It is born of a minute speck of larva. As a child it is far from being beautiful. At that time, it has only one eye and three spidery appendages. Shortly, however, it develops a bivalve shell, two eyes and six legs. Utterly lacking in charm, the creature starts to swim around seeking a domicile.

When it finds a suitable site, it really settles down for life. It becomes a permanent resident, firmly attaches itself to anything that meets its fancy—the body of a whale, a floating piece of wood, or the hull of a ship. Recently, a large ship reported excessive vibration. Once docked, over 200 tons of barnacles were removed, the bottom cleaned and painted. Vibrations no longer existed and the ship increased its top speed by 18 knots.

*Barnacle: Small shellfish found attached to logs, rocks, ships' bottoms, etc.—Dictionary.

—This Month

WHY DO MEN DO IT?

*Since antiquity men have dressed up as females, for private
parties, to appear on the stage, and in public gatherings.
Why do they behave that way? What is behind all the
"horse play." This article gives you the real reason.*

EVER so often our readers send us pictures of so-called men's frolics masquerading in women's dress, which they do, not as inverts, but "just for the fun of it."

When a man, in the privacy of his own home, dons women's dress because he has a vehement desire for it, he always is classed as a *transvestite*. Whenever normal men get together in a crowd and dress up as women they cannot be classified as transvestites, and in many cases the reason that prompts them to do it is difficult to understand, at least for laymen. It seems to be a custom in many big business organizations to give parties ever so often; frequently these parties show a number of men dressed in women's clothes which they borrow from their wives, or female friends, and then the "boys" deport themselves in this attire. College boys frequently give plays in which they are dressed up in women's wigs, and women's finery. As the young men are usually in their 'teens they make up excellently as girls, so much so that often some of them rival the other sex in looks and appearance.

When, however, business executives do this sort of thing they are no longer in their 'teens and are usually between the ages of 30 and 50 and over. They then appear as middle-aged women and the ensuing picture is no longer one of pretty young girls. Often the impersonated women emerge as portly housewives with considerable tonnage, as the case may be.

Sexologists and psychologists have often pondered about this phenomenon and occasionally scientific articles are written on the subject. What makes men behave in this manner? The subjects when questioned about it seem to be surprised that there could be any serious reason back of all this tomfoolery. Most of them seem to think that it is innocent, but good fun, mixed with a lot of "horse-play." That is the explanation of most masqueraders, but we must look deeper for the correct explanation, because there *is* an explanation.

Perhaps the best answer lies in the word "exhibitionism." Men as a rule do not appear in public with bare midriffs, exposed arms, knees and upper portions of their legs. For centuries, indeed for thousands of years, man has been deprived of exposing most of his anatomy publicly, or otherwise, except in the sanctity of his home.

True, men can deport themselves in abbreviated attire on the beaches, but beaches are not to be found universally, except at the seashores and some of our inland lakes. So, the urge for exhibitionism which brings the condition about is not satisfied, hence this so-called "horse-play" is really a sort of subdued, mild sexual exhibitionism by the men who take part in these periodic "frolics."

magazine that this type of "horse-play" is not always as innocent as it appears on the surface.

The writer in this particular case, who has homosexual leanings, reported that he instigated one of these masquerades. The moving idea in mind was that he would get a better look at the physique of a certain man in his organization whom he greatly admired, but never had the courage

"High-point of the evening's entertainment at the second annual Follies was reached when the executive group shed dignity to bare burlesque talent which was enthusiastically received by an appreciative audience."

If you tell these men that this is the real motive, every one of them will become very angry and deny the allegation emphatically. This is a normal reaction because many of man's impulses are masked. As Freudians will tell you, there are a host of subconscious desires in every man and woman which are never recognized consciously. It is quite true that such mild types of exhibitionism usually do not lead to anything that is seriously wrong. Yet it has come to our attention in a letter to the Editor of this

to speak to as far as his attachment was concerned. The affair, where the men dressed up as women, was duly held and it was a source of gratification to the instigator to see the object of his secret love attired in abbreviated female raiment. He later consulted the Editor with a view to find out what could be done in his case as since that affair his desire for the other man had increased violently.

It is to be noted that the object of his attention did not know anything about all this, and whether he knows by the time this is printed, we do not know.

There is a possibility that not all similar masquerading that goes on all over the land is done with a purpose in mind such as the case above described, but it should always be kept in mind that it might be.

The photograph printed here was supplied by the publicity office of a very prominent midwest manufacturing concern employing thousands of men and women. For obvious reasons no name or address is divulged.

Accompanying the photograph was the usual letter which we reproduce here, minus names and locality:

"Front office executives, white-collar workers, and production employees of the ——— Company 'pooled' talent to compose the cast and stage crew of the second . . . Follies, "Hooray, America," which enjoyed a three-night run at . . . Hall in . . .

"The annual Follies production is 'something to shout about' for the folks at the five Chicago . . . plants and laboratories, where fine . . . equipment and . . . devices are precision-made in fulfillment of army and navy contracts.

"High point of the evening's entertainment was reached when the executive group of . . ., including President . . ., shed dignity to bare burlesque talent which was enthusiastically received by an appreciative audience. All agree that the yearly shows, sponsored by the Employees' Activity Committee, make for continuous-performance of good-fellowship and camaraderie between labor and management."

● ● ●

Sperm Movement

HOW do sperm make their way through the uterine cavity and tubes in order to meet and fertilize the egg? Up until a few years ago, it was believed that human sperm made their ascent entirely on the basis of their own wriggling movement.

Five years ago evidence was presented to show that sperm might be aided in their ascent by a pattern of womb contractions. Now, a recent study has concluded that, without the aid of these contractions, human sperm are not able to make the ascent through the womb at all.

The study was made by Dr. William Bickers, Department of Gynecology and Obstetrics, Richmond Memorial Hospital, Richmond, Va. *(Fertility & Sterility,* Vol. 11, No. 3, 1960). Dr. Bickers established his theory on the basis of tests made on a patient whose ovaries had been removed. Since womb contractions result from the action of hormone produced in the ovaries, the womb contractions of this patient could be determined by controlling the administration of hormone.

A number of tests were made shortly after the patient had had coitus. When there was no hormone administered and consequently no uterine contractions, no sperm were found in the womb even up to an hour and a half after coitus. When contractions were present, spermatozoa were found in the uterine fluid, the maximum concentration being reached one hour after coitus had taken place. Dr. Bickers concludes that sperm can move through the cervical canal under their own power, but if no womb contractions occur, they cannot rise above the internal opening of the cervix.

Types
of
French
Prostitutes

*Prostitution is a secret
and large profession in
France. There are
many categories of pros-
titutes who ply their
trade in different ways
and appeal to differ-
ent classes of men.*

by Jean-Paul Clébert

THOSE "in the know" usu-
ally put prostitutes into two
classes. Some are fancifully
called *hetaires,* the old Greek name
for high-class courtesans, and perhaps just to stay within the framework of classical terminology, the
other class is known as *pallaques,*
a term based on an ancient Greek
and Roman garment worn by
women. The *pallaques* are prostitutes who stand on street corners
and on sidewalks nowadays, but
who in former times would have
been inmates of a "house." The
hetaires, on the other hand, are
more discreet ladies who would

*M. Clébert is Editor-in-Chief of
the French medical journal "Problèmes" and a noted French medical
journalist and research worker.*

formerly have been called *demi-
mondaines* (the word is now
passé in French). They are women
who are "kept" by a succession
of lovers. They are the fashionable courtesans who claim that they
make prostitution an art rather
than a means of livelihood.

Secret and "Occasional"
Prostitutes

As a matter of course, officially, prostitutes who do not carry a
card, do not have a file at police
headquarters and do not stand at
street corners, are considered as
"occasional." Actually, this is a
misnomer, since it does not cover
the situation.

A distinction must be made between "occasional" and secret. The

In Paris a special class of prostitutes frequents swanky bars, and are generally pretty and well dressed. They do not solicit but wait for a client to approach them. They are usually unknown to the police. — Photo Serge Jacques, from "Problèmes," French medical journal.

"occasional" prostitute engages in promiscuous intercourse outside of working hours, often even though she may have a husband and a family, simply to supplement a meager budget, to make ends meet.

Besides, there is a whole class of prostitutes who are not generally referred to as such, but, nevertheless, are secretly prostitutes. They have no other means of livelihood, but they are so discreet in their maneuvers that they are not well-known to the police. They do not stand on "hot" corners in front of hotels of dubious reputation. They do not deck themselves out in conspicuous garments, and they do not solicit. Rather, they frequent swanky bars, and are generally pretty and well dressed. They simply wait for a client to approach them.

The fact that they are alone, are nice to look at, and, if need be, may cast an enticing glance in the direction of a potential customer or show a flash of leg as if by accident, is all that is needed to persuade the man he has made a conquest. The matter is discussed with discretion. They drink; they chat. He makes advances and the young woman allows herself to be induced "to finish the night" with the man. It is only later in the course of more intimate conversation that she reveals she is financially embarrassed and has debts. She usually persuades him to "lend" her some money, to invite her to lunch the next day and to buy her presents.

They are really "kept women," but "kept" only for brief periods. They seek clients among their acquaintances. Their customers are rich and substantial. Most of these women try to find a husband or a permanent lover. Their prices are rather high, generally what they think the traffic will bear. Their haunts are on the Champs-Elysées, in Montparnasse and in the Saint-Germain-des-Près district.

The Ladies of Saint-Germain-des-Près

This currently popular "village" in Paris is the scene of a large clandestine trade, but not on a high level. The customers are often men from the provinces who want to feel that they are sophisticated, but are too smart to be caught in the toils of Montmartre or in the districts where the "aristocrats" of prostitution hold forth.

In the Saint-Germain-des-Près bars the girls are all young. Many of them are under age. They are sometimes incorrectly called *existentialists*. Many of them come from comfortably well-off families, but they have "turned bad." It is rare to find professional streetwalkers among them. Their manner of soliciting is almost imperceptible. They spy a man alone at a bar and manage to get him to offer them a drink, which is a normal procedure at such places. They make no overt proposition, "work" only at night and pretend that they do not have any home or that they owe money to their landlady. They all live with a man, who is not precisely a *mackerel* (procurer). Most of their lovers are male prostitutes.

A particular bar will usually have a reputation for the number of girls of "easy virtue" available, as well as for its "pretty" boys. All of them operate with the consent of the owner of the bar. There are also many pickpockets there.

The girls are young and cutelooking. They affect the mannerisms of a "false whore" in the style of the literary heroine, Manon Lesçaut. They wear very tight sweaters and tight jeans. Their fees start at 5,000 francs ($14.00) a night; some of them earn as much as 120,000 francs ($343.00) a month. Clients desiring "special" treatment are not charged extra. If the client wants two women together, the charge is 20,000 francs ($57.00).

Theft is practically always the rule. The innocents are cleaned out, clear to their handkerchiefs. They never complain to the police. Living along the borderline of prostitution, these women lead a "bohemian" life, get drunk when they are not actually working at the job, and constantly change their abodes.

The Artisans

Another category of clandestine prostitutes operates in workingclass neighborhoods. They loiter

Au Salon de la Rue des Moulins (A Parlor on the Street of the Mills), a painting by the famed French artist, Toulouse Lautrec. This scene was supposed to have occurred in a brothel where Lautrec lived and worked from 1892 to 1894.

in cafés. There is nothing to distinguish them from the other women there. They can be detected only after long experience. These women are interested in picking up lovers and forming more or less permanent relationships. They live in furnished "studios" or apartments of their own. They offer love against a lower middle-class background, which has nothing in common with the erotic but close atmosphere of hotel bedrooms.

They even sometimes share the customer's gratification and will sometimes invite him to partake of a meal. Very few of them are attached to pimps. Their prices are lower and they very soon work up a regular clientele, chiefly bachelors.

"Phony" Housewives

Among the clandestine prostitutes are the "phony" housewives who frequent the large cheap markets (such as are found in Clichy Avenue, Daguerre Street or Saint-Honoré Street) in the mornings. They usually carry a market basket with a few vegetables sticking out of it, and they solicit while mingling with the crowd. They cater to a special clientele, who know them.

Then there are the "shoppers" in the big department stores. Many "idle" men are attracted to these stores by the pretty faces of the salesgirls. These "shoppers" are lost in the crowds. They put up no resistance to the men who seek them out and offer them propositions on the spot. They are generally very well dressed. Their favors are expensive. They act very much like unfaithful wives who have secret rendezvous between five and seven o'clock; but they get paid for their relationships.

While the existence of these "secret" prostitutes is well known to the police, they usually escape prosecution and are not subjected to medical supervision.

The Amazons

We must also mention the *amazons,* prostitutes operating among rich but not fashionable men. They are well paid and have a regular clientele. "Kept" women, movie starlets, cover girls, dancers, dress models, and artist's models make up their ranks. They gratify gentlemen over week-end holidays. Each of these women has some one man among her clientele who sees her frequently and is "well placed," so that he can afford her protection from police control through his influence.

Prostitutes in Paris generally belong to different levels of a fixed hierarchy, depending on social and economic factors, and on a certain type of clientele.

Adapted from *Problèmes,* French Medical Journal, March-April, 1955.

● ● ●

LAVATORY WALL INSCRIPTIONS. All of us are familiar with inscriptions found in public toilets. Until Kinsey's time, however, no one thought that these inscriptions might furnish useful information about the secret desires and wishes of the persons who wrote them.

Recently, J. Housden collected all the legible inscriptions he saw over a period of 2 years in 23 lavatories, mostly in Greater London. Surprisingly, the largest number of inscriptions referred to transvestism (desire to dress in clothing of the opposite sex), fetishism (referring mostly to sexual pleasure from wearing knickers or rubber mackintoshes), homosexuality, and masochism (pleasure from having pain inflicted on oneself). Surprisingly, there were more than twice as many references to transvestism as to homosexuality. The author suggests from this that transvestism and fetishism are probably far more common than is usually thought.

—*British Journal of Criminology,* Jan. 1963.

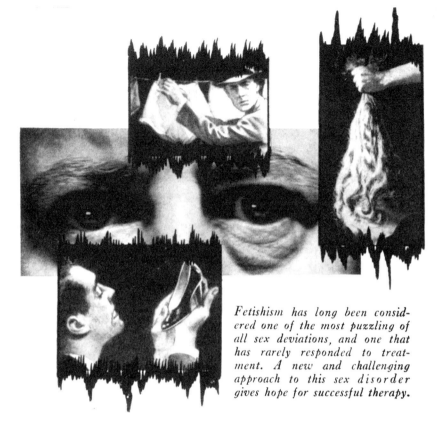

Fetishism has long been considered one of the most puzzling of all sex deviations, and one that has rarely responded to treatment. A new and challenging approach to this sex disorder gives hope for successful therapy.

NEW TREATMENT
FOR THE FETISHIST

by Sarah R. Riedman, Ph.D.

A LOCK of hair, a lace handkerchief, a garter, a certain perfume or the aroma of a pressed flower may all be perfectly normal symbols of love. But

A distinguished physiologist, Dr. Riedman is author of "Physiology of Work and Play," "Our Hormones and How They Work," and co-author of "Story of Microbes."

when any one of these becomes a substitute for the loved one, arousing and even satisfying sexual desire to the exclusion of the person, the resultant state of mind becomes a sexual deviation known as *erotic fetishism.*

In such cases, the fetish itself becomes completely adequate to produce tumescence alone or tumescence *and* detumescence, the latter being an indication of complete sexual satisfaction.

The fetish, or erotic symbol, may be one or several of a great number of objects—hair, nail, apron, dress, hair pin, glove, ribbon, petticoat, fur, some special part of the body such as the foot, nose, or hand, or just an odor. Interestingly, some fetishists have been known to derive satisfaction from a special part of the body, while feeling actual aversion to the individual as a whole.

Occurring in both sexes, but much more frequently in men, it may lead to anti-social offenses, such as compulsive theft of the fetish, or compulsive actions of other types.

Fetishism has long been considered one of the most puzzling in the whole domain of sex deviations. Although many cases have been studied, treatment has rarely been successful. The usual treatment is some form of psychotherapy.

Recently, a new and challenging approach has been reported by Dr. M. J. Raymond, a British physician. Dr. Raymond says: "Of all the sexual aberrations, fetishism is one of the most intriguing, perplexing, and varied. The literature is rich in detailed case reports and in speculation about theories of causation. I have been able to find, however, only three apparently successful results in established cases; one attributed to a cooperative wife . . . one to psychoanalysis . . . and the third to temporal lobectomy (removal of part of the brain). . . ."

He then goes on to describe the successful use of *aversion therapy* in one case, a treatment similar to the antabuse treatment of alcoholics.

Antabuse is a drug which is now commonly used to break the habit of confirmed alcoholism. If a patient takes a drink of liquor after he had been given antabuse, he is attacked by a severe nausea. After a period of such conditioning, the patient may become nauseous at the very thought of alcohol.

In the case involving fetishism, the patient, a 33-year-old British married man, was referred to the hospital after he had followed a woman with a baby carriage and smeared the carriage with oil. It was the twelfth such attack by him known to the police, and this time they were taking a serious view of his infraction.

A previous charge by the Royal Air Force (when he was in military service) of six incidents of slashing, setting on fire or otherwise mutilating either carriages or handbags had led to his admittance to a mental hospital, but more than a year's stay there failed to cure him.

After discharge from the institution, he deliberately rode his motorcycle into a carriage with a baby in it. For this he was convicted of careless driving and fined, but the incidents continued without any sign of abatement.

On examination, the patient said that he had had impulses to damage baby carriages and handbags from the time he was ten. After many hours of analytical treatment he traced his abnormality to two incidents in his childhood.

The first was when sailing a toy boat in a park, he was impressed with a woman's consternation after he struck her carriage with the keel of his boat. The second was when he became sexually aroused in the presence of his sister's handbag.

These two objects became the "symbolic sexual container," the patient showing no other psychotic abnormalities. He related his story with a certain amount of relish.

At this time Dr. Raymond decided to try aversion therapy. He explained to the patient that the aim of treatment was to change his attitude to handbags and carriages by teaching him to associate them with an unpleasant sensation instead of with a pleasurable eroticism.

The patient was first given an injection of *apomorphine* (which induces nausea) and immediately afterwards (before nausea set in) was presented with the objects of his fetishism.

This routine was repeated at intervals of every two hours, day and night, while he was given no food and was kept awake at night with a stimulant. The treatment was continued for seven days and then the patient was allowed to go home. He was to return in a week for additional treatment.

When he came back he reported jubilantly that for the first time he had been able to have normal sex relations with his wife and without the aid of his old fantasies. His wife also noticed a change in his attitude toward her. Treatment was then recommenced with another drug producing the same effect of nausea but without

the sedative effects of apomorphine.

After five more days he said that the mere sight of the objects of his former attraction made him sick. The treatments were again given with carriages and handbags at his bedside.

On the evening of the ninth day he rang for the nurse and implored her to "take them away." The next day he handed over several photographic negatives of these objects which he had carried about with him for years to give him sexual satisfaction.

Six months later he returned for "booster treatment," during which he was shown colored films of women pushing carriages and carrying handbags in the provocative way he said that had affected him previously.

Nineteen months after the treatment he was apparently still getting along without his fantasies, and had not once been in trouble with the police.

Dr. Raymond believes that aversion therapy follows logically from the approach previously found successful for alcoholics. The results obtained in alcoholism are not dependent upon the specific biochemical changes produced by antabuse or any other drug, but upon the establishment of a psychological response.

So also in the case of this sexual fetishism, the patient learned to associate the distasteful reaction to the drug—nausea—with the object of his fetishism, until the latter by *itself* induced the same distaste.

Modification of psychological attitudes are more easily obtained in states of exhaustion and hunger, hence the technique of keeping the patient awake and without food.

In addition, Dr. Raymond refers to the fact that Binet, who was the first to devise the word fetishism, observed that the fetishist seemed to be hypersensitive and to have an unusual capacity for forming conditioned responses. This capacity may be an asset in treatment, as it is a help to forming the aberration in the first place.

This case history and its successful treatment occasioned considerable interest and controversy in the British medical press. Taking issue with Dr. Raymond, Dr. S. E. Smith defended the analytical method, citing cases in which it has been successful, and arguing that the cure of fetishism is not a haphazard procedure depending upon "co-operative wives," etc.

On the other hand, Dr. John W. Fisher considered Dr. Raymond's success in his method "solid grounds for hope that at last we may be able to deal more constructively with that obscure group of psychoneuroses known as the fetishes and perversions and indeed many . . . [other people] who have been wrongly conditioned."

In a communication to the same journal, Dr. Cyril M. Franks picked up another point in Dr. Raymond's presentation. If erotic fetishism is related to a greater capacity to conditioning, perhaps doctors could work out some method of predicting this capacity.

Such an investigation, he says, is currently going on in the psychology department of the Institute of Psychiatry in Maudsley Hospital in London.

Dr. Raymond's therapy and Dr. Franks' investigative study, both early beginnings, may prove fruitful in the near future, just as they engage the interest of the profession today.

Much scientific work must be done before the causes and treatment of this unusual sex deviation are finally discovered.

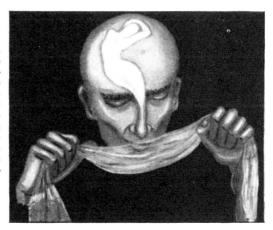

To the stocking fetishist, the odor or sight of a woman's stocking may be sufficient to give erotic stimulation or satisfaction. The stocking has become the symbol of the loved person, and the erotic feelings that usually are felt toward the woman now attach themselves to the fetish itself.—*Original Illustration by Tina.*

SEX APPEAL in MARRIAGE

*Sex appeal varies. Variations in sex appeal
are many. If a wife lacks the sex appeal that the husband seeks, he may become impotent. The story of how a wife
restored her husband's interest in her—
sexually—appears in the following article.*

by D. O. Cauldwell, M.D., D.Sc.

GOLD is where you find it—and so is *sex appeal!* To those who look no more than surface deep the so-called "glamour girls" do not lack sex appeal—they are veritable queens.

Yet, some observant philosopher said: "No man can sleep with a queen."

In marriage, sex appeal between husband and wife is not constant. In only one individual there may be many *variations* in that which constitutes sex appeal.

The late Dr. Wilhelm Stekel gave many striking descriptions of *variations in sex appeal.* One of his male patients was potent only with a woman whose two middle upper front teeth were missing. Some men do not find a woman sexually appealing except in certain specific attire. An erroneous idea has been popularized by the poets to give the impression that only men who are "tall, dark and handsome" appeal to women.

●

Niam-Niam girl (Central Africa) with decorative cicatrices on chest and abdomen. (Photograph by R. Buchta). These Cicatrix designs play a highly important rôle in sexual selection.

High-caste Chinese women with artificially shrunken feet. (From photograph by Ethnic Museum, Berlin.) Diminutive feet at one time caused strong sexual preference among Chinese males.

The purpose of this article is to explain some of the variations of sex appeal in marriage. An excellent "personal story" of one woman's discovery and how it worked was received recently from a reader of SEXOLOGY. She wrote:

"I read the article on Sexual

Right, artificially shrunken foot of a Chinese woman, exterior view. (From photograph by the Ethnic Museum, Berlin.)

WHAT _REALLY_ IS SEX APPEAL IN MARRIAGE?

IT would be most difficult for the average man to explain in simple language what sex appeal constitutes. Scientifically speaking, all animals, humans included, are powerfully influenced by what scientists term "sexual selection."* Sexual selection is the force which makes attraction between sexes and subsequent mating possible in all the species of the animal world. The pictures which the editors selected for this article show a wide range of females who hold a powerful sexual attraction to males of their own environment. One of the curious phases of sexual selection is that certain types, while powerfully attracted to corresponding types in their own surroundings, appear grotesque and repugnant to others far removed from their immediate centers. The article and pictures here presented vividly portray the strange and thought-provoking aspects of sex appeal in marriage as it exists among various races. (*See page 315)

Conflicts *in April '53* SEXOLOGY. *It was good as far as it went, but I do not believe that it was enlightening enough.*

"About two years ago my husband became impotent. He is only 29 years old. He went to see our family doctor who gave him several hormone injections as a tonic. During two months of such treatment he made no progress. He discontinued the treatment. After that he visited several other doctors. His efforts were unsuccessful. The doctors told him that they could not help him.

"By this time my husband was convinced that he was doomed to be impotent the rest of his life. It was then that I decided to see if I could do something about it.

Extremely obese Tunisian woman in festive dress. (After photograph.) Obesity constitutes strong sex appeal for males in many parts of the world.

After reading numerous articles on the subject I concluded that I might be at fault. I sat down and took stock of myself, sparing nothing.

"I had allowed myself to become so engrossed in raising our children that I had seriously neglected my appearance. I had put on 20 pounds of useless weight. I had had my two upper front teeth pulled and had not had them replaced. My hair was long and stringy. I needed a haircut and a permanent wave badly. I did not have a decent dress to wear because every time my husband had given me money for new clothes I had spent it on the children. I had abandoned the use of cosmetics.

"At this point in my inventory I firmly decided to get busy and improve my appearance. I hoped that this might have a helpful effect on my husband.

"First, I went on a rigid calory diet. I had the dentist attend my teeth. A visit to the beauty shop took care of my hair—I came away with a proper haircut and a permanent. I then shopped for clothes and bought cosmetics.

"My husband was amazed at the change in my appearance. He at once started making ardent love to me. He did this every night, but was still impotent. Continuing my improvement, I put forth special effort to stay clean and neat, and within two weeks my husband became capable of having an erection. He ejaculated, nevertheless, the moment intromission was accomplished. I realized, therefore, that he was still partially impotent.

"Feeling that I had made prog-

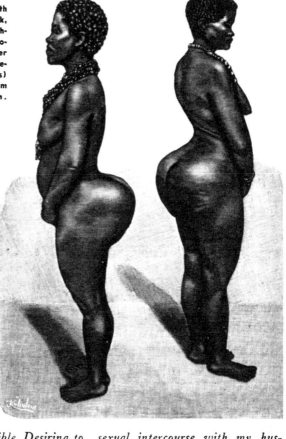

●

ress, I determined to try harder. After many heart-to-heart talks I stumbled onto what had apparently caused my husband's impotence. It happened that, following the birth of our third baby I suffered from a swollen and inflamed womb. This made coitus painful and orgasm impossible. Desiring to save my husband from worry, I neglected to tell him. Thus he came to regard my failure to reach a climax as his fault and the fear of being a sexual failure was planted within him. The feeling thus engendered made him so tense that he ejaculated more quickly each time we engaged in coitus, until he eventually became entirely impotent.

"Medical treatment cleared up the condition of my womb and yet, when I felt well enough to desire sexual intercourse with my husband I found no satisfaction because he was too premature. This was so disappointing that I reminded him to try to exercise control. I did not realize that he was trying desperately to control and that the harder he tried the quicker he ejaculated. That, and my slovenly appearance, was the key to the cause of his impotency.

"Now, under changed circumstances, my husband became sufficiently potent to accomplish intromission and to reach a climax. And, having read that a mildly anesthetic ointment applied to the entire male organ three hours before coitus had helped many men to control and retard their ejaculation, I suggested that my husband get a tube of such an ointment and try it. This he did. I encouraged him not to make any effort to control and assured him that I had complete confidence in his ability.

"All that I have described has done wonders for us. My husband is now fully potent and has such excellent control that I have no difficulty in reaching a climax with him. I have passed this information on to a number of friends and they have found it helpful."

Variations in Sex Appeal

All is well that ends well, and many readers of SEXOLOGY will find help and inspiration in our

Indian girl in marriage-wooing presentation. (From engraving by Sebastian Münster.) Similar presentations are made by a number of mammals, particularly monkeys.

reader's story. At the same time, no specific course of action will solve the problem of a lack of sex appeal in marriage for *all* couples. There are men who are impotent with any but a slovenly-appearing woman. There are men who find no appeal in a woman whose lack of cleanliness causes her body and clothing to give off strong odors, while an untold number of men are impotent with a woman devoid of strong body and clothing odors. The smell of a perfumed female body is exciting to one man but may not be to another. There are men who find sex appeal in their wives only when such wives actually smell "goaty."

The well-known writer, Erskine Caldwell, gave an example of strange sex appeal in a story, "A Swell Looking Girl." A wife who had permitted her appearance to become exceedingly slovenly died. When the undertaker had finished preparing the body for burial the widower went in sorrowfully to view his departed mate. He was amazed. Before his eyes lay the body of "a swell looking girl." The cheeks were rouged, the lips had color, the hair was lovely and youth was pronounced. The husband pleaded that he might have the body of his departed spouse in the house with him alone for "just one night."

Well qualified researchers into the cause of divorce have concluded that although sexual incompatibility is nearly always believed to exist or play a part in marriage failures, this is not necessarily always the case. Many causes of divorce are in no way related to the

sex life between the spouses. Nevertheless, when sex appeal in both husband and wife wanes or vanishes, marriage flounders on the rocks of serious uncertainty.

Husbands as well as wives need to make the most of their sex appeal for their mates. There are wives who find no appeal except in extremely strong males (husbands). Some wives lose sexual desire for husbands who turn out to be less brilliant than they seemed to be before marriage. There are wives who find no appeal in a husband who is not scrupulously clean in body and habits, and it is just as true that there are wives who find their husbands most appealing sexually when they come home from laboring jobs smelling of grease and perspiration.

The adage that "one man's food is another man's poison" applies to sex appeal between married people. The famous sexologue, Judge René Guyon, has written at length about *uterine* and *clitoroid* types of women. According to Guyon there are countless numbers of women who, being what he calls the *uterine* type, are never happy without a "full uterus." Such women find little appeal in a husband who fails to keep them almost constantly pregnant. Fortunate is such a woman who marries a man who finds greater appeal in a wife who is pregnant. It often occurs that the uterine woman expresses a desire for "deep" penetration in marital intimacies. The desire is of *psychological,* rather than of *physical,* origin. The idea (erroneous though it may be) of such a woman is that deeper penetration contributes in a greater degree to the likelihood of conception. The husband of a clitoroid wife may lose his appeal and become repugnant in his intimate relations with his wife if he insists on seeking the utmost penetration.

Certain wives find little sex appeal in their husbands if the latter eliminate foreplay. Other wives, like many husbands, care little for foreplay.

It is surprising to learn that there are so many men who are unaffected by love play (or foreplay) and who are impotent if their thought processes and imagination fail to bring them to erection and capability to perform coitus. The editors of SEXOLOGY constantly receive letters from such men.

There are women who put an end to a courtship promptly if, when kissed by their suitors, they fail to become sexually aroused. There are men who cease their pursuit of a woman they feel they might desire in marriage, if rather close association or body contact fails to cause them to experience an erection.

Loss of Sex Appeal

A confused young man wrote in quest of sexological counsel. He had recently met a young woman with whom he had fallen "deeply in love." At first, just to be near her had so aroused him sexually that he had had strong erections. He had lost little time in proposing and had been accepted. And, he had decided not to have intercourse with the girl until after marriage. (A wise decision.) Soon after he had been accepted, although his love had not decreased, this confused young man had ceased to have erotic sensations when in his beloved's presence. He therefore doubted the advisability of marriage, although he was determined to go through with it.

An experienced sexologist can do little more than *guess* in such cases. The probable solution of this enigmatic case was: The girl most likely reminded the young man—even on the unconscious level—of some female relative toward whom, when he was far too young to have been sexually capable, he had had incestuous desires. For this reason, although not knowing it, he had "decided not to have sexual intercourse with the girl before marriage." He neglected to say whether he had said anything to his fiancée about this. When his engagement became established, his erotic feelings toward the girl became dormant (or absent) because the incestuous element was removed. (He could not have married a female relative in whom he had found such powerful sex appeal.)

Adult Sex Appeal in Marriage

On the genuine adult level of sexuality, sex appeal in marriage comes to be based less and less on certain physical or imaginative characteristics. This level may be reached quickly between some couples while others may require years. There are husbands and wives who eventually blend together so well as to make the admonition that "the two be one" seem true. The more closely the two become blended, the greater sex appeal between them becomes. This does not mean that each becomes so appealing to the other that sexual relations become almost constant or that sex becomes uppermost in their thoughts and in their lives. It does mean that such harmony has been established between them that neither is readily ignored sexually by the other.

Your personal problem, if you have one, may be quite similar to that of our reader whose letter is reproduced in this article. The same kind of remedy may apply. Still, there are thousands of problems centering in disunity and a lack of sex appeal between husbands and wives. Your individual problem may best be resolved from the personal angle—that which you find lacking or unpleasant. The physician who succeeds best is the one who *treats his patients rather than their diseases.* If you have a problem on the sexual plane in marriage, *seek to correct yourself* and your problem may disappear.

All that our reader did in seeking to help restore her husband's potency was good. She was naturally more appealing after she had had proper medical and dental attention and had improved her appearance by a visit to the beautician, donned new clothing and applied cosmetics. Yet, if you have overlooked an important fact, turn back and read her letter again. You will recognize a fact which *she* probably overlooked. It was not her neglected appearance which was responsible for her husband's impotency. Rather it was her own partial frigidity, manifested by willingness *without real desire or a satisfactory culmination.* The husband was led to believe that *he was failing because his wife no*

longer reached a climax. After he became impotent he probably became impressed, consciously or unconsciously, by his wife's neglected appearance. It was but natural then, for him to take notice when she "prettied" herself up. Had the wife remained sexually ardent it is quite possible that her husband would not have become impotent.

In conclusion, let us consider an angle our reader presented, but on which she did not elaborate. This is important because it happens so much more often than it is observed. There are women who, without realizing it, become so "engrossed" in raising their children that they neglect their husbands. That many fail to understand just what has happened is brought out in the letters these women write to SEXOLOGY in seeking a means of reëstablishing marital harmony. The complaint most often made by wives is: "Since our baby came our previous happy sexual relations have practically ended. It must have been something that happened to me when I gave birth to the baby." To this often is added: "Would hormones help me? Would an operation do it?" The answer is that although the husband is loved and wanted, the baby (or the children) have become so great a part of the woman's life as to almost exclude the husband and father except as the breadwinner.

We should not overlook the fact that wives, too, suffer. Some men become more "married" to their work, to business, to a profession, etc., than to their wives. They neglect their wives and thus become sexually unappealing to them.

Is there a solution? There is—but many are strangers to it. It is love, love, and still more love. When there is love enough in any marriage, sex appeal is never a missing ingredient in the formula for marital happiness and harmony.

The FEMALE BREAST

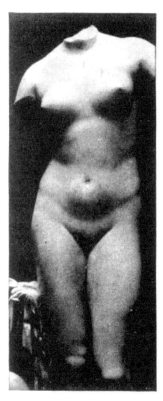

Venus of Cirene. An ancient Greek statue in the National Museum, Rome, Italy. Many artists believe that this Venus represents the most beautiful and perfect feminine proportions.

The breast is one of the most important organs in a woman, physiologically as well as cosmetically. The structure and care of the breast during pregnancy and in ordinary circumstances is described.

by Sarah R. Riedman, Ph.D.

SELF-CONSCIOUS and impatient at the age of fifteen, the teen-ager dons falsies to compensate for what she considers a deficiency in her incompletely developed breasts. Perhaps more resigned, but with no less concern, her mother regards the first signs of sagging of her own breasts as

A noted physiologist, Dr. Riedman is author of Physiology of Work and Play, co-author, Story of Microbes.

a cosmetic liability. The shapeliness of the bosom is as much a preoccupation of the mature woman as of the adolescent.

Whether fashion dictates the severely corsetted Victorian contour, the boyish form of the mid-twenties, or the sweater-girl profile accentuated by the pointed bras of today—the basic interest is cosmetic. While the female breast has been depicted in sculpture and painting as the "spring of life," it has also from time immemorial been looked upon as a woman's most alluring physical adornment. It is said that a marble rose bowl molded from the breast of Marie Antoinette was part of the garden decoration in a French palace.

Standards of Beauty

Standards of bust beauty vary not only with the time but with different peoples. Breasts, like noses, eyes and other physical features, vary with individuals and with national groups. Four main contours are described as *conic, discoid* or bowl-shaped, *hemispheric* and *elongated*.

In Hawaii and New Zealand the small conical breast predominates, while the American Indian woman's breasts are melon-shaped, elongated and drooping. Silesian and Chinese women tend to be flat-chested, and the Yugoslavians and Viennese are known for their beautiful hemispheric type of breast. The discoid type, in which the base is longer than the sides, characterizes the tall blond peoples of northern Europe.

Apart from racial, geographic and hereditary differences, other factors, such as clothing, the weight of the breast, general increase in body weight, as well as strain and stress, all enter into it. Thus South American and West Indian women, accustomed to balancing baskets on their heads, are high-chested, possibly because of the erect posture required; while Mexican women, weighted down with enormous loads on their backs,

have the pendulous breasts associated with stooped posture. During her lifetime a woman's breasts change with her age and motherhood. One who has raised a large family and nursed her children is likely to show considerable change in breast size and shape.

Perhaps more than any other organ, the breast reflects the activity and balanced pattern of hormones (chemicals produced by various glands). Delicately controlled in kind and amount, hormones influence both the function and the structure of the breasts.

"Witches Milk"

At birth and through the early years, the size and structural features of the breast are similar in boys and girls. The gland tissue is scanty in the newborn baby, yet a thin milky fluid called *witch's milk* occasionally escapes, secreted undoubtedly under the influence of maternal hormones. In the ten- to twelve-year-old girl, enlargement of the breast is one of the first signs of growing up. Fatty and fibrous tissues develop at the same time that the glandular cells begin to form.

Each breast is made up of 15 to 25 lobes, arranged radially like spokes of a wheel, and separated by fat which gives it its smooth uniform contour. Large size does not necessarily indicate good nursing potentiality, since the fat may form at the expense of gland tissue.

Partitions of fibrous tissue mark off the lobes and extend to the tip of the breast, giving it shape. Each lobe, in turn, is divided into

smaller pouches (*lobules*) of column-shaped secreting cells. Each lobule opens into a tiny duct (canal) which joins with others to form a series of branching ducts. Fifteen to 20 main ducts converge at the nipple and open separately to the surface.

The nipple contains muscle fibers running circularly. Stiffening (erection) of the nipple occasioned by fear, cold, pain, suckling and sexual stimulation results from contraction of these muscle strands. The sensations aroused from the nipple are like those from the glans penis and clitoris, which contain erectile tissue.

The nipple is richly supplied with nerves which are stimulated in its erection. The area around it is colored and contains oil glands that lubricate the region and protect it from drying and cracking. This area becomes enlarged and its color deepens during the first months of pregnancy, a sign recognized from earliest times as among the first indications of pregnancy.

Phases of Development

There are three major phases in the development of the mammary glands: puberty, pregnancy, and nursing or lactation. With the onset of puberty and the first menstrual period, the breasts grow, becoming fuller throughout adolescence. Much of this enlargement is due to the growth of the ducts, the fibrous network and the nipple. Before each menstrual cycle there is a sense of fullness and sometimes mild pain from the increased blood flow and accumulation of fluid in the tissue spaces.

During the early stages of pregnancy, the breasts grow markedly. The blood vessels are visibly engorged, the superficial veins becoming prominent through the skin. An even greater development takes place during nursing, with new lobules being added.

These menstrual, pregnancy and lactation changes recede at the end of the monthly discharge and after each pregnancy and weaning. After the change-of-life (*menopause*), more connective and fatty tissues develop. This accounts for the increased breast size of the middle-aged woman who has begun to deposit fat in other parts of the body as well. In the elderly woman, the regression of breast tissue, called *senile involution,* takes place.

All these changes reflect the cyclical character of the activity of several glands: the *pituitary, adrenals, thyroid* and *ovary.*

The Master Gland

The pituitary or *master* gland exerts its effects on the others which in turn influence the master gland, accounting for the cyclical activity. While changes in the breast are brought about directly by ovarian hormones, their secretion is *triggered* by the pituitary.

This gland, hardly larger than a pea, is hidden in the skull at the base of the brain. It is controlled by a near-by nerve center in the part of the brain described as the "center of the emotions." Emotional disturbances affecting the pituitary may lead to genital upsets, such as disturbed menstrual rhythm. A woman complaining of painful b r e a s t s (*mastodynia*) is often a thin, nervous, irritable person who may develop breast enlargement resembling that of pregnancy and called *false pregnancy*. On the other hand, an inactive pituitary may result in shrinking of the breasts and premature degeneration of the ovaries and the womb.

Toward the middle of the ovulation cycle, when the egg is discharged from the ovary, this organ releases also a hormone called *progesterone* (*for pregnancy*). Progesterone, like estrogen, is formed only through the stimulation of a hormone from the pituitary—LH (*luteinizing hormone*). Progesterone is responsible for lobular development. Together with estrogen it brings about the full development of the breast.

During Pregnancy

During pregnancy, the *placenta*, the organ that nourishes and pro-

tects the unborn child, also becomes involved, and along with the ovary supplies a large amount of progesterone for the continuing growth of the breasts. The placenta is indispensable for breast growth; if it is removed from pregnant animals, their mammary glands fail to grow.

Toward the end of pregnancy another pituitary hormone, called *prolactin*, w h i c h stimulates the flow of milk, enters the blood. This lactating aid has earned the name *mother love* hormone, because of its effects on both male and female animals. In pigeons and doves

Ewe woman from Togoland carrying water. The custom among some primitive women of carrying heavy loads on their heads develops an erect posture and prevents the breasts from sagging.

it leads to the production of *crop milk*, a milky fluid fed to the young.

In women about to give birth, prolactin appears in the blood and promptly stimulates the flow of milk. As long as suckling continues, prolactin continues to be formed; at the same time the ovary is restrained from secreting estrogen. The upsetting of the balance in favor of prolactin and milk production is the reason for the usual disappearance of menstruation during the first few months of nursing. This accounts also for the popular though incorrect idea that a nursing mother can not become pregnant. *Nursing may tend to keep pregnancy from occurring, but by no means prevents it.*

With the nursing period over, the breast returns to almost its previous size, but repeated pregnancies and lactations eventually cause permanent enlargement and stretching of the woman's breasts.

Undeveloped Breasts

Many women who are emotionally disturbed by their small breasts seek hormone treatment to correct what they consider a detraction from their feminine beauty. Estrogen, if taken orally or by massage into the skin in large doses, can lead to stunting of the ducts. Even more serious is the danger of upsetting the hormone balance, causing more harm than good.

Where hormones are concerned, and particularly the sex hormones, *avoidance of tampering is the best advice to follow.*

Clearly, breast tissue is extremely sensitive to hormone stimulation, and at various times it is a target for almost every hormone in the body. Benign (doing little or no harm) breast disease is almost surely due to hormone factors. *For these reasons hormone treatment is not an appropriate tool in the hands of a beautician, but one to be handled with the greatest care only by a medical specialist.*

Size and contour of the breast have little to do with normal lactation, or with sexual function and gratification, but the part the breasts play in appearance, however exaggerated in the minds of both men and women, raises the question: can anything be done to alter them?

Care of the Breasts

There is practically nothing that will restore the shape of a sagging breast, any more than the natural elasticity of a stretched dried rubber band can be restored. However, a few things can be done to prevent this condition. Among these is the wearing of a proper brassière—not always a simple matter.

A comfortable, well-fitting supporting garment of soft and non-irritating material helps to prevent stretching, sagging and distorting of the natural contour. It must offer support from beneath and in the direction of the firmest anchorage, the shoulders. It should fit the contour of the breasts, separated in the center. The straps must not be so tight as to make a depression on the shoulders. Pleats, tucks, seams, wires and other devices designed to accentuate the nipple cause irritation of this delicate structure. One thing a good brassière must not do is bind, compress or flatten the breast.

To reduce the strain from the extra weight of the breast, proper support is especially important during nursing, and for the same reason, the reclining position is recommended. After weaning, a binder

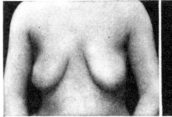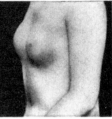

Sagging breasts before and after plastic surgery.

is necessary to prevent pain and distention, and to help "drying up."

Physical exercise, suited to the age of the woman, strengthens all muscles, including the shoulder and back muscles which indirectly give proper support to the breasts. During all vertical exercises a bra should be worn. Only when swimming, or performing athletic exercises in a horizontal position, is this not necessary.

Extremely important is proper posture: the stooped posture of the round-shouldered woman is associated with drooping, flabby breasts. Erect posture, consciously developed whenever one is standing, helps to support them.

General good hygiene, such as cold baths, fresh air, rest, relaxation and sound nutrition are as essential for bust protection as for the health of the body. Drastic reducing diets that result in rapid weight loss may cause sagging of the breast, just as they lead to premature wrinkling of the skin.

Massages, "miracle" lotions and "skin foods" are of doubtful value. Some of these contain astringents which only temporarily "tighten" the skin, and some have oils that are absorbed very slightly, but at best give only imaginary comfort.

Hormone treatment for the small-breasted woman should be considered only as a form of medical therapy in certain cases, not as a "home" remedy.

Plastic Surgery

Finally, there is cosmetic surgery, which, like face lifting, involves plastic surgery of the most skillful type. The operation to reduce size, done in two stages, requires an incision in which the nipple is reset, the skin drawn tightly over the tissue and excessive sections removed.

Plastic surgery to increase the dimensions of small breasts is not advisable. In most cases a small bosom is hereditary. The use of various materials for implants under the breast tissue has been found to be dangerous to the woman's health.

Such rejuvenating procedures are not usually advised except when medical factors (pain from excessive weight, or unusual lack of similarity in shape or size), psychological or economic reasons are sufficiently compelling. In all instances, the reputable surgeon always carefully considers the possibility that the unfavorable medical results may outweigh the cosmetic problem and harm the woman.

BREAST FANTASY — *By Tina*

Some women hope to enlarge the size of their breasts by the application of hormone creams. But they are soon disillusioned—for hormone creams can never bring about this much desired effect. Our artist surrealistically portrays this wish for breast enlargement through the use of hormone preparations. A woman is pouring a liquid (representing hormone cream) from a vessel onto her breasts. In the background is her imagined shadow with the large breast line she futilely desires to obtain.

"I could never love a mere man"—from an Aquarell by the French artist Henry Fournier. From "Le Sourire." This picture well illustrates the love between two women of the Lesbian persuasion.

the
story
of
a
LESBIAN

by Frank S. Caprio, M.D.

Lesbians are female homosexuals. Is there a "third sex"? Why do some heterosexual females (those attracted by the opposite sex) participate in homosexual activities? The answers appear in the following informative article.

A WIDELY circulated book under the title of "Diana, The Strange Autobiography of a Lesbian" is similar in many respects to "The Well Of Loneliness." However, the char-acters in *"Diana"* are not fictitious. Affording insight into human nature, autobiographies have a value to psychiatrists. In *Diana*, the author betrays the unconscious motivations behind what she claims to

About the Author—Dr. Frank S. Caprio is an outstanding author of popular medical articles. He has had extensive experience in hundreds of sexological cases through his private practice and research conducted in some of the world's largest hospitals. His latest book is *"The Sexually Adequate Male"*—in which many sexual problems are refreshingly analyzed. He is joint author, with Dr. Louis S. London, of the valuable volume "Sexual Deviations," which is the first work to cover the many variations of sex abnormalities for the lay reader. Dr. Caprio has the faculty of expressing in a clear manner the many intricacies of modern sexological problems.

believe and has experienced. Many of the scientific contributions which psychiatrists have made are based on autobiographical data gathered from the life-histories of their patients.

In appraising the book from the scientific point of view, much can be learned about the psychology of lesbianism. It reveals how a lesbian (a woman who manifests sexual love for another woman) reacts to various life-situations and gives the reader a detailed cross-section of personality traits common to most lesbians.

On the negative side—like "The Well Of Loneliness" — the book *Diana* gives the reader a wrong idea of homosexuality. It is unfortunate that Dr. Victor Robinson, who wrote the *Introduction*

and who has written much on the subject of sex, made statements that are considered scientifically inaccurate according to modern psychiatry. No doubt this is because the book was published in 1939. Old ideas about homosexuality have been superseded by new ones which are more applicable and scientifically factual. He misinforms the reader when he says: "For though the existence of a *third sex* is now widely recognized, general knowledge concerning the cause and the probability of recovering from homosexuality is inaccurate and confused."

No "Third Sex"

There is no "third" or "intermediate sex," as Edward Carpenter—the famous sexologist, Rob-

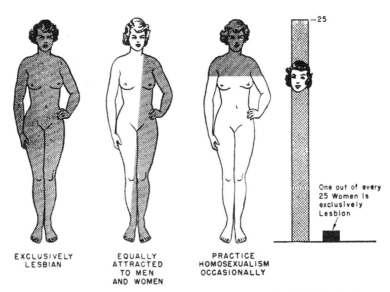

EXCLUSIVELY LESBIAN   EQUALLY ATTRACTED TO MEN AND WOMEN   PRACTICE HOMOSEXUALISM OCCASIONALLY

—25

One out of every 25 Women is exclusively Lesbian

Three classes of Lesbians are shown above—Left, those exclusively Lesbian; Center—those attracted to both sexes; Right—women who are attracted sexually to other women at times. One out of every twenty-five women are exclusively Lesbian.

inson and others would have us believe. *A homosexual component can be found in every human being.* It is either expressed, repressed or sublimated. The term "third sex" gives the reader the impression that the world is made up of men, women and homosexuals. Such is not the case. While it is true the public may be confused regarding homosexuality, psychiatrists know more about it today than they ever did and are gradually making this knowledge accessible to the public.

Dr. Robinson claims that lesbianism is not a question of ethics but of endocrines. This is no longer true, as there are thousands of lesbians who have no endocrine disturbances, and many more thousands of women who have endocrine disturbances and are *not* lesbians. He also states: "There is no danger that the woman biologically craving the male will seek that strange light" (referring to lesbian gratification). There are many lesbians who have a biological craving for the male and participate in homosexual activities—who may be predominantly heterosexual and who are willingly seduced into homosexual practices out of sheer curiosity. Since there are so many variations in the expression of the homosexual component among human beings, sweeping statements are usually inaccurate.

Diana's Family History

While Diana—in her Foreword —refers to herself as belonging to the "third sex," she admits that environment factors played an important rôle in causing an early inclination to homosexuality.

Diana, who was born in Kentucky, came from a home of affectionate parents. The family consisted of three brothers and herself. The father died when she was nine (a psychic trauma in Diana's life). Regarding her father's death she wrote:—"A paradisiacal family life was cruelly blasted by my father's sudden death. Mother's silence terrified us and we wondered if she were going to die too: we were without understanding. What I needed was someone to tell me what to do, or how to stand the silence and mystery without crying. Though my body shook from holding back my tears, I could not let myself give way; father would not have liked it."

She turned to her brothers for paternal affection. During childhood she preferred to play with boys; her nature was tomboyish. Her mother was disappointed when she noticed that Diana displayed signs of masculinity. Diana was very much aware of her lack of femininity as evidenced by her statement: "From the age of twelve to sixteen, these impressionable years were flooded with male habits, male viewpoints, male ideals, and male psychology."

Another psychic trauma (shock) in her life occurred when a boy tried to seduce her. This experience set up a strong feeling of dislike toward boys in general. She had been referred to by this same boy as "seductive looking"—an expression which she hated—and the implication that a woman had to

submit to a man to gratify his physical needs horrified her. This early attitude which she took toward the opposite sex did much to establish her preference for her own sex. The fact that she had been teased by her brothers ("unmercifully" as she put it) made heterosexuality less attractive to her.

She developed her first homosexual crush for a girl named Ruth and experienced a strong craving to caress her. Not wanting to share Ruth with her friends, she became very jealous and morose.

At the age of sixteen, Diana came across a medical book in her father's library that dealt with the subject of homosexuality. She read that homosexuals were "perverts" and at one time were burned at the stake. She became panic-

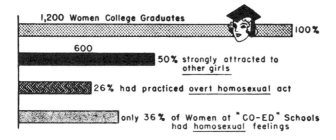

1,200 Women College Graduates 100%

600

50% strongly attracted to other girls

26% had practiced overt homosexual act

only 36% of Women at "CO-ED" Schools had homosexual feelings

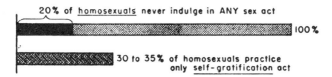

20% of homosexuals never indulge in ANY sex act 100%

30 to 35% of homosexuals practice only self-gratification act

Lesbianism or sexual attraction between females is here shown graphically . . . top graph shows that one-half of 1200 women college graduates were sexually attracted to other females. But only 36 per cent of women at CO-ED schools showed such homosexual feelings. Lower graph shows percentage of homosexuals indulging in sex acts.

stricken and experienced a sickness in the pit of her stomach. She consulted a doctor who examined her to determine whether she had any physical abnormalities. Feeling extremely guilty because of the way she felt toward Ruth, she confessed to her brother Gerald that she had "lesbian tendencies." Her brother tried to comfort her, but she continued to be tormented by conflicts which puzzled her.

She tried more and more to repress her homosexual tendencies: "I ignored with almost fanatic self-discipline, those girls who were particularly attractive to me; I did not want my strength tempted." At the same time she made an effort to develop an interest in heterosexuality and there were certain boys who definitely attracted

her. Incidentally, in every lesbian one can find at the unconscious, if not at the conscious level, a *dormant or repressed desire for heterosexuality.*

Recognition

Diana mentions how lesbians can uncannily recognize one another. This sometimes appears to be true since a lesbian identifies herself with others who have the same observable mannerisms. Lesbians are extremely sensitive and see themselves in the mirror-actions and behavior of another lesbian. This psychological mechanism is referred to as "projection." It explains why some lesbians are actually repulsed by the behavior of the obvious, mannish lesbian. Their repugnance represents a defensive reaction against that which they do not wish to admit in themselves. It is brought out in the book *Diana,* when Jane is repulsed at the idea of Diana visiting a rendezvous for lesbians in Paris. Jane refers to them as being "perverted."

The story continues with Diana having met Carl who wanted to marry her. She gave herself to him, but found that her trial-marriage experiment failed. It did not solve her problem. She discovered she was frigid, which no doubt was the result of her bisexual conflicts. Psychoanalysts have found that many women who are unable to achieve an orgasm from intercourse unconsciously suffer from homosexual repressions which prevent them from abandoning themselves completely to the love-making of a man. These same women, because of their sexual frustration, often turn to their own sex with the hope of finding sexual fulfillment. They use frigidity as a rationalization or excuse for satisfying their homosexual cravings. This is particularly true among wives who have been divorced because of sexual incompatibility.

Pseudo-Frigidity of Lesbians

The inability to respond sexually to a man, common to many lesbians, constitutes a pseudo-frigidity in the sense that they "hold back" unconsciously because of some unresolved conflict. They arrive at the conclusion that heterosexuality and marriage are impossible for them. When they do give themselves to a man, it is more with the feeling of pleasing the man rather than sharing sexual satisfac-tion. This was true in Diana's case. At one point she stated: "Not once in eight months had physical intimacy meant anything to me but the giving of gratification to Carl." She said she was afraid of hurting Carl because of her frigidity. This at best can be construed as a *rationalization*. Frigidity should never be used as a reason for preferring homosexuality to hetero-sexuality.

Diana says that it became easier for her after she recognized that she *was* a lesbian and *accepted* herself as such. Many lesbians claim that they are happy and experience no conflict about their homosexuality, simply because they have accepted the fact that they are lesbians and will continue to live a lesbian type of existence. But this is only a surface or *pseudo-happiness*. Basically, they are lonely and unhappy and are afraid to admit it, deluding themselves into believing that they are free of all mental conflicts and are well adjusted to their homosexuality. Their attitude toward themselves, toward their friends, family, marriage, children, religion and the world in general is an *ambivalent* one (conflicting feelings). They are unaware of their own contradictions which they show in their thinking and behavior.

This unhappiness, common to lesbians, permeates the general trend of the book. Diana's relationships to her various lesbian friends, Jane, Louise and Leslie, all involve scenes of jealousy, manifestations of possessiveness and frustration, a meaningless type of existence with no plans for the future. The book indicates that lesbians suffer from emotional insecurity and are never sure of the love of their partners.

That lesbians often become intimate with wives living with their husbands is portrayed in the example of Jane's relationship to Louise. Louise's husband, Paul, turns to Diana for consolation, does not realize that Diana is also a lesbian, becomes interested in her and matters become more complicated. There are many such marriages that end in divorce, *because the husband is competing with a lesbian who is in love with his wife.* These situations—to avert a scandal — seldom receive publicity. They are generally revealed to a psychiatrist when one of the persons involved begins to suffer from the emotional consequences following the dissolution of the marriage.

In *Diana* is mentioned a lesbian —Eleanor — who commits suicide by taking an overdose of sleeping powders. We recall that in "The Well Of Loneliness" there was also a suicide. When a type of living (homosexuality) causes suicide, it becomes the concern of psychiatrists and society to take steps to improve the situation.

Toward the end of the book Diana meets a girl friend named Leslie, with whom she shares physical intimacies. Leslie's mother becomes suspicious of the relationship, appeals to Diana with the hope that Diana will relinquish her hold on Leslie, in order to give her the opportunity to lead a normal life. But Diana holds Les-

lie's parents responsible for Leslie's becoming a lesbian, tells the mother so and leaves the decision to Leslie. Leslie decides not to return home to her mother and Diana supports her. Leslie attends college. Diana teaches and writes articles and novels with some success. Leslie becomes jealous because she accuses Diana of maintaining her *ghost - love* for a former lesbian friend—Jane. Diana and Leslie visit Jane with the purpose of coming to a final understanding regarding their respective loyalties. One night Diana found Leslie coming out of Jane's bedroom. Diana is heartbroken and tells Leslie that she is through with her because of the betrayal. Leslie finds herself a job singing in a café. Diana and her mother go to the café to hear Leslie sing. Leslie begs Diana to forgive her and the book ends with a reconciliation effected between them.

After reading the book the reader cannot help but come to the conclusion that in all of these lesbian relationships there is revealed a type of behavior similar to what psychoanalysts call "adult infantilism." While some lesbians may be exceptionally talented and have achieved a certain amount of success in a career, for the large part they are emotionally insecure and are unconsciously seeking an *ideal* love relationship, which they never find.

If this book has but one merit—to enlighten the reader with deeper insight into the psychology of lesbianism—its publication is justified.

SEX among the ESKIMOS

In remote regions of the world, Eskimos still practice a uniquely practical sexual morality designed to cope with the harsh problems of existence in the Arctic wastes.

by L. T. Woodward, M.D.

INALUK, a young married Eskimo, had been forced to be away from his home for a period of two years, making a mail journey to far-off Fort Churchill. The day after his return, his wife gave birth to a daughter. It was a delightful surprise for Inaluk, and the happy event caused much rejoicing — though he did express some regret that it hadn't been a boy. It was never discovered who the father of the child had been. Inaluk wasn't at all interested in knowing.

This anecdote illustrates the typical Eskimo attitude toward sex. In the bleak, dreary world of the Arctic, where life is a perpetual battle against the elements and an eternal struggle for food, few sexual restrictions of the kind we know have developed. The facts of life, for an Eskimo, are blunt and hard, and he is completely without

---

Dr. Woodward is a medical author and counselor.

pretense in adapting his sexual code to fit reality.

Eskimos are too busy at the grim business of staying alive to bother with complicated codes of morality. An illegitimate child has no stigma attached; in fact, it is often desirable as an added family member and potential worker.

Marriage is a simple and common institution in the Arctic. The Eskimos regard the unmarried state as being unnatural, and so marriage takes place early. Children are customarily betrothed at birth; as soon as a male child is born, his father buys a wife for him. Should this infant fiancée die, the boy often will have to marry a widow decades his senior, if there are no other available girls his age.

The boy and his child-bride begin to live together from puberty on, as soon as the boy is able to provide food for himself and his wife, and she is able to sew and do the many other feminine chores required of an Eskimo wife. *Hardly any Eskimos above the age of fourteen or fifteen remain single,*

except in communities where the balance of nature has been upset. Getting married is simplicity itself. When the parties concerned have decided that the young couple is suitably mature, the young man merely comes and fetches his bride to his house. There is no ceremony.

When life is as hard as it is in the Arctic, where the infant - mortality rate is incredibly high, early marriage is essential to survival of the group. Therefore, there are practically no restrictions as to the choice of a wife.

Any man, apparently, may marry any woman, though there are various local restrictions on this—for instance, in some places a man may marry any woman except one who bears the same name as he does. (Eskimos do not have differentiated names for males and females.)

Furthermore, in some communities marriage between brothers and sisters is by no means uncommon —making the Arctic one of the few parts of the world where incest is regularly practiced. Also widespread is polygyny in Eskimo communities where the supply of women far outnumbers that of men. The cleverest hunters will usually have two and sometimes three wives, since an unmarried woman is a potential child-bearer going to waste.

Since the Eskimos are an unusually peaceful, practical-minded people, this sort of multiple arrangement is accepted by the two wives without protest or friction.

There are, of course, exceptions; some Eskimos find it more conducive to matrimonial harmony to keep their wives in separate houses and stay with each in turn, and one shrewd fellow contrived to establish a household at each end of his hunting territory, enabling him to have ready sexual companionship without having to traverse the entire length of his wide-ranging hunting path to get it.

Divorce among the Eskimos is so common as to be almost universal; it is a widespread custom to exchange wives with a close friend. When a couple breaks up, the children remain with the mother. This tends to discourage divorce among couples who have sons, since the father is anxious to keep a son to provide for him when he is no longer capable of doing so himself. Marriages which have remained barren any length of time, however, usually are broken up and the partners move on to what they hope will be a more fruitful relationship.

Many Eskimos have three or four wives in as many years by this procedure. But barrenness is not the only cause for divorce. Two young men of a tribe may choose to establish a relationship whereby they exchange wives with each other every year, providing both sexual variety and what is considered "good luck." Both men will firmly insist that they will have bad hunting if they neglect the exchange any year.

Among the Pacific Eskimos, a different form of marriage has sprung up, in which all cousins and brothers can demand the right of intercourse with each other's wives. This group-marriage plan seems to have evolved from a previous understanding whereby, when a man is on a journey, his younger brother will temporarily marry his wife, provide for her, and exercise sexual rights over her.

The women submit to this sort of treatment quite willingly. An Eskimo woman is happy so long as some man is providing for her. There is little emotion in Eskimo life; husband and wife never display any great deal of affection toward each other, nor is there any particular display of anger. Shouting and quarrelling is rare.

Eskimo family life is so organized that each mate is indispensable to the other. The husband makes himself responsible for the hunting, getting food and skins for his family; he also builds the house and makes tools. The wife does the sewing, helps to prepare the skins (she chews them to make them soft enough to sew, and thus the teeth of most Eskimo women wear away to unsightly stumps), cooks, keeps the oil lamps burning, and cares for the children. On rare occasions when the husband is in need of assistance, the woman helps with the hunt. At all times, she works in constant teamwork with her husband.

As a result of the Eskimo system of easy marriage and divorce, sex life is so loose as to approach promiscuity. Exchanging of sexual partners for the night is done openhandedly, and most men eventually sleep with nearly all the women of their community.

Great emphasis is placed both on the need to have children and the necessity to indulge frequently

Eskimo customs permit wife lending, wife trading and, in some communities where women outnumber the men, the practice of having several wives.—*Ewing Galloway.*

in sexual intercourse as a matter of health.

A white sea-captain who visited Alaska tells the story of a young Eskimo man who approached him, saying, "I know that you are too decent and cleanly to do what I wish to have done: my wife is barren, you understand, but if you yourself will not, then command one of your sailors to make her pregnant."

When the white man reproached the Eskimo for making such a seemingly immoral offer, the Eskimo replied, "It is no shame, since she is married, and can have one of your married sailors."

The innocence of such a remark reveals the simplicity of Eskimo sexual customs. The husband has the right to dispose of his wife's body in any way he sees fit, and will frequently lend her out as a token of friendship or as a device to get children. *The concept of "faithfulness" in our sense does not exist, though a wife who disobeys her husband's assignations for her may be considered "unfaithful."*

Customarily, when a traveller from far off, such as a hunter embarked on a long and arduous journey, arrives, he is given a woman. To the Eskimo this is a healthy and praiseworthy practice; the voyager, travelling alone over the Arctic wastes, has had no chance for sexual intercourse, and it is only good manners to provide him with a temporary wife to ease his loneliness. They solve the problem of long sexual abstinence in the most direct fashion.

In some communities this temporary wife is furnished from among the spinsters and widows of the community, but in others, particularly in the Aleutians, the Eskimo householder is required by custom to place his wife at the disposal of any of his guests.

When the Russian fur trappers entered Alaska in the 18th Century and discovered this pleasant custom, they were quick to take advantage of it, thus spreading venereal diseases widely through the previously uninfected Eskimo lands.

Generosity extends into all the regions of Eskimo life, not only in sexual matters. Children always have the right of entry to anyone's house, and are permitted to eat whatever food is there. Women are also given this privilege, in some localities, and all over the Arctic a hunter who has had bad luck will be nursed through his lean weeks by gifts from luckier, more successful friends. These favors are always repaid scrupulously.

It is everywhere a common practice for Eskimos to trade wives with one another, for a long or short period. No jealousy figures into this swapping; rather, it is thought the best way to demonstrate deep friendship. In Greenland, where the Eskimos live together in large communal houses, visitors report a game called "the game of putting out the lamps," and visitors were given an opportunity to take part in this amiable communal sharing.

Other sexual practices are similarly free and easy. Homosexuality exists, though it is not practiced widely except by men who must go for months or years without any female companions. More common and stranger is the custom of Eskimo men sometimes to copulate with animals they have just killed; there also are stories of women sometimes having sexual intercourse with the robust, sturdy Eskimo dogs.

Modesty takes an unusual form among the Eskimos. It must be understood that modesty is strongest among those peoples who do not need to wear clothes but wear them anyway; where clothing is necessary for protection against the cold, modesty in our sense does not fully develop.

The Eskimos are accustomed to going almost entirely naked inside their stiflingly warm winter houses; since the conditions of their lives are such that they can never have any real privacy, nudity is quite common.

There is one modifying factor, though. Although sex is regarded openly and naturally by the Eskimos, and talked about uninhibitedly in front of young children, a curious magical taboo enters into the physical side of sex: *nakedness is perfectly common and acceptable inside the houses (it is, of course, inconceivable outside!) but the sexual organs themselves are considered magical, taboo, and must be concealed.*

This custom apparently grows out of the belief that dangerous magical influences may act on the genitals if they are exposed to public view, not from any desire to keep them hidden from shame.

Therefore, in some parts of Eskimo territory a tiny triangular apron is tied around the waist and between the legs to provide cover; among the Pacific Eskimos these aprons are beautifully decorated with shell beads. But they reveal more than they conceal, and serve as symbolic garments only.

It is a mistake to regard the Eskimos as licentious, immoral people. Their "loose" sexuality stems from purely practical considerations. A hunter bound on a long journey must have some sort of sexual relief; what better show of hospitality could a host make than giving him his wife? Children must be born; if one man cannot manage to produce them, his wife must be re-married and not allowed to end her days barren.

In the free exchange of wives, they are making provisions for continuation of the race—for otherwise, under harsh Arctic conditions, monogamy and simple marriage would never produce enough surviving children.

The Eskimo attitude toward marriage is also based upon the rugged conditions of life. Close working harmony is essential to survival between Eskimo man and wife. If a couple does not like each other, they are neither bound together for all eternity nor required to go through complex legal proceedings. They simply leave each other.

Young people drift from marriage to marriage in much the same way teenagers in America do from one "steady" to another, not settling down until children arrive. In our society, such mores would lead to chaos; in the Arctic, they have evolved from necessity.

It is, of course, the male children who are the most important. A man with many sons has great prestige, while daughters occasion no pride. In fact, if a man already has several daughters and his wife bears another, the baby may sometimes be killed by the father so the wife, unencumbered by a nursing infant, can begin a new pregnancy—with hopes of a son.

The customs of the Eskimo mirror the world they live in. It is a world where nothing is permanent but the snow; there are no landmarks, no trees, no guides of any sort. Everything is frozen and still, and life is a bitter struggle. The Eskimos have no written laws, no government, and no literature. And their patterns of love follow suit. To cope with the problems of existence in the Arctic wastes, the Eskimos developed a uniquely practical sexual morality.

In areas where the white man has made considerable inroads, the easy-going Eskimo morality has in many ways altered. However, in the more remote regions, these practices are still as common today as they were in the days before the coming of the white man.

● ● ●

NOTORIOUS HUSBAND POISONERS

by H. W. Secor

THROUGHOUT history, fascinated attention has been drawn to the mysterious and terrible power of dealing swift death by the use of a few drops of poison. The method apparently was a favorite device not only for

Mr. Secor is Managing Editor of SEXOLOGY *and a medical and sexological author of long experience.*

political assassination, but also for getting rid of unwanted husbands and wives.

As far back as 131 B.C., we are told by the historian Livy, women in high circles disposed of unwelcome husbands in this way. Husbands also made use of this convenient path to freedom, but, as history shows, they took this path far less often than did the wives.

An unusual history of the "art of poisoning" was given recently by Dr. Theodore G. Osius in the *University of Michigan Medical Bulletin.*

The practice was particularly common, we are told, in the 15th and 16th centuries in Europe, with the most famous poisoners being the notorious Borgia and the Medici families in Italy.

From the School of Naples we read of the incredible woman Toffana, who is reputed to have murdered about six hundred people in her long life-time. Two of her poisonous concoctions, known as *Aqua Toffana* and *Aqua Napoli,* were actually sold as cosmetics.

These supposed beauty aids were really made from decomposing hog flesh, to which was added arsenic oxide and corrosive sublimate along with opium. This produced a mixture teeming with deadly bacteria. Two Popes were numbered among her victims and numerous prominent husbands to whose wives Toffana sold the deadly potions.

Finally Toffana was arrested, forced to confess and then strangled. One of her pupils, Hieronomya Spara, was the leader of a secret society of young married women from the best Roman families, whose common bond was a desire to get rid of their husbands. The infamous Catherine de Medici, another Toffana school graduate, was said to have carried her knowledge of poisoning to France from Italy. So terrible was her reputation that people were afraid to eat or drink in her home or even when she was around.

So widespread did this poisoning become that at one time (1679 to 1682) in Paris a special commission of judges listened to poisoning cases. Charges against 442 people were heard during this time but the chief culprits, the members of the nobility, had powerful friends and were seldom punished.

One of the most devilish poisoning schemes used in France in the 17th century was to apply powerful poisons such as arsenic, corrosive sublimate or cantharides ("Spanish fly") to a man's shirt-tail, causing a strong irritation of the skin about the perineum and sexual organs. When a doctor examined the suffering victim, the diagnosis was frequently *syphilis,* for which mercury was prescribed. The "devoted" wife gladly proceeded to administer more mercury to her husband, with death as the ultimate goal.

One notorious poisoner of the late 17th Century was the beautiful Marchioness de Brenvilliers, a French noblewoman. She was acquainted with various poisons by her lover Sainte Croix.

At first she amused herself by trying various experiments with poisoned confections and wines on hospital patients. Next she poisoned her father and her two brothers. Then she turned her attention to her husband.

At dinner, it was reported, the husband used to have himself waited on by a servant specially instructed to watch for possible poisoning. In spite of this vigilance, the husband was given poison a number of times. In each case,

however, the Marchioness was struck with remorse and called a doctor in time to save his life.

According to rumor of the period, the husband owed his life to his wife's lover Sainte Croix, who preferred not to have to marry the Marchioness. Thus every time she gave the husband a poison, the lover gave him an antidote. Eventually, the Marchioness was arrested and sentenced to death for her crimes.

In early England, so intense was the hatred of poisoners that, up until 1542, those tried and convicted were *boiled to death,* a probable basis of the common expression "getting into hot water."

A notorious male poisoner was the Roman emperor Nero. He killed his stepbrother, his mother and his wives by giving them prussic acid to drink.

One of the most infamous poisoning cases in more recent history was that of the French "Bluebeard," Landru, who was tried in 1922 for poisoning a number of women with cyanide and then disposing of their bodies in incinerators. He kept a business record of his victims, which revealed that he promised marriage to and obtained the savings of 283 women.

Fifty per cent of all murders are unsolved each year, Dr. Osius concludes, and it may be that secret poisoning is even now far more frequent than is generally believed.

References

Osius, Theo. G., M.D.: "The Historic Art of Poisoning," *University of Michigan Medical Bulletin,* Vol. **XXIII** (March) 1957.

(Photo page 174 posed by professional model.)

CURIOSITIES

An unusual case where the male of the species carries the unborn young. Here an infant sea-horse is shown emerging from the pouch of a male sea-horse. The female deposits her eggs in the pouch, and the male fertilizes and retains them until they hatch.

A Papuan widow mourning her husband by wearing his skull (indicated by the arrow) slung from her neck.

This spiked blouse was an artist's idea for protection against *frotteurs*, suggested during a wave of frottage in Vienna, Austria. *Frottage* is a deviation in which people take pleasure in rubbing up against others. It most often occurs in crowded places where detection is difficult.

An ancient print depicts a woman being married to a tree in India. The origin of the custom is not clearly known, but it may have been connected with age-old fertility rites.

ODOR

by Edward Dengrove, M.D.

Some deviates are sexually stimulated only by certain odors. What is the cause of this fixation? How does it develop? Will this sex deviation respond to treatment?

TWO persons meet and fall in love. Each is attracted by certain attributes the other possesses, often without being fully aware of just what the attrac-

Dr. Dengrove is a well known medical author and psychiatrist in private practice in New Jersey.

tion is. Insignificant as these may seem to others, the tone of voice, a grace of movement, the color of the eyes, the style of dress— details such as these often play a large part in establishing a love relationship. Usually, one grows to love the whole person. The personality traits or physical charms which sparked the initial attraction then become dear because they are a part of the person loved.

But it sometimes happens that physical characteristics such as body build, parts of the body like arms or legs, or inanimate objects such as articles of clothing, assume a sexual value of their own. When a person is unable to have sexual relations without their presence, or when they completely replace the sexual partner and are alone sufficient to arouse and satisfy his sexual desires, we say that he has a *fetish*. There are *fetishes* of many types; but perhaps one of the strangest is *osphresiolagnia,* a technical term for sexual fixation on odors.

holds for the man who loves and desires her. To the *odor fetishist,* the odor not only increases her attraction—*it is her attraction!*

Sexual Substitute

The fetishist requires no sexual partner for arousal or gratification —he has replaced the usual sexual object and partner, the woman, with a symbol, the *fetish*. To this symbol he is sexually responsive; in its absence he is unable to find true sexual satisfaction.

In *osphresiolagnia,* the symbol is an odor. The most attractive woman will not arouse the interest of a fetishist of this type unless she possesses the right odor; any woman whose odor is right will be desirable to him, no matter how old, ugly, or unattractive she may be otherwise. Thus, the odor fetishist imposes what the

FETISHIST

In the civilized world, we have come to depend less on our olfactory sense and to rely more on our senses of sight and hearing. In the animal kingdom and in primitive societies the sense of smell plays a more obvious rôle. Although we may not always recognize its importance, the olfactory sense has a vital part in courtship, romance and sexual activity. The scent of her body—or of the perfume she uses—may contribute greatly to the attraction a woman

psychoanalyst Otto Fenichel calls "the condition of love"—unless the woman meets the condition, there is no love. For what the fetishist is really seeking is not the woman —but the odor.

In fetishism, as in other sexual deviations, there exists a deep fear of a member of the opposite sex as a love object, and especially fear of genital contact. However, this fear does not kill the sexual urge, which is neither decreased nor abstained from, but which continues unabated and must find expression in another direction. Because of his deep-rooted fear, the fetishist is unable to love and desire a woman in the usual manner. Instead, he substitutes an inanimate object, such as shoes; a part of the body, such as hair; or sensations, such as odors.

Fear of Women

This fear of the female as a sexual object is the result of a complex form of *conditioning*. Psychoanalysts speak of castration fear. It is not unusual for boys to become frightened when they see the female sex organs for the first time, and to imagine that the female, too, once had a penis but had been deprived of it because she was "bad." Or, at some stage in his psychological growth there may have been an incestuous desire for his mother, and a fear of punishment for such forbidden thoughts. Then, if he considers all women equal to the desired mother, the urge for sexual intercourse with them is equally forbidden, and equally subject to punishment. Or it may be that a very dominant mother represents a constant threat to the child, causing his sexual development to be determined in some measure by his fear that a strong woman may emasculate him. Thus, he may learn to fear all women. There is a peculiar complex known as *vagina dentata*, or "the vagina with teeth." According to psychoanalytic theory, some men associate all women with the threatening, dominant mother, and fear that through intercourse, they will lose the penis in the vagina. There may be many other complicated underlying complexes involved.

This fear of the female as a sexual object leads to fetishism when other objects are forbidden. The male homosexual also fears genital union with the female, but he is able to accept sexual relationships with those of his own sex. The choice of the fetish itself is determined partly by chance, and partly by the nature of the object chosen.

For example, a boy may harbor an incestuous desire for his mother —a forbidden sexual object. His mother may use a particularly strong perfume. The child may hear comments made about it, such as, "that perfume's enough to overwhelm anyone," or "that perfume of yours would chase anyone out of the room." Thus the forbidden sexual object is related to a strong odor, and related to the strong odor is the idea of strength and mastery—"enough to overwhelm anyone." Strength may thus come to be related to strong odors; and the grown man may be unable to find sexual gratification with any woman who does not smell heavily of strong perfume. It is not unusual for *transvestites*, men who dress as women, to derive sexual satisfaction from the use of perfume and from female body odors.

Case Histories

Dr. Otto Fenichel, psychoanalyst, tells of a man, a *transvestite*, with a fetishistic preference for certain odors. The man had lost his own mother when he was a little child, and though he had been reared to believe that his step-mother was his real mother, he suspected the truth. His feminine behavior was aimed at showing his father that he would have been a better substitute for his dead mother than his stepmother was. At the same time he feared that his desire to be a woman, if it were to come true, would deprive him of his penis. He tried, therefore, to reassure himself that it was possible to both be a woman and keep a penis.

Dr. Benjamin Karpman records the case of a 33-year-old man who was arrested in a department store for annoying women. It was this man's practice to stand on a crowded "up" escalator. When he saw a woman with an attractive back, he would lean forward to "smell" her. Then he would disappear in the crowd.

He was sent to a hospital for examination. There it was learned that he had lost his mother when he was very young. He had an excellent war record; but when his request for demotion following battle fatigue was denied, he went AWOL. Five weeks later he was apprehended, and put into a stockade. There he became frightened when he began to recognize his own homosexual interest in the younger men in the stockade with him, and he sought relief in phantasies. In one of his phantasies he envisioned a French farmer's daughter, and imagined himself breathing deeply of the freshly laundered dress she wore. This phantasy resulted in erection and sexual stimulation.

The Sense of Smell, a 16th Century engraving. Odor has an important association with sex and courtship.—From AESCULAPE, a French medical journal.

He was pardoned and discharged. Shortly thereafter, he got married, and returned to the United States. He successfully concealed his compulsion from his wife, although it was aggravated by idleness and alcohol, as well as his wife's loss of weight, which caused her body to lose the shape he considered "ideal." After little more than seven months of psychotherapy, this man suffered no relapse, although he had been suffering from this fetish for three years.

Binet, the French psychologist who was one of the first to study fetishism, recorded the case of one of his students who was absorbed in reading one day, when he quite suddenly became sexually aroused. A woman, unknown to him, had

A sexual fixation on odor is believed to play a large rôle in the sexual stimulation of the foot fetishist. From an old engraving.—The Bettmann Archive.

seated herself on the same bench. She had a strong body odor; it was to this odor, not unattractive to him, that he had reacted.

Unusual Odors

Not all the odors desired by fetishists are pleasant ones; sometimes disgusting odors are chosen as the objects of fetishism. Dr. Iwan Bloch tells of an old man who derived sexual satisfaction from smelling his woman servant. He did not desire intercourse with her—the odor of her body was sufficient. He demanded only that she wash no oftener than once a week. When she did, he was able to detect it immediately, and at once dismissed her.

The foot fetishist is most often attracted by the unwashed foot, and it may be the smell which stimulates him. Dr. Karpman tells

of a male homosexual who preferred a partner who had not bathed for several days.

Since the fetishist desires not the woman, but her odor, he can sometimes find satisfaction in objects separate from the person. A large factor in clothing fetishes is perhaps not the garment itself, but the odor which clings to it. Handkerchiefs are often desired by fetishists, as are the more intimate articles of feminine apparel, such as stockings, corsets—or panties. Since the odor of the wearer clings to her clothing, it is possible that the garment is desired mainly for its smell.

There are hair fetishists, who, once they have clipped off the desired locks of hair, derive their satisfactions from handling and smelling it. Certain genital fetishes seem to result from a fixation on the odor of the genital organs.

The sexologist Magnus Hirschfeld recorded cases of women who were unable to resist sexual advances made by any man smelling of the stables.

Kissing the loved one during love-play preceding coitus may be related more to the sense of smell than to that of touch.

To the fetishist, smell ceases to be a component of sexual activity and becomes the *total activity* instead. Usually he makes a ritual of his fetish, and it may lead him to many impulsive acts. He may, for instance, pursue an unknown woman whose smell is stimulating to him, or steal articles of clothing he desires for their odor.

Binet designated those who place great emphasis on the sense of smell as the "type olfactif." Some persons are more sensitive to olfactory sensations than others; but true odor fetishism is due to some experience, perhaps in early childhood, which so conditioned the sexual responses of the individual that he cannot find complete satisfaction in the natural sexual relationship. In all such cases, psychotherapy is indicated.

Treatment

It is valueless to attack the fetish, or to deprive the individual of it. This would only cause him great anxiety and arouse hostility. If the fetishism is to be cured, the trouble must be treated at its source. The individual must be helped to rid himself of his sexual fear of women. The complex attitudes and phenomena of this fear must be brought to the surface; his feelings aired and expressed.

After this fear structure has been demolished, re-education can take place. He can be directed towards the woman as a sexual object, and any further fears can be handled in the working through of the situation. Treatment may take a long time; but it is only through such prolonged therapy that the

Marie de Clèves, Princess of Condé. King Henry III, in his youth, developed a violent passion for this woman. During a ball on a hot evening, she changed chemises, leaving her underclothes, drenched with perspiration, in the wardrobe room. The young prince, walking through the room, was so stimulated by the odor of the chemise that he fell in love with its wearer.—From an old engraving in AESCULAPE, a French medical journal.

direction of sexual desire can be properly channeled, and the person enabled to lead a healthy sex life.

References

The Psychoanalytic Theory of Neurosis, by Otto Fenichel. M.D.
The Sexual Offender and His Offenses, by Benjamin Karpman. M.D.
Odoratus Sexualis, by Iwan Bloch. M.D.

● ● ●

"SEX CIRCUS"

IN Japan the Japanese call Chitose (near the U. S. Air Force base and camp of the U. S. First Cavalry) "the world's most evil town." American GI's have nicknamed it the "sex circus." In it are 564 houses of prostitution, 2,400 prostitutes, 2,000 other girls who claim to be "steady" or "only" girl friends of Americans, and another 4,000 who pour in on paydays. The American commander would like to have a genuine cleanup, with the offending places closed.

—*Tokyo Times*

The serpent has been the symbol of sexual passion for thousands of years. The Christian bishop's staff was originally a rod with a serpent twined around it. Identified in the public mind as a prime cause of expulsion from the Garden of Eden, the serpent has represented sexual forces throughout the intervening millennia. Historically, the serpent is found as a sexual symbol among the Greeks and Romans, and as an object of worship in ancient Egypt. Archeological studies reveal the sexological significance ascribed to snakes by both North and South American Indian tribes. Various religious faiths stigmatize snakes as the beginning of all transgressions. Among African natives serpents have many weird meanings. If certain species of snakes appear in a hut, the husband believes this indicates that his wife has conceived. Many other fantastic but very interesting serpent-sex interpretations are here described by the author, the famed former curator of African Ethnology (Chicago Natural History Museum), who has visited Africa and studied the subject at first-hand.

Sex and the

by Wilfrid D. Hambly, D.Sc.

Curator of African Ethnology (Retired), Chicago Natural History Museum

Antiquity of Serpent Beliefs

MY first interest in serpent beliefs and cults was aroused during a journey in Portuguese West Africa where the Ovimbundu, a Negro tribe, after three centuries of European contact, retain some curious beliefs concerning serpents. I noticed an elderly man wearing a long necklace made from vertebrae of a python. He explained that this amulet would cure his rheumatism, for just as the python is supple, so the stiffened joints of the patient will regain their flexibility. This method of cure is called "sympathetic magic."

A medicine-man — consulted by clients who were worried about their future—used a small divination basket. This he shook to and fro, then paused to see what objects came to the top. He pointed to a small wooden snake, much twisted, and said "This comes to the top to tell me that the man who visits me will have an illness, and will be twisted with pain." In earlier days, dreaming of a snake was a bad omen which meant that the limbs of the dreamer would be

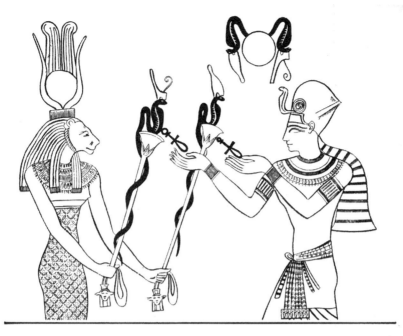

Serpent...

An Egyptian King in the presence of the Goddess Leontrocephale. The Goddess holds in her hand two religious symbols entwined with serpents. In ancient Egypt the snake symbolized fertility and was associated with Phallicism. . . . The King is offering the Ankh (the Egyptian sex symbol of fertility) to the Goddess.—From "Monuments de l'Egypte," by J. F. Champollion.

tied and he would be sold into slavery.*

The serpent is often represented in African woodcarving; this is not surprising when we consider the former prevalence of python worship, especially in Dahomey, west Africa. The Zulus of south Africa still carve elaborate wooden staffs around which one or more snakes are entwined, and they believe that a snake visits a hut to announce a pregnancy. The visitor receives a drink of milk because he

*Hambly, W. D. Serpent Worship in Africa. Field Museum of Natural History. Chicago, 1931.

is the reincarnation of some ancestor who has come to deliver news and a blessing. The fondness of snakes for milk probably gives rise to beliefs that snakes suck the udders of cows, and to numerous legends of snakes that visited women at night to suck their nipples, and in some stories *to impregnate the women!*

The Oldest Serpent Story

In the Book of Genesis is a picturesque account of perhaps the most ancient beliefs relating to sex and the serpent. Adam and Eve were both naked and they were unashamed. Then came the temptation to eat of the fruit of the tree of knowledge. After that there was a sense of shame, and the couple sewed together fig leaves to make aprons.

This story probably has historical relationship to the general beliefs, past and present, of Egypt where serpents played an important part in folklore, religion, and mythology. It is uncertain just when beliefs, fears, and attention to snakes become an act of worship. In Egypt there was a keeping of sacred snakes in temples, and the association of snakes with male and female deities, and such customs may be said to be a form of worship. Technically this worship of snakes is *ophiolatry* (serpent wor-

ship). In Egypt a serpent was not merely associated with a deity, it might be the embodiment of a god or goddess, usually a goddess of fertility and abundant harvest.

In Egypt the snake was associated with Phallicism, worship of the male organ, as the Egyptologist P. Pierret** has pointed out. The ancient Egyptian painting shows three deities. On the right is Reshep, a Phoenician god. The central figure is the Syrian goddess Qadesh who stands naked on the back of a lion, while holding a snake in her left hand. The god Ammon is shown with penis erect: he was patron of serpents which were sacred to him, and some of the serpents, probably those kept in temples, were mummified.

The Serpent and Conception

The Ashanti people of west Africa believe that the python has an influence on human fecundity (productiveness) and this idea they express in a legend. Originally there were two pairs of men and two pairs of women. All the women were barren until a python was sent by the sky god Onyame to inhabit a river. The python bade the men and women stand face to face on the banks of the river while he sprayed them with water. The women conceived and gave their children the name of the river.

The Ibo tribe of southern Nigeria believe that when a snake advances toward a woman, it does so as a sign that she has *conceived*. In this conception there is reincarnation of the spirit of a dead

A Hindu idea of the primeval double-sexed being—the serpents on arm, head and neck are emblems of sex power. Note "ankh" (in crotch)—this is an old Egyptian "sign of life" or fertility. It represents the union of male and female elements. Flower in left hand is another symbol of fertility.

**Le panthéon égyptien. Paris, 1881, pp. 46, 72.

"The Sinfall"—an engraving by Steinbrecher. The temptation of Adam and Eve as related in Chapter 3 of Genesis (Bible) is perhaps one of the most ancient stories pertaining to sex and the serpent. God had forbidden Adam and Eve to eat fruit from the trees in the Garden of Eden . . . but Eve was beguiled by the voice of the serpent and both she and Adam partook of the fruit, for which act they were chastised.

person. The Ibo and Ijaw tribes speak of a tree of life around which a python is coiled at certain times of the year; a visit to the tree at this time causes conception. Hausa women believe that dreaming of a snake means conception. In west Africa several words signify the supposed power of snakes to cause conception. The word *"Bobo"* is applied to a certain group of snakes, and the name is interpreted as *the bearing ones*. There is a group of snakes known as *Sansa* meaning *the procreating ones*. The Fan tribe makes models of snakes

out of clay at a time when boys have reached puberty and are ready for tribal initiation. The sexual side of these rites is emphasized by circumcision and instruction in sexual knowledge, and throughout the ceremonies the models of snakes are *symbols of the male organ*.

Snakes play an important part in the beliefs of several tribes of the Congo region, central Africa. There is a widely spread belief that a snake visiting a hut is an announcement of conception. If a man of the Bangala people awakes

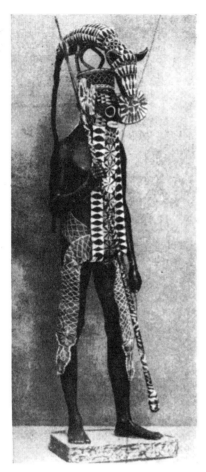

Medicine man of the Cameroons, West Africa. His beadwork ornaments include a large serpent skin as a waistband.—Courtesy, Chicago Nat. History Mus. (Hall D.)

Congo region there is a local belief that rubbing python's fat on the ears and back of a woman will aid delivery of her child.

The idea of ancestors visiting their living relatives in the form of snakes is common among Negro tribes of south Africa. Among the Zulu, harmless snakes enter the huts; these reptiles are *amatongo* (ancestors) and offerings of milk are made to them. The idea of an ancestor taking snake-form and visiting the living to announce a conception, or to give assurance of safe delivery, is common throughout tribes of east Africa.

Python Worship

African beliefs are not confined to ideas concerning snakes as symbols of conception and fecundity. There have been at least two centers of python worship, genuine *ophiolatry,* with ordained priests and priestesses, the keeping of sacred pythons in a temple, and beliefs of the dwelling of a deity within a sacred python.†

The sacred pythons at times escaped from their temples and appeared before young girls, who then danced in a frenzy so that they might be sent to the python house to act as priestesses. Apparently the duties of the priestesses were to feed the pythons and to take part in sacred ceremonies during which the python-god was carried through the streets. There are many folklore stories about the se-

and finds a certain species of snake near him, he assumes that his wife has conceived. The snake that makes such an announcement is respected by sprinkling a little camwood powder over it. There are many instances of the use of snake's fat in preparing magical ointments, and in the northeast

†Duncan, J. Travels in West Africa in 1845-6. London, 1847.
Ellis, A. B. Several works published in the period 1887-1894.
Skertchly, J. A. Dahomey As It Is. London, 1874.
Bosman, W. Description of the Gulf of Guinea. In Pinkerton's Voyages and Travels. London, 1808.

ductive influence of the python over beautiful girls. One writer of the period 1874 speaks of *snake wives* devoted to python-temple service, but in reality concubines of the priests. Ellis mentions two thousand wives of the python temples who were secretly married to the priests. In all rites accompanied by erotic dancing the priestesses give themselves up to sexual unrestraint. They say that the python god possesses them, and it is he who makes them pregnant. The Ijaw tribe of Nigeria had a definite belief that the husband of a priestess in the python-temple was a serpent, and for such a female sexual intercourse with a man was forbidden. Every eighth day the water spirit in python form rose from the river and visited his wife, who was under obligation to remain alone in her hut, and not to go out after dark. A visit from the python god caused his priestess wife to dance in ecstasy and to utter oracles while under spirit possession.

Canon J. Roscoe,* who spent twenty-five years in east Africa, speaks of a python temple on the shore of Lake Victoria Nyanza. A priestess fed the python with milk from sacred cows and she was required to remain celibate, which suggests that the python-husband idea prevails. Moreover, the name of the sacred python was always a *male* name. The special time of python worship was at new moon at which time married men, especially the husbands of barren women, made sacrifices to the python,

and requests for offspring. There is implication of a python-fertility cult in the belief that sacred cows supplying the python with milk belong to the god *Mukasa* whose wife is a female python. At one time the king of Uganda sent the headmen of each district to ask the python to grant many children to the royal house.

Serpent Sex Beliefs Worldwide

Astonishingly similar beliefs respecting sex and serpents are to be found in all parts of the world, and at all periods of recorded history. The serpent is not merely a symbol of human conception, sexual potence, and fecundity; the reptile is connected everywhere with water, rain, the rainbow, and

Native of the French Sudan holding sacred snakes.—*After Hostains-D'Ollone. Mission of the Ivory Coast (Sudan) and French Guinea.*

---

*Python Worship in Uganda. Man, Article No. 57. 1909. Man is published by the Royal Anthropological Institute, London, England.

Sacred house for python worship in Dahomey, West Africa. From Skertchly's "Dahomey As It Is." Serpents have many weird sexual meanings to African and other natives in many parts of the world, as explained in the accompanying article.

●

fertility of the soil. Beliefs relating to human beings are only a small part of many ideas about serpents: but all such ideas are alike in associating the serpent with abundant reproduction.

The aborigines of Australia are a simple stone-age people with few possessions, but they have a rich mythology which includes many ideas about rainbow snakes and ancestors in snake form who are the heads of totem clans. Rainbow snakes guard waterholes and these reptiles can impart a peculiar power to medicine men. In some regions snakes are painted on wood or rocks as part of a rainmaking ceremony.

Egypt is not the only country of the Near East where serpents symbolized fecundity. In Babylon, Serakh was a snake god who was the deity of abundant grain harvests. Arab beliefs about snakes as guardians of wells are widespread: also the idea that the serpent guardian of water can grant conception, or wish barrenness on women. Among the Nagas of Assam, east of India, the dream idea occurs again: a man who dreams of a cobra takes this as an indication that his wife has conceived. Widely spread in India is the belief that women will conceive if they make offerings at small village altars known as *snakestones;* to kill a cobra is sure to produce *sterility*. The Ainu, a primitive people of north Japan, believe that offended snakes cause the evils of childbirth.

America, North, Central, and South, provide instances of serpents associated with human and general fertility. Pueblo Indians believe that the snake clan has descended from the union of a female snake and a man. These ancestors gave birth to snakes which changed into human form. The snake is associated wtih rainfall and abundance of maize. The Hopi Indians have a fertility rite in which rattlesnakes play an important part. Symbols representing corn, rain, and lightning are set out in the kiva (room in an Indian dwelling). Priests of the snake fraternity carry snakes (rattlers) in their mouths, and at the end of the ceremony these snakes are set free to the four points of the compass to induce rainfall.

S n a k e m o u n d s, representing horned or feathered serpents, are found in Ohio and other states. To many Indian tribes the snake symbolized abundant water supply and *fertility,* and in Mexico among the Aztecs the goddess Cihuacohuatl was a serpent woman from whom the earth was peopled. Tonantzin (our mother) was represented in Mexican art with a large male serpent as her consort. African beliefs and ceremonies have prevailed in the West Indies, particularly Haiti, and in Guiana, South America, as a result of the importation of Negro slaves from the parts of Africa in which python worship and snake beliefs were elaborated. Reports state that *voodoo* worship in Haiti included the feeding of a sacred snake, the appointment of priests and priestesses, dancing, spirit possession by the snake god, and consultation of the snake god regarding the future. All this is distinctively African.

European cultures are replete with snake beliefs of the sex-potence and fertility type. French medieval architecture represented folklore stories of serpents sucking the breasts of women, and in Grimm's "Teutonic Mythology" there is a story of a snake creeping into the mouth of a sleeping woman and causing pregnancy. The parent snake became the constant guardian of the child. Siward, king of the Goths, presented his daughter Alfhild with a snake that grew up with her as a guardian to protect her chastity.

Greek and Roman culture was richly endowed with beliefs relating to sex and the serpent. At the shrine of Apollo snakes were fed by a naked virgin priestess. At Epirus the signs for a rich harvest were favorable if the sacred snakes of the temple ate the offerings of cakes and honey. Olympias, the wife of Philip, was visited by the god Ammon in the form of a serpent. The serpent was found lying by her while she slept, and the result of this serpent-human union was the illustrious Alexander the Great, who cried for more worlds to conquer.

Zeus, in serpent form, violated Persephone who then gave birth to Dionysus, himself a god who occasionally a s s u m e d serpentine form. When worshipping Dionysus, women placed snakes in their hair and round their bodies. Greek mythology states that the mother of Aristomenes had sexual relations with a god in serpent form, so also had the mother of Aratus. The serpent was named Asklepios. Such stories are related to the fact that barren women visited the temple of Asklepios. There they slept and were impregnated by the serpent god who visited them in their dreams.

A feature of some Roman snake cults was the test of virginity. Girls were taken to a cave at Lanuvium each year, and there they made offerings to sacred snakes. If the snakes accepted these food offerings the chastity of the girls was proven, and a rich harvest was predicted. The forms of expressing the snake-fertility idea are many and varied.

Why Serpent Symbolized Reproduction

Snakes swim well and inhabit moist places in country where water is abundant, and in dry lands where rainfall is seasonal, snakes hibernate during drought, then come forth in abundance with the first rains. These facts are logically connected with the beliefs that snakes symbolize water and abundance of crops. Female snakes lay many eggs, and these are no doubt found by native hunters, and in case of the viviparous snakes (those bringing forth their young alive) there is a numerous and impressive progeny, alert, and at once fending for themselves. The snake has a habit of shedding its skin,

and I think that this fact might suggest a new life and a resurrection. With regard to mythology, the tales have some factual foundation. There are cobras that spit their venom, hence ideas of *fire-spitting* serpents, and some pythons are of monstrous size, even twenty-five to thirty feet. It is possible that the expanding hood of the cobra suggests erection of the male organ, and we may be sure that the peculiar structure of the penis in snakes has not escaped attention. Every snake has a double penis, and in some species of snakes each half of the penis divides, thus giving a quadruple structure. The male organ has to be withdrawn by invagination (by introversion of the vagina), and consequently snakes remain in the act of copulation for a considerable time.

Beliefs of illiterate people are often scornfully dismissed as meaningless superstitions, but in the case of sex and the serpent I think there is a strong probability that the structure and habits of snakes have provided logical reasons for the world-wide beliefs in the serpent as an emblem of sexual potence, abundant food supply, and human fecundity.

Large wooden serpent, probably a python, carved in wood and measuring about ten feet long. Cameroons, West Africa. Displayed in Hall D, Chicago Museum of Natural History.

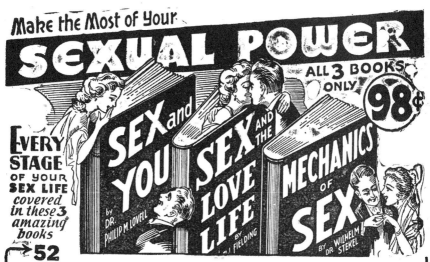

Ten Types of Women . . . .

by Hippocrates, Jr.

WHAT wife does not like to be told that she is different!

Wives want to be loved for their feminine traits and yet be told that they are different from all other women. It is true that discrimination will show that women really do differ from each other, but it is also true that wives fall into certain types. Women have always been regarded as something of a mystery, and the existence of types did not help the solution of the mystery in the least.

With the discovery of hormones (internal secretions in the blood) the problem is not quite so puzzling as it used to be. It is now known by all students of the subject that these hormones play a most important role in the physi-

1. Athletic type. Above is shown Diana, Goddess of the Fruitful Protector of Forests and Animals. From a woodcut at Paris Museum.

2. Masculine type. This is a reproduction of the sculpture: Huntress of the North. From a woodcut by E. Hubner.

Hormones in varying proportions in a woman's system considerably influence her nature. A woman's hormone system is much more complicated than that of a man. The success of a marriage is often due to the man's choice of a woman whose nature is harmonious with his own.

cal appearance and mental makeup of men and women. Part of the mystery of women may be due to the fact that a woman's hormone system is far more complicated than that of a man. *Her varying moods depend somewhat on the hormones released in different amounts according to the stage of her menstrual cycle.*

The principal organs which supply these hormones in the woman are the ovaries, the adrenals, the thyroid, and the pituitary. In the average woman all these glands supply their hormones in just the proper amounts. However, we may all be thankful that the "average" woman just about does not exist, for she is a very drab and colorless person. When the hormones are present slightly in excess or are deficient in a small degree, the girl or woman becomes a person of color and charm. Sometimes these deficiencies and excesses exist to a

3. Sickly type. The Greek Slave. Marble statue by Hiram Powers, Corcoran Gallery, Washington.

4. Romantic type. Above is Venus de Milo, famous ancient Greek statuary found in the ruins of an Emperor's palace at Rome.

5. Seductive type. This is Hebe, Cupbearer of the Gods and Personification of Youth. Sculpture by Antonio Canova.

marked extent, and it is then that the doctors must correct the difficulty by supplying the deficiency or by surgery.

Based on these excesses or deficiencies of the four hormones mentioned above, many types of women can be mentioned. This is really very important for a man to consider, for although women dream that they can change a man by marrying him, no man ever deludes himself that he can change a woman by marrying her. A man had better be cautious in choosing a woman to become his wife, because the type of woman she is before marriage is the type of wife she is going to be. The ten most common types of women are described below.

1. The aggressive, *athletic* type of woman is very commonly met. Her activity can be traced to an excess of adrenalin in the blood. Adrenalin is the hormone secreted by the two glands placed on top of the kidneys. The athletic girl reflects the fresh air and sunshine of the outdoors. She looks best when in simple sport clothes. Quite often she becomes muscular because of her vigorous participation in sports, but she avoids becoming ungainly by maintaining her feminine traits.

2. The utterly *masculine* type of woman who likes to wear mannish clothes is an example of the woman in whom there is an excess of adrenal secretion. She is not athletic, for she does not have the

6. Emotional type. Above is from a sculpture of a statue in the British Museum.

7. The Tall type. Shown here is Venus by Cranach, famous medieval artist.

8. The Doll-face type. Shown above is Psyche. After a statue by W. Von Hoyer.

endurance of the athletic type. However, she does have a great deal of power in her muscles. Very often she has coarse hairs on her chin and around the corners of her mouth. These hairs may be traced to a deficiency of ovarian hormone. It is very common in medical practice to find that women having an excess of adrenal hormone are deficient in ovarian hormone. The two seem to compensate each other in amount so that when one is deficient the other is present in larger amounts.

3. As a contrast to the athletic girl is the weak, *sickly* girl. She seems to be ailing, and lacks color both in her cheeks and in her personality. She is anemic, and prefers to sit passively watching rather than to participate in sports. If she does go into some activities, she tires very soon. Her thin shoulders and flat chest are due to a deficiency of the ovarian hormone. This condition very often exists to a serious extent, so that the missing hormone is supplied by medical treatment, but when the condition is slight the woman often is considered charming in that she is weak and sickly as a member of the "weaker" sex is popularly supposed to be. This idea, of another decade, is rather out-of-date today.

4. The *romantic* girl probably can attribute her nature to an excess of pituitary hormone in her blood. She likes companionship and is socially in demand.

5. The *seductive* type of woman

9. The Maternal type. This is a reproduction of a sculpture of Venus of the Capitol.

10. The Frigid type. Illustrated above is Queen Elizabeth, Queen of England. From a portrait by Hans Holbein. Elizabeth had an anatomical defect and never married.

owes her appearance and feelings to an excess of ovarian hormone. Her well-formed, voluptuous body is physically attractive to men. She is often a man-chaser, as she craves masculine attention. She likes to play the vamp.

6. Everyone has seen the gushy, *emotional* woman. She is easily moved to tears or to laughter. She is restless, and has a tendency to lose weight. Her condition is due to an overactive thyroid.

7. *Tall* girls owe their size and height to the fact that a small gland at the base of the brain, the pituitary, is overactive. The hands are usually large, even in proportion to the large bodies. These tall women are almost always clever, and in general brilliant women are of the tall type.

8. The *doll-face* woman is the result of too little secretion of the thyroid or pituitary, or of both. Quite often while attractive of face and ankles, the doll-face is rather stout around the waist. This type of woman generally keeps her infantile expression throughout life, and is quite sluggish of mind. She cannot grasp deep thoughts. She is the source of the expression, "Beautiful but dumb."

9. The *maternal* type is caused by a combination of too little thyroid and too much ovarian hormones. Her oversize breasts and her stoutness make her easily recognizable. Avoiding of sweets and treatment with thyroid extracts are often of help to women of the extremely maternal type.

10. Finally there is the type of wife who is cold and *frigid*. Her physical appearance and pessimistic attitude are due to a deficiency of adrenal and ovarian hormones. She is less desirable than the masculine type, for she is also neurotic. She is melancholy, and easily discouraged. Although frigid women are seldom positively attracted to men, they do marry with a scheming intention to acquire a breadwinner. They are not affectionate wives. A suitor should studiously avoid such a woman. It is true that in some instances, when supplied with the necessary adrenal and ovarian hormones, such a woman responds surprisingly to the treatment by becoming sociable and likeable, but such a response is unpredictable. The fact that a good marital technique on the part of the husband may alleviate conditions does not always assure a happy marriage. Keep away from this type!

Wives and women about to be married have often asked their physicians if they can be supplied with the means of changing their womanly type. "Can you supply me with the necessary hormones so that I shall become a certain type?" is a question commonly asked. Unfortunately the answer to that is "No." At present enough is known about hormones to replace deficiencies or control excesses of hormones. But the making of personalities to order seems to be still beyond the realm of possibility.

So, for another few years, at least, wives will have to remain in the type in which they were born —the type which seemed attractive to the men they married. It isn't so bad after all. Perhaps the husband who chooses a woman of a certain type "likes 'em that way."

CURIOSITIES

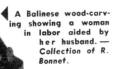

A Balinese wood-carving showing a woman in labor aided by her husband. — *Collection of R. Bonnet.*

The goddess Luna with a "chastity sign." The moon face symbolizes the lunar menstrual cycle. The goddess protects her virginity with the switch in her right hand. The lobster sign represents life or fertility.—*From a 1503 English calendar.*

An early Greek idol, probably a fertility symbol.— *From the Barracco Museum, Rome.*

This wooden carving was found over the door of a hut in which Pacific coast Indians quarantined their menstruating women.

Payment will be made up to $15 for all curiosities in the sexual realm accepted for publication. In the case of two or more identical entries, the one bearing the earlier postmark will receive preference. For full details send for our free leaflet.

EARLY AMERICAN SEX CUSTOMS

Americans of the 17th, 18th and 19th Centuries developed sexual customs which were markedly different from the sex practices of today. This interesting sidelight on our sexual history as a nation will help us better to understand the origin of some of our contemporary sexual behavior.

by Robert M. Frumkin, B.A., M.A.

SEX customs in early America represent, in general, two branches of practices originating from a common stem—that of English culture which, although not common to the Dutch, German, and Swedish settlers of the middle colonies (Hudson Valley, Pennsylvania, and Delaware), was the culture which finally prevailed throughout the country. These two branches of English culture were found in Puritan New England and in the Southern colonies.

In terms of attitudes toward work and leisure, the New England colonists might be designated as a *working* class of people; whereas the Southern English colonists who owned and operated large plantations, by contrast, might be designated as an *aristocratic* class. Whereas the New England colonists lived in village settlements and isolated farms, the Southern English colonists lived

A prominent sociologist, Mr. Frumkin is an instructor in sociology at the University of Buffalo.

on large plantation estates with slaves, hired laborers and tenants. Manual work had dignity in these Northern colonies, but was considered servile in the Southern colonies. Keeping these contrasts in mind, let us review some of the sex, family, and marriage customs of Puritan New England and Southern English colonial times.

Puritan New England

The settlers of the New England colonies came to our shores principally because of religious persecution. Puritans believed that there should be a separation of church and state, and that nonfunctional ritual should not be in religious ceremonies.

In America, however, the Puritans were rigid and orthodox in their religious practices. The religious training of children here was severe. The childhood years of many colonists were heavily overshadowed by the Puritan doctrines of original sin and the punishments of a ghastly hell if the children avoided their rightful duties.

A smock marriage—an early wedding ceremony practiced in colonial New England. The bride stood completely nude in a closet and held out her hand to the groom through a hole cut in the door. Drawing, L. S. Stevens. © SEXOLOGY.

Everywhere there was the explicit and implicit assumption that there was something shameful and immoral in the sexual act. But this emphasis on purity was not only concerned with sex; it permeated every aspect of life. The marriage ceremony became a civil contract, an economic institution. In a sense, to the Puritan, anything which diverted the attention of people from money-making was immoral. Thus, non-functional art, dancing, plays, smoking, drinking— almost any activity or thing which was not immediately concerned with money-making—was evil. It is said that the Puritans regarded money-making as the "most God-given" of occupations.

Among the Puritans there was a strong pressure to marry. Bachelors were specially taxed and penalized in many ways in order to encourage their marrying. Odd as it may seem, a man who was married in those days had more freedom than a single man.

There was among the Puritans a *single* standard of sexual morality — male and female suffered alike the penalties of sexual transgressions. The severest punishment was provided for persons engaging in premarital or extramarital relations. The Puritans did not shrink from prescribing the *death penalty* for adultery with a married or espoused wife. Only in Plymouth and Rhode Island was the law softened to severe flogging or beating. Nathaniel Hawthorne in his classic novel *The Scarlet Letter* told of the added penalty in Plymouth of wearing the scarlet letter "A" upon the breast until death released the adulterer. The records of the Massachusetts Bay Colony show that two persons were executed for adultery in 1644; a third execution is mentioned by Cotton Mather in his famous book *Magnalia Christi*.

Nanette Fabrey and George Guétary starring in a bundling scene which was presented in a New York musical show "Arms and The Girl," some years ago.

In colonial times, parents generally controlled courtship. Puritan law required that a young man, before courting a young woman, obtain her parents' formal permission. For not doing so, he could be fined or imprisoned. Parents in that way controlled who married whom.

Bundling

One well-known colonial courting practice in the Cape Cod and Connecticut valley regions was *bundling* or *tarrying*. This custom was said to be a copy of the similar Dutch practice of *queesting*, which was practiced with the approval of Dutch parents. The custom was said to have arisen from the social and industrial conditions under which courting was done.

It was often supervised by the mother and sisters or both parents, sometimes even the whole family. In this practice, the courting couple would lie together in bed fully or partly dressed, usually separated by a board and covered with a blanket to keep warm. This practice was encouraged, especially among poor families who lived in one-room cabins, to conserve fuel. That economy was the main purpose is proved by this popular verse of the times:

> *"Since in bed a man and maid,*
> *May bundle and be chaste,*
> *It does no good to burn out*
> *wood,*
> *It is a needless waste."*

To the abuses of this practice has been attributed much of the illegitimacy of the times, especially during the period following the French and Indian War when returning young veterans took advantage of this custom to satisfy their long-deprived sexual urges. Yet despite the disrepute into which this practice came, mothers with daughters circulated this poem:

> *"The country girls in clusters*
> *swarm,*
> *And fly and buzz, like angry*
> *bees,*
> *And vow they'll bundle when*
> *they please.*
> *Some mothers too, will plead*
> *their cause,*
> *And give their daughters great*
> *applause,*
> *And tell them, 'tis no sin or*
> *shame,*
> *For we, your mothers, once*
> *did the same."*

Some Puritan clergy defended this practice as being "innocent, virtuous, and prudent," and said that it has prevailed "with ten times more chastity than sitting on the sofa."

Because of improved economic conditions, larger homes, and better social conditions, the practice of bundling was generally abandoned by 1800.

Smock Marriages

Another interesting custom of colonial times was the so-called *smock marriage.* This practice was carried over from England, where it was believed that if a widow were "married in her smock without any clothes or head gier on"

the husband would be exempt from paying any of his wife's debts which she had contracted before marriage. Many such marriages took place in the evening to save the bride from embarrassment. In one case described by W. C. Prime in his book *Along New England Roads,* the bride stood completely nude, wearing not a stitch of clothing within a closet, and held out her hand to the groom through a diamond-shaped hole cut in the door; by this means the wedding ceremony was performed. In Hall's *History of Eastern Vermont* there is another case of a widow who stood naked and hidden in a chimney recess behind a curtain while wedding her groom. Many such marriages were supposed to have taken place where

Robert Owen, 1771-1858, the great 19th Century English Socialist, established an experimental sexual community in New Harmony, Indiana (1825-1827).—*The Bettmann Archive.*

the marrying widow wanted to avoid her past debts.

The Southern English Colonies

Whereas the Puritans settled in the New World for religious reasons, the Southern colonists settled in the New World for political and economic reasons. Aristocratic in their philosophy and way of life, they upheld the religious tenets of the Church of England. Only marriages performed by the Church of England clergy were recognized. Marriage for them was a religious contract, a sacred institution. Yet men had a chivalrous, playful attitude toward women. In contrast to the Puritans who upheld a single standard of morality, the Southern English had a *double* standard of sexual morality. Compared with the Puritan attitude toward sex, however, the Southern English were relatively more liberal. Attitudes were also more liberal toward women in the South. Women of the wealthier families were free to develop the "feminine arts" and become "ladies." Women of refinement were protected and honored by chivalrous gentlemen of the Southern plantation estates. Divorce was extremely rare.

Since the majority of Southern colonists were middle and lower class, it should be emphasized that these contrasting differences, between the Puritan New England and Southern English, apply only to the Southern plantation aristocracy. Unfortunately most of the non-wealthy women of the South were "household slaves" and "breeding animals" like their coun-

terparts in New England. Most married women of the lower and middle classes, both in the North and South, aged rapidly through overwork and too many childbirths, and many died at a very young age. It was not until the Industrial Revolution that a woman's burdens began to be lessened and her status as a human being began to be increasingly recognized.

Utopian Sexual Communities

The Industrial Revolution, which had begun in the late 18th century and was in full force in the first half of the 19th century, led to some bold social experiments, which attempted to substitute for competitive individualism a form of cooperative socialism or religious asceticism. Their object was to rid the world of its inequalities and injustices made sharper by this revolution. The English socialist Robert Owen, who was a great believer in the equality of the sexes, had established New Harmony, Indiana (1825-1827), the land for which he had purchased from George Rapp, another Utopianist. Rapp moved his own religious-socialistic experiment to Pennsylvania where he established a community which he called Economy. Whereas in Owen's community mating was permissible, in Rapp's "Utopia" celibacy was the rule—that is, no sexual relations were permitted. Although the first Rappist group was established in 1815 and had a fairly large following in subsequent years, by 1902 only eight members were left, for an obvious reason—the rules enforcing celibacy. The two best known, yet exactly opposite utopian sexual communities, were those established by the *Shakers* and *Perfectionists*. These we shall now discuss in some detail.

The Shakers

The Shakers founded two communities in the New World in the latter part of the 18th century —one at Hancock, New York, and the other at New Lebanon, New York. The latter still exists today. Ann Lee, sometimes called "Mother" Ann Lee, was the founder of the Shaker movement. She believed that in Christ's second appearance, which was supposed to come very soon, he would appear in a woman's form and that she was that woman.

Ann Lee regarded the sexual relationship as the most sinful of all human relationships. Therefore, chastity was demanded of all permanent residents of the Shaker communities. There was no marriage; the two sexes occupied rooms in separate parts of houses, and when married couples joined the community, they regarded each other as brothers and sisters only. The Shakers were vegetarians and refrained from every worldly vice. Their membership today is about 500. In a sense then, the Shakers were like the Rappists except that the men were the leaders among the Rappists, while among the Shakers the woman were said to have predominated.

In a sense the Perfectionist community founded by John Hum-

Hester Prynne, the heroine of Nathaniel Hawthorne's famous book "The Scarlet Letter," wearing the letter *A* upon her bosom. This was a common punishment for adultery in Puritan New England in colonial days.—*The Bettmann Archive.*

phrey Noyes—first at Putney, Vermont (1838-1847), and then at Oneida, New York, after they were forced to move from Putney. —was a realization of the dreams of socialist Robert Owen for a Utopia in which there was in reality equality of the sexes. Oneida practiced the Perfectionist doctrines of Noyes from 1847 to 1880. The clergy and other high-pressure groups forced the courageous Oneida experiment to end.

Girls did not always rely on the honor system in bundling — sometimes they were well prepared to protect themselves.—From Doten, "The Art of Bundling."

and education of children. When children were wanted, the community decided who should be parents. If longevity and health are evidence of success in this revolutionary type of parenthood and reproduction, the Noyes Perfectionists at Oneida were most successful. For according to reliable reports, the Oneida community was one of the healthiest this nation has ever had. Contemporary family authorities and researchers have deplored the unreasonable prejudices which cut short the Oneida experiment, but none have ever been brave enough to found a "New Oneida." It would take a brave and wise pioneer having the wisdom and knowledge of Havelock Ellis and Bertrand Russell and the courage of Noyes to ever again attempt such an experiment in our times.

The 20th Century

As compared to colonial times, sex relations of today exist more in an atmosphere of free expression and permissiveness, rather than in one of repression and restrictiveness characteristic of Puritan sexual attitudes. Sex is more and more regarded as something that is neither sinful nor shameful, but a necessary, natural, and, indeed, a beautiful and wonderful part of life. In marriage there is greater freedom in the choice of a mate, more respect for the social and psychological needs of prospective mates and less emphasis on the economic factors which played so heavy a rôle in Puritan marriages. Today both husband and wife have more love

According to Ditzion in his *Marriage, Morals, and Sex in America,* Noyes believed that "A free choice of motherhood had to be added to a free choice in wifehood to make a reality of sex equality. The thought was that a man should not embrace one woman exclusively any more than he should hold on to private property. All men in the community should ideally be potential husbands of all women; and all children the pride and joy of all adults." Noyes called this kind of marriage *complex marriage,* which indeed it was.

There were no marriage ceremonies nor permanent ties between couples; the community assumed all responsibility in the support for each other and more consideration for their spouse's need for personal expression. The husband is no longer the supreme ruler, nor the wife the lowest slave.

Today, democracy is heavily stressed in the home. All family members are respected—even children. For all those who say the family and marriage is degenerating, there are thousands more who prove that never in the history of mankind have men *and* women had so much dignity and so much potentiality and opportunity for happiness and self-realization as we have today in America.

References

1. Calverton, V. F.. *Where Angels Fear to Tread*, New York, Bobbs - Merrill, 1941.
2. Ditzion, S., *Marriage Morals, and Sex in America*, New York, Bookman, 1953.
3. Earle, A. M., *Customs & Fashions in Old New England*, London, Nutt, 1893.
4. Frumkin, R. M., "Factors in Successful Marriage: A Review of Major Research Findings," *Journal of Human Relations*, 3, Spring, 1955, pp. 76-79.
5. Goodsell, W., *A History of Marriage and the Family*, New York, Macmillan, 1939.
6. Kirkpatrick, C., *The Family*, New York, Ronald, 1955.
7. Nordhoff, C., *Communistic Societies in the United States*, New York, 1875.
8. Noyes, P., *My Father's House: An Oneida Boyhood*, New York, 1937.

● ● ●

"UPSTAIRS CLUB" GETS YOUTHS IN TROUBLE

SALVADOR J. RAMETTA, assistant district attorney in charge of prosecution at the Adolescents' Court in Brooklyn, stated recently that the upstairs social club is responsible for more sex offenses among young boys and girls than any other one agency with which he has come in contact during his 18 months at the court. He refused to say how many there were in existence but he said the police were closing them up as fast as they got evidence.

"I blame the parents, not the youngsters for these kindergarten call houses," he said at his office. "Somebody should give parents a course in the psychological as well as the physical care of their children. They should be taught to do more understanding and less lecturing."

"If parents had the courage to talk over sex with their children, to understand rather than condemn and to see that the children had plenty of normal physical outlets, things like these upstairs clubs wouldn't exist."

Mr. Rametta saw his first upstairs club a year ago when the Red Flash Club, which held forth in a vacant Brooklyn store, was raided.

"Many of these upstairs clubs are on the street level," he said, "but the majority are upstairs apartments, run so quietly that few of the neighbors realize what they are. That's why they're so hard to locate but we close them up as soon as anyone turns in word. Usually some parent or neighbor calls us. Not even the landlords know what's going on."

In the case of the Red Flash Club a parent called the police.

"The girls didn't make any money," Mr. Rametta said. "It seemed to be some fantastic case of little politics in which 14-year-old girls, who'd belonged to one club, admitted to me that they'd had relations with the Red Flash Club boys in order to put a girl friend of theirs in as president."

He thinks parents pay too little attention to their children during adolescent years.

"What happens is this," he said, "a girl, just as those 14-year-old girls in the Red Flash club case did, comes home from school and finds her mother gone to a movie or shopping. She has nothing to do. Some friend suggests an upstairs club. She goes. She wouldn't have been inclined to go if she'd had something to occupy her mind with at home."

—*Helen Worden in N. Y. World-Telegram.*

MY MOST UNUSUAL SEX CASE

By VERNON W. GRANT, Ph.D.

■ The subject of my most unusual case was a successful journalist of 42 whom I shall call Henry. He was married with two children, very intelligent, and well able to express his feelings about his life-long sexual problem.

Henry clearly recalled a fascination for women's shoes going back to when he was four years old. During grade-school days, he had fantasies of women wearing high-heeled shoes of "dainty design."

At first his interest was entirely esthetic—he appreciated their beauty, but they did not excite him sexually. But by the time he began to masturbate, he found himself using fantasies of shoes.

One day, on discovering some high-heeled shoes in a relative's dresser drawer, he said, "I felt as if I had found a treasure." At twelve, he had dreams in which patent leather pumps were pressed against his sex organs. He also recalls excited reactions to ladies' shoes and a growing appreciation of shapely legs.

His earliest fetish interest apparently was free of a conscious sexual element. The sexual attachment developed gradually. It is notable that Henry was capable of normal emo-

SEX DESIRE FOR SHOES

Dr. Grant, head of the Department of Psychology of the Summit County (Akron, Ohio) Mental Hygiene Clinic, is author of PSYCHOLOGY OF SEXUAL EMOTION.

tional involvement with a woman, free of fetish attraction.

At seventeen he fell romantically in love. He had very intense feelings, but no sexual desires. He suffered a great deal when this relationship ended.

For several years, Henry became absorbed in physical culture, and he developed an exceptional physique. During this time, his feelings toward shoes as well as toward women were relatively weak. However, at age 25 the interest in shoes revived and became an absorbing preoccupation.

He was able to reach climax by fixing his attention on high-heeled shoes, always preferring patent leathers of simple design, and shapely ankles and legs. Movements of the foot and leg, while the woman was sitting or walking, were a source of excitement. He did not care about the leg above the knee.

Orgasms achieved in this way were more intense than those he had in sexual intercourse. Anticipating a normal sex relationship was never as exciting as the opportunity to view beautiful legs with the preferred type of shoes. At especially sensitive moments, Henry was able to reach a climax by gazing at the shoes and legs of a store-window mannequin.

At times, he was somewhat responsive to feminine hands, if they were shapely and well cared for. He also responded to buttocks in movement, but has never been interested in the breast.

The strength of his fetish attraction may be indicated by the fact that Henry repeatedly risked arrest in pursuit of satisfaction. He often drew attention to himself by his obvious intense staring and the length of time he spent in certain public places, such as bus stations and restaurants. He once followed a woman into a store where he previously had been warned that he would be arrested on sight if he entered again.

During a period of unemployment, poor health and low morale, the fetish urge would reach its highest peak. Henry spent days at a time seeking the object of his desire, often to the point of physical exhaustion by prolonged and agonizing efforts to obtain relief, and sometimes suffering severe headaches as a result of nervous tension.

But when, in better circumstances, he was able to satisfy his need with a minimum of strain and anxiety, his fetishism afforded him such fascinated excitement and so intense a gratification that, Henry confessed, he would not wish to be rid of it.

However, it was not Henry's sexual feelings about shoes and legs that made him so unusual, since such fetishism is not uncommon. When Henry encountered the ideal combination of shoes and legs, he experienced much more than a genital-sex reaction. The fetish clearly stirred in him, not sensuality alone, but an emotion very similar to that of being in love. His emotion centered upon the legs and shoes, with an impulse to kiss and caress.

Though the woman who wore the shoes might be attractive in other ways, he was sure she would lose her charm for him without her shoes, or with less attractive legs.

A drawing depicting foot fetishism, taken from a book by Magnus Hirschfeld, the famous German author on sex and human oddities.

A similarity between emotions surrounding fetishism and emotions caused by normal sexual behavior is suggested here. No one would be much surprised at a lover in rapture over beautiful eyes, or hair, or a melodious voice. In the case at hand, the peculiarity lies in the fact that an ordinarily incidental and unnoticed object—namely shoes—has become more important than any other.

Another characteristic of some fetishes is the remarkable power of the object. But we see a normal parallel in the phenomenon of "love at first sight." In both cases, some trait has an immediate and startling emotional impact. In highly-sexed people, moreover, the achievement of climax without contact is not unheard of, though more often occurring in adolescent boys.

Returning to the case of Henry, our shoe and leg fetishist, the solution he finally hit upon to satisfy his urge is of interest.

He once saw a movie based on a search for the most beautiful legs in Hollywood. While watching the film, he experienced great excitement and climaxes.

He then purchased a camera and made films on his own, employing prostitutes whom he supplied with the kind of shoes and hosiery he preferred and instructing them in the manner of walking movements he found most provocative. The films were limited to leg displays no higher than the garter. For several years, he relied almost entirely on this means of sexual outlet.

It has been said that all of us are fetishists to some degree, insofar as we find ourselves strongly attracted to persons with certain types of profile, coloring, or expressions of the eyes, certain mannerisms, and styles of movement or clothing.

In this unusual case, however, the person became wholly unimportant. All of the sexual feelings and emotions of love became associated solely with an item of apparel and minor parts of the body.

"NAKED" AND "NUDE" IN ART

by Magda van Emde Boas

An art historian discusses the many contradictions in people's attitudes toward the artistic nude.

DUTCH papers regularly carry items about petitions against statues or monuments, which in effect always amount to a protest against a naked figure. Perhaps these so-called guardians of public morals are equally active in other countries. In any case, the subject deserves some reflection.

Drawing, painting and modeling of naked male and female bodies are, and have been, part of the education of artists for many centuries. Even during periods of the most fervent puritanism, nobody thought of destroying all the paintings of, for instance, "the day of the Lord" or other Biblical scenes presenting dozens, if not hundreds,

of undressed human bodies. *How then can we explain the contradictions, of which many more could be quoted, in the attitude towards the nude in the arts?*

There are certainly some people who will reject any kind of representation of a naked body as a matter of principle. Let us for the time being refrain from trying to explain such an attitude and its motivations and limit ourselves to the public in general, which is quite prepared to accept the nude in art.

We notice that even the most progressive and the most broadminded person may sometimes be embarrassed by a work of art that he considers provoking in an unhealthy way.

Let me remind you that I am

Mrs. Boas is a well-known art historian of Amsterdam, Holland.

dealing only with real works of art, where form and content are one and where the artist—a talented and sensitive human being in perfect control of his technique—has created something out of a heartfelt need to communicate his feelings, ideas and experiences to his fellow men.

Pornographic drawings or paintings whose special aim is to stimulate the senses are quite a different matter and will not be considered in this article.

Our question then is: *Where in real art is the limit to that which we still experience as art, and at what point and why do other products of human skill become distasteful and embarrassing?*

Perhaps the language we use can help us a bit further. A "nude" is a human body as nature has created it, whereas a "naked" body is associated in our mind with undressing and the taking away of covers and garments.

I should like to suggest that a naked body in art, one that strikes us as being undressed, consciously or unconsciously reminds us of the undressing act and therefore is more likely to offend our feelings than a nude, which presents the human body as nature has created it.

To the first group belongs in any case the "semi-nude." From real life we know only too well that a partly-dressed body is much more stimulating erotically than a totally naked one and the same applies to art as well. Which proves that all the famous draperies and "fig-leaves" used by moralizers as a "cache sexe" (a sex concealment device) lead to the opposite result.

Nevertheless, even a nude can provoke quite different feelings and sensations. Sometimes it is felt that abundant display of female flesh increases the "nakedness." Indeed, a nude by the fa-

The sensuous, fleshy nudes of Peter Paul Rubens, "The Three Graces" (Prado Museum, Madrid, Spain), right, appeal to the senses more than the chaste Venus rising from the sea in Botticelli's famous painting (in the Uffizzi Gallery, Florence, Italy).

284

plicated and difficult to analyze, that is decisive in this matter; the painter from the Catholic Southern Netherlands in the 17th Century has quite a different mental attitude from this great fellow-artist in the Calvinistic North.

I do not think that we can fix by definition what can be considered a "nude" and what is "naked." In addition to the means of expression and the temperament of the artist, there is the attitude of the observer himself and the way he is "conditioned" which have to be taken into account.

Somebody who was brought up to consider the human body as something obscene will certainly react quite differently from a person with a more healthy and sound attitude towards sex.

The thesis that a frustration of our natural impulses leads to a strong reaction in the opposite direction, applies here as well. Perhaps this is the real explanation for some of the persons most fervent in their desire to destroy certain statues and monuments. The pre-conditioning might equally explain why in one country a statue will be considered a "nude" and in another it might appear very "naked."

To continue our example of Rubens and Rembrandt, we might

mous Flemish painter, Peter Paul Rubens, certainly appeals to the senses more than a slender Venus from the Italian Renaissance, and we are inclined to call the Rubens' female more naked.

Still, actual weight cannot be the only reason for this effect; if we had to apply the vital statistics of a present-day jury in a beauty contest between some of the models of Rubens and Rembrandt, for instance, I am sure we would not find them very different.

And yet the sensual appeal of Rubens is infinitely stronger than that of Rembrandt. It is the whole of his vision and conception of women, something far more com-turn to the difference between modern sculpture in Holland and Belgium. Many of the Belgian nudes are very naked in the eyes of a Dutchman and it is hardly conceivable that a Dutch town would put the funny little mascot of Brussels, the "Manneken Pis" (urinating little man) outdoors in a public place.

Another factor not to be neglected is the climate. Even the most beautiful nude in a park on a chilly day makes me shiver. In order to enjoy a work of art, one has to be able to identify oneself with it not only mentally but physically as well, and there are countries where the weather hardly ever permits one to enjoy nudes in the open air. In southern countries this is of course entirely different.

Thus we see that "nude" and "naked" are anything but absolute notions; on the contrary, they have to be used extremely carefully. Just one example to illustrate it: the painting of a naked female may be in perfect accordance with the above-mentioned criteria for a nude, but surround it by males or females who are not only dressed, but very much

so and the nude will become most shockingly naked.

Perhaps this is one of the reasons why Manet's famous "Dejeuner Sur l'Herbe" (Breakfast on the Grass) caused such a scandal. Similar sensations are quite deliberately behind many of the paintings of the Belgian surrealist Delvaux.

I hope I have made it quite clear that the notions of naked and nude do not in any way constitute a verdict with regard to a work of art or the moral standard of an artist. The difference is just the expression of different mental attitudes, based among other things on all sorts of historical and social circumstances.

In his book *The Nude,* the British art historian Sir Kenneth Clark quotes a Professor Alexander as saying: "If the nude is so treated that it raises the spectator's ideas or desires appropriate to the material subject, it is false art and bad morals." *In reply, Clark declares his opinion that "no nude, however abstract, should fail to arouse in the spectator some vestige of erotic feelings . . . and if it does not do so, it is bad art and false morals."*

The "Mannekin Pis"—a noted landmark in Brussels, Belgium—has received innumerable gifts of clothing from visitors to the city, who are shocked by its nakedness.

Curiosities

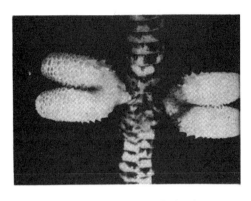

THE MALE SEX ORGAN of the *Both-* ▲ *rops insularis*—a rare and deadly snake found on a tiny island off the coast of Brazil. The organ consists of a double hemipenis on each side of the tail, equipped with strong spines which prevent withdrawal during copulation.

THE FEMALE FIGURE at the ▲ base of this carved drum represents fertility. The sacred instrument is used by the *Bamendjo* tribe of Cameroon, Africa, in rituals of ancestor-worship. — *Courtesy, Chicago Natural History Museum.*

AFTER FIRST MENSTRUATION, girls ▲ of the *Bechuane* tribe in Africa wore these grass or cane bodices around their breasts. —"*Das Weib,*" Ploss-Bartels.

SEXOLOGICAL INVENTIONS

by James L. Harte

Strange are some of the inventions—impractical or harmful—proposed in the past, intended to remedy or improve sexual practices, conditions or defects. Based on information gathered from original sources, the following article describes the inventions and reports the extravagant claims of the inventors.

SEX facts and functions are nowadays discussed freely. Books that would have been concealed a generation ago now appear on best-seller lists. Civic and social groups listen to speakers on subjects that in grandfather's day would have been taboo—even between husband and wife! Dr. Alfred Kinsey has made sex a subject of everyday discussion in the home. The years of the past have brought misinformation as well as knowledge. That this is so is indicated by the beliefs and actions of yesteryear.

Devices to Prevent "Self-Gratification"

Many inventors were misled by erroneous thinking on sexual subjects. Ellen E. Perkins, a Minnesota woman, was granted a U.S. patent No. 875,845, in 1908, for *Sexual Armor*. Her invention was little more than a *chastity belt for*

males to prevent what she explained in her patent application as "the deplorable but well-known cause of insanity, imbecility and feeble mindedness, especially in youth—self-gratification."

This device, which would have done credit to a master of torture, consisted of a metallic crotch in two parts, one clamping over the male organs in front, the other clamping to the rear. A gate, which moved upward to the rear, could be unlocked by an attendant to allow for the obvious. The front plate, however, could not be opened in any way to permit the wearer's hands access to this part of his body, this piece being "perforated so that liquid may be passed therethrough." This metal crotch was affixed to a "flexible leather garment," an arrangement of leather straps over the shoulders and about the waist, to hold the entire device

About the Author—James L. Harte is an ex-newspaper man, now a free-lance writer. His fact and fiction articles have appeared in over 300 magazines, including *Nation's Business*, *Reader's Digest*, *Brief*, *Extension*, etc. He is the author of eight books, two of which were "ghosted" medical books. He is Washington, D. C., correspondent for several journals.

in place. This harness was padlocked just behind the shoulders of the wearer, thus doubly assuring against its removal.

"When properly made and fitted," the inventor described, "this may be worn with very little if any discomfort, and when properly covered by garments the fact that it is being worn will not be noticeable." Expansion of the male organ, she insisted, would be prevented, so prohibiting the *melancholy human tragedy of self-gratification,* ultimately curing this *disastrous practice* while allowing the wearer all necessary personal liberty.

Ellen E. Perkins was not the first to be horrified by the thought of the "tragic effects" of male self-gratification. The files of the U. S. Patent Office reveal a patent (No. 587,994) granted in 1897 to one Michael McCormick of San Francisco for a device which would have inflicted upon the wearer much pain and discomfort.

McCormick called his invention a "Surgical Appliance" to accomplish three purposes: "To prevent involuntary nocturnal seminal emissions; to control waking thoughts; and to prevent self-gratification." This device consisted of a metal shield, shaped to fit the abdomen, held by a belt about the waist, locked at the back. The lower portion of the plate was fashioned into a tubular affair through which "the male organ is passed through." The tube could be adjusted to the size of the organ. Within the tube, protruding toward the organ, were a number of "pricking-points," as described by the inventor. "Now," his patent application explained, "when from any cause expansion in this organ begins, it will come in contact with the pricking-points and the necessary pain or warning sensation will result."

"If the person wearing the device be asleep, he will be awakened or recalled to his senses in time to prevent further expansion." "If through forgetfulness or any other cause his thoughts should be running in lascivious channels, these will be diverted by the pain from the pricking-points." "Voluntary self-gratification will be checked as the wearer cannot find relief without removing the appliance."

Joseph Lees, a Summit Hill, Pennsylvania, inventor, in 1900 (U.S. patent No. 641,979) was concerned with the weird ideas of the time in the matter of sexual habits and he patented a *surgical appliance* which was also of the chastity-belt type. This appliance was composed of a locked "receiver for the penis" fastened to the male body by means of a waistbelt. In the words of the inventor, this device was "especially adapted to prevent nocturnal seminal emissions and which—when worn— will prevent the bedclothes (from) unduly heating the genital organs. In the event of an erection of the penis it will automatically sound an alarm sufficient to awaken even a heavy sleeper. The device may be adjusted to any size of penis and the spinal column and the cords leading to the testicles will also be kept cool while the device is worn."

This inventor, so illogically concerned with keeping the cords to the testicles cool, suggested a single cell battery with connection to contact points within the sheath which held the penis. Erection was supposed to cause the closing of the circuit, ringing the bell attachment.

In 1906 Raphael Sonn, of Georgia, patented a "Sanitary Appliance" (U.S. patent No. 826,-377). This style of male chastity belt was designed to prevent — without interfering with the functions of nature or under *normal* conditions causing discomfort or pain—the practice of self-gratification in males, and the curing thereof.

The Georgian conceived a sheath to hold the male organ, the sheath, of a suitable material of lightness, strength and non-corrosive properties, to cover the organ in its natural state. About the sheath were "clamping members" and "gripping elements." These, upon expansion of the organ encased in the sheath, would close and cause pain and, by this method of torture, prevent the wearer from indulging in the practice. The "clamping" and "gripping" elements were operated by a powerful spring contained in the hinges holding them to the sheath. The entire apparatus would be belted to and locked on the person.

Horace Taggart, of Akron, Ohio, in 1897, invented a device for "assisting anatomical organs" to perform normal functions. A plain, hard-rubber belt, the Taggart appliance was to "produce elastic compression of the dorsal

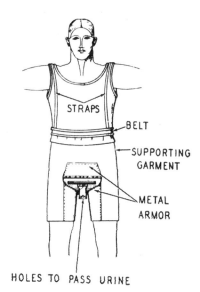

Ellen E. Perkin's patent (No. 875, 845) for male "sexual armor," intended to prevent self-gratification. Worn like a chastity belt, it was locked on the person and had a perforated gate through which urine passed.

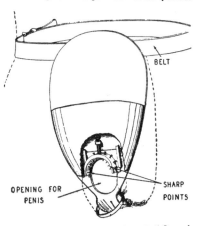

Michael McCormack was issued U.S. patent No. 587,994 for a device intended to prevent nocturnal seminal emissions; to control "waking thoughts," and to prevent self-gratification. If male organ became tumescent, sharp points pricked the skin and discouraged any further erections.

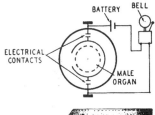

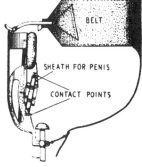

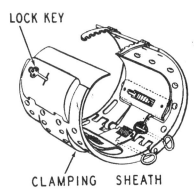

Joseph Lees (U.S. patent No. 641,979) invented a male chastity belt to warn the wearer (by ringing a bell) when an erection occurred at night, in order to prevent nocturnal emissions, etc. Erection caused electrical contacts to close a bell circuit.

LOCK KEY

CLAMPING SHEATH

Raphael Sonn (U.S. patent No. 826,377) patented a device to discourage self-gratification. It comprised a sheath having *clamping* and *gripping* members which, upon erection of the male organ, closed in and caused pain, thus discouraging self-gratification, the inventor claimed.

vein when the generative organs have become so inactive as to refuse to perform their natural duties." This, claimed the inventor, assured that any abnormal or unnatural male organ could achieve proper expansion and maintain rigidity for the purpose of sexual intercourse.

"Coital Aid" Device

A New York inventor, Louis Hawley, in 1907 was granted a patent (U.S. patent No. 844,798) for a "Surgical Appliance" likewise to assist anatomical organs in the performance of their natural duties. "A certain percentage of men," Hawley stated in his application, "are afflicted with congenital or acquired malformations (of the male generative organ) which prevent normal intercourse. Though the organ may be apparently healthy and subject to natural excitement under ordinary conditions, it yet fails in its duties when called upon for the actual performance thereof." Hawley therefore guaranteed his device as a "simple, inexpensive and efficient device for use on the male generative organ during copulation."

This Hawley invention was a sheath, or tubular jacket as he explained, of tough but elastic material which fitted over the male

Horace D. Taggart's patent No. 594,815 —a device for assisting the male sexual organ in performing coitus—comprises a ring of proper elasticity and shape to slip over the penile organ. It is supposed to exert pressure on the dorsal vein and slow up the circulation of blood through the organ, causing it to remain rigid for a longer time.

organ. An opening at one end permitted the protrusion of the *glans penis,* as a supporting web, of elastic material, within the sheath held adhesively to the organ, maintaining rigidity. "Abutments designed to rest against the body and prevent longitudinal movement in that direction," the Letters Patent specified, "when applied to an organ having only partial ability to become erect, the appliance supplies the necessary rigidity for a time sufficient to accomplish the purposes intended, while by reason of the uniform pressure (of the webbed gripping sheath) being exerted on all of the circulatory and expansive parts of the organ the circulation is thereby equalized and there is produced neither sensory anesthesia, blood stasis, or unnatural congestion."

Even in recent years inventors were still concerned with man's inability to maintain his manliness. In September 1915, Lewis B. Hart, of Louisiana, patented a "Generative Organ Appliance" (U.S. patent No. 1,153,072). The patent application stated: "The purpose of the invention is to provide an appliance wherein the generative organ of a male can be stimulated so that an erection may be had, thereby enabling copulation with a female, without discomfort to either, thus insuring satisfying intercourse, irrespective of the advanced age of the male."

Records do not show whether or not the Hart device gave aid to doddering males, nor do records verify the claims for other similar patents. Hart's appliance was "a body, made of rubber, flexible and

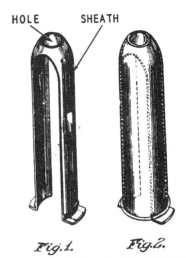

HOLE   SHEATH

Fig.1.   *Fig.2.*

Louis Hawley (U.S. patent No. 844,798) invented a device to assist anatomical organs to perform their functions. It comprised a sheath of elastic material to fit over the penis and by action of supporting (adhesive) webbing inside the sheath, avowedly helped the organ to attain and maintain rigidity for performing marital act.

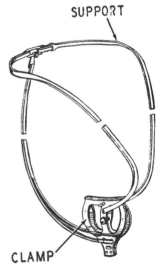

SUPPORT

CLAMP

Joseph J. Martinka (U.S. patent No. 1,328,-176) patented this device for preventing bed-wetting by women. A clamp engaged the labia (lips) of the vulva and compressed them, closing the urethral (urine) outlet.

JAGGED NOZZLE

Josef Flesicher (U.S. patent No. 641,201) patented a design for seltzer-bottle spouts, having sharp jutting edges to discourage its use as a syringe for douching female genital organs. Inventors think of everything!

Lewis B. Hart (U.S. patent No. 1,153,072) patented a generative organ appliance for "stimulating" the penis, thereby permitting copulation to be accomplished—"irrespective of the age of the male," he claimed.

resilient, in the form of a sleeve or truncated cone, so that its outer circumference tapers from one end toward the other, adapted to receive the male organ, the latter being more commonly known as the penis of the male gender." "Hook-like catches," as the Louisiana inventor described them, within the thick cone, held to the male organ and firmed it. The larger end of the cone abutted the body of the wearer, the head of the male organ protruding through the smaller end. With this, the inventor claimed, erection could be maintained at any age and "the act of copulating can be successfully performed without injury to the male or female."

Ellen E. Perkins, she who feared for the sanity of the male and so devised her chastity belt to prevent his self-gratification, admitted that some females likewise indulged in the habit. With slight change, she explained, her device could be locked upon a young woman, to serve a similar purpose. The files of the Patent Office reveal few such contraptions for strictly feminine use.

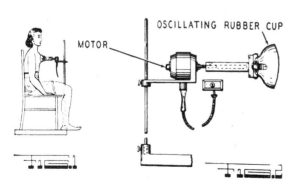

OSCILLATING RUBBER CUP

MOTOR

Peggy Brown obtained this patent (No. 1,-795,073) for a motor-driven bust massager, intended for use in developing the breasts, and also for massaging the breasts to remove lumps formed in the milk after childbirth. Physicians frown on all breast massagers—they can be very dangerous to health.

"Bed-Wetting" Prevention

Perhaps the most diabolic device ever designed to plague the ladies had no particular sexual objective. It was designed "to prevent bed-wetting by women and girls," patented in 1920 by Joseph J. Martinka, of New Jersey (U.S. patent No. 1,328,176). The Martinka invention resembled the ordinary sanitary belt except that it was made of metal and, at the crotch, was formed into a clamping device. The jaws of the clamp were of celluloid "for the sake of combined lightness and strength." This "Surgical Appliance" would be fitted upon the sufferer and locked on. The clamping portion would be "applied in and to engage the labia of the vulva in such manner as to compress and thereby effectually close the outlet of the urethra, thereby preventing bed-wetting." No mention of the internal pain as the jaws of the clamp prevented a natural function was made by the inventor.

Josef Fleischer, of New York, undoubtedly was unconcerned with any woman's pain, but he felt some concern for a less than wholesome habit which some woman might be addicted to, or so he believed. In 1900 he patented a siphon spout for the tops of bottles of seltzer water and similar fizzes, with sharp, jutting edges to the nozzle (U.S. patent No. 641,201). The object of the invention, its creator stated, was to prevent the use of the siphon *"as a syringe for insertion in certain parts of the female body"*—obviously to prevent douching.

"Bust Developers"

Inventors, both male and female, seem to have been concerned with the problem of milady's *bust*. Hundreds of "bust developers" as well as falsies of all sorts, including *water-* and *air-inflated varieties,* have been patented. Most notable of the developers is the intricate device patented by Peggy Brown, a Connecticut lady, in 1929. Hers is a large, complete and intricate device, with twin rubber cups to be fastened to the breasts. The cups vibrate in all directions, thus—according to the claim—aiding by massage in the development of the bust.

Prevalent interest in the feminine form, with television accentuating the cleavage, has brought new ideas for devices intended to enhance the female bosom. As long as there are sex problems there will be inventions claiming miraculous cures.

In the more sexually enlightened world of today we can but look back on those inventions of yesteryear with the same feeling of incredulity and repugnance that comes to mind when we recall the chastity belt of antiquity.

● ● ●

One of the many forms of penile "crutches" offered to the impotent man. These semi-rigid rubber supports, intended to aid intromission, are considered harmful and are not recommended by SEXOLOGY.

A simple home-made apparatus for cold water treatment to restore breast firmness. The method of using the device is shown at left; the construction of it is shown at right.

Sexology, June, 1946

● ● ●

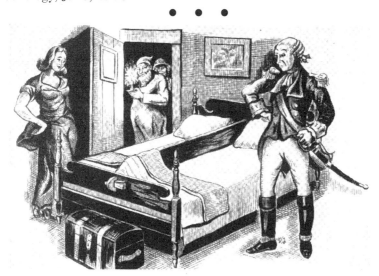

A quaint variation of what we today consider *normal* sexual behavior is the old American custom of *bundling*. A separating board ran through the center of the bed and was supposed to preserve chastity between the man and the woman sharing the bed for the night. Bundling enjoyed its greatest popularity around 1830, particularly in Pennsylvania. A male guest who had to spend the night in a home might have had to sleep with the unmarried daughter of the family. The bundling bed was the answer to the problem.

Sex changes in

aging

*The dramatic lengthening of the life span
of the average adult highlights the importance of scientific study of the process
of aging. Although the outward signs
of age are obvious to everyone, little is
yet known about what goes on inside the
body to cause the changes. Also wrapped
in mystery are many of the sex changes
that take place at various stages of life.*

by E. H. Herrick, Ph.D.

ALTHOUGH aging is com-
mon to all living beings and
begins the day we are born,
it is still a process wrapped in
mystery. We can describe many of
the changes that take place in the
process of aging, but still know
very little about what goes on "inside" the body to cause these
changes. A whole new branch of
medicine, *geriatrics*, has developed
so that aging is being studied as
never before. With the heightened
scientific interest in the subject, the
next few years should tell us
much.

A natural part of aging in early
life is the development of sexual
maturity. For many years it was

Dr. Herrick is Professor of Zoology
at Kansas State College of Agricul-
ture and Applied Science.

believed there were active forces
in the body to prevent this phase
of maturity until a certain age.
These inhibiting forces were supposed to play out, permitting the
body to go ahead and develop
completely.

This early guess has given way
to good evidence that it is the
pituitary gland which starts to produce *hormones,* or special secretions. These hormones in turn
cause the ovaries in girls and the
testicles in boys to develop. There
is now no real question about the
pituitary gland's starting the process of sexual maturity—but we are
still ignorant about what causes
this gland to become active at a
particular age level.

The major sexual maturing
process usually begins about the

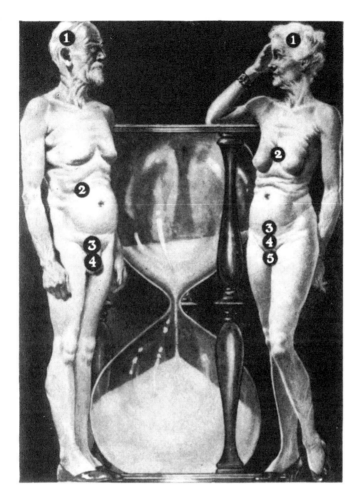

age of twelve in girls. Once the development of the ovaries takes place as a result of activity of the pituitary gland, new hormones are produced by them. One of these hormones produced by the ovaries, estrogen, is principally concerned with such changes of female adolescence as development of the breasts, enlargement of the hip bones, a spurt in general growth and a reshaping of pretty much

Major physical sex changes, as indicated by the numbers in illustration above: In the male, the pituitary gland becomes less active, (1); a gain in weight takes place, particularly at abdomen, as a result of decreasing male hormone, (2); there is likelihood of prostate gland enlargement, (3); there is a decrease in sex hormone produced by testes, less frequent and less vigorous erections, and testicles become smaller and less firm, (4). • In the female, the pituitary gland becomes less active, (1); there is recession of mammary tissue and breasts become less firm, (2); ovaries cease functioning and menstruation ceases, (3); the womb becomes smaller, (4); the vaginal lining becomes thinner and the labial folds smaller and thinner, (5).—*Original illustration by L. Sterne Stevens.* © Sexology.

Changes in the female ovary. At the left is shown the ovary of a nineteen-year-old female. The shriveled ovary at the right is the ovary of a seventy-two-year-old woman.—From *"Das Weib"* by Ploss & Bartels.

the whole body. External parts of the reproductive system develop, and also the internal structures.

Not only does the body change in structure but there are psychological changes too. Interests change and things that seemed important not long before are soon regarded as childish. Girls become very conscious of their age and often drop playmates a year or two younger because they no longer want to associate with "children." They like to feel they are fully adult.

With these changes in interests, boys become important as never before. With the periodic production of hormones, the sexual cycles come periodically too, with each cycle climaxing in a break-down in the lining of the uterus—the menstrual period—about every 28 days.

Changes in the developing boy are just as dramatic but come a little later. With the development of the testicles, male sex hormone is produced. This new material in the body is responsible for the change in the voice, general body development, growth of the beard, coarsening of the skin and toughening of body tissues.

Adolescent boys also have a change in interests. They forget that all things "sissy" were the worst things that could happen to a growing boy. They find that girls are pretty attractive after all. Without the effect of male and female hormones, the main body appearances of the two sexes would be almost indistinguishable.

Books by the late Dr. Alfred Kinsey give much information on the years of life in which there is sexual maturity and activity. There comes a time, however, when physical sex drive lessens in both men and women and the process of aging catches up with a life previously more active.

In women, the "change-of-life," or menopause, is usually much more clear cut than in men, although women show considerable variation in age and progress of change. Most women have at least begun the menopause by age 50, some by 40.

The change in perhaps half the menopausal women is not a conspicuous one. The menstrual periods no longer occur; the end may be sudden or there may be a few irregular periods. The woman may feel very little different from before. If there had been fear of bearing too many children, there is peace of mind. This feeling of freedom may be tempered by a realization that she is no longer young but the common reaction is a wholesome one, with acceptance of things as they are.

The remaining half of the menopausal women experience some, if not considerable, discomfort and mental disturbance. The transition may run through a number of years of irregular periods and associated disorders, or a relatively short time of marked disturbances. The woman may experience "hot flashes" which give her a feeling of "burning up" about the head, neck and shoulders, or more or less over the body. They may last only a few moments or longer. There may be headaches and mild digestive disturbances.

Mental disturbances ranging from mild depression to high nervous tension may occur, with symptoms suggesting the mental disorder of *schizophrenia*. These times of nervous tension may not be recognized by the patient herself and the most tactful suggestion that she needs medical attention may be met by a stormy response. She may feel that those about her are doing everything

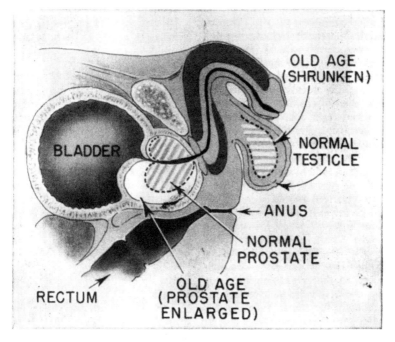

Among the sex changes in men commonly occurring in old age are changes in the testicles and the prostate. Generally, the testicles become less firm and shrink in size, and erections are less frequent. In many men, enlargement of the prostate gland may take place when sex hormone production drops considerably.

possible to make her life miserable and that she is the only one in the household not needing attention. The disturbances cannot be predicted. They vary from very mild to those needing extensive medical treatment.

Menopause disturbances arise from an overactive pituitary gland trying to nudge the unresponsive ovaries into action. Once the pituitary gland gives up and quiets down, the patient again takes up life pretty much as if nothing had happened.

After the menopause, certain changes take place in a fairly regular pattern. The breasts will change in time, for there will be regression of the mammary tissue. The external appearance depends largely, however, on deposits of fat, which is true *before* the menopause as well as after. With deposits of fat present, the breasts may remain little changed in appearance until advanced age. Sexual urge may remain for years after the menopause but this is subject to much variation, just as there are differences in individuals at a younger level.

In advanced age there is regression of the external genitalia. The labial folds (lips of the vagina) become thinner and smaller. Internally, the lining of the vagina becomes thinner and resembles conditions in the pre-adolescent. It is thus more subject to bacterial infections. The uterus (womb) becomes progressively smaller and in some respects resembles the juvenile organ.

Just as ovarian hormones caused the development and maturing of most of the reproductive structures, there is considerable regression of these organs after the menopause when the hormones are discontinued. Once the ovaries have become inactive at the menopause, there is no awakening by any known medical treatment. Egg cells capable of development are no longer present in the ovaries.

Complexions characteristic of the "bloom of youth" are said to be due to an abundance of ovarian hormones. How much credence we can put in this is difficult to say. The claim is made that cosmetic creams containing hormones restore this youthful bloom, but actual proof has not been given.

In men the "change-of-life," *if it actually exists as such,* is usually not an abrupt one. There is a decrease in the amount of male sex hormone produced along in the forties and fifties, but usually the change is too gradual to be recognized well. This is associated with a tapering off in physical activity and sexual drive.

At these age levels the testicles become less firm and actually reduced in size. Erections are less frequent. As a general rule there is reduced fertility but this is one of the most varied features in men. Fertility may remain until ripe old age. Reliable reports of men becoming fathers at ages of seventy, eighty or even ninety are not really rare.

The change in the voice and growth of the beard that began during adolescence are not reversed to any extent. The voice may become thinner and higher pitched, but this may be associated with decline in general body vigor as well as reduced hormone levels. The beard continues to grow if somewhat less actively.

A receding hair line at the forehead and baldness of the hereditary type appear to be a feature of aging, but actually baldness takes place only if there is enough male hormone present. Men completely devoid of male sex hormone do not develop this type of baldness as they approach middle age. Unless men have this family-line type of baldness, sex hormones have very little influence, if any.

A good many men in their late forties take on extra weight. This is due largely to reduced physical exercise and more and richer food. However, the inner-tube-around-the-waist type of obesity is associated with lowered levels of sex hormone. This type of obesity does not regularly occur in men below forty years of age, even with low production of sex hormone.

Enlargement of the prostate gland may take place when sex hormone production has dropped down considerably, but no one knows why most men do not develop this condition even if sex hormones drop to very low levels. It seems strange that the prostate depends on male hormone for its development and maturity, but enlarges to disturbing size in certain individuals when sex hormone plays out.

Experiments on insects and animals to try to determine the effect of sex activity have been quite inconclusive. In fruit flies, mating shortens the life span; but in rats, mating lengthens the life span for the male.

In laboratory animals, the tough connective tissue that develops under the influence of male sex hormone begins to be less tough when the hormone is discontinued. There is every reason to believe that, with lessened production of hormone, the tissues of a man too lose much of their toughness. Other experiments on living animals showed there was greater muscle endurance in animals treated with male hormone.

Although the menopause in women takes place when the pituitary gland is still active, this gland must play a considerable part in the aging process of both men and women. In men the pituitary gland is, without much question, the mainspring of activity of the testes as well as of some other parts of the body. Other glands which become less active as the individual ages—the thyroid, the adrenals and others—undoubtedly also play their rôle in aging.

References

Comfort, Alexander: *The Biology of Senescence,* Routledge and Paul. London, 1956.

Engle, Earl T., and Gregory, Pincus: *Hormones and the Aging Process,* Academic Press, 1956.

Herrick, E. H.: "Tensile Strength of Tissues as Influenced by Male Sex Hormones," *Anatomical Record,* 93:145-49, 1945.

Kinsey. A. C., Pomeroy. W. B., and Martin, C. E.: *Sexual Behavior in the Human Male,* W. B. Saunders, 1948.

Kinsey. A. C., Pomeroy. W. B., Martin. C. E., and Gebhard. P. H.: *Sexual Behavior in the Human Female,* W. B. Saunders, 1953.

Orr, W. H.: *Hormones, Health and Happiness,* Macmillan, 1954.

SEX and **satan**

by Wilfrid D. Hambly, D.Sc.

Curator of African Ethnology (Retired), Chicago Natural History Museum

Witches were supposed to have the power to cause sterility or sexual impotence in an enemy. Witches of both sexes were said to have sex relations with demons. Strange beliefs concerning the association of sex and witchcraft are revealed in the following enlightening article.

WHEN we look into the records of the activities of witches, we must at once abolish the idea that a witch may be any old woman, bent with rheumatism, and having a nose that inclines downward to meet an upturned chin.

Witchcraft is very old, going far back beyond the records of the Old Testament. Witches and wizards were common in western Europe long before the introduction of Christianity into England (597-604). Change from old to new beliefs is a confusing mental process, and it is not surprising therefore that teachings of the Church became confused with the unholy beliefs and practices of servants of the Devil.

It is on record that the priests of Winchester cathedral marched round their edifice against the daily movements of the sun as a protest against their bishop and his conduct. A march of this kind was known in witch's ceremonies as *widdershins,* and was the equivalent of a curse.

Witchcraft spread with the arrival of the *Mayflower,* and was prevalent in New England during the seventeenth century. The Reverend George Burroughs seems to have mingled his Christianity with witchcraft, if it be true that he made puppets (dolls) of wax and clay, and brought them to the witches to be pierced with pins. This was a common device of the witches who wished to harm an enemy.

The Supernatural

Witches and wizards were well organized and widely distributed. All were sworn servants of the Devil, their master, who gave them of his power, taught the spells and routine, whipped them if they dis-

---

SATAN, WITCHES AND SEX — By Tina
During medieval times Witches were thought to have sexual relations with the Devil. This sexual liaison between Witch women and Satan is surrealistically illustrated by our artist. The leering face of the Devil is seen looking down on the figure of a woman (representing the Witch woman), whom he grasps in his hand. The Witch, with upraised arms, caresses the face of Satan. From the right of Satan's face a serpent is seen curving toward the Witch woman. (The snake is a sexual symbol and represents sexual contact between the Witch and Satan.)

obeyed him, and copulated with the women. Presumably the part of the Devil was played by one of the wizards. Christian church members and clerics commonly believed that Satan in various forms could make himself visible.

Witchcraft becomes more understandable when we consider the general background of European life in the Middle Ages. In the absence of natural science, and in view of the opposition of the Church to research in human anatomy, astronomy, and chemistry, explanations of disease and misfortune followed a supernatural trend.

An unseen world was peopled by devils, the imps who served them, fairies, and pixies. The souls of wicked people returned to haunt the countryside. Surgeons consulted the stars to find a time favorable for bleeding their patients (a method used in medieval times which was supposed to cure various

ailments) and by the same means recovery or death was foretold.

When we describe the trial of witches and mention the ordeal to test their guilt it must not be forgotten that such trial was a method approved by the Church. The idea seemed to be that some spiritual power would miraculously save the innocent person.

Witchcraft Is Not Dead

In many parts of Africa today the medicine-man (and woman) is the link with an unseen world of spirits, good and evil. A large wooden image in Chicago Natural History Museum is studded with nails and pieces of iron. The medicine-man in his evil capacity would, by request and on payment, pierce the figure in this way, meanwhile muttering a curse against an enemy of his client.

I have seen a wizard demonstrate his method of discovering a thief. He spun a tortoise shell on a stick and meanwhile mentioned the names of like culprits. He said that the tortoise shell would stop rotating when the name of the real culprit was mentioned. I saw a rain-making dance, and witnessed the questioning of a corpse to find the manner of death, in the hope that the ghost, supposed to remain near the body for a time, would answer the questions.

In literature concerning the history of mankind is an illuminating background for the study and understanding of witchcraft in Europe. A separate study of witchcraft in New England is hardly necessary, for there we find the characteristics of European witchcraft. The New England witches had their "High Frolics" where the Devil appeared in person, sometimes disguised as a deer. Alleged witches had seen the Devil look in at the window. Contracts had been made between women and the Devil. Women were stripped of clothes at their trials and the "marks of the Devil" were discovered on their bodies. All this, and much more we shall find in the reports of trials of witches in Europe in the period 1450-1650 A.D.

Witches and Fertility

Witchcraft was not always hostile to society, in fact there were benevolent ceremonies for making rain, and special dances at which witches and wizards leaped high in the air to stimulate the young wheat by sympathetic magic.

But woe unto the person who offended the witches so that they retaliated by a curse causing sterility or impotence in their enemy. In the year 1608 questioning at trials revealed the astounding fact that witches claimed the power to make male and female sex organs disappear. They asserted they could place a curse on a man so as to paralyze the nerves and muscles necessary to cause erection of the male organ. Or the witches could prevent passage of the semen into the female. These curses were sup-

Sex and Satan in Africa—a wooden figure studded with nails, the property of a witch doctor of the Bakongo tribe, Belgian Congo. The figure is in the Chicago Natural History Museum, to whom we are indebted for this interesting photo.

Witchery in Africa—Medicine man of the Vachokwe tribe at Cangamba, Portuguese West Africa. He is performing a mystic rite to locate a thief and make him return to the village.—*Photo courtesy Chicago Natural History Museum.*

posed to be made effective by use of images and herbs.

Yet primarily the power of witches to cause sterility depended on the dedication to the Devil. Babies, children of witches, were brought to the Devil in early infancy to receive power. At puberty the girls were brought to their master for first sexual experience. At trials of witches in Scotland (1590 A.D.) Janet Clark was accused of taking away the natural function from "men's genital members" and of taking away the "secret member" of Johnne Wattis.

In the Belgian - Congo figure studded with pieces of iron, illustrated in this article, there is a large shell having the shape of the female vulva. This was no doubt used in ceremonies to affect fertility favorably or unfavorably. I have seen a medicine-man of Angola (Portuguese West Africa) give a barren wife a slender neckband of hide to which one or more cowrie shells were attached. The cowrie of this kind is a small white shell with lips resembling the external female genitalia (*labia majora*) and is supposed to counteract sterility.

A curious aspect of a witch's life was that, although she was dedicated to the Devil and had sexual relations with him, she might be a good-looking young woman, married, and the mother of normal healthy children. When not engaged in the ritual of witchcraft she could be a competent housewife. In the New England trials several such women were convicted of witchcraft and executed; the crucial evidence seemed to be the presence of the "Devil's marks" on the body.

The most fearful curse the Devil could pronounce was one that would prevent a woman from obtaining a husband or make her marriage barren.

Sexual Contact with Satan

Some kind of sexual ritual has been common in many religions and has even amounted to worship (phallic worship) of the male organ. The cult of witches was no exception, and accounts are so numerous and so well in agreement that the testimony of ritual *marriage to the Devil* must be accepted as factual. An edict of Pope Innocent VIII (1484) refers to witches of both sexes having sex relations with demons.

It was said that the Devil would not have sex relations with a pregnant woman. The Devil offered to lie with Isobel Elliot (tried for witchcraft about the year 1578) but "forbore because she was with child, but later the Devil often met her and had carnal copulation."

Various witches at different trials agreed that during intimacy the body of the Devil was cold and "his seed was cold." This evidence has led to much speculation. Did the man posing as the Devil wear a suit of cold material? Was the male organ an artificial object? The women who suffered this ritual marriage to the Devil complained of the pain of copulation. One witch said that his organ was of great size and twisted in the form of a serpent. This is an interesting point because the serpent has been associated with fertility, and the Devil was regarded as a master who controlled human fecundity.

To make his contract binding for seven years, sometimes longer, the devil demanded a signature in blood. He is reported to have made an incision on the applicant, sometimes with hoof or claw, for he was armed with both. The client then signed the agreement with his own blood. The Devil slightly scratched an infant who was presented to him, but the child so dedicated was not admitted to the high mysteries until the age of twenty years. The blood covenant has a near parallel in an African custom of blood brotherhood. Two men swear mutual help and undying friendship. Each cuts the arm of the other and the pact is sealed by mingling their blood.

Sacred Animals

The witches and wizards, in common with many members of other religions and cults, had their

The Witches of another day made many strange "spell-weaving" concoctions in their cauldrons. The sex angles of witchcraft were numerous. Woe to the man who seduced a fair maiden and was threatened with punishment by a witch.

sacred animals. The Devil himself took many animal forms, and witnesses at various trials swore they had seen him as goat, deer, dog and many other creatures. This transformation into animal form, a privilege which the Devil be-queathed to his servants, is not unknown in various regions. The Egyptians had many sacred animals including the cat which was worshipped at the town of Bubastis, and on death the sacred animals were preserved as mummies. In west Africa pythons were not many years ago kept as sacred animals that were fed by a priest. A python carried in a religious parade was said to contain the python god himself. In the records there are instances of the animals themselves being tried as accessories of witchcraft, and a death sentence was pronounced.

The court evidence agreed that witches had their 'familiars,' "some hath one, some hath more . . . as like cats, weasels, toads or mice whom they nourish with milk . . . or by letting them suck now and then a drop of blood." Our *black* cat of Halloween seems to be the wrong color, for the cat of a witch was usually a yellow brindled pussy.

In the year 1664 a witch named Alice Duke of Somerset County, England, declared she had a 'familiar,' a little cat that sucked her breast at night, and put her in a kind of trance. Another witch confessed that the Devil in form of a hedgehog sucked her left breast at five o'clock in the morning.

The legal evidence assures us of many contracts made between witches and the Devil, but seldom do we hear of breach of contract. The rule seems to have been, once a Devil's servant always a servant. There is evidence showing the renewal of contracts, but beatings and curses were the lot of those who attempted to renounce their pledge to Satan.

As an exception to fidelity, a witch at Arras in France (1460 A. D.) tried to break her vows. She reported that the Devil beat her cruelly with "a bull's pizzle." This means that the weapon was the dried penis of a bull, which makes a formidable whip. There are also references to the scourging of women by a Devil who used cords.

Witches Orgies

Although an anthropologist would naturally sift the legal evidence given in law court records with regard to orgies, the poets must be credited with the tersest and most colorful accounts of midnight revels of the witch cult. These poetical descriptions are truthful and contain most of the basic elements of witchcraft ritual.

Shakespeare (1564) Macbeth, Act IV, Scene I, pictures a dark cave where a cauldron is boiling. Enter the three witches. "Thrice the brindled cat has mewed, Thrice and once the hedge-pig (hedgehog) whined." Then round the cauldron the witches go, throwing in the many ingredients that go to make a magic brew.

*"Form a charm of powerful trouble
Let the hell broth boil and bubble"*

Macbeth enters and refers to the powers of witches over the winds and waves, and the words express the commonly held beliefs of the period. Court trials sometimes referred to the control of the elements by witchcraft.

The Scottish poet Burns (1759-1796) was well acquainted with the revels of witches. He mentions Tom (a peeping Tom) who crept up near the haunted kirk to watch the midnight revels of the witch cult.

*"And wow! Tom saw an uncou sight
Warlocks and witches in a dance"*

They danced hornpipes, jigs, strathspeys, and reels that "Put life and mettle in their heels. And there sat Old Nick in shape o' beast playing the pipes."

Official records describe the revels which were enlivened by drinking, wild dancing, and promiscuous sexual intercourse between witches and wizards. Some evidence shows that at certain rites a child was sacrificed to the Devil. Many witnesses were ready to swear that they saw witches depart for the meeting flying on poles or broomsticks ,and that magical ointments rubbed on the wood made this feat possible. There were also magical words to promote an aerial flight. In New England there were general meetings of witches in a field near Salem village.

Some rites for blessings or curses were performed at these general assemblies, but a witch might also go through a ritual in private. Testimony was given (1487) that Janet Wischert, in a secret place outdoors, stooped down and threw her clothes above her head so that she was naked from the waist downward. She then threw stones forward and backward to symbolize her control over rainfall. The record refers also to a witch scraping a hole in the ground, urinating therein, and then performing a magical ceremony with incantations.

Usually the assemblies began at midnight and ended at cockcrow. Witches and wizards said goodbye to the Devil by kissing his posterior, and then all took a homeward flight on their poles and broomsticks.

Trials and Punishments

Legal procedure had to be based on definition of a witch or wizard, and in English law this seems to have been a person who has conference with the Devil, to take counsel (from the Devil), or to do some act (in obedience to the Devil).

Evidence of shame in alleged witches is lacking. On the contrary a person either entirely denied guilt or gloried in martyrdom. The accused knew well that torture and death might be their lot, yet they adhered to their faith and appealed to the Devil sometimes "in such a blasphemous manner as is not fit to mention."

The penalties for witchcraft were indeed severe, but many accused persons spoke freely and even proudly of their association with the Devil, whom they definitely regarded as their God.

M. A. Murray states that in English and Scottish trials torture was not usually given. In England the death penalty was hanging, then burning the body and scattering the ashes. Convicted witches of Scotland were strangled at the stake, then burnt; or they might be burnt alive. The French courts almost always imposed the penalty of burning alive, which was the terrible fate of Joan of Arc.

Trial by ordeal was a procedure that any accused person might have to face. This method of testing guilt has been common in many parts of the world, and everywhere there seems to be the basic idea that God, ancestral spirits, or some other unseen power would protect the innocent. The ordeal for witches was by water. In the presence of a minister of the parish the thumbs and big toes of the convicted person would be tied crosswise. The victim was then tossed into pond or river. Normally such a person would sink, and if that happened innocence was inferred. But a witch, being abnormal and aided by the Devil, would float even though tied in such an atrocious manner.

Crucial Evidence of Witchcraft

After testimony had been heard in court the order would be given for the body of the accused to be searched for evidence known as "the Devil's marks." These might be small reddish-blue spots that were indelible, and M. A. Murray suggests that the marks were tattooing. This is a feasible idea because many persons attested that the Devil, at dedication, made his mark by scratching or pricking.

But more important as evidence of witchcraft was the presence of extra breasts, teats, or nipples on the body of the accused, in parts where such organs never normally grow on a human being. The first evidence of this kind that came to my notice was in a record of the trial of an alleged New England witch named Mary Easty on whose body the female searchers appointed by the court found a "teat." This discovery sealed her doom, and the death penalty was imposed. In the annals of prison life, I do not think there could be a more dignified and convincing appeal than that penned to the judges by this unfortunate woman.

Despite protests, the judges of England and New England continued to convict on the presence of these so-called "teats." M. A.

Murray states that this kind of evidence is lacking from the records of France and Scotland.

In Suffolk, England (1665) six female searchers stripped the accused and reported that they found a teat on her belly, and three more in her "privy parts."[1] At the end of one teat there was a little hole which seemed to have been sucked recently. Some white, milky substance was exuded from this teat. This exudation was described as "witch-pap," and by some witches was admittedly used to suckle their animal familiars (imps). Teats were sometimes found on the bodies of alleged wizards.

Three women searched the body of Elizabeth Sawyer and found a teat above her fundament (the buttocks). Scientific articles in the *Journal of Anatomy* and the *British Medical Journal* report the presence of extra breasts (*polymastia*) and of extra nipples (*polythelia*) —a condition well known to students of Physical Anthropology. The condition of such extra breasts is not too rare.*

*See SEXOLOGY, page 582, April 1952. (Extra Breasts on Women, by H. Winfield.) Also, page 276, Dec. 1946, SEXOLOGY. (Extra Breasts in Women, by Maxwell Vidaver, M.D.)

Reference Books

Fowler, S. P.—Salem Witchcraft, Boston 1865. Contains 1. Wonders of the Invisible World, Being an Account of the Trial of Several Witches (1693). 2. More Wonders of the Invisible World. The former work by Cotton Mather, the latter by Robert Calef.

Murray, M. A.—The Witch-Cult in Western Europe, A Study in Anthropology. Oxford, Clarendon Press, 1921.

Salzman, L. F.—English Life in the Middle Ages. Oxford University Press, London, 1926.

News of the Month...

Sexology, June, 1939

Juvenile Bride Fails to Appreciate Law's Protection

A 15-year-old bride at Mt. Holly, N. J., was dragged by courtroom police from the arms of her husband with such force that she struck her head against a door jamb and was knocked unconscious. Eleanor Layton, junior high school student had just heard her husband, 32-year-old John Rafka, a soldier on furlough from Camp Dix, held in $2,000 bail on a charge of seduction brought by the girl's mother, Mrs. Bessie Layton. Rafka had eloped with the girl to Elkton, Md. When she flew to his arms, attempts to separate the pair ended with the girl unconscious at the feet of two township officers. Revived, Miss Layton went home with her mother, but insisted she would "run away" and join her husband at the first opportunity.

—New York Daily News.

• • •

Sexology, May, 1960

Bar License vs. Homosexuals

THE license of a bar may not be suspended or revoked simply because homosexuals patronize it, a ruling by the San Francisco District Court of Appeal declared recently.

The decision came in a case instituted after a tavern in Oakland, which had a large homosexual patronage, had its license revoked by the local Department of Alcoholic Control. The Department had charged that the tavern was a resort for homosexuals.

The Court ruled that before such a license could be revoked "there must be improper, illegal, disgusting or immoral acts of conduct committed on the premises to the knowledge of the licensee."

Sexology, July, 1960

Grandma Prostitutes

GRANDMA prostitutes? Yes—it happened in Italy recently where the police cracked down on a ring of "call grandmas," according to a Milan, Italy report. Believe it or not, the prostitutes arrested were all over 55 years old, with one prostitute believed to be 73 years of age. Many of the clients were found to be young men.

• • •

Sexology, June, 1952

Marriage or Jail

THE Arab News Agency said recently that Gov. Ashshami of Hodeidah Province, in Yemen, Arabia, had ordered all bachelors and single women of his province to get married or go to jail. The Governor issued the order because he was worried over the low population of his province.

• • •

Sexology, August 1961

"Picture-Bride" Racket

AN official of the Hawaiian Longshoremen's Union has exposed a "picture-bride" racket which preys on lonely Filipino longshoremen.

Basis of the swindle is the custom of picking out a Samoan girl as a bride from a series of pictures offered by a "marriage broker." The man makes his choice, pays for passage from Samoa to Hawaii, and waits. When the girl arrives, more money is requested to prepare for the marriage and other "expenses." If the arrangement is concluded the marriage takes place. Shortly thereafter the girl "disappears."

• • •

Sexology, January, 1947

Routine Twins

IN Tallahassee, Fla., 98-lb. Mrs. J. W. Dabney had her fourth consecutive set of twins in just under four years.

—Time Magazine

SEX STIMULATING
DRUGS

Old German woodcut shows witches brewing a charm.—*Bettmann Archive.*

How successful is man's age-old quest for drugs that can heighten sexual desire and ability?

**by Kenneth Walker
M.D., F.R.C.S.**

THROUGHOUT the ages, man has had three wishes: the wish to increase his sexuality and potency; the wish to escape, for a time, from the toils and the worries of the daily struggle for existence; and the wish to renew his youth.

In his never-ending search to reach the first goal, the use of aphrodisiac drugs has played an important rôle.

In ancient Egypt special fertility rites were organized by the

Dr. Walker, a distinguished British surgeon, is author of "Marriage" and "The Physiology of Sex," and co-author of "Sex and Society" and "Sexual Disorders in the Male."

priests and these included methods of stimulating sexual desire. These methods were professional secrets which were passed down from one generation to another generation by word of mouth.

So also in ancient Greece, dancing, the taking of large quantities of wine and possibly of other aphrodisiacs, formed part of the worship of the god Dionysius.

In later years some of these priestly methods passed into the keeping of medieval magicians, sorcerers and witches and it was to the witch that the young man or woman went in search of love-spells.

All through the ages the witches and "wise women" have been con-

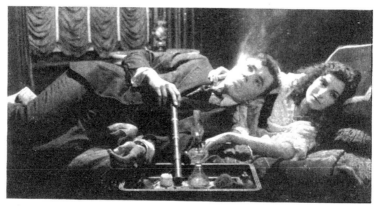

Narcotics, which have often been used as aphrodisiacs, are highly dangerous and lead to addiction. Here an early movie, showing two of its characters smoking a narcotic drug, portrays the evil effects of drugs.

tributing many valuable remedies to the medical pharmacopoeia—a good example is digitalis, which is used as a heart stimulant.

So many herbs were discovered by women of this kind that a special book was published in the eighteenth century under the title of *Herball*. In his interesting little work on medieval medicine, *Passport to Paradise*, Bernard French tells us that this early predecessor of *British Pharmacopeia*, gave descriptions of the belladonna plants, with their purple flowers, which were then growing in the marshes of Piccadilly and of the marigolds and the poppies which were particularly plentiful in the lush fields of Paddington.

At a later date, when increasing foreign trade brought to England plants from abroad, confidence was transferred from home products to extracts made from strange foreign roots and flowers. Not only were these foreign plants more remarkable in appearance than the more familiar home plants but they had high-sounding

and melodious names such as *yohimbine*, *cantharides*, and *hashish*. Moreover they were so rare and so difficult to come by that only the experts managed to obtain them.

Now, there was a general principle in medieval medicine—and to some extent it lingers on in the medicine at the present day. This principle is that *"the rarer, the less easily obtainable and the more costly the remedy, the more likely it is to do good."*

It was because they possessed these three qualities in a very high degree that gold dust, pearls dissolved in wine, powdered mummy from Egypt and powdered rhinoceros-horn from Africa were regarded as being exceedingly powerful remedies.

The old principle of "sympathetic magic" also applied to some of these new drugs. According to this magical principle: "Like cures like."

For example, just as heart-shaped leaves were known to do good to heart disease, so also was it thought that powdered rhinoceros-horn would benefit men suffering from sexual weakness. Consequently rhinoceros-horn was imported, ground into a powder and taken by the mouth. It became a very popular, if expensive, remedy for impotence, and it is still being used in some parts of the world, for this purpose.

Aphrodisiacs are said to produce their results in several different ways: by irritating the genital organs; by stimulating the central nervous system; and finally by altering the mental state.

The first of these three ways in which aphrodisiacs are said to work will be studied first.

A good example of an aphrodisiac of this kind is cantharides. This extremely irritating drug is obtained from a beetle known as *Spanish Fly,* an insect which is found in Southern Europe. From it is extracted *cantharidine,* a whitish powder which when applied to the skin is so irritating that blisters soon appear. Cantharides were formerly used in medicine as counter irritants for such conditions as inflamed joints.

For a great many years cantharides have had this reputation of possessing a powerful aphrodisiac action. After being taken by the mouth they are eliminated from the body by means of the urine. In the process of the urine being voided it irritates the bladder and the urethra. This irritation evokes erections through reflex action.

It also causes intense discomfort to the unfortunate patient and has been known to have fatal results. It inflames the stomach and the bowels, evokes vomiting and diarrhea and produces congestion of the kidneys.

No one but a madman would take an aphrodisiac of this kind and only a criminal would prescribe it for anybody else. Santorin, a less irritating drug extracted from the dried flower heads of *artemis maritinea,* acts in a somewhat similar manner though it is far less dangerous.

Nux vomica and its active principle, strychnine, is an example of a drug which has a stimulating action on the central nervous system. As a result of the stimulating action, it possesses some aphrodisiac qualities.

It was introduced into European medicine by the Arabs and at first was used only for the purpose of poisoning animals. But it was found that when taken in small doses it increased the sensitivity of both the muscles and the nerves.

It likewise had a stimulating action on the brain, so that after taking it sensations became finer and more acute. For this reason nux vomica and strychnine are still being used by physicians in the treatment of impotence.

Its value as an aphrodisiac is very difficult to assess, for the drug is usually given to the patient with the doctor's assurance that it is a very powerful and successful remedy. *Consequently it is impossible to decide afterwards whether the improvement following its use has been due to the drug itself or whether it is the result of suggestive action on the patient.*

Alcohol, cocaine, hashish and opium have all been used as aphrodisiacs. Their chief action is on the brain and on bringing about a change in the patient's mental state.

Alcohol has markedly different

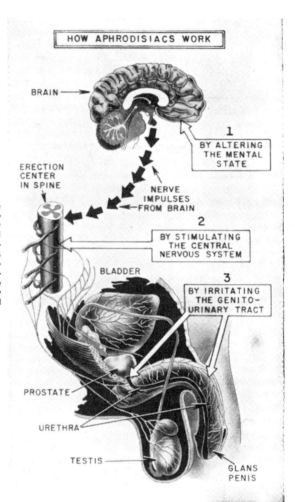

Aphrodisiacs produce their effects in three different ways: (1) by affecting the mental state; (2) by stimulating the central nervous system; and (3) by irritating the genito-urinary organs. None are truly effective; many are dangerous and often deadly.

effects on different types of people and the Arabs were right when they said of it that it "makes a man more so." Alcohol is likely to uncover and to accentuate a person's essential characteristics.

For instance, if a man is by nature aggressive, he is likely to become still more aggressive and to pick a quarrel after a few alcoholic drinks. If, on the other hand, he is rather sentimental in character, he will not quarrel but will become still more sentimental and even maudlin.

Alcohol also helps a weakly-sexed man by restoring to him his self-confidence and this is often highly necessary. A glass or two of wine is likely to be very helpful to a man who has lost confidence in himself, *but he must not drink too much or all sexual desire and capacity will then disappear.*

When taken by mouth, cocaine is a stimulant of the nervous system. It is likely also to arouse erotic ideas in a man and also, to some extent, in a woman. It has a reputation for banishing fatigue, both physical and mental, and for overcoming sexual inhibitions of various kinds.

It is believed to exert its aphrodisiac action on a man by producing vascular engorgement of his genital organs. Yohimbine acts in a similar manner, and is still used by some physicians in treating impotence. *But cocaine is a highly dangerous drug which leads to cocaine addiction and it should never be taken internally for any purpose at all.*

What is true of cocaine is equally true of opium, morphia and hashish. They are all habit-forming drugs and they should not be prescribed as aphrodisiacs or for their effect on the mind.

It may well be that they actually do what it is claimed that they do, namely remove certain inhibitions and at the same time increase sexual desire, but their continued use leads to a degradation of the person taking them, so that he loses all will power and all sense of moral responsibility.

Moreover these drugs have the disadvantage that although they sometimes have the effect of stimulating desire they may in the end defeat the very purpose for which they were taken, by rendering the individual quite incapable of carrying out sexual intercourse.

Hashish has yet another defect. Different samples of it possess such different potencies that it is very difficult to estimate what doses should be taken.

Throughout history, man has diligently sought far and wide for miraculous remedies, but in the end his search has always been thwarted. Either the action of the drug he has found proves erratic and uncertain or else the taking of it leads to his physical and mental degradation. In other words, man's search for an aphrodisiac has been attended with as limited success as has been his search for the Philosopher's Stone and the Fountain of Youth.

Nor should any drug ever be taken except on the advice of a physician. There is no such thing as a short cut to Paradise, though I have no doubt that the search for these two mythical entities will still continue. But the path to Paradise is long and tedious and so also is the treatment of some of the cases of impotence. There are no shortcuts to either goal.

● ● ●

Wrong Use of Sex

"MOST people use sex to release hate, or only to express themselves, rather than to express love in the personal relationship of marriage."

—Dr. Mary S. Calderone in lecture at Morehead College conference on marriage.

MALE SEX MACHINE

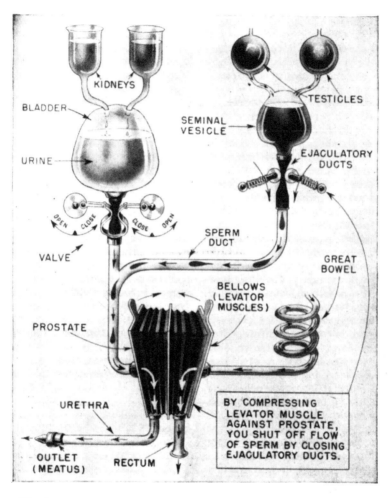

This diagram endeavors to represent mechanically, so far as is possible, the organs of the lower body, which are self-powered. The urinary system expels fluid in one way, through the urethra and meatus; the reproductive system expels it in another way, through the same tube with different motors, there being a double valve system in the prostate gland. The bowel system does not employ the same discharge pipe, as in some forms of life (like birds), but the same muscles clamp down on it. The result is that, when the levator muscles are contracted firmly, they stop emission in the male, as well as other forms of excretion. This is one of the methods of controlling premature ejaculation. © SEXOLOGY.

Sex Difficulties—Causes and Cure

By FRANK LEIGHTON WOOD, M.D.

THE editors of this magazine receive each month hundreds of letters from worried readers who seek the solution of problems pertaining to sex or the married state. Fortunately, many of these problems are of easy solution. The most difficult are those which pertain to mental states or impressions. Because these unfortunates have neglected for years to seek advice, they have formed habits of thinking and living which are very difficult to overcome. Many a woman, because of neglect or misinformation on the part of her mother, has gone into matrimony with the impression that its intimate relationships are something to be endured rather than shared. Because her husband has been no better informed, she has gone through years of married life in a state of frustration and unhappiness, the victim of various neurotic conditions; until, perhaps, too late, she has learned accidentally, from some other woman, of the happiness she has missed and may never participate in.

Likewise, young men, because of vicious habits contracted in childhood, and the sense of shame and wrong-doing which often results, not infrequently develop a characteristic mental state and personality which includes bashfulness, timidity, introspection, and, eventually, a sense of inferiority. This unfortunate complex or personality may become so accentuated and fixed that its victim may find it difficult to look anyone in the eyes, to feel at ease with anyone except his own immediate family, or to converse with or even speak to girls or young women. In order that such a problem may be graphically presented, we shall discuss the case of one of our readers, whose letter follows:

"I am a young man of twenty-six and, from about six to eighteen years of age, I practiced self-abuse two or three times each week. Then I began to consort with public women, at about the same frequency. I never worried much about the self-abuse, but I am now worrying about what I believe to be the effects of it. The symptoms I have read about seem to fit my case exactly. I am shy of girls, am embarrassed in their presence and often blush. I hate to meet strangers. I quit high school after three weeks because of this timidity. I have often gone out of my way to avoid meeting girls on the street. I am very tall and awkward, very self-conscious of my appearance and often feel that people are making remarks about me. I can't keep a job very long because of these things, but always want to quit and go to a new place. I work in restaurants and hate to meet customers, especially when there is a crowd. I feel that people are watching me and I can't stand it. I dream of doing great things but have no confidence in myself, can't take responsibility and have no hobbies or special interests except that I want to be on the move. Sometimes I feel that I am going crazy, and that I ought to place myself under observation in the

thing to a sympathetic adviser. It is possible that simply the telling of his story—getting the load of anxiety off his mind by passing his troubles on to someone else—has helped him to see a little more clearly the possible solution of it. He has been ashamed to tell his story personally to anyone, even to

A young man who is nervous in the presence of women, even total strangers, who are customers is under a severe handicap in business as well as in social life.

State Hospital. What do you think I should do?"

This man has a definite *neurosis* bordering on insanity, yet it seems likely that, with a little sympathetic advice and direction, he may be restored to normal. He has voluntarily taken the first step necessary to a cure by confiding everything to a physician, but he found it easier to write about it. How many people there are who go on for years with a secret worry or wrong rankling in their hearts, ashamed or afraid to confide in someone; when simply telling their troubles or confessing their wrongs might make clear to them how unimportant these things were, or point the way out of their difficulties.

Many a man has secretly worried so long about what was a relatively unimportant matter that he has finally become insane, or committed suicide, and all because he has not understood himself or his problem and all that was necessary to save him from such a fate was simple confession. On the other hand, there are people who bore us terribly with their tales of woe. If we are well informed and charitable, we humor them; for by listening to the recital of their troubles, we help them to unload the burden from their hearts and minds and, by so doing, we may save them from insanity or suicide.

The next important thing, about confessing one's problems to someone who understands such things, is that one learns more nearly the exact nature of them and this is likely to make their solution sometimes possible without further assistance. An army medical officer during the world war was stricken with a strange malady which disabled him for active duty but presented no definite physical signs upon which a diagnosis could be founded by the hospital staff. The patient, being a physician, understood his own condition but, since the staff could find no direct evidence of the disease, they refused to accept his diagnosis and classified him as a malingerer. Although he suffered severe pain, he was permitted no relief and, as a result of this injustice, developed a neurosis and became hysterical at times. After a few months he was discharged

and came under the supervision of the physicians of the Veteran's Bureau of his home district. These doctors were discerning and sympathetic, listened to his statements, and, in a short time, he was on the road to recovery.

This young man who has written us is right in his belief that his past practice of self-abuse is responsible for his present neurotic condition and, having explained the nature of his case to him, we believe he should be able to help himself to become normal again. One of the worst things about the practice of self-abuse is that it is nearly always accompanied by a sense of shame which, in time, often develops into a definite feeling of inferiority. This is because one knows instinctively that it is wrong to abuse the functions of the body. Since he has not learned that nearly all men and most women have practiced this habit at some time in their lives, he feels ashamed of himself and inferior to those who are as guilty as he is of this offense against nature. He fears that his guilt may be seen in his countenance and he is afraid to look people in the eyes. This young man is very tall and, being self-conscious, is doubtless awkward, so that he attracts attention. Naturally, because of his fears and timidity, this worries him, so that he feels a constant urge to escape from prying eyes. This has been going on for so long that escape has become an obsession with him. He did not, for a long time, recognize the danger he was subjecting himself to by encouraging this obsession; but he has come to realize at last that unless something is done about it, he will become insane.

The cure of this condition lies in following a course exactly the opposite from that which brought it about. This young man gave up the practice of self-abuse several years ago, but substituted for it one which is more vicious, more dangerous to health, and probably as harmful to him, personally, but in a slightly different way. Whether he was advised by a physician to do this, or not, we do not know, but we *do* know that many physicians give unwise and vicious advice; for promiscuity in young men is not only dangerous, but unnecessary. Continence in them is possible and healthful.* Consorting with public women, at best, is little more satisfactory than self-abuse and is more immoral and degrading. It did not help this young man to recover from his feeling of guilt and inferiority, although he probably felt that he was pursuing a more manly course.

The first step, then, in the mental rehabilitation of such an individual as this young man, is the practice of absolute continence; so that he need not feel ashamed to look anyone in the face nor fear or resent the scrutiny of curious eyes because of his personal appearance. Self-confidence will, in a measure, be almost immediately restored and, although he will still be bashful and self-conscious in the presence of girls, it will not be as

*See "Is Promiscuity In Young Men Necessary?" July, 1937, and "Is Continence Compatible With Health?", May, 1939, issues of The Facts of Life.

difficult for him to overcome his reticence in this respect when the opportunity offers.

In this connection, we are reminded of the experience of a boy of nineteen who, while he acutely desired the friendship and companionship of girls, could not overcome the feeling of inferiority and bashfulness brought about by secret practices, early poverty, and continued adversity, although he was bright, intelligent and attractive in appearance. While he was visiting an aunt, this wise woman divined the young man's predicament and decided to overcome his bashfulness at one stroke. She gave a little surprise party for him and invited a number of young people, including some very attractive girls. At her instigation, the old-fashioned game of postoffice was played, and two of the girls were induced to enter into a plot to pay s p e c i a l attention to the honor guest. As a result, he was kissed so much that he was thoroughly cured of bashfulness in one evening and, at the same time, recovered a great deal of his self respect. In fact, he enjoyed the experience so much that he was inclined, for some time thereafter, until he regained his true poise, to be rather bold and over-demonstrative toward the opposite sex.

The average young man who has been beset by the fears and worries brought about by unnatural sex practices until they have become an obsession, often needs more than an explanation of the natures of his condition to bring about a cure. After he has overcome his sense of shame and inferiority to some extent by clean and moral habits, he next learns that he must mix socially w i t h both sexes and cultivate the friendship of young people, particularly that of decent girls and young women. For such a person to win his way back to normality, he must fight all the way and principally against his own established habits of reticence and solitude. If he has relatives who are in a position to help him, he may solicit their aid and, like the wise aunt referred to in the foregoing, they may be very helpful. Not having such a help in time of trouble, he may have to work out his own salvation. How shall he go about this? By compelling himself to attend respectable social gatherings of every kind and trying to adapt himself to the society of decent young women. He may take dancing lessons, if necessary, so that he can attend public dances, always remembering that while many nice girls go to such places, one has to be careful about becoming on intimate terms with girls until he knows something personally about their family background, personal

habits, and character. He may attend church of any denomination and cultivate the acquaintance of the pastor, make him a confidant and seek his assistance in the rehabilitation of his damaged personality as well as his aid in making desirable friends and acquaintances. In addition to all this, he should occupy his mind during his spare moments with useful studies, interesting and instructive reading or with healthful sports or hobbies. This will help to keep his mind off sex matters and his past mental condition.

In summing up, we wish to impress most strongly upon the person of either sex who is beset with worries, fears or a sense of inferiority because of personal problems, that is the first and most necessary step in the solution of these personality problems is to share them with someone else. If everyone, young and old, would seek an intelligent and sincere confidant whenever seriously worried over any personal problem, much immediate unhappiness, subsequent misfortune, and mental and physical ill h e a l t h might be averted.

● ● ●

NEED OF SEXUAL KNOWLEDGE

IN all civilized communities throughout the world, marriage is regarded as the basis of society. It has survived many centuries, and whether it is looked upon as a sacrament or as an economic alliance it remains a necessity in any and every social system. Yet important as is this alliance between two individuals, there is no undertaking entered into with so little consideration for the fundamental physiological facts.

Many a marriage has been wrecked at the outset because one or both of the parties was ignorant of the functional responsibilities in a union of such close intimacy between two members of opposite sex.

—*Health and Strength (London)*

famous
TRANSVESTITES

Man or woman? History records many cases where the true sex of an individual has been revealed only at death.

by Eric J. Dingwall, M.A., Ph.D., D.Sc.

A "female husband" who, under the assumed name of "James Allen" was married for 21 years without once disclosing her sex. — Copyright E. J. Dingwall.

N EWSPAPERS today so often report cases of persons being found dressed as members of the opposite sex that the question is constantly being asked: *"Why do they behave in this way?"*

Although the question is simple, the answer is not. *Transvestism,* as it is called, means "cross-dressing" and merely describes what occurs. It does not explain anything.

To begin with, it must be clearly understood that there is no one explanation which can refer to all

A noted British sexologist, Dr. Dingwall is author of "The American Woman," and editor of the English edition of the monumental three-volume work by Ploss and Bartels, "Das Weib" (Woman).

cases. It is true, however, that one or two broad generalizations can be made. It seems clear that there must be some deep inner drive in the individual to assume the outward behavior and rôle of the opposite sex. Some not only wear the garb of the opposite sex but also take on its occupations; and occasionally it is only at death that the true sex of the person is revealed.

Although it has been said, I do not know on what authority, that possibly about fifty per cent of male transvestites have homosexual inclinations, the remainder are probably what can be called intermediate types, although in some the pleasure and satisfaction of cross-dressing is not accompanied by any conscious sexual gratification.

In some of the simpler cases the practice may arise from events in childhood, in which the boy or girl has been made to wear clothes of the other sex. But even in these cases it would seem likely that there is something more involved. In every case of transvestism there lies some form of sexual deviation, of which the cross-dressing is but an indication.

Apart from the cases of physically normal men and women who find relief and satisfaction in this practice, there are, as is to be expected, some cases of persons whose anatomical make-up is irregular. In these cases, it is often not easy to say at birth precisely to what sex the infant is to be assigned. In later life the individual may prefer to discard the former dress and take on that of the sex to which he has now decided to belong.

It will thus be seen that there are many reasons behind transvestism. Some of the most famous cases, which came to light only after death, cannot now be explained at all. *Perhaps one of the most curious of these is the strange case of Dr. James Barry.*

If you were to turn the yellowing pages of the British *Army List* for July 1859, you would find under the "Army Medical Department" the name of James Barry, M.D., heading the list of names of Inspectors General of Hospitals. In August the name disappeared and we read that Dr. Barry had retired and had been placed on half pay.

This entry was one of the last concerning this eminent army physician, who died in 1865 and who, some fifty years earlier, had

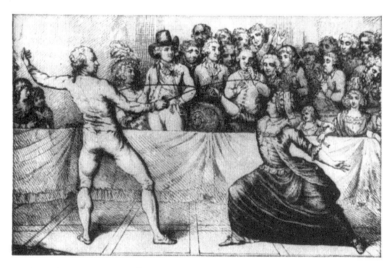

One of history's most famous tranvestites, Chevalier d' Eon, dressed in woman's clothing, engages in a fencing match before the Prince of Wales. The French government insisted on d'Eon's wearing female dress.—*Bettmann Archive.*

qualified as Doctor of Medicine in Edinburgh.

He was a hard-working student and made but few friends, keeping much to himself and refusing to join in the rough horse-play and boxing bouts that were common among his fellow students. Rather prim and proper, he had a melancholy expression, but was so successful in his studies that promotion was assured. For this purpose Barry decided on a military career and he rapidly rose in the Service. Posted to Malta, he soon took his place in the life of the garrison, although some people remarked that there was something peculiar about him.

Next Barry was sent to South Africa. Here he was not only staff surgeon to the garrison, but the medical adviser to the Governor General.

His eccentric behavior was as noticeable as it had been at Malta. On one occasion his behavior actually led to a duel, in which neither side, fortunately, was severely injured, but which resulted in Barry becoming more difficult and excitable than before. Indeed, things came to such a pass that he was sent back to England in disgrace.

As usual, however, influences from high quarters were soon brought into play, and Barry was offered another job which took him first to St. Helena and then to the West Indies.

One day, when ill in Trinidad, he had gone to stay with a friend and had given orders that he was not to be disturbed on any account. Two other medical officers

Army doctor James Barry was a woman who successfully masqueraded as a male for over fifty years.—From the Munnik portrait.

who were worried about his illness decided to go to see him in spite of the ban upon visitors. When the surgeon entered the sick room he found the patient asleep and, turning down the bedclothes to sound his lungs, discovered that James Barry was a woman!

Awakening, Barry was thunderstruck and exacted the most solemn promise that the two visitors should keep silence. This they did until after his death.

When Barry returned to England to retire from medical practice he lived in London. One day he fell ill with what may have been acute dysentery. Refusing medical attention and alone with John, his faithful colored servant, James Barry passed away on July 25, 1865. John called in a woman to take care of laying out the corpse of the Inspector General.

She had hardly begun her task before she called John back. "General indeed!" she remarked. "This corpse is a woman." The authorities were summoned, who confirmed the sex and ordered an inquiry.

Who was James Barry? We shall probably never know. Rumor had it that she was the daughter of a Scottish nobleman. As to the reasons why she decided to enter medicine and live as a man, it is difficult even to hazard a plausible guess. We know nothing of her early life as a girl and the story that an early and disappointing love affair with an Army surgeon, which not only brought her a child but complete disillusionment, is not confirmed.

Unfortunately we have no evidence as to whether Barry was or was not normal physically. Sir William Osler, the famous physician, did his best to obtain the record of the inquest, but the whole of the papers relating to the case had disappeared from the Army medical files.

Another very similar case was that of James Allen, a woman who also lived in the early nineteenth century. At an early age, she donned male attire, marrying a young woman in 1807. She carried on exclusively male occupations, such as groom, inn-keeper, and common laborer performing heavy work on the London docks.

Her sex was discovered only when she died as the result of an accident. The body was said to be entirely normal. Her "wife" stated that she had an idea that Allen was not quite what she called a "proper" man, although none of the physicians who had attended her during her lifetime seems to have had the slightest suspicion of her true sex.

Both Barry and Allen seem to have been physically normal women. Similar cases of physically normal male transvestites are well-known. The most famous of these is, of course, the Chevalier d'Eon, whose male sex was verified at his death.

Born in 1728, he led a remarkable life as a young man in both diplomacy and politics. But rumor that he was really a woman started in London society, where bets were made upon his true sex.

He added to the mystification by giving a party dressed as a woman, in black silk and diamonds, and a few days later embarking for France in his military uniform. When he arrived in France he was told that he was a woman and ordered to wear female clothes, the Queen actually ordering for him a magnificent headdress from the Royal milliner.

Many famous transvestites were known during their lifetime to be intermediate types sexually. The cases of Anne Grandjean and Henrica Schuria are good examples. Both lived many years ago, and in both the clitoris was so much developed that in infancy sex was doubtful.

Anne had a miserable life. She never knew what she was, but she did know that she preferred women to men and was able, partially at least, to satisfy the women with whom she lived. Her case was considered by the legal authorities, who decided that she was female and ordered her to be whipped, since they declared that by her actions she had profaned the sacrament of marriage.

Anne appealed to a higher court, as she did not want to be considered female, but it was decided that she was, and henceforth she had to wear female clothes.

The same sort of thing happened to Henrica Schuria, whose physical organs were very similar to those of Anne. She dressed as a soldier and served in the army, and when she came home she also lived with women. When it was discovered what she was doing she was condemned to death, but finally the sentence was reduced to whipping and she was forbidden to live any longer with the widow with whom she was co-habiting.

Nowadays, there are so many cases reported that transvestites are almost too well-known to excite much comment. In England examples are very common. In 1916 a man who was called up for military service was found to be a woman; and in the same year another soldier when absent without leave was found later to have been brought up and dressed as a girl ever since childhood.

In 1932 a woman died who had lived as a man for twenty years, both marrying and doing heavy manual jobs, while in 1948 a woman who had lived as a man for thirteen years was found guilty of murder. In 1954 a young woman, said to have normal sexual organs, was so determined to dress and behave as a man that she finally married another girl in an English church. When the facts were discovered they were each fined but were not otherwise punished.

Thus does transvestism continue now as it has always done, not only in the so-called civilized societies but also among primitive peoples. Although occasionally innocent people are deceived and possibly harm results, it seems clear that transvestites generally do little harm to anybody and deserve much more sympathetic understanding than they usually get.

● ● ●

FEMALE BUSTS

W E are far too preoccupied with female busts, declared Dr. Goodrich C. Schauffler, a gynecologist teaching at the University of Oregon. He recently told a Chicago congress on gynecology and obstetrics: "Anomalies of the breast in childhood call for more attention from physicians in the present age because of the emphasis by modern advertising and the press (and Hollywood movies) upon this semi-respectable sex appendage. I was recently asked to see a ten-year-old girl, scarcely into adolescence, who was wearing miniature falsies and was already the subject of a bosom inferiority complex. As physicians we must under no circumstances disregard the psychic—I might even say the psychotic—influence of such matters upon our youngsters. It can be exceedingly serious. Recently, in my own practice, I had a case of an attempted suicide and several rather serious total derangements caused by real or fancied breast irregularities."

by Maurice Grevé, M.D.

*The problems described in
this letter are typical of
hundreds of case histories to
be found in the files of
sexologists. An experienced
physician and counsellor
analyzes some of the many
causes of marital disharmony.
All too many persons, he
shows—through ignorance or
carelessness—are suffering
needlessly from*

Sex starvation

EDITOR, SEXOLOGY:
    *I am bringing you a real problem
indeed. If you can help me in any way,
I'll be eternally grateful to you.*

*I married very young, not knowing
anything about sex relationship, and
not knowing that women could and
did receive benefits the same as men.
After several years, and hearing other
married women talk of their experiences, I realized that I was missing
something that went with every marriage. I might say here that I thought,
subconsciously, something was wrong,
as my nerves started to go back on me,
and I had a vague but troublesome
feeling. Of course I told my husband;
he also was surprised, as he is not
sexually inclined, requiring physical
union very rarely, much less often
now than when we were first married.*

*I had been informed that certain
techniques must be followed and after*

*trying several different experiments,
I finally realized my goal. But the
problem is this—although I am certainly of an affectionate, happy and
passionate nature, it takes an unbelievably long time for me to reach
the climax. Therefore I receive sexual satisfaction rarely. My nerves are
getting worse, and sometimes I can
hardly bear the longing for the sexual expression denied me. I find that,
immediately after an unsuccessful
union, and in fact, for several days
after, this reaction is more intense.*

*I believe if my husband were more
vigorous sexually, things might be different. He seems perfectly healthy,
otherwise.*

*I have been very frank in the hope
that you can help me and others who
have the same problem. If you can
help us, we both will be more than
thankful.—Mrs. J. M., Pennsylvania*

BEFORE AND LATER

Pictured at left is an average happy couple soon after marriage. Romance and love are still ebullient as before the honeymoon. Biological intoxication reigns supreme. The lovers view each other only through glamor-colored glasses. . . . But Time rolls on inexorably. . . .

A FEW YEARS LATER. As seen below, the "happy" couple is no longer the same. Time has taken its toll. Disillusion has overtaken the erstwhile lovers. Intimacy has bred not contentment but contempt. The letdown in personal appearance of both is profound. She in curlers, face smeared, ragged négligée—he unshaven, unkempt, with toothpick dangling—no wonder romance departed. Unfortunately for them, this couple has not as yet learned —as millions of others have not either— that people are like cars. Cars, like people, need constant grooming, cleaning, polishing, and, above all, care and understanding. A little "oil" will smooth the rockiest roads. But it is the high-octane "essence" that is essential for a long and pleasant trip.

If people gave as much care, love and thought to their husbands or wives as they do to their cars, there would be hardly any divorces and little strife in married life. And, after all, a new car may not be better than your old one!

THE problems which our correspondent describes are very real ones, indeed, and affect millions of individuals, year after year. They are, without doubt, directly responsible for destroying hundreds of thousands of happy marriages, filling our institutions with neurotics, producing a great deal of ill health in those of stronger nerves and, in general, creating strong feelings of hostility between marital partners.

Husband and wife have failed to establish harmony in their sex relations, while the wife is suf-

The late Dr. Grevé was a physician and sexologist of the city of Luxembourg, in the Grand Duchy of Luxembourg, Europe.

fering from what we may call "sex starvation."

The problem is not a new one —it is as old as humanity itself. Biologically, nature invented the physical act to propagate the race. The instinct, for such it is, of physical union, is simply the means to an end—and that is *offspring*. After this instinct has been satisfied over a number of years, the libido begins to wane. This, of course, is speaking only generally; there are, to be sure, exceptions.

Biologically speaking, the woman often is less sexual, to a degree, than the man. It is unusual for the female, after she has borne a number of children, to have as great a sexual appetite as she had before the advent of the children. This, again, is speaking of the majority—yet there are a goodly percentage of women in whom this is not the case. Nor should such women be called over-sexed. A better term perhaps is "full-sexed."

A full-sexed woman may demand sexual relations several times a week, up to or past middle age; whereas the over-sexed woman will desire the same relationship even more frequently, often past middle age, and sometimes past sixty. There is nothing abnormal or unnatural about the full-sexed woman, however, particularly if she is a healthy female. The over-sexed woman, however, may be called unusual; yet the percentage of such cases is not very great. Our letter writer's need for greater frequency indicates that she is a full-sexed woman with a healthy but unsatisfied sex appetite.

The male—again I am speaking of the average—if he is healthy, and if his mind is free, will find sexual relationship gratifying, up to and past fifty years of age, several times a week. This is not abnormal, but may be termed natural in a healthy individual. With sickness intervening, or if a man is of the nervous kind, and worries a great deal about business or other matters, his libido suffers and his sexual appetite is sharply reduced.

Again, in this matter, however, there is no fixed rule. I have seen in my practice individuals where even ill health and worry did not seem to interfere with their sexual life. Frequently, the relationship was cut down somewhat; at no time, however, did it cease. These again, were strongly-sexed men, or might perhaps be called full-sexed.

In intimate relationship between the two sexes, there is no hard and fast rule. What is good for one may not be good for the other. What is normal for one, may be abnormal or impossible for another, and what holds true for man, can be observed in domestic or wild animals as well.

Thus, for instance, a grieving dog who has lost his master will not only refuse to eat, but also refuses to have any relationship with a female dog at that time. *There is, therefore, not only the physical, but the psychological condition to be recognized in all sex problems.*

I come now to the delicate problem of a man's relationship with his wife; and here I must at once call attention to what is well known in Europe—that the average American male knows relatively little of the *sex technique* in his relations with his wife. In my former practice in the United States, I had an excellent insight into the problem, and I observed what others had found long before my time. That is the biological act, with most American husbands, seems to be chiefly for their own personal gratification, with little regard to the needs of their wives.

There is no need for me to go into lengthy explanations of the sex act, foreplay, and all that goes with it, since there are a number of excellent books on the subject. Suffice it to say that, in many cases which have come under observation, the man as a rule is at fault because he has not learned the most important part of the love act. *This is that love and attraction, between man and wife, will not last for any length of time if the consummation of the love act does not result in climax for both parties involved.*

As mentioned before, not all women are alike. Some women will come to climax in the act in a few seconds; others may take 15 minutes or more. It is, therefore, necessary for the two parties to act in harmony, if the optimum result is to be achieved. Of course, if the husband is selfish and cares only for his own desires and gratification, he will not consider the feelings of his wife. In due time, he will either wreck her health, or what is worse, she will be driven by necessity to someone who will be more considerate. Biologically speaking, this is exactly what happens in a large percentage of cases.

Whether the husband knows about it or not makes little difference; the percentages are against him.

In the case of such husbands as the one described in the letter, it is important to discover, first, whether there are any physical reasons responsible for his obvious lack of vigor and sex drive. If such is the case, the man should undergo a thorough examination by his doctor, or urologist, and have a heart-to-heart discussion of his problems with him.

If a physical defect is discovered, it should naturally be corrected. If there is a deep-seated emotional disturbance which is preventing the male from being aroused sexually, it should be diagnosed and treated.

Perhaps what is required is merely rest or relaxation from overburdening business problems. Perhaps what is needed is healthful exercise, particularly outdoor exercise, to restore abating vigor. If a man has no disease, and no serious affliction, then his case may simply be a sort of sexual *lethargy;* in a less elegant term, this means "laziness."

And now I come to a point that will probably surprise or shock most women. I make the statement (not as a speculation, but from observation and intimate knowledge of many cases) that, in fully 80 per cent of the cases, *the woman is to blame.* This seems like a mass indictment, but it is true, nevertheless. Again, let us look at the problem closer, and see the causes.

It will usually be found that, if the wife thinks back, she will find she had normal biological relations with her husband *when they first were married*. Little by little, the condition changed until, after a while, the husband became as described in the letter of our correspondent: "not sexually inclined, requiring physical union very rarely, sometimes as little as once in three or four months."

Why this change? Is it possible that the husband found someone more attractive than his wife? Let us give him the benefit of the doubt, and assume that he had not.

What else could have happened so that he no longer found his wife as attractive as in the years gone by, and therefore lost his sexual appetite? Speaking bluntly, but from a biological standpoint, *sexual appetite is not different from any other appetite.* If you eat the same sort of food day in and day out you will become tired of it; irrespective of the fact that the food is good, the sameness begins to pall after a while. Perhaps the food is not served attractively, in an attractive setting? If you serve a fastidious man a steak on a broken or unclean plate, on a table which is not set well, on a soiled table cloth and without salt or pepper, he is apt to lose his appetite, *even though the steak is very good.*

Perhaps this will give the modern wife a hint. There is such a thing as sexual attractiveness. It has been stated by many writers on the subject that man is more aesthetic than woman. If this is so, what does the average woman do to make the sex act attractive to the husband? Little, if anything.

Most women do not seem to know even the first rudiments of sex hygiene.

The woman just married requires very little to create sexual allurement. She is still fresh and young. Little by little she loses this freshness and, what is more important, she does not realize that sexual hygiene becomes, not only important, but a matter of life and death so far as her love life is concerned.

Most men have a sensitive olfactory sense, and here we come to the delicate subject of body odors. The bride of two or three months has, as a rule, a fresh odor; but the sexual life and age soon change this. Perspiration sets up a definite odor which may be subconsciously distasteful to the husband; but, most important, the secretions exuded by the female organs are often quite malodorous and offend many men. Of course, a woman who has been properly instructed by her doctor will know this, and will take due precautions. She will bathe often; she will use certain perfumes which attract her husband; and, most important, she will douche regularly with a solution (supplied to her by her physician) to get rid of the annoying mucous secretions which, frequently, offend the man's olfactory sense. This is particularly true after woman's monthly period.

While several large books could be written on the subject of female odors, attractive and repellent, this is by no means the only point in our discussion. There are other considerations.

When a wife has her hair done

up in curlers, which disfigure her in the eyes of her husband; when she greases her face and hands with some toilet preparation or fails to take off the cosmetic from her face and lips, she should not be unduly surprised if she is not sexually attractive in such a make-up. Of course, any considerate husband would be loath to tell her all these things, because he does not wish to offend her; but the result, in the end, is that the sex attraction is killed, and the very thing that the woman strives for—i.e., attractiveness—is turned into its opposite, and becomes aversion or repulsion.

There are a hundred different subtle points, all along the same line, usually disregarded by women. Unattractive, soiled, or torn night-gowns, bed-sheeting not overly clean, body hair (many men are repelled by hair on the female body) and offensive breath (due often to eating foods such as, for instance, onions or garlic, or odor due to defective teeth, etc.) very often subconsciously kill the desire of many otherwise normal men.

Then, there is another most important point, not to be forgotten, and that is the *timeliness* of physical union. A hardworking man may be so tired out in the evening, that the biological act is no longer attractive to him. Indeed, a psychologist well versed in sexual matters, once pointed out that the one and only favorable time for sexual relationship is after the two parties have gone to bed and have slept for an hour or more. This, when practiced (and it must be practiced to be successful) frequently produces excellent results. Sleep refreshes; *it invigorates,* too, most powerfully.

In sum, one can see that the correction of disharmony in sex relations is a cooperative task for both husband and wife. It requires taking into account not only physical factors but also the psychological and esthetic considerations that make for a heightened sexual attractiveness and gratification.

(Photographs of this article were posed by professional models.)

• • •

According to the Chinese legend, Pi-kou breast-fed both his young sisters. The illustration appeared in a Chinese book published in 1856. —From "Das Weib," by Dr. Max Bartels.

BREAST FEEDING FATHERS

The development of feminine breasts in the male is a phenomenon that is not too uncommon. Cases where fathers have actually suckled their babes, however, are exceedingly rare. A number of such cases are described by a famous anthropologist.

by Max Bartels, M.D.

CHARLES DARWIN, the author of the theory of evolution, drew attention to the fact that the breast-glands of a man

Dr. Bartels, a famous German anthropologist and anatomist, formerly of the University of Berlin, is co-author of the classic and monumental work, "Das Weib" ("The Woman").

are rudimentary organs in that they are insufficiently developed and functionally inactive. It should not appear too improbable when rare cases are reported in which the mammary glands of some men secrete milk.

The swelling of the breasts of male children in the first days of their lives, and the secretion of a milk-like liquid, the so-called *witch's milk*, is well-known. Furthermore, the breast-glands of boys swell and enlarge during puberty. The development of feminine breasts in the male is quite possible. Such cases are called *gynecomastia*.

A number of such cases have been described in recent times.* They prove beyond doubt that this growth of the breasts and development of real milk-producing glands is a fact. Breast secretions in most of these cases consisted of milk-like products. However, real milk has been secreted, according to medical reports, in some instances. At any rate, there is no reason to reject in advance the possibility of a father's nursing a baby in rare cases.

Some medical observers have reported a number of instances of milk-secreting breasts in men. Dr. Schenk knew a man who secreted a rich supply of milk during his youth and up until his 50th year. Dr. Walaeus gives a similar report of a Flemish man of 40 with one enormous milk-producing breast. Abensina saw a man giving so much milk from his breasts that they could make cheese of it. Cardanus says that he saw a man of 40 who secreted so much milk that a child could be nourished with it.

Alexander Benedictus, an anatomist who lived in Verona (Italy) at the end of the 15th century, wrote:

"Maripetrus, a member of the sacred order of knights, related that

a certain Syrus, whose infant son survived his wife's death, often gave him his breasts to appease the hunger of his crying son, and that, after continuous suckling, his nipple dripped with milk, of which— to the wonder of the entire city —he afterward had an abundance."

In the Icelandic *Floamanna-Saga* it is written that Thorgils, a chief with the nickname *Oerrabeinsstjupr* (Scarred Legs) went in the 10th century to Greenland, having been called by Eric the Red the discoverer of Greenland. His wife Thorey died there in bizarre circumstances after she delivered her son Thorfinur. During the night Thorgils wanted to keep watch over the baby, and he expressed his sorrow that his son could not live long and that he could not help him. He decided to try breast-feeding the infant. First came blood, then *blanda* (whey) which continued to flow until finally milk was expressed. So the child was nourished.

According to Weinberg, the *Talmud* (Sabbath 53) also contains an observation about this matter, and Rabbi Singer tells it as follows:

"A man lost his wife and she left him a baby, yet he was not rich enough to take a nurse. Then a miracle happened — his breasts grew like the two breasts of a woman, and he suckled his son."

These are old stories about which there can be doubt. But Alexander von Humboldt gives a report of more recent observations about a peasant of the village Arenas in New Andalusia:

"This man suckled his son with

*See SEXOLOGY, issues of September, 1948 and October, 1949.

his own milk. When the mother fell ill, he took the baby into his bed to quiet it and he pressed it against his breasts. Lozano was 32 years old and until then he felt no milk in his breast. But the sucking of his nipple by his son produced an accumulation of the liquid. The milk was thick and very sweet. The father, astonished by the swelling of his breast, gave it to his son, and he suckled it for five months, twice and three times daily.

"He attracted the curiosity of the neighbors, but did not think of profiting by this curiosity, as would have been done in Europe. To preserve this event for posterity, an official written record was made which we saw, and surviving witnesses have assured us that during the whole time when he was suckled by his father, the

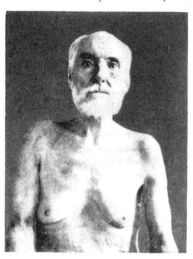

An example of gynecomastia, or enlargement of the mammary gland in the male. Such a condition can often be improved by surgery. — From "Geschlechtskunde," by Dr. Magnus Hirschfeld.

boy had no other food. Lozano, who was not in Arenas when we were visiting the missions, called on us later in Cumana. He was accompanied by his son, who was then 12 or 13 years old. Mr. Bonpland, who carefully examined the breast of the father, found that it was wrinkled like the breasts of a woman after she had suckled a child. He noticed that the left breast was particularly distended, and Lozano explained that this was because the two breasts did not supply the same amount of milk."

Dr. John Franklin reports the following case:

"A Chippewa Indian left his tribe to catch beavers. His wife was his only companion. She was in her first pregnancy. She was surprised by labor and gave birth to a boy. She died three days after the delivery. To save the life of his son, the man fed him with a brew of stag meat. To keep the child quiet, he held it against his breast. This produced a flow of milk from his breast, and he was able to nurse his child. His son grew, took a wife from his tribe and had children. My informant saw the Indian when he was an old man. His left breast was still unusually large."

Although there can be no doubt about the veracity of these stories, it must be noted that the reporters did not personally witness these occurrences. More important, therefore, is a report given by the well-known Greek anthropologist Bernhard Orenstein to the Berlin Anthropological Association:

"In the year 1846 I lived in

the small coastal town of Galaxidi in the Bay of Amphissa with the ship-builder Elias Kanada. This man was of so colossal a build, that I have seen nothing similar in Greece. Whenever his small, weak and tuberculous wife lacked milk, and their little boy, who was not quite 2 years old, cried, his father gave him one of his heavily developed breasts with the tenderness of a mother. The little one suckled it noisily until he was satisfied. Many a time I saw the big man wipe milk from his breast."

This report gives scientific confirmation that, at least in very rare cases, fathers have actually been able to breast-feed children. Such cases represent extremely interesting anthropological phenomena.

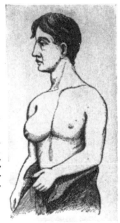

The young man shown here reveals an excessive development of the mammary gland in one breast. Such enlargement, though not to the degree shown here, appears often, without apparent cause, during adolescence. — *After the anthropologist Morgan.*

● ● ●

South Sea Customs

AN interesting study has been made recently of the sex life and customs of an isolated and primitive South Sea island people, known as the Marquesans. The study was reported recently in *Natural History* by Dr. Harry L. Shapiro, chairman of the Department of Anthropology of the American Museum of Natural History.

The attitude of the Marquesan is far more liberal toward sex than in most societies. A limited period of sexual freedom is granted to the youth of both sexes. As young men and women reach maturity (the ages of sixteen to eighteen for girls and slightly older for males), they form a class that is rather like a club.

Sexual experimentation was not only permitted, but even encouraged, although it was expected that the couples would eventually pair off in a permanent marriage.

All offspring, regardless of legitimacy, were warmly welcomed and adopted. There were practically no unmarried persons and most marriages seemed to work out well. There usually seemed to be no objection on the part of the husband if the wife took on an additional husband.

Foreign visitors were apparently received by the young girls with the same sex freedom as was shown their companions. As a result venereal diseases brought by the Europeans spread through the whole community. Since they had developed no immunity to the various new diseases, their first effect was devastating. In a little over a century, only 1,600 persons remained out of a community of 100,000 (1930). Since then, modern medicine has led to a slow rise in population.

One of the unusual practices of the Marquesans is the art of tattooing the entire body with intricate designs.

Two psychiatrists analyze...

obscene, pornographic letters

I. An Analysis by J. Paul de River, M.D., F.A.C.S.

THE writing of obscene and pornographic letters is comparable to the writing of obscene and pornographic literature. In both cases, the authors derive stimulation, sometimes even satisfaction. The primary goal of these pen works is usually to arouse sexual feelings within the writer. Secondly, the writer often wishes to shock his reader (imagination relishes this thought) and, of course,

A well-known criminal psychiatrist, Dr. De River is author of "The Sexual Criminal," Founder and Director of the Sex Offense Bureau, City of Los Angeles, Consultant Alienist to the Municipal and Superior Courts (L. A.), and Instructor in Criminal Psychiatry and Sexology, Calif. Peace Officers' Training Institute, U. of Cal. at Los Angeles.

to acquaint his reader with or perhaps introduce him to sexual deviations. In doing all this, the writer's ego is inflated by the feeling that he possesses a certain hidden power.

Some of the writers of pornographic letters are highly - sexed masturbators who have been sexually frustrated. Many have an organ inferiority which has caused them frustration as well as an inferiority complex. They turn towards sexual aggression in the form of sadistic torture to their victims through the writing of obscenity. They also enjoy the masochistic torture inflicted upon themselves by the building up of fancied dreams which they know will never come true.

There are others, especially

T HERE exists very little literature on obscene and pornographic letters, although such letters are fairly common all over the world. Letters of this type are frequently sent to prominent personalities, particularly stage and motion picture actresses.

SEXOLOGY, during the past 25 years, has received its share of such letters. In the early years following the establishment of the magazine, these letters were quite plentiful and became almost a routine matter. During the past ten years there has been a marked abatement of such missives, probably for the reason that sex education has become more widespread.

The letters, however, never completely stopped. Recently a particularly voluminous, as well as shocking, example was received by the editors. It was a six-page closely-written letter in which almost every other expression was an obscene four-letter word, This particular writer used a great deal of ingenuity, and his fertile, if misguided, fantasy went to great lengths to invent every imaginable type of sexual situation, the result of a sadly deviated mentality. The letter ran the entire gamut from rape and incest to sadism and masochism — in fact, there

Why are such letters written? What is behind the motivation of these authors of pornography? Are such people dangerous?

SEXOLOGY posed these questions to two distinguished psychiatrists with wide experience as sex criminologists. Their comments are printed here.   *—The Editors*

among older individuals, who are impotent. All that they have left to dwell upon is the mind picture of obscenity or filth which they attempt to build up through dream phantasy to satisfy their sexual cravings.

Then there are those whose sexual impulse is weak and insecure. For these individuals some unique or exceptional sexual practice is necessary in order to afford them an outlet for their weakened sexual libido. This they attempt to accomplish through sexual phantasy or through the transfer of this phantasy into the writing of obscene letters.

It should be remembered that in certain individuals very often the mental side of the sexual excitement and release is sufficient without the mechanical involvement of the genital apparatus. In other words, they obtain sexual satisfaction in the fancied experience, without sexual intercourse. This process is termed *psychic (or mental) masturbation.*

Into this practice there enter particularly abundant and varied, not least of all deviated, phantasy forms. Obscenity, erotic reading, and the corresponding pictures stand in close relationship to psychic masturbation.

The authors of obscene and pornographic epistles are by and large sexual psychopaths rather than sexual neurotics. There is a pathological deviation of the sexual impulse.

Most often, the writers of obscene and pornographic letters are found among men. The same type of individual who writes obscene letters frequently indulges in the collection of obscene art. Often they are imaginative geniuses.

Usually we find that they belong to the uneducated or so-called lower classes of society, but occasionally we encounter a highly intellectual individual resorting to this practice. We also find that some of the authors of these letters are less than average in general knowledge but in matters pertaining to sex knowledge and mental ability they are far superior to the ordinary person.

Regardless of the mentality of the obscene letter writer, we do know that a strong *sado-masochistic* element exists in his makeup. Sadism is manifested in the bold act of writing the letter in the first place and the desire to shock or perhaps mentally torture the reader with detailed descriptions and illustrations of sexual deviations.

Masochism (the desire to inflict pain on one's self or the desire to suffer) is discernible when we realize that the author of an obscene letter may actually experience a degree of pain or suffering in the writing of his letter. This may come about during the composition of the letter, or may follow the letter writing in the form of self-reproach, disgust, or regret that he has indulged in this act. However, the sadistic element is the stronger of the two.

There are also evidences in such persons of *exhibitionism* and *tri-*

olism (the tendency to perform the sexual act with several partners or in the presence of several partners). In some of these individuals there is a strong component of *narcissism,* or self-love.

By and large writers of obscene and pornographic letters are a menace to society in so far as they write such letters. Certainly one realizes the damage caused when one of these letters is sent to an innocent victim who is utterly unaware of the existence of such deviated sexual practices.

Occasionally we find a writer of obscene letters who, having the necessary sexual drive (he may even be highly-sexed), becomes aggressive, attempting to carry out his dream life of sexual deviations and sadistic fancies. We find this among those who have been frustrated due to some physical inferiority, not necessarily sexual.

When such an individual does resort to actual rather than fancied acts of aggression, he is usually a prowler and a peeping-Tom, or *voyeur.* He may even go so far as to force entry and commit rape if the opportunity presents itself.

Thus, the writers of obscene and pornographic letters must be considered as sexually criminal deviates. They possess a pathological passion for fabrication and a morbid passion for prestige. By enshrouding themselves with a veil of mystery, they attempt to inflate a weakened ego and compensate for sexual frustration.

II. An Analysis by Clifford Allen, M.D., M.R.C.P.

WRITING an obscene or "dirty" letter is really equivalent to a small child's shouting out obscene words to shock adults. Freud, long ago, pointed out that for a man to tell a girl a "smutty" story is a *symbolical* sexual assault. This is the basis of such letters—to shock or sexually excite whoever reads them. To be shocked is to defend oneself against the sexual provocation, whereas to be excited is to accept it.

One must not confuse this type of letter with the "poison pen" type in which respectable people are accused of imaginary sexual misconduct. The letters we have in mind are the ones filled with obscene words and describing sex behavior of an outrageous kind.

Psychiatrists do not have too many opportunities to examine the writers of such letters, but occasionally patients will confess that they have done something of the sort. They reveal that they have obtained a sexual thrill at the idea of upsetting someone else by their writing.

What sort of people write obscenity? They are not the gay Lotharios, or the pretty girls with dozens of young men at their feet. On the contrary, such letters are usually written by the shy, timid, fearful young men, too frightened to approach a girl. When they are the product of a woman's mind, they are written by the frustrated spinster or the hysterical girl who is forced to live (what she dares not do in actuality) in the secret fantasies which she commits to paper.

Probably immaturity and frustration are the two fundamental motivations which persuade the

Dr. Allen, Consultant Psychiatrist to the Dreadnaught Seamen's Hospital, Greenwich, London, and to the English Ministry of Pensions, is author of "Modern Discoveries in Medical Psychology" *and* "The Sexual Perversions and Abnormalities."

lewd - minded writer to produce such literature. Exhibitionism and perhaps unconscious sadism may be present. When the letter-writer describes rapes, as if he were the victim, or she the aggressor, there may be a homosexual element present. However, all these are symptoms of immaturity.

Since the letter writer prefers obscenity to sexual approaches, there is in many cases actual impotence or frigidity present, with a resulting frustration. Usually such letter-writers are far too timid to indulge in sexual adventures or ask anyone to marry.

These letters often describe sexual attacks, rapes and ill-treatment which the writer is obviously enjoying in fantasy. *Will fantasy ever turn into reality and the attacks become factual?* This is rare. However, I once had a case of a girl who had a similar fantasy but did not commit it to paper—she made complaints. Twice she charged that she had been raped by young men; on each occasion the man was convicted and sentenced. Only on the third occasion was her integrity suspected and her accusation rejected. She was ordered to have a medical examination, found to be schizophrenic and committed to a mental hospital.

One further point is of interest. It is rare to find any form of wit or humor in obscene writing. I have only seen it once. This was in December one year when someone had written on the door of a public lavatory, which was covered with obscene inscriptions, "We wish all our readers a Happy Xmas and a prosperous New Year."

SEXOLOGY readers frequently ask what difference there is between self-gratification and the normal marital act. Our illustration shows the difference graphically and scientifically. The obelisk on the left pictures the degree of difference in gratification to that of the one at the right.

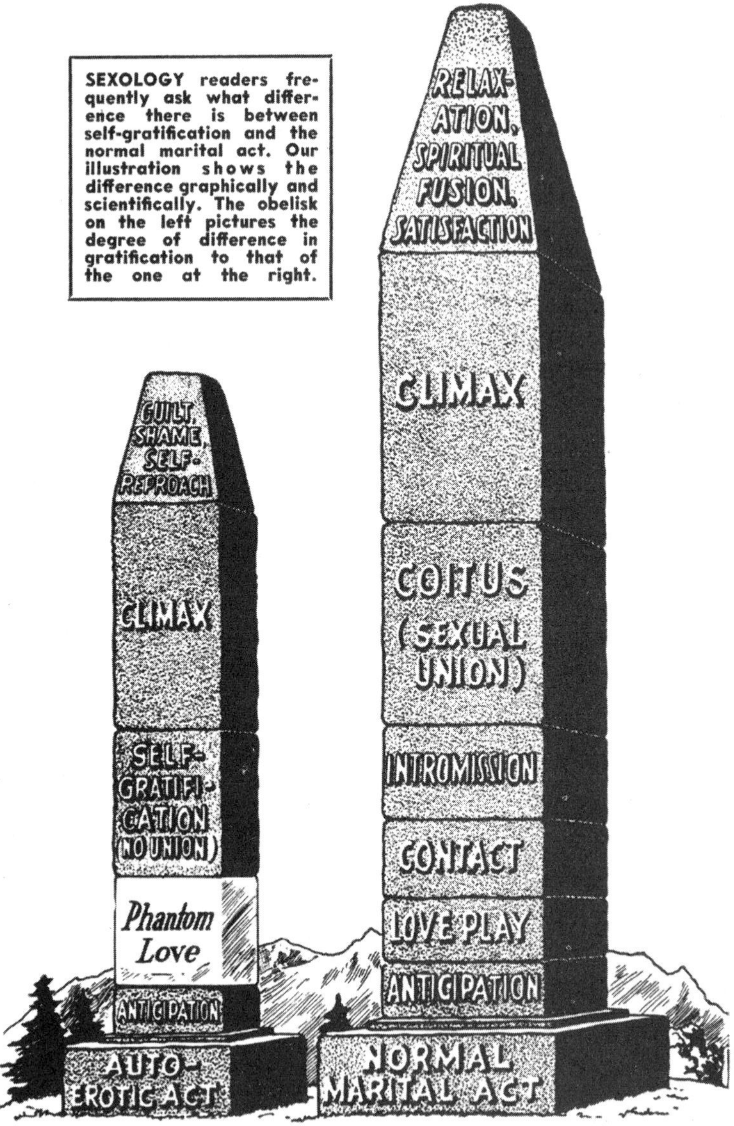
GUILT, SHAME, SELF-REPROACH
CLIMAX
SELF-GRATIFI-CATION (NO UNION)
Phantom Love
ANTICIPATION
AUTO-EROTIC ACT
RELAX-ATION, SPIRITUAL FUSION, SATISFACTION
CLIMAX
COITUS (SEXUAL UNION)
INTROMISSION
CONTACT
LOVE PLAY
ANTICIPATION
NORMAL MARITAL ACT

Note that the gratification derived from the auto-erotic act is only about 60% as much as that of the normal marital act. (Height and girth of obelisk.) The blocks in each illustration give the approximate measure of satisfaction derived from each part of the act; thus Anticipation has the smallest percentage of the total act. Note particularly that in the autoerotic act the following important functions are missing entirely: "Love play, contact, and intromission." Instead, the self-gratifier must conjure up an imaginary phantom-lover. The end result as shown in the apexes of the two obelisks differs vastly. *The left one is entirely negative*. The one on the right wholly positive. Self-gratification is an infantile act.

When does Sex Life End?

*More and more,
it is being realized
that age is not
the decisive factor
in ending sex
interest and activity.*

by D. O. Cauldwell, M.D., Sc.D.

Ewing Galloway

ONE of the common questions which have been put to this author is the effect of age on male virility. Even men in their early thirties, worried about some failure of their sexual power, have asked, "Is it my age?"

Potency depends upon a great many things, mainly the emotional state of the individual. *Age in itself is not the decisive factor.*

One of the most remarkable illustrations of this fact in this writer's experience occurred several years ago on a visit to Florida.

As I was driving slowly along

Dr. Cauldwell is a prominent sexologist, Medical Adviser to SEXOLOGY Magazine and Editor of its Question and Answer Department.

the road in a small, almost wholly Negro community, I noticed two white-haired colored people approaching their house from a nearby field. Stopping in front of the building I requested water for the car's radiator. Doing this gave me a chance to converse with them.

Although he did not look too old, I was amazed to find out that the age of the man was 103—to prove it he showed me the certificate which he had received on emancipation. His wife too had been born a slave and hence was well in her nineties.

When he discovered my connection with SEXOLOGY magazine, which he read from time to time, he put several questions to me, giving me a chance to ask some in return.

I inquired whether he could tell me at what age a couple should cease their sexual functions. "I suppose when they get tired of a sex life," was his reply. Apparently he and his wife had not yet tired of sex, because they still were sexually active and satisfied.

This experience of finding persons of greatly advanced years still retaining their sexual desires and abilities has been repeated many times. Occasionally it is dramatized when one reads of men in the seventies and eighties who have just become fathers. One of the oldest men to become a father in modern medical history was a 96-year-old

Confederate War veteran married to a young wife.

The most famous case in history was that of Thomas Parr, who came to be known as "Old Parr."

Parr was born in 1483, just nine years before Columbus discovered America, in Salopp, England. He died, as the inscription on his tomb in Westminster Abbey tells us, at the age of 152.

As a young man, Parr was a roué and for more than a hundred years he was reputed to be a threat to the ladies. When he reached the age of 80, he decided it was about time to marry and settle down. He lived with his wife for thirty-two years until her death.

When he was 100 years old, it was discovered that Old Parr had an affair with another woman, and, according to the custom of the day, he had to do public penance at the door of the church, wearing a white sheet.

Eight years after the death of his wife, Parr married again—this time at the age of 120. *He had*

Javier Pereira, who estimated his age of 167, was apparently not too old to enjoy kissing a pretty airline stewardess.—*Wide World.*

children both by his first and second wives.

Javier Pereira, a Colombia, South America, Indian, was said to be 168 years old when he died early in 1958. (Unlike Parr's case, however, his age was never authenticated.)

During a visit to New York City a short while before his death, newspapers noted that Pereira showed a "lively interest" in the girl reporters who followed him around.

It is amply clear that age is not the decisive factor in ending sexual activity. In most cases, the sex life ends when it is willed by either man or woman, husband or wife, to end. Throughout life there are lapses. These may be due to the fact that nature called a halt. They may be due to psychological misconceptions. They may be due to an unfavorable physical condition of either man or wife, or both, or to serious illness requiring a long period of convalescence. If both husband and wife have healthy mental attitudes, lapses are relatively unimportant. This is particularly true when both are deeply in love.

Many aging persons feel that there is something wrong in their having strong sexual desires. Thus, they often hesitate to seek counsel with a physician when faced with a sex problem in their marriage.

For example, sometimes the interest in sex declines in one of the partners before it does in the other. Perhaps the husband is still highly potent while the wife may have lost her interest in sex life after her change-of-life. Or perhaps the wife still desires marital relations, but the husband has lost his sexual vigor and ability. Since they are reluctant to bring the situation before a physician, the unhappy state continues.

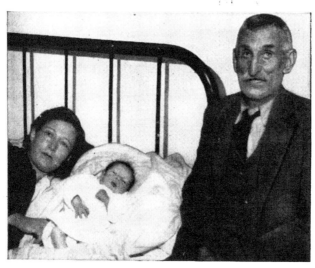

George Isaac Hughes, 96-year-old Civil War veteran, is shown with his wife and their new-born daughter. He is the oldest man to become a father ever recorded in the United States.

"Old Parr," who married his first wife at 80 and his second at 120 years of age, had children by both wives. From a painting by the famous artist Rubens.—*Culver.*

Many times a widowed man or woman in later years feels the need to marry again only to find their families strongly against the idea. This is an unrealistic attitude. The older person will benefit emotionally as well as physically from a happy marriage at this time of life.

It should be realized that it is perfectly natural for persons in their seventies and eighties to show strong sexual interest and derive continued satisfaction from sexual intercourse. Such an attitude can do much to help keep alive a gratifying relationship between man and wife and enable them to continue to share all the satisfactions of marriage and the gratification of marital relations.

● ● ●

Ejaculatory Impotence

ONE of the rarer cases found among men suffering from sexual impotence is the inability to ejaculate during the sexual act. Often the patient suffering from ejaculatory impotence can sustain an erection for a considerable time, and in the marital act the female partner may realize a satisfactory orgasm, but the male fails to achieve a sexual climax. Some males with this condition are able to engage in self-gratification with an emission but cannot achieve ejaculation in coitus with a female partner.

A recent article in the *Journal of Urology* by Drs. Alex H. Kaplan and Morris Abrams of the Washington University School of Medicine discusses this type of impotence and its therapy. They point out that no discussion of the inability to ejaculate has appeared in the urological literature during the past fifteen years.

The authors stress that, in ejaculatory impotence, organic factors play little or no rôle, and the most prominent factors are emotional ones. The patient afflicted with this ailment reacts sexually by unconsciously withholding and refusing to give of himself. Usually psychotherapy is essential in clearing up the trouble.

A study of the family and personal history of the patient is recommended, once a diagnosis has been made. Also the physician is urged to give the patient friendly encouragement, and listen to his description of his family situation. This knowledge may help considerably in treating the disorder.

The authors describe in detail one case of a patient suffering from ejaculatory impotence and the therapeutic methods by which his condition was relieved.

YOUR SEX QUESTIONS ANSWERED

● **Use of Proper Words (271)**
Sexology, January, 1935

Editor, SEXOLOGY:

I have a problem I have been wanting to write about for some time, but I am afraid to put it in writing for fear I might be arrested for misuse of the mails. Just what words or terms am I allowed to use that won't be considered obscene? I judge the subscribers writing to you are very careless with the words they use.

M. D., California

Answer:

The question of what constitutes obscenity or lewdness is not hard to understand, if you simply take the intension of the writer and his ability to use the correct words in explaining his troubles to the Editor. Up to the present time, we have answered several thousand letters. Many of them come from persons of the highest education; others from persons of no education at all. When we consider that they are intentionally offensive in their tone and vocabulary, we simply destroy them; but, if men (or women) write in a sincere manner, we try to help them without regard to the degree of their education or ability to express themselves in the proper scientific terms. (These terms, however, are carefully explained and illustrated in each issue of the magazine.) SEXOLOGY secured mailing rights from the United States Postal Department after that Department thoroughly investigated the magazine. You can see, we could not send the magazine through the mails if they classified it as obscene. We would not edit it and publish it if

would not edit it and publish it if we thought it obscene. We feel that we are offering a valued service to the public in making it possible for them to obtain such information; and the Question and Answer department has been of great help to thousands of our readers. You need, therefore, have no hesitancy in writing to us.

—Editor

● ● ●

● **Breast Changes (6182)**
Sexology, August, 1963

Dear Doctor: Before giving birth to my first child I had normal - sized breasts. Since the baby was born, my breasts have gotten so small that it changes my entire appearance. I thought in time they would come back to normal size, but they haven't. Is there anything I can do?

Mrs. Z. R., Massachusetts

Answer: It is not too unusual for the breasts to change in shape and consistency after the birth of a child. You did not tell us whether or not you nursed the babies. While this sometimes brings about changes, it is actually not at all inevitable. The change in size and shape and consistency of the breasts may very largely be a hereditary matter. If your mother or your paternal grandmother had difficulty with the size and shape of her breasts, you possibly have inherited that characteristic.

If you are underweight, the gaining of a little weight and exercises to increase the firmness of the muscles near the breast might very well help. Otherwise, the best possible thing we can suggest is the wearing of an adequate bra to restore normal shape to the chest and make your clothes appear better. While there are operations performed to pad the breasts, we do not feel that these are generally successful or desirable. They are satisfactory only in a relatively few cases.

● ● ●

● **Masochistic Flagellation (3242)**
Sexology, November, 1951

Editor, SEXOLOGY:

I am a physician. One of my patients—a man more than 70 years old—acutely desires erection daily. He wants to know how to encourage erection, which, without orgasm, satisfies him sexually. A few years ago he found that erection was almost impossible. He objects to associating with women and also objects to intercourse as a means of securing erection. He found that he got erection by having two or more women spank him vigorously—several women, because this arrangement kept him from undesired intercourse. He has since discovered that he can get the desired erection by self - punishment — hitting his abdomen with the back of a hairbrush. Yet this sometimes fails to bring about the erection desired.

(1) How can he insure erection? Perhaps mental pictures are best. (2) Is it unwise to have frequent erection—perhaps daily? It would seem that this patient had better do this than to use others (as women) to satisfy him. His present method does not corrupt or involve others, and emissions do not often take place.

Dr. F. T. F., Florida.

Answer:

Your patient is a masochist. He will fantasy (make mental pictures) regardless, and the same is true with reference to flagellating himself if he can get it done. A great many masochists engage in self-flaggelation. Apparently it is not so much a question with him how to insure erection as it is how to have what he wants otherwise. And, he will largely have this regardless of all circumstances for the simple reason that people of his turn of mind live largely in their fantasies.

It certainly is not injurious to have

daily or more frequent erections. The age of the patient is of little consequence. Some 70-year-old men practice self-gratification, or have sexual relations daily and their health, if not promoted, certainly is not impaired.

—Editor

● ● ●

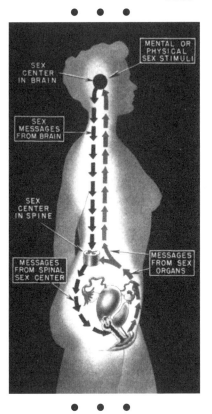

● ● ●

● **Female Masturbation (1405)**
Sexology, March, 1942

Editor, SEXOLOGY:

A girl friend of mine has confided to me a secret—one which she would not tell her own mother. She is in her twenties, good-looking, intelligent, with a sensitive nature and a shy disposition. Yet she is quite passionate—so much so that she had to satisfy her physical cravings artificially. She had been brought up in a respectable home, with fine surroundings, and was unwilling to indulge in pre-marital intercourse; so she has carried on this practice for seven years. She is not a Lesbian, or abnormal, but as desirous of the attentions of the opposite sex as any girl could be. Her habit has caused her to develop an inferiority complex, and worry a great deal; yet she will not consult a doctor. As a result of the habit, there has been an enlargement of the *labia,* and she is afraid to face marriage and the reactions of a husband which, without any experience she cannot anticipate. She thinks hers is the only like case in the world. What can we do to help this girl? Surely, her life should not be wasted on this account.

Mrs. H. W., Illinois

Answer:

There are a great many women who abuse themselves to excess, far more than the average person realizes; and there is no doubt that, when it is carried to excess in the female, there is an enlargement or *hypertrophy* of some of the external sex organs. At the same time, the young woman you mention is rather complimentary to the anatomical knowledge of the average man. A competent physician on examination might see that the external genitalia were larger than normal and he might suspect that the cause was masturbation but the average man would never realize these things, because he has not the proper medical and scientific training. So I do not think that your friend would have anything to fear if she did marry; unless she married a physician, her husband would never realize the condition. But I would advise her to consult a woman physician, and take treatment to reduce her solitary sex urge. She needs sympathetic medical advice, and medicine, and should have no trouble in securing this from a physician of her own sex.

—Editor.

● ● ●

● **Testicles and Sexual Capacity (4135)**
Sexology, October, 1955

Editor, SEXOLOGY:

Although my sex urge and sex life are healthy, I notice that my testicles are about twice the usual dimension. I have no pains in or swelling of the scrotum. I have never had the mumps, but several times have had gonorrhea.

If both testicles were removed, would sexual desire or ability be absent?

Mr. F. E., Florida.

Answer:

There are numerous causes of enlargement of the testicles. For instance, *lymphogranuloma inguinale,* a venereal disease of the tropics, often produces *elephantiasis* (enlargement) of the genital organs. To learn the nature of your condition consult a

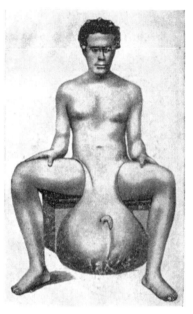

Elephantiasis (enlargement of the testicles), is often produced by lymphogranuloma inguinale, a genital disease of the tropics. —Photo reproduced from "Bilder-Lexicon."

physician and have him examine you.

It is not desirable to have the testicles removed. If sexual desire and capacity are satisfactory before the removal of the testicles, there is a good possibility that sexual ability will not be retarded early. Castration does not affect sexual desire, which often continues to be as strong after as before the operation. In some castrated men, sexual capacity remains healthy throughout life. Many, however, have a tendency to lose their sexual ability a few years after surgery.

—Editor

SEX EDUCATION
ON THE BEACH

by Justus Day Wilbur

Bathing beaches are, in a sense, schools for ana-
tomical sex education. Children and young people
see the human body naturally displayed. Every
form, shape, size and age is represented on
the beach. This is a wholesome development.

A WESTERN STATE visitor to New York's famous *Jones Beach,* teeming with thousands of men, women and children, was surprised and somewhat shocked. "As beach attire they actually permit mere trunks for men and extra-brief bikinis for women," he exclaimed. "We haven't yet allowed these out West."

"Come now," we urged, "don't you really find it rather educational to see human beings almost exactly as Nature made them? I don't think there actually is any sexual immodesty here, do you?"

"I quite agree with you," replied this intelligent man (an edu-cator); "it is interesting. I almost become an anthropologist as I look. The various types of people, nearly naked, become not just impersonal humans, but very definite individuals. The fact that they are 'undressed' seems to make them actually more interesting. I look at a boy and say, 'There is a slender undernourished youth.' I look at a pretty young girl, and say to myself, 'What a pity—she has such poor posture!' I look at an elderly overweight man and I say to myself, 'What a serious handicap—I must never let myself get to such a figure.'"

My friend had caught the idea:

Cooling off at a famous bathing resort. The brief swimming apparel for men and women provides an education in the body contours and struc-tures of both sexes. Glamor is natural and illusion about the human physique cannot exist at a bathing beach. This helps mating selections of young people to be wholesome and realistic.—*Wide World Photo* our bathing beaches of today—most of which have been increasingly liberal in permitting simple bathing clothes—are really places where one can become acquainted with the human race, minus all the clever arts of the modern clothiers who are adept at making the human figure seem like something it isn't, and regimenting us all into standard habiliments—mass camouflage.

Beaches Rid Us of Illusions!

Particularly, it seems to me, our modern bathing beaches are useful during the mating years, in ridding each sex of unrealistic illusions about the other sex. If there is any false notion about the body of a man or woman left after viewing it on a July noon under the intense glare of the sun, with the woman wearing a scanty bathing suit, then it is fantasy indeed.

Young people, particularly if there are no brothers or sisters in the family, definitely need "bathing beach education" to make them know the opposite sex *as it actually is* when almost entirely unconcealed. The normal sex imagining of young people requires precisely such discipline as a bathing beach handily affords in order to avoid a kind of "honeymoon disillusionment" that is nearly always unfavorable to good mating. When young people see each other often in modern bathing clothes, they have already traveled halfway or more in the direction of easy adjustment to the other sex in the physical sense. They do not develop the various neurotic reactions arising from unrealistic ideas about the human body; as, for example, husbands or wives who cannot stand seeing their mates nude, or refrain from looking at their uncovered breasts or other parts, or who become over-excited at almost any uncovering, and associate sin or lust or immodesty with it; familiar reactions 50 years and more ago—but still too widely met with.

We have only to remember how recent are the new standards. They are hardly two decades old, with many communities even today prohibiting bare chests for men bathers, or brief suits for women. And in Europe it was certainly no more than two or three decades ago that famous seaside bathing beaches like Ostend (Belgium) still used the bathhouses on wheels, drawn by horses. This compelled bathers to be almost fully clothed on the beaches, and rather full coverage was insisted on even in bathing suits for the few moments when they emerged, close to the water, to go into, or out of, the sea!

I submit that the frank gazes of young people upon the opposite sex in fairly scant bathing clothes are a helpful preparation for a successful marriage. The young people, with their natural teen-age sensitivity and concentration upon physical contour and personality, see every kind and character of physique—with all the other personality values which freer disclosure unveils (posture, energy, vitality, health, color, form, absence of the screen and crutch of clothes). There thus emerges *a reliable sense of natural physical mat-*

ing preference, the kind and type of contour, size, posture, constitutional build and category, which they can and do most definitely respond to. The girl who would naturally be most attracted to a muscular athletic, extrovert type sometimes finds that her unrealistic ignorance of male physique has tricked her into marrying an introverted, physically weak type, whose padded shoulders and manner hid the truth, *until the honeymoon!* Such a *misfit* could not pass the *bathing beach test!* The young man who thrills to a well-rounded form and well-molded breasts may also be tricked by clothes into believing his girl is what he prefers, whereas the bathing beach would have revealed her true anatomy.

Variety in Physical Choice

We must not forget (as I have explained in SEXOLOGY, January 1952, in an article on *"Sex and Physical Contour"*) that deep in our minds as we grow up there are developed certain basic choices as to the physical type of the opposite sex which excites our imagination most. Bathing beach familiarity with numerous men and women of many sizes, proportions, curves or contours, will bring this preference forward *realistically,* so that the young person understands better what he prefers in a member of the opposite sex.

A woman with whom I discussed this subject looked a bit disconsolate and admitted that many women *avoid* bathing-beach attire in fear of just such masculine judgment, feeling that "their curves" are not alluring enough, (or are *too* curvaceous!). But this is mere hypersensitivity. Young men, lacking attractive physiques, often have the same fears. Preferences are of many kinds, for fat and lean, curves or lack of curve, tall or short, flat or bosomy, etc. The important thing is that bathing beaches of today clarify the preference and make that preference familiar and even more attractive than before.

Listen to a group of young women discreetly commenting to themselves on young men in shorts passing by. "I like a solid, chunky fellow like that one," you'll hear a girl say. "I'd have confidence in him."

"Oh, but he's not tall, dark and handsome, like that man over there," says another girl. "That's my type."

"But look at his legs," is the critical remark of another girl, "just pipe-stems; *he's weak.*"

Young men make similar self-educative comments as they view young women passing by.

Aid to Marital Happiness

Granted that selection by physical contour alone is no infallible mating recipe, the point remains that the young folk of the mating age are very highly conscious on this subject, and that the more familiar they become with the frankly-disclosed contours of many men and women—as at bathing beaches—the more likely they are to make a satisfying lasting marital choice. There is a great difference between the *reality* of the opposite sex, as it stands scantily clad, and the image a naïve young person's sexual imagination can create. Lack of disclosure—at least to the bathing costume point—before marriage, could drive out every bit of romance on the honeymoon.

The fact that in beauty contests the contestants are judged in bathing suits is evidence that their charms could hardly be evaluated reliably any other way, short of nudity! The great vogue of "cheesecake," as the theatrical world calls photographs of women in scant clothes or exposed limbs, is evidence that young men want to see women in revealing costume. Women show similar interest, as the "life-guard fixation" among women demonstrates. We like nowadays to see more clearly what we let ourselves in for! Nor do we like to be unpleasantly surprised on our honeymoon. The modern bathing beach is a show-window of young charms and helpfully offers an education in physical preferences. Not for anything would we consent to wrap up the opposite sex again in all the appalling, obscuring and deceptive accoutrements—the bustles, 14 petticoats, and other garments that were standard in our grandparents' day. Sexology and hygienic progress would be set back too far by such retrogression!

● ● ●

BOY OF ONE YEAR REACHES PUBERTY

A BRITISH physician, Dr. Frazer, has reported a case of a boy of one year old who reached full sex development, believed to be the youngest on record, as a result of disease of the adrenal gland. At six months, the sex organs began developing, the limbs enlarged, the voice became deep and the appetite enormous. At 12 months "he was more virile than the average male" as shown by special test for hormones. However, the mind showed no advancement. The growth of the bones was equal to five years, that of the teeth two years, that of the sex organs 18 years. Operations on the tumor were performed at the age of 18 months; but the boy failed to survive. The prostate gland, seminal vesicles, and penis were found of adult size.

Sexology, August, 1940

● ● ●

SPIES USE HOMOSEXUALS TO GAIN SECRETS

COMMUNIST envoys to the United States were recently accused of holding all-male sex parties, to which effeminate American guests (homosexuals) were invited, in an effort to obtain secret government information. No female guests were invited, according to one witness; the liquor flowed freely and the diplomat host suavely turned the conversation to politics after the guests were intoxicated. The diplomat who reputedly resorted to this nefarious practice was said to be Teo H. Florin, former first secretary of the Czechoslovakian Embassy in Washington, D. C. Mr. Florin was requested to leave this country several years ago.

—*Associated Press*

Humans with TAILS

by Maxwell Vidaver, M.D.

Some human beings are born with tails. This is a THROW-BACK *to our remote animal ancestors. Such cases give us greater understanding of man's evolution.*

RECENTLY a child was born in a hospital in London, England, with a well developed tail two inches long. Men with tails or *caudal appendages,* apparently extensions of the lower spine, have frequently been reported in medical records. An unusual case was presented in the *Journal of Heredity,* by Dr. Taku Komai, of the National Institute of Genetics, Misima, Japan. An *Igorot* native with a tail was discovered about 1917 in the Philippine Islands. The tail measured several inches in length.

In another instance cited by Dr. Komai, that of a native *Dyak* in Borneo, the tail measured about 2¾ inches long and 0.8 inch in diameter. The tail was hairless and wrinkled. The natives said there were some others in the neighborhood having similar tails.

The late Dr. Vidaver was a prominent physician and author who was formerly Editor of SEXOLOGY.

Their neighbors sometimes spoke of the Dyaks as *ape-like,* because many of them were tailed.

Interestingly enough, while pictures of tailed children have appeared in medical literature, those of tailed *adults* are very rare.

Drs. Gould and Pyle in their *"Anomalies and Curiosities of Medicine"* give several descriptions of men with tails. In some cases, the tail appendages were merely fleshy protuberances; but in others, the caudal appendages contained distinctly jointed portions. The tails in many instances resemble more the tail of a pig, than that of a monkey. Drs. Gould and Pyle report the case of a Chinese boy who reputedly had a tail a foot long.

One of the most recent instances of a human tail was reported in the *British Medical Journal.* An otherwise healthy child was born with the vestigial appendage; after the child had reached the age of

11 months the mother finally decided to seek medical advice. The tail was successfully amputated by surgery. The tail in this child was more than a simple fold of the skin (as occurs in many cases) and measured about 3 inches in length. The tail moved and could be wagged slowly from side to side.

Many weird stories about people with tails have been told to travelers in various parts of the world. In Central Africa, for example, the *Niam Niams* were reputed to have smooth hairy tails 2 to 10 inches long. Dr. Bartels (*Archives of Anthropology*. 15:45-131, 1884) gave a summary of tailed humans which included 116 cases, of which 52 were males, 16 females and 48 of unrecorded sex. Later, Dr. Schaffer added 92 cases which he believed relatively authentic.

In Gould and Pyle's work there is cited the story of a missionary, George Brown, who in 1876 spoke of the formal breeding of a tailed race in Kali, off the coast of New Britain. In their description we read that the *tailless* children were slain as soon as they were born, so they would not be exposed to public ridicule. Another fabulous story tells how canoes were built for the tailed men in the East Indies, which had holes in the benches to accommodate the tails of the rowers! A tailed race of princes were said to have ruled

Rajoopootana. Another story cites a tribe of tailed natives among the primitive Indians of Paraguay.

Biological Origin

Biological and medical records have called attention to similar cases from time to time. A tail in a human being is regarded scientifically as a frequent unusual anatomical formation—not of course a regular deviation, but happening with sufficient frequency to attract some medical attention.

Long before the theory of evolution was promulgated by Darwin, men were born with tails. These births were considered on a

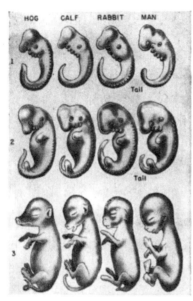

Development of the fetus in four different species of mammals. A tail develops in all human embryos, but usually disappears at a later stage of growth.

par with other human monstrosities, and the close relationship between man and the rest of the animal kingdom remained unperceived.

The births of children with tails are considered cases of *atavism* (the reappearance in an individual of the characteristics of a remote ancestor). Man is no doubt descended from some far removed ancestor who possessed a useful tail; and that occasionally there should be a reversion to earlier forms is but natural.

The spinal structure of a man is similar in every respect to that of other animals with backbones (*vertebrates*). The *coccyx*, the end of the spinal column, is made up of a number of "grown together"

bones, similar to the bones found in the tails of other animals. In man they are *rudimentary* (in an undeveloped state), nature through ages of evolutionary selection having discarded the tail as an unnecessary appendage in human beings.

Dr. Maynard M. Metcalf, professor of biology in the Woman's College at Baltimore, in his work on "Organic Evolution," states (page 163): 'It is interesting to know there have been instances in which a human being has retained, in an abnormal condition, the muscles of the ancestral tail."

The American Text Book of Surgery calls brief attention to the occasional births of children with tails, and suggests their early removal by surgery. If the tail is of appreciable length, owing to man's peculiar mode of existence, it will interfere with a comfortable sitting posture. Amputation of this accessory appendage is very simple; about the same as cutting off a dog's tail.

Rudimentary Organs

From an embryological standpoint, every human being begins life with a tail! Strange as it may appear, the unborn child, in its development in the womb, passes through many phases of evolution. In the first half of the second month of life in the womb, it does not differ essentially in appearance from other animals!

One marvels why humans are not more frequently born with tails. The infrequent occurrence of this anomaly is the result of ages of slow elimination. Nature takes a long time to completely rid the animal system of organs that have become unnecessary. Probably by this slow careful process, the tendency to atavistic creations (throwbacks) is diminished; or it may be these vestiges are retained for future use, in case changed conditions make their re-employment desirable.

There are a number of structures in the human body that have become obsolete. The human ear is endowed with rudimentary muscles capable of moving the ears— muscles which have lost their usefulness. By continued effort, however, these muscles can be developed sufficiently to obtain a limited degree of voluntary motion of the ears. Many a school boy has accomplished this feat, to the great enjoyment of his classmates.

Everyone knows of the *appendix*, which is another instance of an organ that has fallen into disuse. It is the remnant in human beings of a second intestine or bowel which still exists in certain species of animals. Not only is it absolutely useless in man, but at

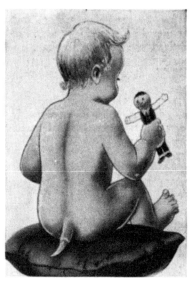

Baby with a tail, an unusual case reported by an American physician in 1901.

times it becomes a menace to his existence. How long Nature will persist in reproducing this unnecessary pouch, no one can determine; though eventually it will disappear entirely.

The *plantaris muscle*, situated in the calf of the leg, is a mere cord,

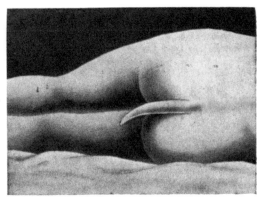

A child with a flexible tail which was movable at will. Appendage measured 2¾" in length and was amputated six months after birth.

having no muscular power, and not useful for walking; yet it has survived the passage of time. In four-footed animals, this muscle is highly developed and extremely useful.

Hair on the human body, a relic of our animal ancestors, is unnecessary; for man has learned how to clothe himself as protection against elements. Yet it still persists, and in many instances reaches luxuriant growth, almost equalling the hair of other *pri-* *mates* (higher animals, including man and the apes).

All this evidence of the close relationship of man and the rest of the animal world is proof that the birth of human beings with tails is highly interesting, but far from astounding to the scientific mind.

In the age of the atomic bomb, we can agree with Samuel Butler when he said, "If our minds should become visible, we would see that they too have tails."

● ● ●

SEXUAL EFFECTS OF ALCOHOL

By T. Bowen Partington, F.I.L., F.R.E.S.

THERE can be doubt that alcoholism does affect the married state. Occasionally, however, the sexual relations form an exception to this rule. The copulative faculty of the alcoholic need not necessarily be materially impaired. And yet alcoholism, if it is accompanied by frequent attacks of drunkenness, is capable of seriously impeding the exercise of sexual intercourse.

The real alcoholic is languid, tired and irritated, and is in a mental and physical condition which deprives him as much of the desire for sexual gratification as of the ability to perform the act. In the not very rare cases in which alcoholism has reached the stage where drunkenness alternates with exhaustion there is sometimes a complete stopping of all sexual intercourse between the married partners. There is created a nervous debility which is capable of producing inability to perform the marital act. Yet the desire is present, and it is because of this that the alcoholic often seeks in his intoxication special excitements to sharpen his impaired power, and this craving for excitements makes him a pervert. In this way he becomes an exhibitionist, or he is driven to commit immoral acts with children. Into this latter method of gratification he is, perhaps, also influenced by the circumstance that in the presence of sexually inexperienced persons he has no need to be ashamed of his infirmity.

Very remarkable is the intimate association between alcohol and sexual diseases (venereal diseases). As the alcoholic makes up his mind more readily and with less caution to indulge in sexual intercourse outside of the married state, more than the individual who is sober, he is also more subject to the dangers of such intercourse. And what sexual disease means to the married man as regards his own health and happiness, the health of his wife and that of his offspring, we need not enter upon here.

—Abstracted from Health and Strength (London)

A remarkable case history of a prostitute whose true sex is never suspected by the men who seek his services.

MALE "CALL GIRL"

by Robert Wood

THE following story is a true account of a career which must be almost unique. It concerns a young man who is now 26 years of age and who is known as—"Miss B." The facts were obtained by personal interview.

B. was born of poor parents and brought up in a working class district of London. Until the age of puberty he appears to have been a fairly normal boy, although perhaps slightly effeminate in his tastes.

Gradually, however, he became more and more dissatisfied with the male rôle and more and more

Formerly Editor of the Journal of Sex Education, *London. Mr. Wood is a noted English sexologist, medical author and adult educator.*

feminine in his tastes and habits. When he was with other boys he felt that he belonged to the opposite sex, and when he was with girls he felt himself to be one of them.

As time went on he experienced an increasing desire to dress and to live as a girl. As he was, during that time, living at home and depending upon his parents these tastes could be indulged in only occasionally and furtively.

As soon as possible he left home and secured unskilled work as a shop assistant. As he was, by this time, of distinctly feminine appearance he sought employment dressed as a girl, and for the first time was able to enjoy living permanently in the feminine rôle. His true sex was not suspected and his new friends and associates accepted him as a woman.

Anatomically, B. is undoubtedly a male. The male organ (which is now habitually kept strapped up) is rather small, but is in other respects quite normal. On the other hand, the pelvis is somewhat wide for a male, and there is no growth of hair on the face.

B. does not seem to be disturbed by his external signs of masculinity and has never desired an operation for the removal of the genital organs. He is, however, a confirmed transvestite of an extreme type. In other words, although physically a male, he experiences an overwhelming urge to dress and live as a woman. The abnormality is a psychological one, but he finds it an essential condition of happiness to abandon the male rôle completely.

His chief cause of physical dissatisfaction appears to have been the absence of female breasts. To remedy this he embarked some years ago on a course of hormonal treatment. Apparently as a result of this the breasts became larger, and B. now manages to give a realistic impression of possessing a female bosom.

On the whole, it may be said that B. gives a most convincing performance as a woman. In features and build, in the size of the feet and hands, and in bodily movements there is nothing about him to suggest the male.

Partly on account of his unusual position, and partly through loneliness, B. began to frequent clubs and bars where people of the London underworld gathered together. It became clear to him that not only was he accepted as a woman by both males and females but that he was regarded as an attractive one by men who never suspected his true sex. B., who did not take kindly to working long hours in a poorly-paid job, began to ask himself if he could not make a living out of this attractiveness. *He decided to become a "call girl"!*

It is necessary at this stage to make a very important point in this case-history. B. is not, and never has been, homosexual in his feelings. In fact neither men nor women attract him sexually in any way. He is, in his feelings, neither homosexual nor heterosexual, but narcissistic (self-loving).

The only love-object that he has is his own body, and the only person that he finds in the least attractive is himself. He is quite indifferent to heterosexuality and feels a distinct aversion for homosexuality. His attitude to homosexuals is uncomprehending and slightly censorious. They are to him "queer," "odd" and "different."

B. identifies himself entirely with the other call girls in the district. They accept him as one of themselves and do not suspect that he is a male. He remarked rather complacently, "We are a normal lot round here."

It was about five years ago that B. began his fantastic life. He took a ground floor apartment in a large old house in a rather shabby quarter of a large city, for which he pays about $60 weekly. He built up his connection through personal contacts in clubs and bars and also by discreet advertising.

These advertisements, carefully worded, were put in display windows in small shops and also in small weekly papers of doubtful reputation. Those on the lookout for such items quickly grasp the meaning of the thinly-veiled offers of "personal services."

From the financial point of view, B. has been very successful. He has a number of regular clients, keeps a personal maid, and runs his own automobile, and estimates his income as being between $450 and $500 weekly.

On the whole B. seems well content with his life. He saves only a little, but seems to have no fears for the future. He smokes rather heavily, but drinks only very moderately and never gambles.

How is it possible, it may well be asked, to maintain this fantastic rôle with "her" clients? They, it must be remembered, imagine that he is in fact what he appears to be. The answer is that B. caters for the most part to sexual deviants, that is for those men who do not desire ordinary sexual relations with a woman.

Some of these require the services of a "masseuse." Many of them are fetishists interested only in certain parts of the body, or in certain types of clothing. B. possesses a very extensive wardrobe. He can, if required, dress as a ballet dancer, a Victorian governess, a nun, a circus girl, or a lion-tamer.

He possesses a large collection of rubber shoes, boots, sheets, rubber gloves and hats. In B.'s opinion most fetishists are rubber fetishists of one sort or another, and this act is the most popular one in his répertoire.

In addition to these clients there are the sadists and masochists, that is to say those who wish to inflict pain on their partners, and those who wish to suffer it in some form. B. does not enjoy pain, and therefore takes very few sadistic clients; these he makes pay heavily for their pastime.

For his masochistic clients, however, he possesses an extensive collection of lashes, dog-whips, horse-whips, canes, birches, pincers, spikes, heavily-nailed boots, and shoes with sharp and fantastically high heels. He also keeps a large stock of corsets, handcuffs, chains, ropes, furs and silks.

During his career he has become adept at playing the rôle of the imperious, dominating woman with her slave, or that of the cruel and severe school-mistress; this last rôle is extremely popular.

One of his most unusual clients was an elderly business man. He came regularly about twice a year. He brought with him a large quan-

Male prostitutes have been found in many large cities of the world. Here a typical Parisian male prostitute is shown.—Photo by Papon, from the French medical journal "Problèmes."

Prostitutes are often sought out by clients who wish them to perform bizarre or deviant acts. Some males, known as masochists, derive sex gratification from being dominated or beaten by a woman, as shown in this water color by R. Schlichter. —*From Bilder-Lexikon.*

tity of bandaging material, and insisted on being swathed from head to foot in the fashion of a mummy. Even his lips had to be tightly sealed with adhesive tape.

In this condition he was left on a bed for two hours. After this B. undid him, and he departed apparently well-satisfied. *For this unusual service he paid the sum of $450!*

B. would seem to be a person of average intelligence but limited education. Psychologically he appears to be decidedly hypothymic (emotionally undeveloped). At times he gives the impression of a condition which has, in the study of delinquency, been called "the affectionless type."

B. has never married and no love affairs have occurred in his life since early adolescence, and these were not of a serious nature. In his world there is no loved person —neither man nor woman. While he has many acquaintances and a few friends these latter do not seem to be really important. It is convenient and agreeable to know them, that is all.

He thus gives the appearance of being self-sufficient, and needing neither to give nor to receive love. He has strong and frequent sexual urges, but these are never satisfied with another person, but only alone and with himself as love-object.

B. is mildly amused and inter-ested in the charades that his clients pay him so well to perform. He neither likes, dislikes nor despises them. Occasionally he experiences sadistic emotion, and if a client incurs his hostility or dislike, that client, if a masochist, receives good value for his money. Hurting in such a case becomes a pleasure.

In concluding the interview B. made one very interesting remark. The clients to him are anonymous and faceless men. He does not remember their names or anything individual about them. "Some of them come to see me time after time," he said, "but I never remember their faces, and until they remind me I imagine that I am meeting them for the first time."

Courtship Customs

Rules and modes of courtship are different today than they were 50 and 100 years ago. Courtship customs of the past are described and compared to modern premarital sex conduct.

by Robert Wood

THE word *courtship* may be defined as the regular and intimate association of two persons—one of each sex—with a view to marriage. Although in our society this is an established custom, among some peoples it is quite unknown. Where it has been practised it has taken various forms, and many important changes have taken place in courtship customs in our own society during the past two hundred years.

The Puritan code held that sex was for procreation only and regarded amorous contacts as "sinful dalliance." Any sexual activity outside marriage was wicked. The family was patriarchal; the choice of a mate and courtship customs were controlled by the parents. This code sought to make sexual irregularity an offense against the law. In England in 1650, for instance, under the Puritans, fornication could be punished by three months' imprisonment.

Under this code *early marriage* was encouraged, bachelors were often persecuted and *virginity* was

Formerly Editor of The Journal *of* Sex Education, London, *Mr. Wood is a noted English sexologist, medical author and adult educator.*

highly prized. A father considered that he was carrying out the will of God in disposing of his daughter. Any young man who wooed a young woman without permission was guilty of "inveigling." In Massachusetts a fine was imposed for the first two offenses and imprisonment for the third. Whipping, a fine, or imprisonment might also follow "necking" or "petting."

The frantic efforts to control sexual behavior do not appear to have had much success. Professor Folsom quotes from the records of one New England church in which, out of "200 persons owning the baptismal covenant, 66 owned to pre-marital sex relations." In 1642 the Elders of Connecticut found so much "sexual license" that legislation against it was considered hopeless. *Compulsory marriage* was one of the punishments for fornication by a single man and woman.

Courting Sticks

George Riley Scott refers to a method of courtship practised by the Puritans in the Connecticut Valley during the 18th century. This consisted of a "courting stick" about one inch in diameter and 6 or 8 feet long. It was hol-

Photo by Underwood & Underwood

low, and fitted with mouth- and ear-pieces. Courtship took place in the presence of the whole family. The couple, seated on either side of the fireplace, were forced to whisper their endearments through this primitive telephone. One of these "batons of propriety" is said to be preserved in Long Meadow, Massachusetts.

Bundling

A custom about which much has been written was "bundling." Common in England, Scotland, Holland and Scandinavia, it was brought to America by the Dutch and the Puritans, and seems to have become common, especially in Connecticut and Pennsylvania. It found favor chiefly among the poorer people, whose houses were small and cold.

In such houses there was usually a single bed, used by the family and guests. In order to save fuel and candle, the lovers lay together in bed, wearing all, or at least part, of their clothing. This practice was carried out with the full knowledge and consent of the parents. Many devices were introduced to increase the safety of the practice, such as placing a low board between the lovers, or using a bolster. Some parents tied the girl's ankles together, or wrapped up the lower part of her body.

In these circumstances kissing and other forms of love-play were inevitable. Although sexual intercourse was not permitted, many illegitimate children resulted from this tantalizing situation. Bundling reached its heyday about 20 years before the American Revolutionary War. In some parts of Britain it continued until 1847, and it caused a scandal in the Orkney Islands in the 1930's.

Seventy-Five Years Ago

In the days of our grandparents a great deal of the Puritan code was still intact. The rules of courtship were fixed and simple, and the meetings of young people strictly supervised and regulated. A formal introduction was necessary, and the young man would ask the girl's father for permission to call on her. These visits were made with the family either present or near at hand. The young man would soon be asked his intentions; if he became the accepted suitor the couple would be given more freedom. On the whole there seems to have been more premarital freedom at this time in America than in Europe.

The rules of sexual behavior were strict. Practically no caresses were permitted until the engagement, and then only of a very restrained kind. Sexual intercourse before marriage was condemned, but there was a great deal of it. Pre-marital coitus was regarded as less serious when it involved the girl's betrothed.

After the giving of the ring the official engagement began, and no rivals were then tolerated. To break the engagement at this stage was regarded as very serious and most unusual. The chaperone never seems to have been as common in America as in Europe — a fact often deplored by American writers on etiquette. The system of chaperonage was widely practised in Europe in Victorian times, and then rapidly declined. Emily Post now refers to it as a "lost convention." Professor Folsom speaks of it as still lingering in conservative circles. "There has been," he adds, "a tendency to use a sex-abhorrence sentiment in girls as a substitute."

By 1890 the older patterns of courtship were beginning to change. Henry Seidel Canby called it "a

In early American Colonial days, a "courting stick" was the means of private communication between a young woman and her suitor when he visited her home.

golden age of confident companionship." Mixed excursions became popular and courtship was romantic. French observers commented on the freedom of American girls, and also on their apparent lack of passion. Canby thought that the sex morals of the working girl of the 90's were much the same as those of the society girl or college girl of 1930.

Reasons for Changes

Among recent factors making for change have been the breaking down of the old taboos concerning the discussion of sexual topics, the declining authority of the family and the waning power of the Puritan code. Burgess and Wallin point out the influence of free association and contraceptives in bringing about changing patterns of courtship behavior.

Mechanical inventions have also played their part in recent changes. Among these have been the telephone, the motor car, and motion pictures. In the past, communities were small and the members were known to one another. The conventions governing courtship were rigid, and community supervision difficult to escape. All this has changed, and E. S. Turner expresses the opinion that "in a startling brief time the closed car has done more to change courting customs in the western world than anything else, not excluding the cinema." Burgess and Wallin say that "mobility is the keyword to the change." The closed car has provided a mobile private parlor, Popenoe in his research found that 25 per cent of men questioned proposed "while riding or driving."

The erotic aspects of courtship and other types of association have also moved to the forefront, and "necking" and "petting" have become parts of the folkways. "Petting" now often involves anything short of actual sexual intercourse.

Dating

"Dating," which began in the second decade of the 20th century has also become an important custom. The object of this practice is to enable young people to find satisfaction in each other's society without committing themselves to any serious engagement. In the past when a couple had been out a few times, no other young man was supposed to intrude. This exclusiveness has no place in "dating"; if it should become exclusive, it ceases to be "dating." Many boys and girls appear to begin this practice at the ages of 13 or 14.

A much criticized aspect of "dating" is "rating." This means the choosing of the "date"—not because of any particular liking for the boy or girl in question, but because of the status that he or she rates. Prestige is gained by being seen with a "campus queen," or with a boy with money, an automobile and an impressive athletic record.

The accepted code of behavior, according to Burgess and Wallin, seems to permit a good-night kiss on the 2nd or 3rd date. "Necking" is considered suitable for repeated "dating" or "going steady," and "petting" is reserved for engaged couples. In general, sexual intercourse is reserved for marriage.

Courting. — Early
French engraving.

Needless to say, this code is often transgressed; heavy petting and sexual intercourse frequently take place among unmarried couples.

According to Dr. Kinsey, the increase in "petting" and in pre-marital intercourse constitutes the greatest difference between the old patterns of behavior and the new. He found that the greatest difference in pre-marital sex activities occurred between women born before 1900 and those born in the 20th century, the incidence of virginity at marriage having fallen by 50% in the latter group.

Premarital Coitus

Other studies suggest that, although virginity at marriage has decreased, especially among women, there is no general tendency toward promiscuity. Most of the pre-marital intercourse takes place between engaged couples.

The Burgess and Wallin study finds that about one out of two couples have had pre-marital sex relations. About 50% of the men had had sexual intercourse with women other than their fiancées, whereas this was true of only about 10% of the women.

A similar decline in virginity seems to have occurred in England. The Mass Observation Report of 1949 showed that 59% of men and women had experienced some form of pre-marital or extra-marital sexual intercourse—40% of single men and 38% of single women had had sex relations. Thirty per cent of the people questioned believed that sexual intercourse outside marriage is permissible in certain circumstances. They did not all declare this to be right, but they admitted they practiced it. A survey by Seebohm Rowntree published in 1951 states that in 1939 one bride in 6 was pregnant on her wedding day.

It is too early as yet to evaluate some of these changes. Many people will, no doubt, tend to condemn them; and for the older generation modern times are always "out of joint." Actually, social conventions, institutions and customs are constantly in a state of flux. It may well be that the young people of today will evolve a pattern of sexual behavior which will be freer, happier and more realistic than that of the past. In any case they are merely manifesting what Havelock Ellis called "the very conservative habit of change."

men who prostitute their wives

From a psychiatrist come these strange cases of three men, who for deeply-hidden reasons, could not have satisfactory sex relations with their wives until they had degraded them to the level of common street-walkers.

by Edward Dengrove, M.D.

MOST men assume with the exchange of the marriage vows the obligation to honor and respect their partner in marriage—an obligation the man zealously guards and willingly fulfills in expression of his love for the woman who is his wife. Most men—but not all. For there are men whose marriages are dominated not by the desire to honor and cherish their wives, but rather by the need to degrade them.

Such was the case with Tom C., a handsome young man of thirty-two who, exceedingly embarrassed, came to a psychiatrist's office seeking help. He related the following story:

For several years he had been married to an attractive woman four years his junior, with whom he had had two young children. His marriage had been a happy one up until the last six months.

Then their sex life had taken a most unusual turn.

Almost every Saturday night for the last half-year he had persuaded his wife to accompany him to the swankiest cocktail lounge in town, dressed in her most alluring costume. Once there they separate. He takes a table and orders a drink; she seats herself at the bar. Although she is constantly within his sight, there is absolutely no communication between them.

Tom's wife is a beautiful woman and, dressed as she is for these excursions, quite seductive looking. To all appearances, she is alone. Eventually, then, she is approached by someone who offers to buy her a drink. She accepts his invitation, and allows him to "pick her up." After a while she remarks that it is getting late, and suggests to her new acquaintance that he take her home.

As his wife and her companion leave the bar, Tom follows, trailing them to his house in his car. His wife invites her escort in "for a nightcap," and when they enter the house Tom stations himself at a window through which he can see into the living-room, where the rest of the drama will be enacted. His wife leaves the other man momentarily while she goes upstairs on some pretext or other, and soon returns clad only in the flimsiest of negligees, which conceals none of her charms. She allows this man to make love to her.

At this point, Tom strides into the house; the other man is startled,

---

Dr. Dengrove is a well-known medical author and psychiatrist in private practice in New Jersey.

and his wife pretends to be. Having thus interrupted the lovemaking, Tom immediately proceeds upstairs to bed. Meanwhile, his wife explains to her companion that Tom is her brother, returned home earlier than anticipated; she suggests that her friend had "better leave now." He does. She goes upstairs to Tom, who is now sexually aroused, and they have intercourse.

Tom explained to the doctor that it was only after witnessing such events that he was sexually potent; without this stimulation his potency was weak and variable.

His wife admitted to the truth of Tom's story, but insisted that she participated only because she wanted to preserve the marriage for the sake of the children. Since this was a recent development in their sex life, she was hopeful that Tom would soon "get over it."

Why should a husband subject his wife to so degrading an experience? Why should he need to see his wife in the intimate embrace of another man in order to be able to have intercourse with her? And why should any woman agree to take part in such a relationship?

First, there was the possibility that Tom had strong homosexual tendencies of which he was not consciously aware. If this was so then, although not actively seeking a physical relationship with another male, Tom was indulging that urge by observing another man in a sexual situation with a woman. In that case it would be, not his wife, but rather her companion who was the object of Tom's vigil at the window.

Then, there was the possibility that by forcing his wife into a situation where she would have to submit to the sexual advances of any casual partner, Tom was reducing her to the level of the common prostitute, making her seem less respectable than other women.

Or *voyeurism* (the need to "peep") may have been the motivating factor, in which case the important element would have been that Tom, concealed, was witnessing intimacies not usually meant for the eyes of a third party.

In psychiatric therapy it became evident that all three of these possibilities played a part in Tom's sexual deviation. His father was a successful business executive, the head of a company he had himself built over many obstacles. Tom was employed by his father's firm in an executive capacity, and through his position with the business gained in his adult years far more of his father's attention than he had ever enjoyed as a child. His father had been so preoccupied with business matters that he gave his children but little of his time, and even less of his love.

His mother, attempting to "make up" for the father's failures as a parent, was over-indulgent, and Tom was terribly spoiled. He had one sister; there was a great disparity in their ages and he never developed any feelings of closeness with her. Because his mother was so subservient to all his wishes and so fearful of his father, Tom developed a great contempt for women, not unlike his father's attitude.

And then, one day when he was a young boy, Tom burst into his parents' bedroom and surprised them in the sex act. Witnessing that parental coitus stimulated him sexually, and coupled with his contempt for women, led also to the development of conflicts centered around homosexuality. This tendency remained hidden, coming to the surface only during his psychiatric treatment.

The sexual situation into which Tom forced his wife was, then, the result of his subconscious attempt to recreate a situation which he had experienced in his childhood, when he had interrupted his parents in the marital act. And it also allowed him to express the disgust he felt for the female, to say to his wife, in effect, "This is what I think of you; you are no better than a prostitute."

As for the reasons why Tom's wife allowed herself to be party to such events, we cannot with authority say, since she did not enter into psychiatric treatment, feeling that she did not need it. We can only suppose, therefore, that she permitted such degradation for some deeply unconscious reasons of her own.

The outcome? Tom's wife finally decided that she had put up with the situation long enough, and refused to engage in their Saturday night jaunts again; whereupon he left her, terminating both his marriage and his visits to the psychiatrist.

The second case is that of the young man we shall identify only

"The Procuress," by Paola Carrocciola. — Photo Vasari.

as James L. James was an office worker, thirty-five years old. His position did not afford much financial remuneration, but he had an excellent financial sense and through shrewd management and clever investment built up an income far beyond his limited salary. He was brought to the attention of a psychiatrist by his wife Marie, who sought the doctor's advice and help.

Her husband frequently drank to excess, she complained, and when he was drunk he was also angry and mean. After his last binge he had returned home in a nasty mood and had struck her. It was for this reason that she wanted him to receive psychiatric help. Prodded gently by the psychiatrist, who observed that she was not being entirely frank, Marie finally revealed the true reason for her coming. James, she said, insisted that she have sexual relations with other men. Afterwards her husband would demand to know *all* the intimate details of those relationships. When she described them fully, he became sexually stimulated and had relations with her. If she refused entirely, or hesitated to answer some of her questions about the most personal details of her affairs, he became furious, sometimes striking her in his anger.

"He wants to make me feel filthy and low — like a streetwalker," Marie said. "At least, that's the way I feel about it, and he knows it!" Her husband, obviously unwilling to discuss his strange kind of sexual preference with the psychiatrist, refused to return after his first visit.

The third case is that of Roger W., a man of middle age who had been married only a short time. Roger had been the financial support and the emotional mainstay of his mother until her death, and it was only after her passing had relieved him of all responsibility to her that he had married. His mother, who had been quite a belle in her youth, remained a charming and attractive woman always, vain and demanding of those about her. Roger, an only child, had been trained to dance attendance upon his mother, as his father had always done.

Here again, it was not the man but his wife who was the first to seek help. Roger's bride, obviously distraught, told the psychiatrist that, though she loved her husband and wanted to be a good wife, she could not have marital relations with him under existing circumstances. For during intercourse, when she yearned to hear him express his love for her with fond endearments, Roger instead abused her with obscenities.

"I cannot repeat to you, doctor," she said, her voice trembling, "the awful names he calls me."

Consultation with Roger disclosed that what his wife described did indeed take place. It disclosed, too, that Roger's potency was weak; he had difficulty in effecting intercourse. He insisted that he loved his wife, and did not want to see his marriage terminated.

Roger's attachment to his mother was far stronger than that of most men. Nor was it healthy, for it incorporated the kind of love Roger should have felt, not for his parent, but for another woman. Roger envisioned his mother as the symbol of pure womanhood, and the only kind of woman he would marry was one he could see in her image. But once married to a woman he regarded as fine and worthy as his mother, Roger was sexually impotent with her, because subconsciously he equated her with his mother, with whom a sexual relationship would be unthinkable. But by hurling obscene words at his wife and addressing her in language never used to a lady, Roger reduced her to a level far below that of his mother. Thus he made her appear unworthy of his respect—temporarily—and so capable of receiving his sexual love.

When he concluded psychiatric treatment, Roger was able to enter into a mature and satisfying relationship with his wife, for he had rid himself of his unhealthy attitudes and his conflicts over his sexual desires.

Unlike the other two men who had refused to undergo the necessary treatment, he no longer felt the need to debase his wife and degrade her to the level of a common street-walking prostitute.

This illustration depicts a street scene in a red light
district where the prostitute is shown as disease
and death masquerading in the dress of the prostitute. From an old European engraving.

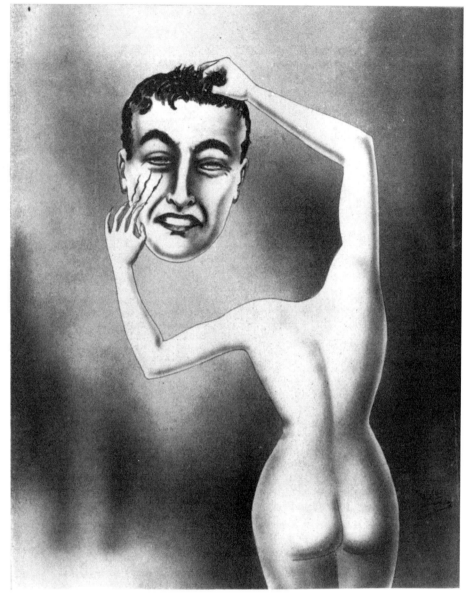

SEX AND PAIN ENIGMA — By Tina

In many marriages it is not uncommon to find one or both partners, during intense sexual stimulation, exhibiting slight sadistic or masochistic tendencies by biting, scratching, or in various other ways deriving satisfaction from pain. The headless figure of a woman symbolizes the momentary loss of mental control during ardent love play. This results in the release of dormant sadistic impulses inherent in all humans. The man's face with the scratches represents sexual satisfaction through pain.

SEX and PAIN

Algolagnia is a sex aberration of a person—either a sadist or a masochist—who can find satisfaction in love or sex only when inflicting pain to the sexual partner, male or female. The following article indicates the nature and variety of such cases.

by T. Bowen Partington

A MAN and his wife recently consulted me. He is 40 years old; his wife is 38. Their married life is a happy one and they are very much in love. They told me that their marital relations are quite satisfactory. Always when they have relations they are completely undressed. Before they engage in preliminary love-play the husband flagellates her buttocks. The wife admitted that generally he hurt her and at times she cried out, but, as she said, "I am gratified by being aroused in this manner—sexually." Occasionally she has a climax as she is beaten. Then the husband kneels and his wife whips his buttocks in a similar manner which in turn sexually arouses him. They asked me if their conduct was *abnormal*. I told them that I knew of other married couples who acted in much the same manner.

Desire to Inflict Pain

From time immemorial, love has been connected with everything gentle and tender. Yet it is true that in many men and women there exists a subconscious streak of cruelty—a desire to inflict pain. Even in a normal healthy man there is a slight inclination to hurt his partner in love. The same is true of woman—with the additional longing to be hurt by her lover. This explains the biting and other slight injuries sometimes inflicted on each other by lovers at the height of sexual excitement. I remember seeing the bosom of a woman bearing quite visible bite marks made by her husband. She said she was gratified by the biting.

The custom of biting is common among primitive peoples. Erotic bites are known in many parts of the world. Sadism is an aberration in which sexual satisfaction can be derived only by inflicting mental or physical pain on the sex partner. It is *an abnormal deviation* from a primitive instinct that is inherent in mankind. The desire to inflict pain on the beloved and the longing to suffer a little pain are traits, which appear in many sex acts.

When an individual cannot find

Catherine de Medici, who is said to have derived great pleasure in having the ladies of her court whipped before her eyes—a trait of the sadist. Undoubtedly she obtained sexual satisfaction from witnessing such scenes.—Picture by French artist Hopwood Se.

first to clearly describe the form of sexual deviation (masochism) in which satisfaction is derived only by being cruelly treated.

Flagellation

Here, of course, we are more concerned with masochism as a preliminary to, or as a substitute for, normal sexual relations. Perhaps the most common form of pain the masochist craves is flagellation (whipping) from the hands of his wife or mistress. Dr. W. Hammond reports in *Sexual Impotence in the Male* a man who paid three prostitutes to tread on his bared chest. Many a prostitute can tell of men who pay just to be given a severe whipping. Many a brothel has a supply of straps, whips, etc., used for flagellation. Some bedrooms of married couples contain a whip or strap which the husband or wife will use at times.

How far the desires of a masochist could go is well shown by the case of Mr. X., a technologist, quoted by Krafft-Ebing. He thus described his masochistic fancies:

"I am lying on my back on the floor. She stands over my head with one foot on my chest or she holds my head between her feet so that her undraped form is directly in a line with my vision. Or she sits a-straddle on my chest or on my face, using my body as a table. If I do not obey her commands promptly she locks me up in a dark room alone. She introduces me to her friends as her slave and turns me over to them as a loan. She makes me perform the lowest menial work, wait upon her when she arises."

satisfaction in love unless the act is accompanied by the infliction of pain, either on himself or on the partner, *this is a form of sexual abnormality!* Such people are called *algolagnists.* The two phases of this are *sadism* and *masochism.* Those who find it necessary to inflict pain are the *sadists,* a term derived from the Marquis de Sade, a notorious Parisian deviate of the eighteenth century. His writings describe cruelty and horror committed under the influence of the love lust. The *passive* algolagnists—those who can derive sexual satisfaction only when pain is inflicted on them — are known as *masochists.* This term was coined by Dr. Krafft-Ebing. It was apparently suggested to him by the descriptions of the aberrations found in the writings of Sacher-Masoch (1836-1895). Leopold von Sacher-Masoch was the

Many masochists find satisfaction in *passive* flagellation. I recall one case; a married man with children. During his masochistic craving he would rent a room, hire several prostitutes, who sexually mistreated, then flagellated him. He would beg for mercy and pretend to resist the beating. This would go on for two or three days till his craving had subsided, when he would return home to his unsuspecting wife and children.

Symbolic Masochism

There are cases of *symbolic* masochism where the victim is satisfied with merely imagining situations of masochistic practices. As an example of this: almost every three months a man, about forty-three years old, would visit a prostitute and pay her well. She had to undress him, tie his hands behind him and put a bandage over his eyes. Then she would shut the windows and doors of the room and leave him in the room alone, helpless on the sofa. About half an hour later she had to return and unbind him, when he would go home, completely satisfied. For this she was well paid!

There are persons who do not wish to suffer any actual pain, but are satisfied if they have sexual intercourse with a *domineering* partner. I have met some men like this who like to be "mastered" by the female partner: told what to do in the course of the sex act and

A camp of German Flagellant Brotherhood of penitence of 13th Century. Laymen in Italy, France and Germany went from town to town stripped to the belt. After singing penitent songs they whipped themselves until blood appeared.—*Bettmann Archive.*

made to do just what the woman wants; conversely I have known a number of women who can *want* a great deal of rough treatment in the course of the sex act.

Many men want to be subjected to the attentions of women like the heroines of Sacher-Masoch's stories. This is not *true* algolagnia but should rather be called *ideal masochism,* as Krafft-Ebing points out. Personally, I think sexual relations would be often more mutually pleasing if at times the wife were to take the initiative and not let all the suggestions as to love-play, etc., come from the husband. In turn the normal man I am sure, at times, likes to be told what to do by the woman he loves.

So far in this article I have dealt mostly with instances of *male* masochists but it should not be thought that masochism is not found or is very rare in women. Possibly a trace of masochism is

The masochist has the strange desire to be whipped by a stalwart woman, from which act he derives sexual satisfaction. The same applies to a woman masochist.

present in every woman. Many women find satisfaction in a certain amount of pain during love-making and the sexual act. If masochism is found in men, *it is produced in women rather as an exaggeration* in the domain of her normal sexual sensations, for it is to a great extent in harmony with her passive sexual rôle. It is notorious that some women like to be beaten by their husbands, and are not content unless this is done. Some women have confessed to me that they like to be "roughly handled" by their husbands in the preliminary love-play and during the act itself. Lucian, the famous Greek writer of ancient times, makes a woman say:

"He who has not rained blows on his mistress and torn her hair and her garments is not yet in love."

In this connection, Krafft - Ebing was once told by a Hungarian official that the peasant women of the Somogyer Comitate do not believe themselves rightly loved by their husbands until their ears have been properly boxed. A case described by Dr. Stekel will be of interest. It is of a woman who in spite of many lovers and ten years of married life found herself to be completely frigid and unable to reach a climax. Then, one day, she happened to come across a man who had the habit of biting his sexual partner's ear - lobes. He did the same to her and this produced such an intensely satisfactory sensation that she at once reached a climax.

It is now agreed by sexologists that sadism and masochism are two of the commonest forms of sexual abnormalities.

Sadism Is Older Than Mankind

André Tridon tells us in *Psychoanalysis and Love* that *"cocks during the act of mating peck cruelly the back of the hen's head. Tomcats bite the necks of their mates. Toads, at times, choke the female to death in their clinging embrace."* In olden times, as in the case of certain savages of today, brutal force was used to overpower a woman and satisfy the lust of the domineering male. It is when these old possessive and submissive instincts *break the bounds of normality, that the pathological stage of algolagnia is reached.*

The giving of pain increases the sexual satisfaction of a sadist. It may even culminate in an orgasm. The horrible cases of lust murder are probably due to this abnormal form of sexuality. The "Jack the Ripper" type of sadist may first attack women, then kill them. In milder cases, the mere cutting of the girl's clothes may suffice to produce satisfactory sexual gratification and even to induce an orgasm. But mere cruelty is not sadism. It must have a sexual connotation. Actually, there are two groups of sadists. Those of the first group practise sadistic acts as a substitute for normal sexual intercourse: but with the abnormal types of the second group, sadism precedes, accompanies or follows coitus; among this group flagellation is common. Such men will willingly pay a high price to prostitutes if they submit to whipping or other acts of cruelty. Many

Parisian brothels provide customers with air-filled rubber tubes with which to "torture" their sexual partners. But not all sadists are so easily satisfied and often insist on real flagellation.

Sadism may take very strange forms. In its worst it may drive the half-insane pervert to acts of utmost violence, strangulation and even murder. Perhaps it is to this abnormality of the sexual instinct that we must attribute the brutal crimes of Jack-the-Ripper and the more recent ones of "The Düsseldorf Monster" Peter Kurten, who was sentenced to death in 1931.

Many sadists are unaware of their abnormality. This may be called "unconscious sadism" and it is well represented by a case quoted by Dr. Chapotin. A male deviate always frequented a dirty little café where drinks were abominable and the seats were hard and uncomfortable. He went there solely because of the gratification aroused in him by listening to the foul language used by the very ugly woman cashier against a certain waiter. He tried by all means in his power to get the waiter into trouble, and when he had been foully abused by the hateful woman, the deviate would leave the café, mentally and physically satisfied. As I write this, I recall a case in which the man who insisted that during love-play with his wife and in the act itself he compelled her to refer to what is taking place and their respective sex parts by the filthiest of words; this excited the husband intensely, though the wife told me she loathed

having to use such language, but the husband always insisted.

Sexologists talk of "symbolic sadism." This has been described as "imaginary sadism." Actually, there is little to choose between the two terms. I know a case of a man who would regularly visit several prostitutes whose faces he would lather and then remove the lather with a razor, pretending to shave them. In no way were the girls hurt. Just this pretense was enough to excite him sexually and bring on an ejaculation. This is *symbolic* sadism. The imaginary act of shaving was symbolic of his latent sadism. This pretense must have had some symbolic meaning for the man. In the same way, the manifestations of sadism may be only imaginary. Sadistic fancies and daydreaming may suffice. And many men—and women too—indulge in such. Many such men imagine during coitus that they are mistreating their sexual partner. Others have violent erections and even reach a climax on seeing girls beaten or tortured in other ways. But they never take any active part in brutal acts. The mere sight of cruelty is stimulating enough for this type.

Although masochism is especially to be found in men, sadism is equally common in men and women and perhaps, in many respects, a sadistic woman is more dangerous, more cruel than the male. As historical examples, we have Catharine de Medici and Messalina. The former found satisfaction in seeing her maids of honor flogged in her presence Women are known to have confessed to abnormal satisfaction at the sight of their own children writhing under the whip. I recently read of a woman who would strip her 10-year-old girl naked and whip her on the slightest pretense. The notorious Mrs. Elizabeth Brownrigg was hanged at Tyburn (London) in 1767 for the sadistic murder of many children.

In milder forms of sadism, the woman may be satisfied with only biting her partner during the sex act. This is much more common than many would think. I recall one man showing me his arms and his chest to let me see the marks made on him by his wife who, he said, during intercourse and as her excitement grew, would repeatedly bite him. Women are far more inclined to bite in the sex act than are men.

My experience is that some women seem to develop sadistic inclinations during the time they are menstruating. In this article I have mentioned extreme cases of sadism and masochism. But that they exist in a modified form none can deny and I have seen such cases existing even if in a mild way. I have evidence of many cases where in the love-making between men and women, the husbands will incline to some form of sadism, whipping the wives being perhaps the commonest. Naturally there are some wives who will resent it, but on the other hand there are women who seem to like it, even demand it. I know of a case where if the wife commits a minor offense in the home, her husband will order her upstairs where she must remove her clothing and then bending over a chair, she has her buttocks whipped. Some women are mild sadists and are most aggressive on the marriage bed.

What constitutes pain in one set of circumstances becomes gratification in another. The ambivalence of satisfaction and pain causes acts—which in any other relation would be resented—to be accepted as indications of love during the sex act and its preliminaries. Slaps and blows are frequently accepted as caresses; scratches and bites form part of the love-play which is expected, even though such behavior is often misunderstood by many.

• • •

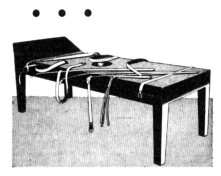

A whipping table used by sadists and their victims. —After Hirschfeld.

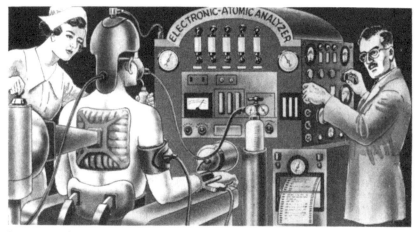

By means of electronics and atomic tracer elements it is now possible to completely analyze humans, particularly for glandular information. This gives doctors a true index for masculinity and muliebrity—sexual index.

What is your true sex?

An outstanding scientist and pioneer in Sexology discusses masculinity and femininity: the biological and psychological sexual factors in the "normal" person and the sex deviate; the elements in the human organism behind male and female characteristics; the rôle of electronic-medicine in sex determination.

by Hugo Gernsback

Member, American Physical Society;
American Society for the Advancement
of Science.

BIOLOGISTS, sexological scientists and researchers increasingly have come to the conclusion that there is no such individual as a 100% male or a 100% female.

There is a scant amount of literature on this subject. Even Kinsey, in his two published volumes, has little to say on the varying degrees of *masculinity* and *muliebrity.**

*The term *muliebrity* instead of *femininity* is here used for its sexological connotation. In anatomy, *muliebria* means the female genitalia. Muliebrity means womanhood, also the state of being a woman, or of possessing full womanly powers—correlative of virility. (From Webster's New International Dictionary.)

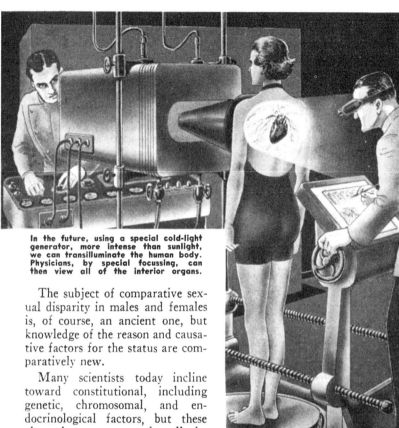

In the future, using a special cold-light generator, more intense than sunlight, we can transilluminate the human body. Physicians, by special focussing, can then view all of the interior organs.

The subject of comparative sexual disparity in males and females is, of course, an ancient one, but knowledge of the reason and causative factors for the status are comparatively new.

Many scientists today incline toward constitutional, including genetic, chromosomal, and endocrinological factors, but these alone do not account for all the involved facts. Psychological factors, environment, the child's early training, and other considerations also play a large rôle.

Let us take an apropos example. Many parents dress their young children in clothing of the opposite sex. Boys are dressed as girls and girls as boys. Boys may be made to wear long girls' dresses and long hair, often beyond the age of 8. Girls may wear boyish haircuts and pants. Accordingly, in their most important and formative periods, these children become strongly influenced not only physically but psychically. The boys begin to feel themselves as girls, the girls as boys. Here psychosomatic effects begin to impress themselves strongly upon the child's personality and it becomes difficult to throw off the early inculcation in later life.

Indeed, in many cases, such children growing into adulthood become what I have termed *conditioned transvestites*. We sexologists, who have seen literally thousands of letters from transvestites and have talked with dozens of them, have been deeply impressed with the fact that so many of the cases were *transdressed* in their childhood.

I repeat what I have stated many times: "Parents, beware! You are playing with dynamite when you dress your boy as a girl or vice versa."

To correct an almost universally erroneous view, transvestites are *rarely homosexual*. But a man may feel a compulsion to dress up in female finery, complete with nylons and high-heel shoes. He must satisfy this urge or life will become intolerable. Satisfying this desire usually brings vicarious sexual relief. However, aside from this minor deviation—transvestites can be excellent husbands (or wives), provided their mates can learn to tolerate and live with this eccentricity. A high percentage will not.

What are the important and outstanding characteristics of masculinity and muliebrity? To put it bluntly:

A male is as male as the prevailing state of his testes; a female as feminine as the prevailing state of her ovaries. This statement is by no means all-inclusive of all the facts. It is at best an approximation; but it may stand until further research is forthcoming.

To illustrate the above *quasi* axiom, let us look at an eunuch —a castrated male. He is at best

only a 40% male. Having no testes, he generates only very little of the all-important male hormone, *testosterone,* as well as little of some other hormones. If he was castrated as a child, his lower leg extremities have grown disproportionately long. He usually has a high, feminine voice. He walks with a feminine gait, and his body has little, if any, hair. Moreover, he may think like a woman. His body may become rounded like a woman's and he usually takes on fatty deposits paralleling the female physique. Most important, the total absence of testes precludes his begetting offspring. The degree of these changes depends upon whether castration was performed before or after reaching maturity (puberty).

Now let us look at a castrated female, who lost her ovaries by disease or by surgery, or who— in a rare case—was born without any ovaries. Having no ovaries, she no longer generates sufficient vital female hormone, *estrogen,* and perhaps some other hormones. Such a woman—depending on her age — may acquire a male-like, low voice. She sometimes will grow hair on her body, particularly on the legs, chest, and face. She cannot menstruate. Her skin may lose its female softness and her gait may become more masculine. The total absence of ovaries physically, types her as a woman past her menopause, regardless of her age. This also means total barrenness — she no longer can procreate. She is now a 40%— or less—woman.

By way of correcting another

fallacy, neither *adult* eunuchs nor castrated women lose their libido, if they were castrated *after* puberty. If married, depending on their age—both can carry on satisfactory marital relations. If castrated in early infancy, they may never acquire libido.

Incidentally, too, science today can minimize some of the difficulties existing in both castrated sexes: the eunuch thus can be made—to a degree—more male, the castrated female more female, by the administration of specific hormones. (*Note.* This can be done effectively *only by a physician.*) Obviously the castrated cannot procreate offspring.

We have above considered extreme cases — castrated individuals, either 40% male or 40% female—or less. Now let us consider the run of the mill—the so-called "normal" individuals. We may find at the top, perhaps 90% males or 90% females. The percentages given here are wholly arbitrary—so far science has no accurate yardstick and it may be many years before we have exact scientific data.

However, we do know for certain why there is not likely to be a 100% individual of either sex. The reason: Both males and females—all animals for that matter, with perhaps few exceptions—have in their bodies both male and female hormones. The average male thus generates not only testosterone but estrogen as well. So does every female. *But* the amount of estrogen in the male is comparatively small. Likewise in the average female there is pro-

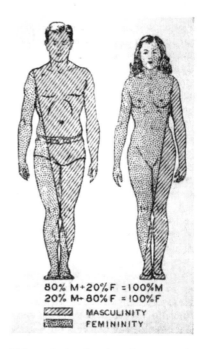

80% M+20% F =100% M
20% M+80% F =100% F

▨▨▨ MASCULINITY
▨▨▨ FEMININITY

Male and female elements appear in every man and woman. Some of these factors are biological; others are psychological in nature. The individual's early training, experiences and emotional relationships often play a large rôle in determining psychological masculinity and femininity. The presence of some degree of femininity need in no way detract from a positive biological maleness. And a woman may be biologically feminine to a high degree while possessing some masculine factors.

duced only a small percentage of testosterone.

Now if the male and female hormones are carefully measured and reduced to percentages, why won't we have a good yardstick to calculate the masculinity and/or the muliebrity of everybody?

The problem is far more complex. There are the chromosomes which determine sex originally— XX chromosomes in women, XY in men. Furthermore, as we have hinted above, there are a number of other hormones, besides the primarily male and female ones. And new ones are discovered every year. Many of these hormones play a significant rôle in our physical makeup, and, in conjunction with the male and female hormones, make us the individuals that we are.

The chemistry of the animal body is highly involved and depends on scores of factors, such as evolution, heredity, alimentation (i.e., the foods and liquids we ingest), the metabolism caused by the foregoing, light, heat and surroundings, as well as others lesser known.

In addition, there are a number of psychic factors, as we have already seen, all of these contributing to the sum total of our final sexological makeup.

We can therefore readily understand that there must be thousands of varied degrees of masculinity and muliebrity between the castrate 40% and the top 90% "normal" individual.

There are, for instance, the group known as *bisexuals*. They are neither male- nor female-sexed in their libido, but both. Accordingly, they may have satisfactory cohabitation with either sex. They may be placed at the 50% to 70% scale on our yardstick. Yet the average bisexual may *outwardly* appear as a normal male or a normal female. Even after an exhaustive autopsy, bisexuals for all practical purposes may appear as either normal average males or normal average females, at least in the anatomical sense.

In still another classification, we may have *anatomical* bisexuals, such as the not-too-rare pseudo-hermaphrodites and the very rare *true* hermaphrodites, who actually have more or less complete male and female generative organs in a single body.

Then we have another category, a subgroup of transvestites, who have an overpowering drive to change their sex permanently. There are many individuals of this type, both males who desire to become females and females who want to become males. Dr. Harry Benjamin, of New York, uses a special term for this group: *Transexualists*. These individuals are quite distinct from transvestites who have only one desire, i.e., to dress in the clothes of the opposite sex. Transexualists, however, are fierce in their desire to change their sex *by means of surgery*. Nothing else will suffice.

Occasionally such persons (if outwardly male) have themselves castrated and completely emasculated to rid themselves of all evidence of maleness. (Christine Jorgensen is in this class.)

Frequently these persons feel that they are females in male bodies. This has often been confirmed by surgeons, who in normally appearing males have found ovaries or partial ovaries in their abdomens.

Finally, when it comes to types, we must not forget the large group of homosexuals. Mistakenly, the popular view is that homosexuals of both sexes are anatomically different from heterosexuals. This is pure nonsense. There are as many differences in homosexuals as there are in heterosexuals. There are as many 90% male—and female—types of homosexuals as there are 40% types. Some of our best athletes, boxers, wrestlers and football players are homosexuals. Even Hercules, according to mythology, was homosexual! He was known to have loved a beautiful youth named Hylas.

There are, on the other hand, the feminine-looking, sissy homosexual male types as well. Among the female homosexual types there are the mannish ones as well as the demure, delicate types. But all belong to their own respective sexes—the average male homosexual is still anatomically a male. The same is true for the female homosexual.

It is certain that in the not-too-distant future medical and sexological science will untangle the present uncertainty as to the *true* status of every individual's sex.

People have a right to know their true sex status. Their peace of mind, their happiness are involved in it. Untold millions of neurotic individuals can trace their difficulties to sex disparity in their makeup. Conversely, once we know how to grade individuals as to their true sex, *we will be better able to remedy the existing individual deviations from the normal.*

Electronics coupled with atomics will most likely bring the solution. Electronic circuits have already been devised whereby many parts of the human anatomy may be explored successfully without the necessity of operations.

More important, electronics gives us many tools to explore and accurately grade all of our glands, hormone-producing and otherwise. Thus accurate indices as to their all important rates of secretion can be had.

Atomic tracer elements coupled with electronic devices even now are unraveling many hitherto unknown or little understood facts of our internal anatomy. This new science, electronic-medicine, is making spectacular strides.

In due time, too, I foresee entirely new techniques to explore the deepest innermost recesses in our bodies. The X-ray was the first tool to *indirectly* view the inside of our bodies.

In the future, the medical technician will *actually* see all of your interior organs and will watch them work.

This will be done by means of a device placed directly against your body. It will be a light source, several times as powerful as the sun—but it will be *cold light.* The light source will be so strong that it will transilluminate the thickest part of the body. Thus the physician by accurate focusing can actually see *in three dimensions* your heart as it beats. He can also see the heart's interior and watch the working of the heart valves. He will watch the actual working of many of your glands, either with his own eyes, by photography, or by motion pictures.

When that time comes, *and it is coming,* we will at long last know what makes us tick.

News of the Month...

Sexology, December, 1946

The Nude Churchill

CHURCHILL'S fondness for doing his morning work in a dressing gown finally resulted in a scene unique in American annals. It was during a stay at the White House that Roosevelt entered Churchill's room, to find him nude, about to begin shaving. The Englishman was quick to point out the historic significance. "This is probably the only time in history," he declared, "when the Prime Minister of England, in the nude, has received the head of another great state." —*Coronet Magazine*

● ● ●

Sexology, November, 1962

It Didn't Help

A 39-YEAR-OLD German student has been sentenced to 10 months in jail for seducing more than 100 women and girl students, according to a Reuters dispatch. Nikolaus Reissig, of Tuebingen, convinced the women that he had been advised by his doctor that only love could cure his ailments.

Reissig has bad eyesight, a defective leg, and is only 60% fit for work.

● ● ●

Sexology, November, 1960

Effects of Air Conditioning

ACCORDING to a recent survey, the rate of pregnancy in air-conditioned homes is significantly above the rate in non-air-conditioned homes.

This finding was reported by Prof. John R. Watt of the Department of Mechanical Engineering, University of Texas, after studying two communities which were similar except for air conditioning. Prof. Watt was not prepared to explain the reasons for the difference in pregnancy rate.

Sexology, November, 1958

Obscene Letter Writers

A COLLEGE professor of history was sentenced recently by a Federal Court judge to a suspended one-year prison term for mailing obscene letters. The court placed him on probation for five years and further ordered him to submit "to regular and continuous psychiatric treatment for your mental and emotional condition."

The offender was a member of a correspondence club whose members exchanged descriptive letters about their sex lives and desires. Eight other members of the club were arrested, reports the Newark, N. J., *Evening News*.

● ● ●

Sexology, June, 1952

"Picture-Bride" Racket

IN London, England, the magazine *Tailor and Cutter* complained that the summer exhibit at the Royal Academy of Art was unfair to the tailoring industry. The display included 94 nudes. —*United Press*

● ● ●

Sexology, January, 1947

De Luxe Chastity Belt

ONE of Hetty Green's (famous Wall Street tycoon) most bizarre possessions was a $20,000,000 jewel collection, including a gold helmet ornamented with emerald peacock feathers, a diamond-studded chastity belt, and a box of unset gems. —*Magazine Digest*

● ● ●

Sexology, August 1961

Bigamy in Britian

MORE than 20,000 Britons have more than 40,000 mates, according to the London *Pictorial*. British bigamists outnumber those of other monogamous countries by about 20 to 1, the report continued.

The paper called "the stable and unemotional British . . . the most notorious race of bigamists on the face of the earth."

The *Pictorial* cited unnamed "marriage guidance experts" as the source of the estimate.

why I am a FETISHIST

Why does a Fetishist prefer inanimate objects to human beings on which to fixate or satisfy his sexual desires? Fetishism is a transference of love from a person to some object which represents that individual. Although a fetishist may understand the sex feelings of average men, most men find it difficult or impossible to rationalize fetishism. In this illuminating article, written by a "boot" fetishist, the reader is given a rare insight into the mind of a real fetishist. As there are many millions of various types of fetishists, it is necessary that we should study their behaviorism in order to better appreciate the tremendous gamut and complexity of the incredible phenomenon which we call SEX.

by "Boots"

MY indulgence in that erratic form of behavior known as fetishism is, I believe, the result of my being an inadequate homosexual, in addition to suffering from "a deep-seated hidden hunger for love and affection which has always been denied me."

The subconscious desire within me is to love and be loved by masculine persons — my fetishes symbolize manhood. For example, a white lily is a symbol of purity; the lion is a symbol of courage. I am a homosexual; my particular fetish became "a symbol of manhood." Thus, an inanimate object, which is cold and lifeless, becomes through symbolism the token of "a warm, friendly, human being."

Fetishism is a throwback to some vaguely remembered incident of early childhood in which the fetish of today then played an important part. Poetically, it is similar to saying, "The Song is Over, But the Melody Lingers On" — or "You Keep Coming Back Like a Song." In my case it happens to be :

Just stray, sweet bits of happiness,
 Scattered through the years gone by.
With boys in boots, their kind caress—
 These memories cannot die!

Many factors contribute to this peculiar form of eroticism. Among these may be found an "extreme inferiority complex," or actual inferiority, or some mental or physical defect, however slight, which may bring upon one the thoughtless ridicule of companions. The emotional balance and stability of an overly sensitive person's entire future life may be involved. With a childhood background of maladjustment among those who are endowed with healthy and normal reproductive powers, the dormant seeds of fetishism may find fertile soil in which to fully mature and form the prevailing "sexual pattern."

It is difficult to kill a full-grown weed whose roots extend deep down in the earth. Likewise, it is not easy to destroy a fully developed sexual urge whose roots extend far back to early childhood days.

The Significance of Fetishism

Cargo may be transferred from a small boat to a huge ocean liner. Fetishism is a transference of love, and all that love may be, from a person to some object which represents that individual. This may result from complete frustration of the love instinct, along with all its inhibitions. If the loved one cannot be had *in person* for the satisfaction of one's emotional needs, the fetishist has no other alternative than to express love by proxy by means of his fetish instead of the persons themselves.

Mankind has an innate desire to worship a higher and more powerful intellect than his own. Thus a rubber boot fetishist with very pronounced feelings of inadequacy and inferiority which cause him to withdraw from others and to experience at frequent intervals spells of "mental depression," as well as to suffer at times from a well-defined case of nervous exhaustion, demonstrates by his idolizing the boots of other men that he holds the owners of the boots in high esteem. His seeking to identify himself with the original wearers of the boots is like saying that "Other men are superior to me," like giving other fellows "a pat on the back" by "kissing their boots."

Identifying One's Self With Others

As Edward Podolsky, M.D., pointed out in his article on fetishism (February 1953 SEXOLOGY) the fetishist must feel that he possesses some part of the body of

"My own fetish is men's solid rubber boots, preferably the boots of farmers. This can be better understood when it is learned that I was born and raised on a farm. . . . "

another, or something that represents that part, in order to experience any degree of sexual satisfaction. The feelings and emotions related to friendship, love and sex, are often as closely intertwined as ivy that clings to an old oak tree. The *demarcation point* where one emotion ceases and another begins is difficult to define. To some it is a question of whether love and sex are separate things, or whether the two are closely and inseparably blended together. An indulger in this strange anomaly craves something which seems to be most intimately associated with the person or persons of his affections in their daily living. My own fetish is men's old rubber boots, preferably the boots of farmers. This preference can be better understood when it is learned that I was born and raised on a farm. Many of my early boyhood playmates wore rubber boots. In identifying one's self with others a person must feel that he shares the hopes, ideals, toils and troubles, as well as any success of those whom he secretly admires. One unfortunate aspect of homosexuality is that of unrequited love in which the affection one man feels or holds towards another can not always be reciprocated.

Life was meant for love, and without love there cannot be happiness. If the reality cannot be had, there remains only the symbol of happiness (the fetish).

I mentally share the lives of other men by means of what I call "my buddy's boots," and by wearing them without socks for the satisfaction of tactile contacts

—I then become truly "A barefoot boy with boots on."

Sentimental Love

There is a certain fascination, pride and charm for many home lovers who dwell in a very old and antiquated house in which many generations of people have lived. A similar satisfaction and pride is found by "the buddy boot lover" while wearing old rubber boots which other men have worn for countless thousands of hours. If the companionship of the men themselves is not available, *the symbol or proxy is ever accessible.* The boot fetishist in his leisure hours may at will find satisfaction in the "make-believe comradeship" of "Tom, Dick or Harry" as he chooses. On a stroll along the banks of a country stream or while wading in the placid water, the "barefoot boy with boots on" may experience vicarious gratification by wearing "Tom's old rubber boots."

In imagination, however, the boots are Tom himself who shares the same interests as the fetishist. The reason for this strange psychology of "companions by proxy" can be found in the expression, "There is method in the man's madness."

Some Pathological Aspects

Flower lovers with an intense love for a certain species of flower would in their day-to-day living routine be constantly on the lookout for their favorite posies and be greatly elated whenever such blooms were discovered. The boot fetishist, through his unconscious, continual search for his fetish, has the odd habit of always glancing at the feet of laboring men to see if they happen to be wearing rubber boots. There is a secret satisfaction in seeing other men wear that type of footwear that has so strangely affected the sexual life of the homosexual boot lover.

Erotic and nervous tension with a mild form of muscular rigidity is caused by seeing men or boys wearing boots, due no doubt to "secret sexual frustrations" which they arouse. The boot wearers unknowingly and without the slightest knowledge or suspicion of the nervous irritability they are causing another, are possessors of truly tantalizing boots. This same "nervous sex-craving complex" is also caused by hearing the dull "clumpety clump" sound of men walking in loose-fitting boots, or by standing or sitting close to men wearing rubber boots. Perhaps this "nervousness of desire" feeling is closely related to what a normal sex-hungry man might feel at seeing a pretty girl on a bathing beach, or a bevy of chorus girls, and of being so near and yet so far from the fulfillment of his secret desires. Ripe, luscious fruit can be picked only by those who have some claim or legal right to it. *Common sense demands that one exercise moral restraints over the sensual desires of the body.* Average men have a "safety valve" in this respect by being able to talk things over among themselves. They can "let off steam" in their daily working together and joint sharing of risqué stories. The boot fetishist believes he has an understanding of the feeling of normal men in their need and desire for women. The misfortune is that most men find it difficult or impossible to understand the feelings of the fetishist.

What Understanding Could Mean

A serious, mature knowledge of all phases of sexuality, including its deviations and many and various ramifications as understood by intelligent persons with open minds, and free from unjustified bias, would go far toward the development of a more healthy, more wholesome, more tolerant society. Proper sex education would help eliminate such "ghosts of the mind" as guilt complexes with their attending mental conflicts and various neuroses (nervous disorders).

Our prevailing society is too much inclined to make "moun-

There are many types of fetishists. When it comes to shoe fetishism, there is by no means unanimity. As noted in this article, some are interested only in rubber boots, others only in high-laced shoes, still others only in high-heel feminine shoes. Recently a fetishist wrote: "I would not mind having book supports in the shape of shoes with 6-inch heels on my desk." As it is questionable whether such bookends are made, Sexology has illustrated the idea here.

tains out of mole hills" in regard to many sexual habits which are no more than *individual harmless eccentricities*. However, one cannot alter or destroy a mental idea in a split second of time as one can so easily flood a dark room with brilliant light at the mere flick of a switch.

Prevailing Attitudes

What are the prevailing attitudes toward the sexual deviation known as fetishism? Apparently it largely depends not only upon a thorough knowledge of the subject, but also upon one's own inherent qualities of tolerance and forbearance, and to whatever degree one possesses a "live and let live" philosophy. Much of what an adult person believes is the result of moral indoctrinations which began from the time of one's birth in which one frequently heard the often-repeated words *good* and *bad*. Thus were formed mental ideas and impressions which will exist until death in the minds of countless individuals. For this reason *tolerance cannot be taught*. It must "come from within" as a result of one's own environmental circumstances, personal experiences and individual feelings. Therefore, as one feels compassion, love and tolerance for one's less fortunate fellowmen, so will vary the prevailing attitudes towards all types

of fetishists. The most commonly accepted public attitudes are that fetishism is a form of sex degeneracy, a mental illness, or an inexcusable abnormalness. As a book is considered good or bad according to the interpretation of various critics, so the evil and harmfulness, or the therapeutic value and necessity of fetishes will vary according to differences of opinion among doctors, psychiatrists and people in general.

If a hungry person cannot have a whole loaf of bread, he must try to satisfy his hunger with the crumbs which come from it. Fetishes are the love beggars' crumbs of happiness. However, it is a kind of happiness that is forever *incomplete*. Fetishes can never be more than mere symbols to represent or picture a "warm, friendly, human being" mentioned at the beginning of this article. It is *not* fetishism the fetishist wants, but human beings with all of their love, loyalty and affections. The only possible cure for the particular type of fetishism of the homosexual boot lover would be a replacement of the symbols with the reality. Yes, the *boots* could be tossed out the window when loving *men* came in at the door. This dream of happiness, however, seems like a remote impossibility, so the fetishist must resign himself to his fantasies and his dream world.

● ● ●

● **Sex After 65 (6284)**

Dear Doctor: My wife and I are over 65 years old but still we like to have sexual intercourse very much. Please give us advice in this case. What should we do?

Mr. J. C., California

Answer: There is no reason why you and your wife should not continue having sexual intercourse as long as you desire to do so. Recent surveys have dispelled the old myth that the sex life suddenly vanishes when a person gets older.

What is your S.Q.?

*Sex Quotient

by Mark Tarail, B.A., M.S.

Chief Clinical Psychologist, Gracie Square Psychiatric Hospital (N.Y.)

BY taking this test, you can measure your sex knowledge. Check whether the answer to each statement should be *Yes* or *No*. Compare your answers with the correct answers below. Give yourself 10 points for each correct answer and add the results. Your final score is your S.Q.

A score of 50 or less indicates *inadequate knowledge;* 50 to 60 equals *good;* 70 or 80 equals *excellent;* 90 or above equals *unusually superior.*

(YES) (NO)   1. Does breast feeding cause cancer of the breast?
(YES) (NO)   2. Are marital relations harmful during menstruation?
(YES) (NO)   3. Can a man with one testicle be fertile?
(YES) (NO)   4. Does variety in sexual relations heighten sex stimulation?
(YES) (NO)   5. Are birth control measures needed several years after a woman has reached the menopause?
(YES) (NO)   6. Are aphrodisiacs recommended in cases of lack of sex desire in females?
(YES) (NO)   7. Can a virgin use a sanitary tampon during menstruation without injury to the hymen?
(YES) (NO)   8. Is curvature of the male genital organ to the side unusual?
(YES) (NO)   9. Is the hymen tough and difficult to stretch in all older women?
(YES) (NO) 10. Could a male with a short organ have satisfactory marital relations?

ANSWERS:

1. NO. In fact, it is generally considered preferable for both mother and child.

2. NO. Sexual relations during menstruation are safe for both husband and wife.

3. YES. He may father children of both sexes.

4. YES. Monotonous repetition results in psychological fatigue.

5. NO. Cases of pregnancy are so rare that there is no basis for fear of pregnancy.

6. NO. Most substances are useless. Some are extremely dangerous.

7. YES, if the tampon is inserted properly. A slight stretching of the hymenal opening may occur.

8. NO. Some curvature of the organ is an extremely common occurrence.

9. NO. There is no general rule, women differ in this as in all other respects.

10. YES. Regardless of measurements, a sex organ which erects and remains erect for the sexual act is entirely adequate.

Sex Behavior of
DELINQUENT GIRLS

WHAT are the sexual characteristics and motives of delinquent girls? Some answers to this question have been given by Dr. James Galvin in the *Journal of Nervous and Mental Diseases*. Dr. Galvin, a psychiatrist connected with the Colorado Psychopathic Hospital, made an extended study of three delinquent girls in the hospital. The girls had belonged to gangs of mixed sex, which generally follow a well known sexual pattern.

In the gang groups, individual girls and boys pair off, but the pairs do not always stay together for lengthy periods. A great many of the girls in the groups have experienced sexual intercourse and a few of them have even been prostitutes.

If the girls are challenged by other members of their gang, they feel they must face such challenges —*no matter what they involve.* To demonstrate their courage they may indulge in fights, drink all sorts of alcoholic beverages, engage in unnatural sex acts—or even in "assembly line" sexuality. Sometimes a girl, on a dare, has sexual relations with all the boys in the gang. The girls dread being called "chicken."

Actually these delinquent girls are fearful of sexual intercourse— they are afraid of contracting venereal disease and of becoming pregnant. They also develop a strong guilt complex based on the fear that they may not be able to bear children; that "good" men may despise them, and so on.

Such girls (and their boy friends in the gangs) often use marijuana and drink heavily. They depend on these as a sedative before a fight or a sexual orgy.

The three girls examined gave clear evidence of a desire to conceal most evidences of femininity. They had competed with the boys in the gang in many masculine ways, even fighting them physically. They were extremely reticent when questioned about menstruation, although they had no hesitation in discussing prostitution, the use of drugs, or being in jail.

An exception to this denial of femininity by delinquent girls, however, is their mode of dress. They were accustomed to exhibit their breasts and buttocks by wearing extremely tight trousers and sweaters, with exaggerated brassieres, padded if necessary.

It is interesting to note, that in spite of the promiscuous sex pattern of gang life, each of the three girls had fantasies of normal married life.

Each time the girls entered into a new relationship with a boy, there was a period during which she was attracted to the boy because he was kind to her, not fresh, and did not damage her fantasy that this was "true love" that would lead to normal marriage.

However, as the relation developed, the pair would soon agree that marriage had to be postponed. Since they could not marry because of their youth, the lack of parental understanding and "persecution" by police and social agencies, they felt justified in having premarital relations.

Both parents and society were viewed as hostile and unsympathetic —this justified theft, prostitution or drug peddling as means of procuring the money they needed.

The girls studied showed a pronounced fear and dislike of homosexual activities. Some of them had had experience with homosexuality in institutions and suffered beatings rather than participate in homosexual practices.

A common factor in the history of these delinquent girls was that they frequently had poor homes and family relations. Many of the mothers were poverty-stricken and had been deserted or mistreated by their husbands. The girls did not have any recollection of their father as a guiding influence in their early lives.

What kind of men do such delinquent girls admire? They do not admire the ordinary type of man, whom they call a "square." The man they idolize is the one who manifests the courage to break the law. He must show, not dare-devil courage, but the courage to defy the usual rules of good conduct.

The therapist's job in treating these delinquents is not an easy one. Once he introduces any evidence based on morality, religion or philosophy, he will find future treatment almost impossible. He can make headway only if he can concretely demonstrate to the girls that their antisocial behavior results only in pain for them while socially accepted actions lead to pleasure and satisfaction.

(Photo posed by professional model.)

DEVIATIONS
in sex expression

Many persons have tendencies to depart from conventional sex relations. When does such a departure become sexually abnormal? Variations are often helpful. Any such variations should be mutually satisfying. What is the borderline between neurotic and ordinary deviations?

by Frank S. Caprio, M.D.

Part I

THERE is considerable confusion today as to what is *normal* (or *average*) in sex behavior and what is *abnormal* (or *unusual*). Lack of information as to what is sexually *acceptable* and what deviations are *prohibitive* constitutes part of modern man's sexual inadequacy.

In all human beings there is a tendency to depart from conventional sex relations, according to Freud, who said:— "Probably there is no healthy person in whom there does not exist, at one time or another, some kind of supplement to his normal sexual activity, to which we should be justified in giving the name of 'perversity.'"

Since the dawn of Man, it was believed that any sex act which did not lead to the procreation of the human race was abnormal or unusual. Later, society accepted certain variations of sex expression as usual, provided they ulti-

mately led to the act of coitus. Others expressed the opinion that if a particular sexual activity was preferred to coitus or took its place as a mode of gratification, then it was unusual. This would mean that if a couple engaged in mutual self-gratification rather than coitus, then such an activity was called a "perversion." *Incidentally the derogatory term "perversion" is now considered obsolete.* It has been substituted with a more charitable term, "deviation."

According to many psychiatrists, whatever sex technique is resorted to in the privacy of the marriage chamber, that brings *mutual satisfaction,* may be regarded as normal or usual. Drs. Abraham and Hannah Stone, authors of *Marriage Manual,* feel that there is no particular routine to follow but that "one should preferably develop one's ingenuity and skill and make sex life a mutual adventure."

Sexual deviations may take many forms. Some of these misdirected sexual expressions may involve fetishism (sex worship of objects instead of people); flagellation or whipping of sex partner; tearing clothes off sex partner; stealing female underclothes off lines; sexual exhibitionism; peeping at women in the act of disrobing, etc.—© SEXOLOGY Illustration.

In fact variations often help to restore or maintain the potency of the husband.

Some sexual aberrations are due to a neurotic condition—those, for example, that involve inflicting pain or suffering pain (sadism and masochism); exposing one's sexual parts in public (exhibitionism); incest, homosexuality, transvestism (putting on the clothes of the opposite sex); pedophilia (sexual love of children); fetishism (self-gratification with inanimate objects for sexual stimulation; such as, a lady's shoe, undergarments, gloves, etc.); bestiality (sexual relations with animals), and many others that are regarded by psychiatrists as unusual.

To differentiate between that which is normal or ordinary and that which is unusual one must take into consideration the nature and motivation of the particular sexual act, as well as the attitude of the persons involved. The late Dr. A. A. Biill, the world-famous psychoanalyst, was of the same opinion. He found that deviations from the normal were frequently encountered in the "intimate lives of otherwise normal people." He goes on to say, "we call them *perversions* only when they absolutely dominate the picture, that is, when they are fixed. Occasional indulgence in these acts does not stamp those practicing them as abnormal."

Wives, whose husbands are afflicted with a deviation of a neurotic or bizarre nature, should consult a psychiatrist. Their husbands are undoubtedly suffering from a sexual neurosis and are in need of psychiatric treatment. I recall a case that came to my attention several years ago in which the wife sought advice because her husband insisted on slapping her and tearing off her underclothes, prior to intercourse. It proved to be an expensive deviation. The husband had to imagine that he was raping his wife against her will and obtained erotic satisfaction by subjecting her to humiliating acts before he could experience a sexual climax.

Case Histories—No. 1

The following case illustrates what I mean by an abnormal or unusual deviation.

It concerns a young man, age twenty-six, married, whom I shall call Jim. He was referred to the writer by his attorney for a psychiatric examination because of having gotten into difficulty with the law. He was charged with disorderly conduct. It was discovered that for several years he suffered from a not very rare sexual complex: he stole women's undergarments from clotheslines.

During his early adolescence, at the period of sexual awakening, he was fascinated by panties which his sister had carelessly left about in her bedroom. He became sexually stimulated and entertained fantasies of what women looked like, clad only in panties. This led to an interest in advertisements of women's lingerie and as he grew older, he developed the idea of acquiring ladies' panties by stealing them from clotheslines. This complex became his hidden secret and he felt marriage would cure him of his affliction. But unfortunately, not being sexually well-adjusted, he made excessive sexual demands to such an extent that his wife developed an aversion for intercourse. His wife suspected that there must be something wrong with him sexually. He would accuse her of being cold because she refused to have marital relations every night. They became more incompatible and because she refused him on many occasions, he felt justified in returning to his old habit of stealing feminine undergarments. The law finally caught up with him. However, the Court decided to give him an opportunity to avail himself of psychiatric treatment. While Jim was cooperative and wished to be cured, his wife decided to leave him and seriously considered seeking a divorce on the grounds that her husband was sexually abnormal. One can understand how difficult it is for a wife to tolerate a sexual aberration in a husband, particularly when the security of her marriage is threatened by the possibility of his being institutionalized. Many wives are confronted by this very problem. Many men charged with indecent exposure are married and have children. Others are homosexual and deprive their wives of sex satisfaction. All husbands who have a serious sexual aberration, that brings them into conflict with the law or prevents their wives from achieving sex gratification, are sexually inadequate and are in need of psychiatric treatment.

In the above case we have an example of a husband who forfeited the love of his wife because of a sexual aberration that existed before his marriage.

He is responding to treatment favorably and is developing sufficient discipline to enable him to make an adequate sex adjustment for the future.

Case No. 2—Molested Women

In another instance, a young man had been arrested for molesting women by making indecent advances and obscene remarks. Being married and the father of four children, and never having been arrested previously, the Court decided to have him submit to psychiatric treatment in preference to sending him to jail or a mental institution. He said he had never received any sex education and ap-

parently had failed to satisfy his wife sexually. He accused her of being frigid. Actually he was a poor sex technician and had never learned the elementary rudiments of lovemaking. He was given a complete lecture course in sex technique and before his treatment ended he had learned through self-analysis the psychological factors that led to his sex complex.

Since treatment he has never gotten into difficulty with the law, and his wife reports that she is glad that he sought psychiatric assistance because he had become a changed man. She has been happy for the first time since they married, and was responding successfully to his lovemaking.

He was so satisfied with the progress he had made that he wrote me a letter informing me that he had purchased a new home, had been promoted in his employment and was certain that his sex life was permanently under control.

This case is one wherein the wife was patient and gave her husband an opportunity to be cured of his sexual aberration. If the husband is cooperative and places himself under psychiatric supervision, the wife, particularly if she has children, should give her husband a chance to be restored to normality. If treatment proves ineffective or he discontinues treatment, then she is naturally privileged to make other plans. This holds true in all cases of neurotic sexual aberrations.

(Part II of this article will appear in the July issue of Sexology.)

DEVIATIONS

In this concluding part of Dr. Caprio's article we learn more about "Peeping Toms" and married men with a "self-gratification" complex. The treatment of such sexually deviated individuals is discussed. They can often be cured by psychotherapy.

by Frank S. Caprio, M.D.

PART II

IN the first part of this article we learned what may be considered usual and unusual in sexual expression. As it was explained: there is in all human beings a tendency to depart from conventional sex relations, as Freud pointed out. In this second part of our study we note some further examples of sexual deviations, such as "Peeping Tomism" and other interesting cases which frequently come to the attention of our police courts.

Case No. 3—"Peeping Tom"

The Court recently referred another case to the writer that concerned a young married man, the father of a child, who was arrested for "peeping" into ladies' washrooms. He would hide, bore holes into walls of public lavatories and observe different women entering and leaving.

On one or two occasions when he was caught he pretended he was a carpenter or a plumber making repairs in order to avoid suspicion. However, one time when he was seen looking through a peephole, the woman screamed, attracted attention and he was placed under arrest.

This young man was religious, attended church regularly, was well-educated, a good provider and previously had never gotten into difficulty with the law. His wife was very devoted to him and was stunned when told by the police that her husband was a "Peeping Tom."

Because the Judge regarded this case as a "sympathetic" one—there was no evidence of any criminal tendencies—he was placed on probation with the stipulation that he avail himself of psychiatric treatment.

His sexual deviation, technically referred to as "voyeurism," a French term meaning "looking," was traced to experiences in childhood and early adolescence con-

in sex expression

sisting of looking through the keyhole of the bathroom while his sister took a bath. This premature sex stimulation became a fixation with him, to the extent that he always harbored a secret wish to spy on innocent women while they occupied ladies "rest rooms." Such cases of voyeurism as well as "indecent exposure" are very common. Most sexual deviations of an unusual nature indicate sexual immaturity. Dr. Stekel regarded them as manifestations of "psychosexual infantilism."

The Peeping-Tom patient appreciated being given the opportunity to learn successfully to control his voyeuristic impulses. He studied the subject of sexual aberrations, acquired a scientific understanding of their origin and development, and was finally able to give up what he agreed was a "senseless way of satisfying a sex urge that began in childhood." He was convinced that for a husband to consider himself sexually adequate he first had to achieve sexual maturity. He also expressed a genuine wish to make his marriage a happy and successful one. He loved his wife and child and said that they meant everything in the world to him. He proved his love by his cooperation and favorable response to treatment.

Case No. 4—"Self-Relief" Complex

One patient, married and the father of a nine-year-old boy, consulted me because of his inability to find satisfaction in marital relations. He claimed that he had been unable to discontinue the practice of self-gratification which started during his adolescent years. He also confessed to certain deviations which his wife apparently had no knowledge of. His sexual fantasies were sado-masochistic in nature. His sexual inadequacy as a husband was due to his preference for self-relief.

In describing his sex life, he said:—

"During the age of adolescence, I indulged in the habit daily and sometimes twice a day. This act was accompanied by looking at lewd pictures or by thinking of certain girls or women.

"Unfortunately, I continued the habit after adolescence and still do, even though I'm married. I would often attend theatres and reach a sexual climax during the showing of scenes of women lightly clad. Very often I would feel ill-effects, such as a strain in the testicles after prolonged periods of self-stimulation for an extended period of time, perhaps two hours before reaching a climax. I would not expose myself in the theatre, but would manually stimulate myself.

"Throughout the summer, window-peeping was my main source of sexual satisfaction. There was a particular woman whom I would watch. This woman lived in an apartment at ground level—with a deep patch of woods in the back ground — so that there was no chance of being observed or surprised in the act of watching her. I knew this woman's routine and at about bedtime I would watch her undress in the bathroom. I watched this same woman all summer in various states of undress or exposure.

"For a short while I stole women's undergarments from clotheslines — such as brassières, slips and silk stockings—and would then use them to stimulate my sexual desires.

"On many occasions when I was unable to see anything by peeping into windows, I would come home and indulge in self-gratification, although I could have had normal intercourse with my wife.

"I would imagine having women that I knew and liked as captives in my fortress and making their position so desirable that each liked being there and being my mistress. But the dreams and fantasies that aroused me most were those wherein some person who had been mean and quarrelsome to me were my captives, and I would compliment them only to humiliate them and then satisfy my sexual desires."

This patient proved to be quite conscientious. He developed rapid insight into the psychological causes of his sexual problem and responded favorably to treatment. He made a satisfactory heterosexual adjustment and successfully gave up his desire to practise self-relief, preferring to resume sexual relations with his wife.

The hysterical reaction of teen-agers to the rock and roll gyrations of Elvis Presley undoubtedly has a sexual element in it. This is a type of mass hysteria that has taken hold of the adolescent imagination at many periods in history.
—*Wide World Photo.*

elephantiasis

A startling manifestation of one venereal disease is the extreme swelling of the genital organs. A VD specialist discusses the symptoms, causes and treatment of this ailment.

by Leo Rosenhouse

THE massive enlargement of sexual parts, specifically in the region of the groin, often leads to complications far beyond the extent of personal embarrassment. An enormous increase in the size of the genitals, medically known as *elephantiasis,* is a serious condition and may cause a person to take to bed, because such swelling causes considerable pain, limitation of movement and emotional stress.

There are many causes of elephantiasis. Not all of them are associated with sexual problems. However, the majority of cases of elephantiasis in the temperate zone (North America) are almost specifically due to the venereal diseases; a lesser-known venereal disease, *lymphopathia venereum,* is the prime offender.

This disease is believed to be caused by a virus. It is usually contracted through sexual intercourse, although it may be spread by innocent means. Children may

acquire the ailment from simple contact with infected bedfellows, infected clothing, or the touching of sexual parts with contaminated douche tips and rectal nozzles. Elephantiasis in children has occurred from the carelessness of domestic workers and parents. It is possible that a newborn child may acquire elephantiasis shortly after birth because of infection from its mother during fetal life; but the point is open to question among venereal-disease experts.

In the United States, elephantiasis is more common along the southern seaboard and the Gulf of Mexico. The disease is frequently noted among sailors and prostitutes. Men who seek sexual satisfaction after coming into port often consort with women who have been exposed to lymphopathia venereum. By acquiring this venereal disease, sailors make themselves subject to elephantiasis.

Gonorrhea

Other venereal diseases also may cause elephantiasis. In the female, an enlargement of the lips of the

Mr. Rosenhouse is a VD investigator on the staff of the Department of Health, Sacramento, Calif.

408

Sexology, February, 1956

vagina might be due to gonorrhea. The labia swell to enormous size. Granuloma inguinale, one of the obscure venereal diseases, may result in extreme distress to men by causing an enormous enlargement of the scrotum. A man's testicles and scrotum may swell twenty times the normal size, making walking almost impossible. Dressing properly is an arduous task. Men in this condition usually rely upon suspensory aids to support the scrotum and help relieve the pain. Lymphopathia venereum may also cause swelling of the scrotum.

One public hospital recently reported this incident: A construction worker, a hod carrier, appeared before an industrial accident commission board and asked for compensation for a hernia he claimed was acquired while on the job. The board routinely referred the man to the public hospital where clinicians revealed he had lymphopathia venereum; this apparently was the real cause of his elephantiasis.

The construction worker was promptly placed under treatment for venereal disease. His swollen scrotum was reduced in size so it no longer resembled a well-formed hernia. Health officials traced his infection to a prostitute, who on examination presented a beginning elephantiasis. She had a greatly enlarged vaginal lip (right *labia majora*), but also was suffering from a serious ulceration of the involved tissue. Scientifically, this condition is known as *esthiomene*. Genital elephantiasis with ulceration may also be found in men.

Elephantiasis in Women

Women who suffer from elephantiasis and esthiomene are often in great pain. Relief of symptoms is difficult. The condition may persist for weeks or months, and the ulceration may spread to involve the rectum and buttocks.

Elephantiasis in the female has peculiar characteristics. The labia and clitoris are usually involved, while massive swelling is confined mainly to one side of the vulva, or one vaginal lip, or perhaps the clitoris itself. Extreme swelling of these parts will produce fever, chills, abdominal and joint pains.

Tissue will balloon out and expand until the skin seems ready to tear from tightness and pressure. Swollen tissue takes on bizarre appearances. The skin may become rough and pimply, like a cockscomb, and as wartlike as a toad's skin; or it may remain

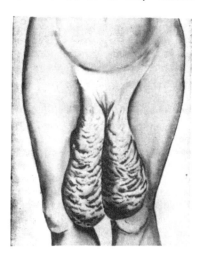

Elephantiasis of the labia majora (large lips of the vagina).—After Scangoni.

smooth and glistening, but painful to the touch. Any bit of friction or rubbing of the thighs against the swollen parts may cause extreme pain.

When the cause of elephantiasis is a venereal disease, swelling is usually attributed to an inflammatory condition which blocks lymph channels in the groin, preventing the movement of fluids. In the case of lymphopathia venereum, certain areas of the groin are invaded by scar tissue causing constriction and obstruction; unusual swelling therefore occurs.

Not long ago, a young man, still in his teens, appeared at a health department after complaining of a swelling in his groin. He blamed this condition on inflammation acquired while he was walking through a patch of poison ivy. Examination revealed that his sexual organ had swelled to gigantic size; in order to walk, he had secured it to his thigh by means of gauze bandage. Elephantiasis in this case was caused by lymphopathia venereum. Most of the surrounding tissue in the groin appeared normal.

Non-Venereal Elephantiasis

Non-venereal forms of elephantiasis may also create serious sexual problems. Enlargement of the scrotum occurs when tissue in the groin is infected by an organism known as *Filaria bancrofti.*

Pregnancy with toxic complications has been known to swell the genitals to tremendous size. Women may acquire a temporary elephantiasis from injury; a severe blow to the pelvic region in an au-

tomobile accident has been known to produce massive enlargement.

Motorcyclists who are subject to frequent injuries of the scrotum, build up scar tissue which may lead to elephantiasis.

In the equatorial zone, elephantiasis is fairly common, but the cause is attributed to disease brought on by poor hygiene and sanitation, rather than by any condition of sexual promiscuity. Surprisingly, once a venereal disease such as lymphopathia venereum is acquired, the gigantic swelling that accompanies elephantiasis may develop within a few weeks.

Treatment

Although such drugs as aureomycin, chloromycetin, terramycin and the sulfonamides are helpful in the treatment of elephantiasis, an extremely enlarged sexual organ is rarely reduced to normal size without the aid of surgery. The process must often be repeated.

A woman with massive vaginal lips (*elephantiasis vulvae*) often undergoes plastic surgical repair of her labia. Successive operations may be necessary in order for her genital anatomy to resume its natural shape.

The impact of elephantiasis on the sexual behavior of men and women is truly significant. No other condition so dramatically terminates sexual activity. Swollen sexual organs render a person mechanically impotent. The size of the engorged organ and its offensive appearance prevents performance of the sexual act. Chronic elephantiasis, that of the recurring variety, can leave a person helpless, and frequently, utterly useless.

Treatment for elephantiasis, other th·n surgery, is a long-drawn-out affair and may involve X-ray, physical therapy, and the use of chemical agents like *corticotropin,* as well as the antibiotic drugs.

There is always the danger that complications caused by elephantiasis may lead to permanent scarring and destruction of tissue, malignancy, and in extreme cases, fatal gangrene.

Public health officials differ as to the prevalence of elephantiasis induced by venereal disease. The unsightly ailment is more common in women. The anatomy of the female reproductive organs may have something to do with this fact, since women reach a chronic stage of elephantiasis more often than men.

The age group most likely to acquire the disease is between 20 and 30 years. Among military personnel, sailors, more often than soldiers, acquire elephantiasis.

One in 200 persons with venereal disease may acquire elephantiasis, but figures are not often consistent. In Los Angeles, an eight-year study of 31,353 male patients with swellings of the scrotum produced only two cases of elephantiasis.

The study points out that the disease seems to be regional, with more cases in certain sections of the country than in others.

Women who have enlarged labia, a characteristic sometimes present following adolescence, should not assume the condition to be elephantiasis. The tissue swelling caused by this disease is far more

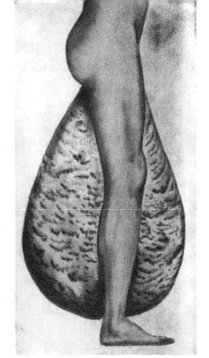

A case of elephantiasis of the testicles.—*After Näglesbach.*

extensive than any well-developed sexual organ. The same is true of a woman's breasts. A large bust should not be related to the massive tissue caused by elephantiasis. The disease usually swells an organ or tissue *ten to fifteen times its normal size.* This expanse of tissue often causes permanent damage.

As the groin is most frequently involved, vital functions, such as urination and bowel movements, are seriously impaired. Any large or unusual swelling in the area should be immediately investigated.

Early treatment and care can do a great deal for the relief of pain caused by elephantiasis. Prompt treatment insures protection against the spread of this disease.

The Rubber Fetishist

by David O. Cauldwell, M.D., Sc.D.

Many persons, as a result of early experiences, suffer from a "short circuiting" of their sexual responses. Known as "fetishists," they receive their greatest sexual gratification from certain parts of the body or even from inanimate objects.

WHAT happens when a fetishist marries a typical, ordinary, sexually well-adjusted individual? A recent letter to SEXOLOGY dramatizes poignantly the anguish and self-torture that fetishism can bring in its wake.

The letter follows:

"Sir:

"I want to know if it will be possible to receive an answer through your magazine's *Question and Answer* section.

"I am married, 34 years old, and I have a strong passion for any kind of rubber apparel, such as raincoats, gloves, etc.

"Every time I see a man wearing some rubber apparel, I feel a voluptuous sensation that is lulled only when I am satisfied.

"Some time ago, while buying fish, I was waited upon by a blond sailor with nothing special about his person except that he was wearing high rubber boots, with trousers and coat of the same material.

"He touched my leg with his. I was wearing nylon stockings and my sexual arousal was so strong I almost fainted. He stared at me and invited me to accompany him. After all such encounters I feel a deep sense of shame and pain.

"What could be the reason for my sexual attraction to rubber apparel?"

"Mrs. O.S.L.A."

←

A symbolic representation by Tina of the sexual fixation of a rubber boot fetishist.

Fetishism is a sexual aberration in which an erotic response is stimulated and gratified by a fetish. A fetish, according to one standard medical dictionary, is "a personalized inanimate object, love object, or any maneuver or body part which, through association, arouses erotic feelings."

The woman who wrote the above letter, obviously a rubber fetishist, appears to have an urge so uncontrollable that she must satisfy it without regard for her marriage relationship.

Must fetishists, then, sacrifice all hope for natural, healthy marital relations? Is it possible to maintain the vows of matrimony and still achieve the satisfaction that fetishists crave?

There are as many kinds of fetishists as there are types and kinds of fetishes. According to Havelock Ellis, fetishism, which he simplifies by the term "erotic symbolism," falls into three categories: love of parts of the body; love of inanimate objects; love of acts or attitudes.

Both Ellis and Krafft-Ebing include fetishism as an element of healthy love. The latter states that "the germ of sexual love is probably to be found in the individual charm (fetish) with which persons of opposite sex sway each other."

So does Wilhelm Stekel, who describes "hands, feet, ears, the voice, the eyes, the complexion,

Dr. Cauldwell is a prominent sexologist, Medical Advisor to SEXOLOGY *magazine and Editor of its* Question and Answer *Department.*

odor, breasts, and other parts of the body" as natural fetishes.

But this correspondent is obviously a rubber fetishist, one of many, it would seem, judging by the many case histories of rubber fetishists that fill sexological literature.

Rubber fetishists are often excited by the smell of rubber, as well as by its sight and feel. This writer is familiar with the case of a young man in whose premarital experience it had always been possible to satisfy his great desire for the stimulation afforded him by the smell of rubber. Yet after marriage he was practically impotent because the smell of rubber during the foreplay and marital relations was absent. He was positive that his bride would not countenance his wearing of rubber garments of any kind. He was advised to conceal rubber near the bed in such a manner as to permit him to smell it during intimate periods.

Another case involved a fetishistic wife who explained that her husband was a traveling salesmen who was often away from home. At such times she went to bed alone wearing rubber drawers, and, she claimed, always experienced a climax. She feared reporting this to her husband, whom she described as "understanding" in most cases. Another wife, her husband reported, "insists that we wear plastic or rubber clothing before marital relations. Otherwise sexual relations do not satisfy her." And from England, a merchant marine officer wrote to SEXOLOGY recently regarding his wife's desire to be fully clothed in rubber clothing during sexual relations.

Fetishism, rubber or otherwise, is no more common to women than to men. One young man wrote to SEXOLOGY prior to his marriage expressing his fear that his bride would neither understand nor accept his desire to smell and wear rubber during sexual relations. He stated that he would be ashamed ever to mention it to her or to permit her to learn about it. On the other hand, he feared impotence if he did not indulge his fetishism.

Fetishism is of psychological origin. Rarely does the victim recall the early associations responsible for its development. But these early associations result, in the fetishist, in a kind of "short circuit." That is to say, instead of developing the usual sexual responses to the opposite sex as he (or she) grows and matures, the fetishist suffers a "short circuiting" of these responses, or a transference from the opposite sex to some object, body part, or attitude.

How this "short circuit" comes about so that, for example, a young woman is aroused by the odor or sight of rubber rather than by a sexually attractive young man in the flesh is difficult to analyze and even more difficult to explain. In some way the young person (perhaps early in childhood) learns to associate sexual excitement and gratification with the fetish.

If this is repeated sufficiently while the personality is sexually undeveloped, a "short circuit" can

be set up which may harden in adolescence and maturity into a fixed pattern of behavior, or "way of life." We then have a *fetishist!*

Perhaps for a classic example of the development of a rubber fetish we must turn to SEXOLOGY of February, 1954. In that issue, an article entitled "Why I Am a Fetishist" by "Boots," relates the author's childhood and early youth.

"Boots" had lost his father when a very small boy and had been reared on a farm by his mother who was so fanatically religious that she had neglected her son and household duties in pursuit of her religious faith. The boy was raised around men and largely in the barnyard where animals were his best friends.

Around the barnyard the men invariably wore rubber boots. When he first engaged in self-gratification he did so embracing a rubber boot with a mixture of odors of the barnyard and rubber. Later, when he was on his own, he devised fancy stationery with the caption, "so-and-so's Bootery." He advertised in farm journals for old rubber boots, stating that he would give to any farmer who sent him such a pair, two new pairs of boots in exchange. Eventually he had an assortment of rubber boots which were his greatest delight. As he obtained more money, he advertised from time to

time and added to his collection of fetishes.

According to leading psychiatrists, psychoanalysts, and sexologists, fetishism becomes excessive or pathological (illness) only when it "pushes the whole love object into the background and when the fetish itself becomes the object of sexual arousal and satisfaction. For example, when a lover satisfies himself with the possession of a woman's shoe and considers the woman herself as secondary or even disturbing and superfluous."

Thus, it can be seen that fetishism is, like so many other aspects of human personality, a habit—but a deeply ingrained one. It can be a minor whim or caprice, or it can develop into a full-blown sexual aberration. It can affect the marital relationship to any degree, from a very little to a great deal. What is important, in any discussion of the individual fetishist, is the direction in which his (or her) fetish is taking him.

Stekel feels that this direction is invariably away from healthy sexual adjustment. "Fetishism," he states, "always develops into a depreciation of the female (or male) regardless of the causes."

But like all habits, fetishism can be limited, if not cured, as can other forms of sexual deviation, drug addiction, alcoholism, etc. All these are habits, and just as habits can be learned, the latest scientific thinking tells us that they can be unlearned. This is a simple way of describing the breaking down of the "short circuit" in the fetishist and the substitution of the opposite sex for the fetish as the object of sexual love. This is done by a process best described as unlearning followed by relearning, or sexual re-education.

Except in very mild cases, the fetish habit is difficult to break simply by an effort of will-power. Of course, there are many case histories of fetishists who have been able to do this. One who did was the young man mentioned earlier in this article. He was so ashamed that his new bride would discover his craving to smell and feel rubber prior to sexual relations that he overcame it after a few months. Of course this cost him great mental anguish and required deep understanding on the part of his wife, since he was almost impotent until he had mastered his unnatural passion.

But for most fetishists who have gone farther along the path of their deviation, trained help is required to go through the process of unlearning the fetishistic "short circuit" and relearning healthy sexual responses. Fortunately this help is available from trained medical men and counselling centers.

References

Blakiston's New Gould Medical Dictionary, 2nd ed., McGraw-Hill, 1956.

Ellis, Havelock: *Studies in the Psychology of Sex*, v. 2, Random House, 1942.

Krafft-Ebing, R.: *Psychopathia Sexualis*, Physicians and Surgeons Book Co., 1922.

Stekel, Wilhelm: *Sexual Aberrations: The Phenomena of Fetishism in Relation to Sex*, v. 1, Liveright, 1940.

● ● ●

TEEN-LOVE LESSONS SHUT BRITISH SCHOOL

IN Eccleshall, England, a magistrate's court recently decided to close a school whose boys and girls discussed sex and entered each other's bedrooms at night. The court held that Robert Copping, 29, bearded headmaster of Horsley Hall, and his partner, Edward Reynolds, 31, were unfit to be in charge of the school's 22 pupils. It also ruled the children were being kept in an environment detrimental to them.

The council's lawyer said boys and girls visited one another's rooms at night and there was constant talk of sex among them. The pupils are in the lower teen-age group. D. E. Evans, defense attorney, said: "One of the most astonishing features in the case was that not a single parent had been called to say they were dissatisfied with the way the children were treated." —*Associated Press*

E X H I B I T I O N I S M — *by Tina*

A psychological-impressionistic study of exhibitionism, as seen through the eyes of a sur-realist artist. At the left we see the bizarre and leering exhibitionist, whose grotesque head indicates his warped sexuality. The black spot on his body symbolizes his indecent exposure, which the enormous hand tries to shield in self-justification. His shocked female victim is symbolized by the enormous eye, the horror in what it sees, expressed in the flash. The falling leaves represent violated shame and pride of the victim.

MECHANICS OF SEXUAL ODOR

Sweet scents, throughout the ages, have been associated with love. Sexual odors, pleasant or unpleasant, are likewise closely associated with love and sexual relations. The feminine odor, though varying among individuals, has certain distinctive characteristics. Sensation of smell are often more impressive than sensations of sight. This article gives many interesting facts concerning the odors of sex.

by Milton Francis

ODORS are either pleasing or displeasing. Odors that are pleasing to some persons are displeasing to others.

Smell is essentially associated with matter. It is important to man, as well as animals, in determining the desirability of food. Through smell, animals get warning of pursuers and are aided in finding sex.

Among animals, *sexual* scents are a distinct class of odors. The most definite animal odors are those in the region of the genital organs and the anus. These odors and others of a sexual nature belong to the capryl group (this group comprises capric acid: a crystalline fatty acid). Such odors, as well as the odors of secretions of the female sex organs, odors of the male fluid containing reproductive cells, and of perspiration, belong in the class of odors known as *goat smells*.

The odor of the stinking goosefoot (a plant with strong-scented foliage) and the odor of some varieties of cheese resemble the odor of secretions from the female vagina. The odor of the male seminal fluid is similar to the odor of sourweed (the sheep sorrel) and also resembles the odor of the blossoms of the Spanish chestnut tree.

Among animals, the differences between the sexual odors of the male and the female are of importance for discovering the opposite sex during the periods of sexual excitement.

There was formerly a widespread belief that a man with a large nose had a large male organ and a passionate nature. This erroneous belief was discredited more than a hundred years ago. Many large-nosed men lack sexual vigor and some are sexually impotent.

The odor of linen or underclothes sexually arouses some men, because such odors are associated in their minds with the erotic act.

Some male animals have specially developed glands: the *cas-*

toreum of the beaver (preputial glands), and the musk gland of the male musk deer. During the mating season these glands become more active, as do the glands on the sides of the male elephant, which become enlarged and discharge a musk-like substance. Such odors attract or excite the female. Billy-goats and male deer have strong characteristic odors.

Burdach reports that the stag always approaches the female against the wind so that he may smell the female odor. If the fe-

This illustration shows the musk ox. The secretion of the substance, musk, which is used in perfumes, is taken from the glands of the musk ox. These glands are located in the vicinity of the sex glands. Only the male provides musk.

males flee, he will remain standing with extended head and open mouth, pleasantly sniffing the female odor.

It has been reported that odors are the cause of sexual perversions, especially homosexuality, among animals.

Albert Moll reports peculiar friendships between animals in a zoo and women. He is sure that animals can distinguish the sex of human beings. Male animals generally seem more friendly toward women. Charles Darwin, English naturalist, wrote that many apes are excited sexually by the odor of some women. Probably they detect in such odor a similarity to the odor of female apes—and draw false conclusions.

The friendship of a female dog for a man is greater than the friendship of a male dog for a man; the reverse is true for women. Bulls can be more easily handled by women than by men. A male dog, during the menstrual period of his mistress, is more friendly to her—undoubtedly because of the odor.

In 1886 Augustin Galopin wrote that when one smells a woman, one becomes sated with the living perfume of her. An amorous assimilation via the nose is prompt and exceedingly impressive.

The odor of the female genitals, according to Albrecht von Haller, has an exciting influence upon men. The distinctive *feminine odor* is considerably characterized by vaginal odors, which are not very penetrating except during the menstrual period. Male genital secretions have distinctive odors.

The typical sexual odor is not present until sexual maturity. In women it differs during puberty, marriage and the menopause. The odor of the unwedded virgin of marriageable age is said to be very pleasant to most men.

The odor of a girl changes when she falls in love. It becomes more pronounced.

The odor of a married woman differs from that of a virgin. Sexual activity causes a change in personal odor.

Red-haired women have a stronger odor than brunettes; blondes have a milder odor. The odor of brunettes has been compared to that of ebony wood; that of blondes to the odor of amber.

In men and women who exercise restraint in the indulgence of sexual desire, the natural scent is more intense because the sexual secretions retained in the body are partially exuded through the skin.

The feminine odor during menstruation is unpleasant to many men. Jäger describes it as similar to the odor of old herrings; Molin thinks it is like the odor of onions.

Just before, during and immediately after sexual intercourse, the odor of the body becomes more intense. Returning home, a certain blind man, through his sense of smell, realized that during his absence his daughter had been enticed to surrender her chasity.

The fact that prostitutes have a definite odor—an unpleasant rancid odor—has long been recognized. Perhaps it is partially due to the odors of the men with whom, as prostitutes, they associate.

Where many women congregate, the feminine odor becomes much more intense. This is noticeable at dances as well as in harems.

The masculine odor is more pungent in strong, vigorous men than weak men. The odor of semen and the odor of the secretion of the glands of the prepuce (this secretion is smegma) belong to the

capryl group ("goat smells"). The odor of smegma (the cheesy matter which collects between the glans penis and the foreskin) has an unpleasant effect.

The sexual importance of the odorous secretions of the glands of the prepuce is indicated by the large development of these glands in males of the musk family: the musk deer, the musk ox, the beaver, and the civet cat.

The male seminal odor, mildly similar to the billy-goat odor, ap-

The musk deer, just as the musk ox, also exudes a secretion from the glands located near the sexual glands. This, however, occurs only in the male animal. Musk odor is one of the most powerful of all odors. It can be diluted into almost infinity and yet give off a strong odor.

pears at puberty. It is a peculiar and penetrating odor. As the sex function declines, the odor disappears.

The odor of the masculine beard and mustache inspires sexual love in many women.

The sexual odor of eunuchs (men whose testicles have been removed) differs from that of normal men. It lacks the odor of semen and the penis odor (the odor of smegma). The odors of castrated animals (steers or oxen and geldings) differ from the odors of bulls and stallions.

A strong feeling of sexual dislike may be caused by a bad odor

The sense of smell is less developed in women than in men. Remarkable is the fact that masturbation causes the sense of smell to become keener.

This illustration shows the so-called nose rubbing of Aborigines. There is a purpose in connection with nose rubbing—which really is sniffing. Aborigines sniff each other to become acquainted with each other's odor.

of husband and wife. Albert Moll reported that a man became sexually impotent because of such an odor of his wife.

A man whose sense of smell is exceedingly keen and discriminating will largely be guided by odors. His sexual desires will be influenced by the odor of a woman. Regardless of her beauty and attractiveness, his feeling toward her will be one of dislike if her odor is objectionable to him. Though she may be ugly, old and stupid, if her odor is pleasing to him he will consider her satisfactory. Such a man will irresistibly pursue every woman in whom he finds the odor that most pleases him.

There are men—handkerchief fetishists—who acquire, often by stealing, women's handkerchiefs. Such men like to smell these handkerchiefs because they contain the scents of their female owners—the true feminine odor.

Krafft-Ebing reported an interesting case of handkerchief fetishism: that of Caspar Eiles, a baker of Vienna. In his youth he had masturbated excessively. Once, in a crowd, he became sexually excited by a young girl, pressed against her, and experienced an erection. However, he merely stole her handkerchief. Thereafter the acquisition of women's handkerchiefs became his method of sex satisfaction. When he was arrested he had in his home hundreds of women's handkerchiefs. He said that acquiring a woman's handkerchief meant as much to him as though he possessed her sexually. His peculiar association of sex with smell caused a perverse sexual impulse.

The peculiarly seductive, intimate character of women's undergarments is largely due to their feminine odors. Lovers sometimes exchange articles of clothing, or locks of hair, so as to have the pleasure of smelling them.

Albert Moll recorded the case of a shoe fetishist—a young man who took shoes and stockings from girls and passionately smelt them till ejaculation occurred. At night he would furtively enter a girl's room, take her shoes and stockings, and return them after he had masturbated with her stockings.

A famous foot and shoe fetishist, Retil de la Bretonne, French author, clearly explained that the odor of the shoes of a woman caused him to become sexually excited.

A certain sportsman, according to Charles Fere, would approach a woman who, with uprolled sleeves, was working in a field. After getting his hand in contact with her armpit, he would walk away as he happily smelled the moisture on his hand.

In perversions of the sexual impulse, the greatest impressions are those of the sense of smell. Many masochists (sexual perverts who are gratified by being cruelly treated) are sexually excited by the feminine odors of their mistresses.

According to Jäger, homosexuals cannot find sexual satisfaction with a woman because to homosexuals the whole woman smells bad, particularly her breasts and lap.

According to Symonds and Pierre Loti, soldiers and sailors are attractive to homosexuals because of their pungent masculine odor: the result of the close proximity of many soldiers in barracks, and sailors aboard ships.

Charles Baudelaire, a poet of a hundred years ago, was sexually perverse. His great passion was the love of odors; he revelled in erotic odors. The sexual odor of women—the feminine odor—sent him into an intoxicating passion.

Aura seminalis and *aura ovulalis* are terms given respectively to the odor of semen and the odor of the ovary.

South Sea Islanders, by their sense of smell, can readily identify the sex of a stranger. Among primitive peoples the nose greeting or nose kiss has as its underlying purpose: smelling. This form of greeting is found in Greenland, Lapland, India, the Malayan archipelago, New Zealand, and the South Sea Islands. Its purpose is to inhale the odor of a friend or a dear one.

Amber and musk, as perfume, have long been known as sex stimulants. Amber, the transparent fossil resin of pine trees, is a hard yellow or yellowish-brown gum.

From animals are derived perfumes:

Ambergris. Substance derived from the sperm whale.

Musk. The secretion of the glands in the vicinity of the sex glands of the male musk animal.

Civet. Substance secreted from a pouch located between the rump and genitals of the civet cat.

Castor. A substance of a penetrating smell consisting of the preputial follicles of the beaver and their contents.

(To be continued in our next issue)

THE WEDDING CUSHION

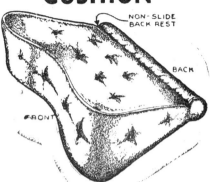

NON-SLIDE BACK REST

BACK

FRONT

MECHANICS OF SEXUAL ODOR

Part II of this article gives more interesting facts concerning the odors of sex. Sensations of smell are often more impressive than sensations of sight. There is no doubt sexual odors—whether pleasant or unpleasant— are closely associated with love and sexual relations. Throughout the ages sweet scents have been associated with love. One needs only to read poetry of the old masters to see this.

PART II

by Milton Francis

WOMEN undoubtedly were the first to use perfumes as cosmetics and as sex stimulants. In primitive times sexual odors were of greater significance than today. Men preferred women whose feminine odor was strongly developed.

Human sexual odors are penetrating and unpleasant. Women have used, as substitutes for their deficient natural scents, the pungent aromatic odors of musk, civet, castoreum (castor), and amber. These are the oldest known perfumes.

The odorous *Chenopodium vulvaria* (the stinking goosefoot) is a plant having a vulva-like odor; adolescent boys smell it with considerable satisfaction.

Egypt, in ancient times, was the home of the most skilled perfumers. Egyptian women had perfumes for their hair, mouth, and private parts.

"The ancients," writes Dr. Iwan Bloch, "knew no love without perfumes."

Paul Lacroix states that in ancient Rome many perfumes as sex stimulants were of great erotic importance. Both lovers, after washing with perfumed water, would apply fragrant ointments and oils to their bodies, and would interrupt the love act to repeat such applications of perfumed essences.

Not until the sixteenth century, according to Paul Lacroix, did the desire for cleanliness arise among respectable women. Until that time women would boast publicly that they never washed their genitals and that they left that practice to prostitutes.

In ancient Egypt the system of polygamy (having more than one wife at the same time) caused sexual competition. Hence the perfuming of the male and female genitals became a common practice. In Europe, in the sixteenth century, the genital organs were perfumed and the pubic hairs were carefully combed and shaped into small crisp curls.

Louis XV, famed lover of Madame Du Barry, increased his affection for her by perfuming her genitals with amber.

In ancient times, the male homosexuals, the pederasts (sexual perverts who have sexual intercourse with boys) and male prostitutes perfumed themselves, and they do so in modern times.

Men who become sexually excited by women's perfumes are known as perfume fetishists. Some men, of course, may greatly dislike certain perfumes.

Perfumes have been used as remedies for sexual maladies: impotence, sterility, and anaphrodisia (absence of sexual desire).

The nature of the association of sexual emotions with the sense of smell widely differs among individuals. The ability of human beings to detect personal odors, and their reactions to them, also differ greatly. Those who lack the sexual significance of odors and do not react to them lose a desirable part of love.

Those whose sense of smell is highly developed belong to the "olfactory type." Smell, as a sexual stimulation, was more important to primitive peoples than sight.

The personal odors of normal, healthy, clean individuals vary considerably. Sexual repulsion is caused by an unclean body, a bad breath, a displeasing tainted breath, and lack of personal hygienic care.

Here is convincing proof that each individual has his own special smell: a dog, by the sense of smell alone, unerringly follows the trail of his master or mistress and always recognizes him or her.

Especially among Orientals and tropical races, human beings can detect individual differences between personal odors.

Pleasing to many persons is the odor of the hair and the body of a dear one in close proximity. The odor of perspiration may be attractive or may be disliked. This odor—in many women it is an "animal" odor—is especially noticeable in the armpits. Women are often unaware of it. A lover who at first finds such an odor displeasing may, when sexually excited, find it very stimulating. Personal masculine or feminine odors disliked by some persons may be pleasing to other persons.

A certain married woman can readily determine the temporary mood of her husband by the odors from his skin! She says that this odor, when he is in a good humor, is slightly sweet; when he is tired the odor is sour; when his mood is angry or excited the odor is sharply bitter.

A cultured, sensitive woman quickly ended an illicit love affair when she found, at the first act of sexual intercourse, that the odor of the man's semen was displeasing to her.

The odors of menstruation, though they vary, have certain feminine characteristics. By hygienic care these odors can be subdued but not wholly eliminated, because to a certain extent they are present in the woman's perspiration and breath.

To most people the menstrual odor is agreeable; to some, when sexually excited, it may be attractive, to others repellent.

To a couple sexually intimate, the sexual odor of the genital organs is attractive. (This odor is stronger in women than in men.) However, the tainting of this odor by uncleanliness arouses sexual dislike.

Important as a genital odor is the odor of the semen of the male. It varies, both among individual men and among races. The odor of the semen of youthful Caucasians is fresh and exhilarating; in mature men the odor is more pungent.

The odor of a man's semen is not unpleasant to himself, but the odor of another man's semen is often obnoxious to him. A woman is excited and stimulated by the odor of the semen of the man she loves.

The odor of semen is often noticeable by a husband in the breath of his wife within an hour after sexual intercourse, though she may not be aware of the odor. In one instance this breath odor, when noticed by a husband, stirred his imagination and caused him to repeat the act of sexual intercourse.

The sexual impulse is considerably influenced by genital odors. Though such an odor, when first detected, may be unpleasant, it is likely to be pleasing when sexual emotion has been aroused.

To make personal odors more agreeable, there are perfumes classified as *masculine* scents and other perfumes classified as *feminine* scents. The masculine scents stimulate the female; the feminine scents stimulate and attract the male. *Negative-masculine* and *negative-feminine* scents neutralize objectionable personal odors.

Some persons use certain perfumes to excite their own sexual emotions. Women, according to an authoritative writer, are the experts who use perfumes to excite sexual desire in themselves.

The typical *masculine* scent—its purpose is to sexually arouse the female—is musk. Musk is very odorous and should be used only when diluted and in combination with other odors. The odor of musk is often displeasing to men.

The scent of lavender is especially effective in one respect: it neutralizes unpleasant odors of the female genital organs. A recommended practice is placing tiny bags of the fragrant dried lavender blossoms among linens and undergarments. Lavender water and other toiletries having this scent are also popular. They were, however, much more popular with women a generation ago than today.

Genital odors are increased by alkalis and are decreased by acids. Genital odors are neutralized by lavender, camphor, and bitter almond.

Each person should choose perfumes that harmonize with his or her personal odors.

Scents and perfumes are frequently mentioned in the Song of Solomon in the Old Testament, particularly in the love passages.

In ancient Greece the *hetaerae* (illicit lovers of the better class) and in Rome the courtesans (prostitutes) used perfumes, unguents, and ointments.

Perfumes were constantly used

by ladies during the Middle Ages and later were used lavishly by women of the nobility: queens, princesses, etc.

It has been said that the Marquise de Pompadour, mistress of Louis XV of France two hundred years ago, spent a million pounds (about five million dollars) a year for perfumes.

From time immemorial sweet scents have been associated with love.

A French writer truthfully remarks that perfumes, powerfully acting on the nervous system, prepare it for gratifying sexual sensations and emotions. The influence of perfume in infancy and old age is of lesser importance than in youth and the prime of life and when love predominates.

● ● ●

Having enmeshed her prey, the "spider-woman" (symbolic of women who rape men) proceeds to vent her lust on her victim. — Illustration by Tina.

● **Bust Developers (423)**
Sexology, September, 1935

Editor, SEXOLOGY:

I enclose a clipping of an advertisement for "Beautipon Cream" to enlarge the user's bust 3 to 6 inches, and ask if you think it advisable to get a supply, for I have practically no breasts to speak of? Or would "Ironized Yeast" be of any value? I am married, 25 years old, and have three little boys; but I have always had a flat, undersized form, and I would like to look more womanly.

Mrs. E. S., New Jersey

Answer:

I consider that practically all the advertised creams, and other preparations recommended to increase the size of the female breast, are fraudulent. It is simply something that cannot be done in any such miraculous manner as the advertisers state.

Often, with an increase in weight, there is some increase in breast development; so, if you are underweight, I would advise a liberal increase of eggs, milk and butter to your regular diet. Also deep breathing exercises and exercises of the arms and chest muscles will help. In addition, massage your breast once a day with a small lump of ice, ending by bathing with rubbing alcohol. All this can be done at home, with little or no expense, and will give you more benefit than any amount of the advertised medicines and ointments.

—Editor

● ● ●

● **Resemblance of Married Couples (3724)**
Sexology, April, 1954

Editor, SEXOLOGY:

I am 49 years old and have never been married. After closely observing married couples, I noticed that the couples whose marriage is lasting have facial features resembling each other. Those who get divorces seem to have dissimilar facial features. I am becoming friendly with a woman 45 years of age. Though we seem to have similar traits, we do not resemble each other in facial features. If we marry, is it probable that our marriage would end in separation?

Mr. W. E., Missouri.

Answer:

Your letter concerns the subject of telegony, a branch of scientific study. The theory is that when people live together long enough they eventually have a resemblance to each other. It is not until people have lived for some years together—as a married couple—that this seems to apply. Naturally, the marriages which have lasted for some years are considered as lasting.

Look at couples just married and you may fail to find any resemblance. After one becomes acquainted with couples who have been married a number of years (or even when one thinks so) thinking of one reminds us of the other and vice versa. No wonder we associate a resemblance of the features *when there may actually be none!*

Another way to look at it is that when people begin to age and when they reach extreme old age especially they appear to resemble each other more than ever. But this applies to actually old folks in general. Place any old man and woman together—side by side—and you will see resemblance. Think of them as a married couple and the resemblance seems more striking. There are many optical and psychological illusions and telegony offers plenty of them.

The only reason for failure of the marriage you have in mind would be because you have lived too many years alone and are rather set in your ways. An unmarried woman of 45 even though she may have been married may be set in hers. If you two can adjust accordingly you can have a lasting marriage. Do not depend upon resemblance to assure success in marriage nor expect failure in marriage because of lack of resemblance.

—Editor

● ● ●

● **Involuntary Excitement (445)**
Sexology, October, 1935

Editor, SEXOLOGY:

I am 17 years old, and in good health, except that I am a little underweight; but I am troubled frequently by sexual excitement, especially when I think about girls. It seems as if I have no control over my sex desire; a doctor told me it is simply nervousness, and gave me some medicine, but it doesn't seem to make any difference. Can it be due to masturbating at an earlier age? I wear a supporter to protect my organ against irritation and to make me less embarrassed when in company. I am afraid to go swimming or in the shower with other boys, for fear of comment, and it worries me. Is saltpeter good to take for it? I am afraid to take it without advice.

J. M., Pennsylvania

Answer:

I do not think that you should worry over these involuntary erections of your sexual organ. It is simply a normal, physiological expression of sexual activity—somewhat like a muscular exercise preparing the organ for its more serious work of married life and necessary for its development and growth. The more you think about it, the more you worry about it, the more it is apt to bother you. I would not advise any medicine to stop it; as any drug which would be powerful enough to do the work would be apt to do you more harm than good. Just keep your mind as much as possible off sexual subjects and become indifferent to the entire matter that is worrying you, and I think that it will adjust itself as you grow a little older.

—Editor

● ● ●

● **Pseudo-Hermaphrodite (3761)**
Sexology, June, 1954

Editor, SEXOLOGY:

I am 23 years old and am almost certain that I am a pseudo-hermaphro-dite. My breasts are too large for a male and my voice is as high-pitched as that of a teen-age girl. Sexually, I prefer men, but even this I find dissatisfying. To be a complete female is my only aim. Would it be advisable for me to

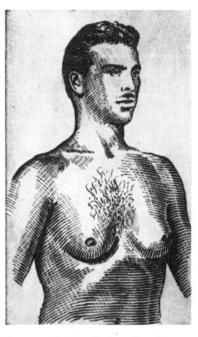

Gynecomastia (female type breasts on a male) may be due to glandular imbalance, malfunctioning liver, tumor, etc. They may be reduced in size by plastic surgery and by eliminating basic cause of the condition.

find an endocrinologist who could determine whether I am really a pseudo-hermaphrodite and could be changed as in the case of Christine Jorgensen?

Mr. R. W., Ohio.

Answer:

Even if you are a pseudo-hermaphrodite you are probably of the male sex. There are few pseudo-hermaphroditic females. If you did not see the article about the "Christine Jorgensen" case in our March, 1953 issue, by all means do so. In the Christine case there was no sex transformation. Our article bears the title: *Man Becomes Woman.* That, of course, is poetic license. No man can become a woman.

Any good physician should be able to diagnose your condition. Many males have large breasts. The condition is known as *gynecomastia* — a condition often discussed in our columns. Many males have high-pitched voices.

—*Editor*

● ● ●

● **Flagellation Desire (5021)**
Sexology, November, 1958

Sir:

I am 40 years old and separated from my wife. I have a very frequent strong desire for someone (male or female) to take me across their knees and give me a good old-fashioned sound spanking. Is this desire unusual or is it fairly common among both sexes?

Do you believe this craving is hereditary? I remember being spanked by my father (only when I deserved it) as a boy, and he made quite a ritual out of paddling me. He was not brutal about it, and I enjoyed it, secretly.

I have been advised that two avenues are open to me. One—to try to be cured, which I believe is impossible, since this desire is so deep-rooted in me. The other is to find someone who will administer the spankings I seem to require. I have a chance to remarry (not to my first wife) and I have reason to believe this prospective marital partner (through her devotion, understanding and willingness to please) would satisfy my desires for this old-fashioned punishment.

Mr. H. R., Penna.

▲

No form of sexual activity is hereditary. Masochism, sadism and other forms of sexualism which are deviations are the results of early environment and experiences. Spanking often causes a condition such as yours, since the nerves that are stimulated in spanking are connected with those involved in sex arousal.

Where there is a possibility of a "cure," it is always preferable to attempt it. In the long run this leads to the greatest permanent satisfaction for both marital partners.

You asked whether the desire to be spanked is unusual or whether it is fairly common among members of both sexes. Since masochists do not openly advertise their dispositions no evaluation of their number is possible. It is, however, by no means rare.

—*Editor*

● ● ●

● **Sex-Change Operations (6183)**
Sexology, August, 1963

Dear Doctor: From all outward appearances I am male, but I am totally female in all my desires. It has come to the point where it is almost unbearable. I have a continual desire to change my sex. If I knew of some worthy person that needed a male organ, I would be tempted to give it to him if it could be grafted on him. Sometimes in the future I want to go to a doctor who has had experience in this type of operation. Is it possible?

Mr. J. P., Texas

Answer: It would be impossible to remove your penis and graft it on to anyone else. The nervous and blood system connections are so intricate, and cells from different individuals have such built-in resistances to each other, that this would be an utterly impossible thing to attempt to do.

Doctors in the U.S. who have performed such operations are quite reluctant to do them. The few who do them will undertake them only after the individual has had a thorough psychiatric workup to determine whether or not it is desirable. The expense is very considerable due to both the surgical fee and the hospitalization expenses. Psychological or hormone treatments may ease your tension.

● ● ●

● **Wimpus (3605)**
Sexology, October, 1953

Editor, SEXOLOGY:

Is there on the market a mechanical device that will maintain erection? Will you please describe it?

Mr. B. C., Nevada.

Answer:

There is no mechanical device on the legitimate market in U.S. such as you asked about. We understand that such devices are barred from interstate commerce and that practically all states ban their manufacture and sale.

One device, commonly known as a "wimpus," consisted of some form of support to be placed on the underside of the penis with bands, or half bands holding that support to the penis. SEXOLOGY has always condemned such devices because they involve danger both to the wearer and to his partner. *They do not tend to restore or increase potency—in fact, they contribute to complete impotency of the partially impotent man.*

We have frequently published illustrations of these devices. A man who suffers from a weak erection (poor potency) should consult a urologist. If

The "Wimpus" (no longer sold in the United States) was a fraudulent device which was supposed to help maintain erection for impotent or old men. In this the device failed completely. It was made of semi-hard rubber, but was still flexible.

the urologist finds nothing wrong, psychological counsel may help.

—Editor

● ● ●

● **Nudity and Sex (5280)**
Sexology, June, 1960

Sir:

I find that most of my friends will dress and undress in front of their husbands, but prefer to be clothed during marital relations. Some of them say that they and their husbands have never seen each other totally unclothed.

Are these women really ashamed, or are they pretending to be? Isn't it natural for man and wife to want to see each other unclothed in their most intimate moments?

Mrs. R. H., Penna.

Kinsey and his co-workers in their monumental study of sex in American life pointed out that the educated class usually had intercourse totally unclothed. The farther one went down the scale towards less and less education, the more the tendency was for both husband and wife to keep their bodies covered and rarely to see each other nude. They found some instances where a couple had been married for many, many years and neither had ever seen the other unclothed.

It is a perfectly normal desire on the part of both male and female, to want to know just what the other looks like and, within the framework of marriage, there should be no real objection to this. Males especially have a desire for observing the body.

Each couple must work these problems out for themselves, but in general stimuli that help to bring about the greatest marital satisfaction should not be discouraged or considered wrong or immoral.

—Editor

● ● ●

● **Virginity of Fiancée (2171)**
Sexology, June, 1960

Editor, SEXOLOGY:

I am engaged to a beautiful girl. We have steadily kept company more than four years. I have never had intercourse with her until a few weeks ago.

I had been away for twenty months without coming in contact with any women. On my first night home, we had intercourse. She said she had never had intercourse before, but all the symptoms of a first intercourse were missing. The act was normal and later she admitted there was no pain.

Do you think it is possible for her to have lost her maidenhood previously?

Mr. J. R., California.

Answer:

There is no invariable rule in these matters. Many a bride has found satisfaction and not suffered in her first embrace. Only a certain percentage of hymens are painfully and bloodily ruptured. Your experience does not necessarily prove your fiancée was not a virgin. *—Editor*

431

Sex in Handwriting...

by Lorenzo J. Chieco

Mr. Chieco is a practicing graph-ologist and handwriting consultant.

Editor's Note: *In presenting this article, we wish to point out that it departs from our usual well-authenticated scientific material. Grapho-analysis is not yet a science. Some individuals, however, believe that it is possible to diagnose personality by studying a person's handwriting. Many psychologists, on the other hand, believe that this is not possible because handwriting is often determined by other factors besides personality.*

A word of caution to the reader.

Do not jump to a quick conclusion that after reading this article you will be able to analyze the sexual characteristics of any letter-writer or of any friend. It takes an expert's long training and practice to master this art—and even the experts are frequently proved wrong.

HANDWRITING is not just a form of drawing and a complex motor activity. Medical experts and psychologists now know that although our handwriting is influenced by our occupation and by the way we have been taught, the way we write is *primarily* due to the way we think and feel. To those who read "between the lines," handwriting is a mirror of the whole personality.

Male-Female Temperaments

Most of us generally believe that "masculinity" is linked with aggressiveness, outdoor activity, and interest in things scientific and mechanical, and that "femininity" is associated with tender emotions, sedentary activity, and an interest in esthetic and humanitarian activities.

But as we know, such viewpoints do not always agree with biological facts. Psychologists Lewis Terman and Catherine C. Miles found that occupations are commonly related to the sex temperament of individuals. Sportswomen and female engineers, for example, are more "masculine" than clergymen and male artists. And male dressmakers and domestics are more "feminine" than women scientists or sportswomen.

From this we may infer that if athletic or engineering ability is found in a handwriting, the writer is likely to be highly masculine in temperament. And if high art aptitude is found in a handwriting, the writer is apt to be of feminine temperament. None of us are 100 per cent pure male or female in temperament. Because of the non-biological differences of the sexes, and because handwriting is mainly a reflection of mental and emotional traits, handwriting, contrary to the beliefs of many, *cannot reveal the writer's physical sex.*

Types of Handwriting

Experience shows that persons who prefer to make their pen strokes broad and heavy are sensuous. Farmers, animal breeders, epicures and painters often write this way. Casanova, Lord Byron, Lady Hamilton, Marquis de Sade, and Sacher-Masoch—all noted for their sensuousness—wrote in this manner.

Thick, heavily inked strokes cover much of the writing space, suggesting that the writer has an exceptional sensibility for touching

Lady Hamilton, the British adventuress who was the mistress of Lord Nelson. Her handwriting indicates a sensuous personality.—New York Public Library Picture Collection.

or being touched. The sense of touch, itself, of course, is a profoundly sexual sense. These strokes are produced either by holding a pen far from the nib, in a semi-relaxed manner, or by using a pen with a blunt or wide nib.

Every person has an individual way of manipulating a pen. Those who write a great deal choose a pen with care. Many persons become attached to a particular pen and some persons have been known to develop a fetishism in connection with writing instruments. A few individuals have reported that the writing process itself produces in them gratifying or seemingly voluptuous sensations.

A good sample of handwriting is like a human face. In its own way it laughs, cries and warns.

Strong Sex Drive

A heavily inked writing that is blotchy or muddy may reveal a person whose nature is permeated or dominated by the sexual impulse. It may indicate an uncontrollable sex appetite. Second only to hunger, sex is the most powerful of human drives and in some men its influence on the personality is almost stronger than the desire for food. It is one of the tremendous forces which mold a man's mental habits and social attitudes.

This sensuality, shown by blotted, smeary, ink-filled circle letters, loops and other strokes, may also reveal drug-addiction or over-indulgence in eating or drinking. Like other traits, sensuality, of course, is not an exclusive one possessed by any particular strata of society. You find it in the scripts of such persons as Mirabeau, Edgar Allan Poe, Thomas Cochran, Hitler and Giles de Retz (*Bluebeard*).

Homosexuality

Accurate information concerning sexual behavior is obtainable only by a consideration of *all* the

Hitler's blotchy handwriting reveals lust and emotional instability. — *New York Public Library Picture Collection.*

features found in a handwriting. Sexual deviations are never revealed by any single sign. They are logically inferred by a special set of indicators in addition to expression of difficulties in personal and inter-personal adjustment.

Homosexuality—a complex condition comprising a variety of elements—is discerned only as a result of thorough evaluation. Frequently, but not always, it is observed with a trait-cluster composed of jealousy, clannishness, esthetic inclinations and marked emotional sensitivity.

At the Magnus Hirschfeld Clinic in Berlin, H. J. Jacoby examined the scripts of thousands of sexually deviated persons. His conclusions that homosexuality is not postitively disclosed by handwriting in all cases, has been confirmed by other analysts.

Sudden pressure in the final strokes of words is one of the characteristics sometimes found in the handwriting of sadists. The various types of fetishism, transvestism and other sexual aberrations are not capable of disclosure from handwriting as far as is known at the present time.

The Zones

From ancient times man has generally divided phenomena into three main parts. The world has been divided into three regions: heaven - above, earth - middle, and underworld-below. Man's body has been divided into three regions: head-above, thorax-middle and abdomen-below.

These three sections have acquired special meanings. The upper (heaven-head) is symbolic of mental and spiritual forces. The middle (earth-thorax) is symbolic of social activities. And the lower (underworld-abdomen) is symbolic of material interests and impulses

This handwriting reveals a powerful sex urge.

from the deepseated unconscious.

This idea of triple organization has affected our minds to such an extent that we project this concept upon the formation of our letters.

In handwriting analysis, the *upper zone* refers to upper loop letters such as b, t, l, etc. *Middle zone* letters are those without loops, such as e, o, m, etc. *Lower zone* letters are those with lower loops, such as f, g, y, etc.

When a person emphasizes a zone, he reveals that the forces associated with that zone have a special importance to him, according to students of handwriting.

Lower Zone and Pressure

The lower zone symbolizes material values and the impulses related to the sexual sphere.

The lower loops can exhibit a variety of forms and signify anything from sexual evasiveness to sexual aggressiveness. Lower loops that are long, large, and well-rounded designate a vigorous sex drive and a vivid sex imagination.

It is interesting to note that in the history of the alphabet, the very shapes of the letters conveyed a certain meaning. The letter *I*, for example, represents Man (the body erect), the male principle, the phallus. By adding a head to the *I* you have *P*, representing paternity, potency, etc.

In modern day handwriting we unconsciously portray the male principle by stressing the vertical downstrokes of the lower zone. Generally speaking, it has been discovered that pressure in this area is an index to a person's libido (sexual urge).

Men who experience periods of impotence often make their downstrokes of the lower loop letters without pressure or size emphasis, but with a marked pressure in their left-right strokes (as in dashes or t-crossings, usually made from left to right). In many instances, a lack of downstroke pressure in masculine scripts may indicate sexual sublimation.

Where lower zone downstrokes are highly left-slanted in a right-slanted writing, opposition to or frustration by natural heterosexual union is sometimes noted.

Excessive pressure of the downstrokes suggests over-compensation, and may reflect sexual inhibition

An analysis of this handwriting indicates that the patient possesses deepseated sexual anxiety and inhibitions.

or insufficiency. Downstrokes that are too short may reveal incapacity of the lower limbs, early sexual *trauma* (injury) or disorders of the sexual organs.

Alfred Mendel found that persons who are bisexual usually stress both the vertical and the horizontal strokes of the *t*.

A single stem instead of a completed loop may point to a rejection of sex, while failure to close the lower loops may be due to inhibitions. In persons suffering from sexual anxiety, the upward return stroke of the loops may approach the downstroke, but does not cross it or reach the base line.

Pictorial Symbolism

Sometimes a person has an occupation, hobby or fixed idea that becomes so much a part of him that consciously or unconsciously he expresses it in his handwriting by a unique formation or flourish.

In the realm of sexual symbolism, Mendel reports the case of a young girl who was obsessed with the idea of giving birth to a child. In her writing she began to make letters whose contour resembled that of a human embryo.

Aleister Crowley, poet, writer of erotica and drug-addict, notorious for his black magic masses and sexual orgies, rather blatantly revealed the dominance of sex in his life by the muddiness and the phallic-shaped *A* of his signature.

Whether for detecting the existing or potential sex criminal, for diagnosing psycho-sexual disturbances, or for estimating sexual compatibility in marriage, the science of handwriting analysis is considered by some to be of value.

References

Jacoby, H. J., *Handschrift und Sexualität* (Handwriting and Sexuality). Berlin, 1932.

Mendel, A. O., *Personality in Handwriting*. New York, 1947.

Mendel, A. O., "Symbolism in Handwriting." *Psychoanalytic Review*, July, 1949.

● ● ●

CHANGE OF SEX LAW

AN English law of 1953 provided that the sex of a person might be officially changed if a doctor declared under oath that he was of the opinion that the registration of sex at birth had been an error and that it was necessary to correct it.

The law was adopted only for those cases in which there was a registration error as a result of physical anomalies or administrative error. However, says the French magazine, *Science et Vie*, many British doctors have been interpreting the law much more broadly.

In a few cases they have been certifying a change of sex where they felt that the *psychological* sex was different from the apparent physical sex. The opinion of the doctors has been the one that prevailed.

The officials are obliged to accept the decision of the doctor, who has to answer for his decision only to his own conscience. There is, however, a problem which has to be met. Since the psychological "women" are women in the eyes of the law, what should be done if one of them decides to get married? In principle, nobody could oppose it. The problem has not yet been posed. Some doctors feel that these "women in men's bodies" have a profound horror of everything which concerns sexuality.

When midgets marry.......

Midgets may marry other small people or persons of average size. Many midgets have children of average size.

by Chandler Davis Marsh

IN my home town, the sister of one of my boyhood friends eloped with a midget from a circus that toured our county. It was quite a scandal. Her family felt much worse than if she had run off with a scoundrel of usual size and development.

And yet for years afterward they continued to be a happily married couple and had two children, both sturdy, healthy and of average height.

Maybe this young woman had an exaggerated "mother-complex" and was attracted by the "cuteness" of the small man. At any rate, she was devoted to him, and apparently felt no shame or embarrassment because of the great disproportion in their sizes.

Science states positively that midgets may have children of average size. Midgets have been known to marry persons of average size and have average children, or to marry other midgets and have normal offspring.

Mr. Marsh is a professional writer on medical and sexological subjects.

Dwarfs

The medical name for midgets is *dwarfs*. There are several different types.

The *thyroid dwarf* or *cretin,* is the direct result of under-functioning of the thyroid gland. He is usually quite ugly and mentally dull, ranging from stupidity to outright idiocy.

The *pituitary dwarf,* on the other hand, is caused by the abnormal functioning of the pituitary gland, which is situated at the base of the skull in a little bony cavity or cup. It secretes a hormone that controls growth; when the hormone is deficient, the skeleton fails to develop to average size. This type of dwarf may have usual or above-average intelligence, and be clever and witty.

Among the non-thyroid dwarfs there are also two kinds: the deformed, *rachitic* (pertaining to rickets) dwarf, and the graceful, well-proportioned but tiny dwarf —who is the only type to be properly called *midget.*

Dwarfs of the first category are

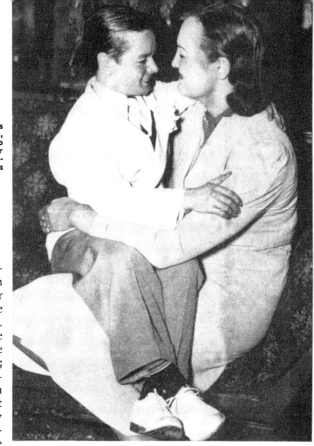

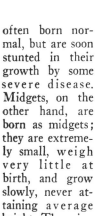
Billy Curtis and his wife, Lois de Fee, six-foot night club bouncer, shortly after their marriage. — *International News Photo.*

often born normal, but are soon stunted in their growth by some severe disease. Midgets, on the other hand, are born as midgets; they are extremely small, weigh very little at birth, and grow slowly, never attaining average height. There is another important difference between the two. The deformed dwarf whose bones are twisted and misshapen is usually sterile and impotent. But the midget may be healthy sexually, and may be the father of children whether married to an average-sized woman or to another midget. As we said earlier, the children may be of average size.

The midget Robert Skinner, 25 inches tall, and his wife, 26 inches tall, had 14 normal well-formed children.

In the European courts of the past, midgets were very popular with the kings and queens, and enjoyed positions as court favorites. It is possible that their popularity was due to their size, or perhaps their wit. Some authorities say that many of the high rulers of those days were mentally not far removed from morons, and that the midgets pleased them as toys or playthings would please a child today.

Famous Midgets

Some midgets have become quite famous and occupy a prominent place in history. The smallest dwarf on record was a tiny woman named Hilany Agiba, only 15 inches tall. The wife of Charles I of England had her favorite, Geoffrey Hudson, 22 inches tall, who was first presented to her in a pie. The pet of King Stanislaus of Poland was a French midget who was 29 inches tall when fifteen years old. He became engaged to another midget who was 30 inches tall, but he died at the age of 22 before their marriage. His forsaken little fiancée lived to the age of seventy-three.

Some of you may have seen the paintings of the Spanish artist Velasquez, who immortalized the dwarfs of the Spanish court. These dwarfs do not belong to the pituitary or midget group; they were hunchbacks, victims of thyroid deficiency, rickets and spinal tuberculosis.

Who can forget the most renowned of American midgets— Barnum's pride and joy—General Tom Thumb? Tom was born in Bridgeport, Connecticut, in 1838. Though of usual size at birth, he ceased growing at the age of five months. His height was 21 inches. Tom was a great success and favorite wherever he appeared, invariably drawing huge crowds to his concerts (his voice was pleasant, although somewhat nasal). It was his greatest boast that he had kissed more than a million women in England alone, and added to that number daily. He married a midget in 1862 and lived happily for 21 years after the wedding.

Jack Glicken climbs upon a desk to bestow a post-wedding kiss upon his blushing 400 lb. bride, Mildred Monte, at the N. Y. C. Municipal Building.—*International News Photo.*

Most midgets resent being called dwarfs because the word is associated in the minds of most people with the notion of deformity, while midgets are well-formed and shapely. They have no symptoms of cretinism, or rickets; they are simply of smaller dimensions than usual-sized men and women.

Midgets usually do not live very long, but some of them have reached a very advanced age. The French midget, Richebourg, who passed in and out of Paris during the French Revolution disguised as a baby in his nurse's arms delivering important messages which he had memorized, lived to be ninety. Mary Jones, an English midget, lived to be one hundred years old.

Pygmies

The tribes of stunted Africans and Malayans, often mistakenly called dwarfs, are in reality *pygmies*. A pygmy is a member of a race of people who are naturally very small—4 feet 7 inches to 4 feet 10 inches. Their tribes are widely scattered in Africa and in the Malay Peninsula. But their size is a natural racial trait, while dwarfism is a result of gland-misbehavior.

Midgets have always been popular with average-sized persons. Children especially like them, perhaps because they feel a kinship of perspective and physical viewpoint with them. Those persons who ridicule midgets fail to realize that there are thousands of borderline cases of gland-deficiency who may go through life undiagnosed and unsuspected.

Midgets are usually normal in every respect except size. Their marital relations, sexual capacities and reproductive abilities are like those of average-sized people.

the

sex life

of

VICTOR HUGO

Victor Hugo was a combination of a great literary artist and a sexual glutton, swayed uncontrollably by his passions. His illustrious reputation was marred by the many scandals caused by his insatiable sex appetite.

by Lester Speiser, B.A.

THE world knows Victor Hugo as one of the great French men of letters, the author of *The Hunchback of Notre Dame, Les Misérables* and many other famous classics. Hugo has also long been a subject of great interest for sexologists, both because of his many romantic liaisons and because of his contradictory sexual nature.

On the one hand, Hugo was a "choir boy in love," as one biographer put it, exalting and idealizing the spiritual ideals of love. On the other hand, he was a sexual glutton, openly unfaithful to his wife with actresses, shop-girls, servants —every woman who took his fancy.

Hugo was the kind of person

who in his youth could complain to his fiancée that she lifted her skirts too high when she tried to avoid dirtying them in the streets (perhaps showing too much of her ankles). "It seems to me," Hugo chided her primly in a letter, "that modesty is something more precious than clothes."

He was also the kind of person, who in his later years, was completely unabashed at being caught red-handed in an affair with another man's wife by the outraged husband and a police officer.

In one of his early letters to his future bride, Hugo contrasted the "pure and ardent" love he felt with the notion that most men had— that "love is only a carnal appetite which is overcome by gratification."

Despite this contempt for "carnal appetite," Hugo claimed that he had "knowledge" of his wife nine

Mr. Speiser is a high school teacher of English now specializing in the field of guidance.

separate times in the course of the first night of marriage.

Havelock Ellis describes the child Victor Hugo as melancholy, frequently found crying in corners for no particular reason. At school he was the smallest child there, under the care of the schoolmaster's daughter. His earliest recollections were of being taken in the morning into her bedroom and placed on the bed, where he would watch her put on her stockings and dress. One could only hazard a guess at the profound effects of these incidents on the impressionable Hugo.

Hugo's chaste courtship of the young and beautiful Adèle Foucher in the years 1819 to 1822 and the early years of his marriage gave little hint of his conduct that was to come later.

The courtship, a stormy one, was opposed by a domineering mother

whom he adored and equally opposed by Adèle's father. As it prolonged itself, his natural instincts yearned for gratification and he began to rebel against his "celibacy." That very same year he wrote Adèle passionate letters expressing the natural impatience of a young suitor to marry the mate of his choice. But he steadfastly ruled out the idea of pre-marital relations with her.

Josephson describes Adèle as rather tall, slender with a round head, very dark hair, a beautiful moonshape forehead and brilliant black eyes. Her nose was aquiline and delicate; her lips red, fresh and warm. Her complexion was dark olive. No one could blame Hugo for his passion, and finally (but not until his mother, Adelè's greatest rival, had died) he married her on October 12, 1822.

And for ten years he lived in bliss, raising children, enhancing his reputation as a writer . . . seemingly embodying the idea of the perfect husband.

Then, however, the unpredictable gyrations of life began to intrude on Hugo's paradise. He became increasingly busy with work in the theater. In July of 1830, Hugo's second daughter was born. There followed long months of fatigue and semi-invalidism for his wife, resulting in a physical separation from which he undoubtedly suffered greatly.

Hugo was beginning to realize the intellectual incompatibility which existed between himself and his wife. It was a year of literary triumph. Adèle valued his material successes but understood little of his work. To top it all off, Saint-Beuve, a famous critic and a dear friend of Hugo's, admitted to him that he was in love with Adèle. Saint-Beuve was remarkably ugly. It hurt Hugo's pride that his wife should respond to Saint-Beuve.

Leon Daudet, a famous writer and grandson of Victor Hugo, wrote "Cloudy Trophy" which concerns itself with this and later parts of Hugo's life. The book is based on the collected correspondence of Hugo, **Saint-Beuve** and the love letters of Hugo's wife to Saint-Beuve. The revelations of this book point up the contradictory nature of Hugo, who, although tiring of his wife and already involved in many extramarital affairs, makes love to her so that he can remonstrate **with** her over Saint-Beuve.

Hugo's plea apparently had little effect on his wife, since by this time Hugo had been openly unfaithful with innumerable women. But the affair between Adèle and Saint-Beuve did not last very long. After a complicated involvement encompassing a near duel with Saint-Beuve, Victor convinced his wife to end her liaison.

This did not prevent him, however, from having numerous "minor affairs" with various women. Daudet describes how Hugo one evening observed a young lady, who had just been mauled by a man, burst into tears because a policeman seemed to believe the man's complaint that she was soliciting.

Hugo stepped into the picture and extricated the girl from her difficulty. The young lady, Fanny Fantin, invited him to her house where he spent the night. But he vowed never to go back because he was afraid of falling in love with her!

This ever-changing, many-sided genius of French letters continued in this manner. There is no doubt that he needed his wife and deeply loved his children. He was involved in politics and French artistic affairs. He was one of the prominent personalities of his day. But the other side of him reflected his insecurities, searching, and his irresistible attraction to and for beautiful women. It had won for him Adèle and, no doubt, also played a part in his estrangement from her, though he was to remain married always.

Adèle Foucher was a milestone in Victor Hugo's life. His other romantic involvements were nothing more than escapades; that is, until he met Juliette Drouet, the second major milestone in his romantic life. He met her in a theater office, while awaiting to assist in the final selection of a cast for one of his plays. Afterwards he recalled meeting her before at a theater ball. Six weeks later she became his mistress.

This liaison endured with remarkably few mishaps for fifty years and, in fact, ended with Juliette's death in 1883. They evoked a passion in one another that was grandiose in its scale. Victor wrote vivid poetry celebrating the beauty of Juliette. His letters were passionate, expressing deep joy in their relationship. Hugo was unashamed

in the uninhibited expression of his feelings. And Juliette Drouet responded in like manner. She swore eternal loyalty to him and was true to her word all her life.

And what about Adèle? She stands as a monument to wifely patience. Victor himself told her about Juliette. She pardoned him! They are described as weeping together! Adèle had resolved that it was owing to his genius that he should be free "to use other women." Had he not been faithful all during their engagement and for at least ten years in their marriage?

Adèle continued as the queen of Hugo's household, at the head of the table, caring for the children and watching over other interests. And Juliette continued as his "queen of love."

Do not assume, however, that with Juliette Drouet there ended for Victor Hugo any further romantic attachments. No indeed! While it is true that his relationship with Juliette was by far the sun in the solar system of his passions, Hugo had other lesser stars dotting the sky. While his need for Juliette never slackened, the novelty of her constant companionship wore off.

Hugo was Juliette's religion, and she sequestered herself from the world for years, seeing only the object of her adoration. Her beauty faded a little; the "outside" world beckoned Victor, and he became entangled in a number of liaisons. Juliette was jealous and she did all she could to counter his numerous outside distractions.

Perhaps the most colorful escapade during those years was the scandal Hugo got himself into with Léonie Briard, pretty and impressionable wife of a French portrait painter. The famous writer was always the object of admiration by the women he met. At this period he was also restless as a result of the death of his much adored second daughter.

Thus, one day in July, 1845, Paris was rocked by a partially hushed-up scandal. One newspaper, the *National*, put it this way: "An illustrious personage who combines the laurels of Parnassus with the ermine of the peerage has been caught in criminal intercourse with a certain well-known painter's wife."

Josephson writes: "A certain sofa, according to legend, also played a notable part in the affair, for underneath it was posted a dull but patient police officer, invited by an outraged husband."

Daudet related how the officer fell back in astonishment when he heard Hugo say to him haughtily: "I am the Vicomte Hugo, a peer of France, therefore inviolable, and responsible only to the upper chamber." The lady was completely naked and Hugo in his nightshirt.

Adèle, his wife, took the whole affair calmly and was even delighted because she saw how jealous Juliette had become over it. Hugo had been involved in three households at once—his home, his retreat with Juliette and that of Léonie Briard. He even tried to win over the lady friend of his son, Charles, one Alice Ozy, an actress. But in this he was unsuccessful.

From time to time, Hugo's sexual gluttony impelled him to make amorous expeditions on week-ends to a small town where he could watch the young women scrub floors. He even had an affair with a certain Mary, the extremely attractive wife of a butcher. Daudet points out how attracted she was to him and how with little effort he won her over.

(All this, mind you, while he was completing a difficult chapter of *Les Misérables*, a haunting story exposing the cruel system of French justice, and with Juliette standing over him, jealousy gnawing at her heart.)

But there was no doubt that Juliette *and* Adèle were the two important women in his life. They played complementary rôles in Hugo's existence. Adèle was the devoted mother, a gracious hostess. There is no doubt that he continued to love her quietly.

Juliette, on the other hand, was more beautiful than Adèle and more important, possessed of the wit, sparkle, fire, sensuality and passion that his wife lacked. And it is also true, that after Juliette's death in 1883, Victor Hugo never wrote another word. He died, in fact, two years later on the twenty-second of May, 1885. However, Hugo noted in his diary written three months from his death at eighty-three, *eight separate occasions of sexual relations* during that last year.

We cannot in this short space begin to tell you the story of Victor Hugo. The amazing thing about his life is that his passions, his escapades, his romantic liaisons, were only a small part of a rich and useful life, woven in and out, so to speak, in the broad loom of his existence. At his death, police lines were necessary to control the million people who watched the funeral procession pass.

In Victor Hugo we see the combination of a great literary artist and a man swayed uncontrollably by his sexual passions. He was a contradictory figure whose reputation was made by his illustrious literary gifts, and marred by the scandals in which he was involved by his sexual gluttony.

● ● ●

ARMY USE OF SALTPETER?

QUESTION: I have been informed that the Army puts certain chemicals in the food, probably some potassium salt, which greatly reduces sexual desire and the number of erections. I have been unable to learn anything about this. However, since being a patient here and eating away from home for a few weeks, I find that is definitely the condition in myself. It has never occurred to me before and there is no physical reason for it now. Is this assumption correct, and if so what preparation is used? Is there such a drug that can be used without permanent harm to the individual?—Lieutenant (MC), U.S.N.R.

Answer: Saltpeter is used and has been used for years in curing most meats for both civilian and military use. The amounts used and the reasons for its use by the Army are identical with the use to which it is put in food to be eaten by civilians. Saltpeter is not used by the Army for its popularly reputed anaphrodisiac action (decreasing sexual desire)—a reputation not justified by the facts.
—*The Journal of the American Medical Association*

Sexology, October, 1946

● ● ●

NEW "ELIXIR OF YOUTH?"

AN extract made from cow embryos is now being used experimentally in therapy of the aged. The discovery of the reputed rejuvenating effects of this extract is credited to the French physiologists, Leon Binet and Colette Jeramec-Tcherna. They reported the results of their research to the French Academy of Science.

The report declared that in making the extract, the embryo is removed from the cow's uterus; then it is crushed and the pulp is converted into a fluid in a mixing machine. During this operation the embryonic substance is kept cold to preserve it. After an antiseptic is added to destroy any bacteria, the extract is ready for injection.

The reported effects, when the extract was injected in aged patients, were that their mind was enlivened, their muscular strength was improved, their healing properties were speeded up, etc. Apparently the extract helped such aged people to burn body fuel faster, thus providing more ready energy. The discoverers of this extract claimed that their experiments appeared to prove that the worn out human body benefits by the injection of the embryonic extract. It is obvious of course that many more tests are needed.

WHAT IS YOUR S.Q.?*

*SEX QUOTIENT

by Mark Tarail, B.A., M.S.

BY taking this test, you can measure your sex knowledge. Check whether the answer to each statement should be *True* or *False*. Compare your answers with the correct answers below. Give yourself 10 points for each correct answer and add the results. Your final score is your S.Q.

A score of 50 or less *indicates inadequate knowledge;* 50 to 60 equals *good;* 70 or 80 equals *excellent;* 90 or above equals *unusually superior.*

(T) (F) 1. Sexual intercourse during pregnancy is dangerous both for the woman and for the unborn child.

(T) (F) 2. Impotence, or the inability of a male to engage in coitus, can usually be cured by eating certain foods.

(T) (F) 3. Psychological factors can cause sterility.

(T) (F) 4. The offensiveness of certain sexual practices is determined not so much by the act itself as by social attitudes and customs.

(T) (F) 5. Pyromania (a compulsion to start fires) is often an expression of a blocked sexual drive.

(T) (F) 6. It is established that an unborn child can think and have feelings.

(T) (F) 7. Sex dreams are unnatural in older persons.

(T) (F) 8. Women lose their sexual desire after change of life.

(T) (F) 9. A male child is not capable of having sexual intercourse.

(T) (F) 10. The majority of marriages usually end in divorce.

ANSWERS:

1. FALSE. Under normal circumstances, most doctors would permit sexual intercourse up to the last few weeks of pregnancy.

2. FALSE. When diet is adequate, food will not affect potency.

3. TRUE. For instance, previously infertile couples have sometimes conceived children after adopting a child.

4. TRUE. Societies are known to differ in their evaluation of specific sex practices as natural or unnatural.

5. TRUE. Many pyromaniacs experience sexual satisfaction from starting and observing fires.

6. FALSE. Most doctors believe that consciousness begins at birth.

7. FALSE. Sex dreams are natural and are experienced by all human beings at all ages and stages.

8. FALSE. Menopause, or the cessation of menstruation, has no direct effect on the sex drive. In some women sexual desire is increased.

9. FALSE. Even very young children do have erections and are capable of having sexual relations, though usually without orgasm.

10. FALSE. Approximately one out of every four American marriages taking place at this time will end in divorce.

Interpreting Milady's Legs

By PETER BANG-ABBOT

ANALYSTS of character and of temperament and disposition have taken the bumps on the head, the features, the shapes of and lines on the hands and many other bodily factors to tell what men and women really are. The old doctors, rather short on science, but long on observation, took "humors" as indexes of health and indicators of treatment. Here, however, is a new idea —reading the personality from the legs which, as any illustrated magazine or rotogravure supplement will tell us today, are the most important and conspicuous features of human anatomy. What do you think, Reader? Does your experience show you that, as "the apparel oft proclaims the man," the legs are the interpreter of the woman?   —EDITOR.

"**T**HE history of feminine fashion is the history of human civilization" — or so at least says Chateaubriand, with the innate chivalry of the Frenchman, somewhere in his works. And this remark is still justified today, after 140 years, even though it must be taken with a grain of salt. The woman of to-day works, plays golf, follows some other type of sports, or dances; not because she wears her skirts above the knee but, on the contrary, she wears her skirts above the knee because she works physically in one or the other capacity. Thus her leg has become a matter of public concern.

Why is it then that there is no primer of "Milady's Leg" in existence? It is astonishing that the female leg has in no way received the homage due to it. If I dare undertake to fill this gap and to write down a classified index of legs (not to talk about the relationship between the exterior and character of the bearer), I am fully conscious of the limitations of the attempt to theorize, in spite of all expert knowledge and long study of the subject.

Medical men with psychological ambitions, who have more opportunity of studying the secrets of the female body, cannot miss the close relationship existing between the build of body and the character. Regarding the legs of the female species, this relationship begins already with the thigh. Beach observers who during the summer have the advantage of beholding this, under normal circumstances, concealed member of the female anatomy, should make their observations not only with the intention of an understandable private admiration, but rather with the purpose of getting to the bottom of the soul of the female sex which, so often, is decried for a "puzzling sphinx nature." Such a task, I am sure, would at least be as enjoyable as instructive.

The thigh can be divided into three general types: we have to differentiate between "strong, powerful thighs," "slender thighs" and "short thighs"; in the case of the last, the length of the limb is in striking contrast to the proportions of the physique.

Our analysis result of the relationship between thighs and characters limits itself to a few remarks; these embrace, however, the principles of the structure, or, rather, the main pillars of the interior decoration of the human body.

sonality that it is unbelievable that character experts have so far given so little attention to this ingenious phenomenon.

If up to now a "meaty" knee has been considered solely as a store room for fat, and as a symbol of physique in general, we must now add to this definition a psychological observation; namely, that the "meaty" knee is a

From left to right, as our author classifies leg types: (1) The Flower-Pot legs; (2) the Stick legs; (3) the Dream legs; (4) the Doll legs. Do you find your ideal among these, or must you turn to the opposite page?

marks; these embrace, however, the principles of the structure, or, rather, the main pillars of the interior decoration of the human body.

Strong, powerful thighs mean a firm temperament, and a firm basis of mental faculties.

Slender thighs exclude bodily strength, but point to a well-developed brain.

Short thighs belong to spiteful and envious females.

But let us go on—down. Don't the knees have to tell us anything? They have, indeed! Perhaps even more than the thighs. Results of comparative observations showed such a surprising resonance between the female knee and the per-

sign of weak character and of especially showy femininity.

A fleshless, bony knee symbolizes strength, desire to be active and good physique. Yet another observation shows that it may also mean a certain frailty in life; the absolute relation of the latter quality to the former has so far not been clarified.

The "crooked" knee also belongs in this class of body members. Analytical material h a s thrown light upon this problem, too; inasmuch as such knee structure is peculiar to ladies full of guile, and those whose character is rather on the weak side.

There is, of course, much more **material in existence about the** female leg which, for this reason, can be treated more correctly and explicitly.

We shall have to differentiate between the following types of the species leg:

(1) The Flower-Pot Legs: they are strong and powerful, and run in an almost straight line from knee to foot, like the utensil whose name they bear. Because they do not wrinkle. The owner is usually very sensitive and nervous. This type of leg is sometimes also a sign of a certain decadence; the possessor is not very suitable for marriage. This kind of limb may often be found on very intelligent women, with lively and thoroughly active brains, but mostly in larger towns. Temperament: choleric.

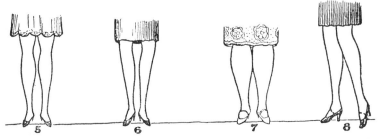

(5) The Circus legs; (6) the Baroque, or Bow legs; (7) the Champagne Bottle legs; (8) the Ideal legs, our author says, and it is difficult to quarrel with his choice. In his own original way, the writer undertakes to match these limbs with the psychology of the possessors.

not exhibit any thinning down towards the ankle, the genial curve is missing. Their owners are predestined for hard work. In character these ladies are good-natured, dependable, attached, and sometimes a little blasé, small and greedy. Temperament: phlegmatic.

(2) The Stick Legs: they are the extreme opposite of the former, very thin, and without any visible calf. They may be symbolic of a certain physical and mental weakness. Yet, u n d e r given healthy circumstances, and if provided with the necessary muscles, they may not be unsuitable for the exercise of sports. If they are very thin, the stockings must be pulled up all the way so that they will

(3) The Dream Legs: Since the fashion of short and still shorter frocks in the last 25 years, which has put female legs—so to say—in the showcase for the benefit of the male species, we know that this type does not only appear in fairy-tales and nude paintings of beauty-loving and beauty-thirsty artists. (Its complete description, if you can muster sufficient interest, can be found at great length in old French books like the "Chevalier de Faublas" and the "Droll Stories.") These legs are unbelievably beautiful; "they are really an anatomical impossibility." Only the artist of a time which knew the female leg by mere hearsay could permit himself to tell us

that. In its absolute finished beauty, this type of leg is still very rare. Yet it is the ideal of all chorus girls. The owner can be thought of only as *"grande amoureuse."*

(4) The Doll Legs: the owner is not the sportswoman type, and the muscles are rather undeveloped. While the form of the leg is attractive, it has something which may be termed infantile and loose. Like dolls' limbs, they make you feel as though they were stuffed, and that when the stocking bursts the shavings will appear. The owner is good-natured, good-mannered, shy, soft and, generally makes a satisfactory wife. But she ought to wear rubber stockings and go in for leg massage for psychological as well as medical reasons — Temperament: phlegmatic. Mentality: not very talented.

(5) The Circus Rider's Legs, or for short the Circus Legs: They have calves, curve, slender ankles, and yet the certain something is missing. They are mostly too short and too curved to be called perfect from an aesthetic point of view. They contain some error in the laws of proportion, and thus there is something ridiculous about them. Some of their owners are to be treated with caution because they go in for practical jokes and maliciousness. Experts claim that they have been very successful with massages for the purpose of perfecting the form of this type of leg. Temperament: melancholic.

(6) The Baroque Legs (owners are popularly known as bow-legged): According to latest fig-ures, this type is almost extinct. The inventor of the short skirt is not to be found among its followers. Due to modern baby hygiene and sports, the bow-legged lady becomes a rarity. If it does happen, it is the fault of the parents, who ought to be punished by a jail term. The owners are not suitable for stage or screen careers. Temperament: also melancholic.

(7) The Champagne - Bottle Legs: thin ankle and strong calf give this type a certain sensuous curve. Owners will usually claim (wrongly) that their legs are ideal because they unite strength with beauty; but they forget that their extremities do not live up to the laws of proportion. Their character is inclined to be obstinate, stubborn, full of life, and also energetic and conscious of a goal. Temperament: choleric.

(8) The Ideal Legs have to conform in every detail with the modern ideal of slenderness and racy curves. These are especially suitable for dancing and, before all, for sports, especially tennis, driving and swimming. They are a valid excuse for modern fashions. The outstanding representatives of this type are often social climbers, because captains of industry like them as wives, and motion-picture directors as stars. The owners of this ideal type are self-conscious, independent, free of prejudice. They exhibit propriety in character, but are difficult in marriage. They are correctly called the inventors of short skirts. Temperament: sanguine.

It remains to be said that the foregoing classification includes only the fundamental types of the species. In nature there are, however, any number of types which in reality are mere crosses between the types, mentioned. From an aesthetic point of view we find ourselves confidently on the road of progress.

One thing, important to our analytical observations, must be reported briefly; this is the growth of hair on the legs, which can frequently be observed. As important as this is for character reading, very little can be said about it. Whatever we know, however, is faultless. Growth of this hair on the thighs, as well as on the legs generally, means an almost irresistible inclination towards sensuality.

Finally, we want to investigate the feet. Here we can make use of only a rough classification, and a short outline of character interpretation:

Into the first category fall the "large, decisively formed and strong feet" which symbolize their owners as strong women of strong character.

The second group consists of the "small, graceful feet" which point towards boldness and impulsiveness and, sometimes, maliciousness.

The third embraces the "small, but fat feet, undecided in their outline" which belong to the typically "weak sex"; *i.e.* to women of soft temperament and weak, unstable character.

In the fourth and last category we place the "long, narrow feet" of whose owners nothing disadvantageous can be reported. Still, men ought to be warned. All observations prove that the distrust and caution, with which they have been treated instinctively for centuries, are not without cause.

The modern character interpreter will have to learn and exercise the trade of the shoemaker, if he desires to obtain further results in the latter field and make additional conclusions on the connection between feet and character. He would also have to work as a shoe salesman, for the identical reasons. As far-fetched as this demand seems, be sure that success would follow.

What do you know, dear reader? A modern scientist of the analytical type must know a lot.

● ● ●

INTERSEXUAL GOATS

REVIEWING the published data on intersexual goats, Dr. S. A. Asdell believes that the intersexes (animals showing characteristics between the typical male and female condition) are *all modified females.*

His data support the view that intersexuality is due to a recessive gene which modifies female development, but does not affect male development. All the intersexual goats he has seen have been hornless. It thus appears that the gene for hornlessness is closely linked with the gene for intersexuality. (A gene is an element of a germ cell transmitted from parent to offspring. Genes are carriers of hereditary traits.)

—*The Journal of Heredity*

MALE BECOMES

The life story of one of the most widely publicized cases of sex change in recent history.

by Tamara A. Rees

Robert Rees as a U.S. para-trooper at the age of 19.

JUST about five years ago—in November, 1954—newspapers in this country carried the sensational headline, "G.I. Paratroop War Hero Returns a Woman."

This was part of the world-wide publicity given my case on my return from Holland, where I had managed to obtain surgery which enabled me to assume the female rôle—a goal which I had sought for many long years. Few of the true facts, however, were reported and there was much coloring added to my story to increase public interest and circulation figures.

There remains a great deal about patients with transsexual desires like my own that puzzles the medical profession. In the case of the *transvestite* (who desires merely to wear the clothing of the opposite sex), recorded case histories have been cited where the patient was dressed and treated as a girl during infant years. As a result,

Miss Rees is the author of "Reborn."

FEMALE

Tamara Rees as entertainer at the age of 32.

it is believed, an attachment for this attire is established.

In certain cases of *transsexualism* (where the person wishes to change his sex), this might also have some bearing but in my case such a background did not exist.

I was neither an only son nor one of a family of boys only, where the parents might have wished for a girl, nor was I surrounded by all females. Our home and social life was always quite normal and yet my problem manifested itself at the early age of five years.

For a playmate I chose a little girl about my own age. Her dresses were always freshly starched and very lovely. I would sneak through the fence, much to the anger of our governess, to play with this little girl and her fine collection of dolls and lovely white doll house. I deeply envied this girl her bright ribbons and pretty dresses and I could never quite understand why adults never wished me to play with her dolls and that lovely little house. I wanted all of these things for myself and said so. Until later years this incident was forgotten by my parents and I sup-

pose that they thought that I had outgrown the stage.

Other events during this period of my life are hazy and of no great importance. My next recollection of any marked difference between me and other boys my age was about the period when I was nine years old. I was then attending public school in East Los Angeles and was considered above average in scholastic ability.

I took little interest in group activities and much less in games played by boys. I preferred to sit and read or single out one or more of my girl classmates to play with. We would play "jacks," jump rope or climb on the various kinds of schoolground equipment. At home I was quite content to pass the time in reading books or occasionally helping my mother with various household tasks.

While I was seldom given the opportunity, I took an early interest in learning to cook and bake. Today I excel in both departments and enjoy turning out a good meal or a fine pastry.

It was obvious from my ninth year that I was destined to be a small underdeveloped person (I am still only 5' 3½", weighing 116 pounds) and that I would be small of waist and wide of hip. It is therefore quite understandable that together with my mannerisms and obvious lack of interest in masculine activities that the boys should make me the butt of cruel jokes and their hazing.

It was also at about this stage of my life that I took up the practice of secretly dressing in my sister's and mother's clothes. This fact was never discovered by anyone, so far as I know.

I shall never forget my first school Halloween costume parade. My costume was that of a Spanish female dancer and it was complete with earrings, lipstick and high heeled shoes. What a sensation I made among the boys at school! Each year after that I lived for the day that I could again publicly appear costumed in my beloved female rôle.

Life was a succession of many unpleasant events for five years.

Days and nights often found me in lonely tears of angry frustration and self pity. By my fourteenth birthday I had become withdrawn and resentful of society. Undeniably I was a problem child.

When I was in my last year of junior high school my parents, suddenly aware that there was a problem which they could not fathom or cope with, took me to the first of many psychiatrists. He was a perfect specimen of the type often caricatured in the movies. *I never could have told him what my desires were or confessed that I had now taken to stealing articles of feminine apparel from clotheslines.*

After only a very brief conversation and without benefit of either a physical or psychological examination, the psychiatrist told my parents, "This child is merely underdeveloped and wants to be like the big boys."

Nothing could have been further from the truth. I now knew that there was a definite difference between a boy and a girl and in my mind I now felt that I should have been a girl.

The psychiatrist recommended a series of injections "that will help him to develop" and this treatment was promptly embarked upon. The result was far from the expected. I became more frustrated and restive.

In a period of enraged discouragement because I had failed to conform to the expected demands of my parents, my father took me out on a back country road one evening and beat me severely with an apricot branch. The cuts and marks of that beat-

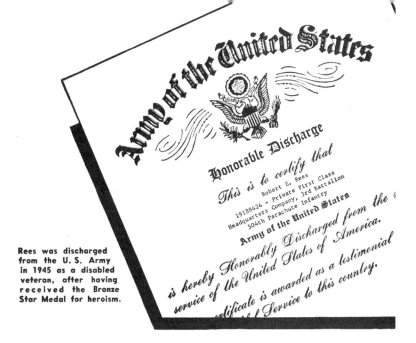

ing I was to wear for many days and the scars of resentment I carried for many years. The following day I ran away from home, to an environment completely alien to any that I had known.

My next year-and-a-half brought me into contact with the homosexual, the deviate, the alcoholic, the rich man, poor man, beggarman and thief. I make no pretext that I remained innocent. Perhaps it was my very ignorance which protected me from the homosexual or the temptation of finding someone who had a professed interest and understanding of loneliness. Fortunately, sexual expression in the physical sense has never been a part of my problem.

In early 1940 I returned to the home of my parents, since I wished to enter the Civilian Conservation Corps (C.C.C.) and this required the consent of my parents. Since they felt that they could neither understand nor control me and that I would be a disquieting influence on my brother and sister they gave in to my request.

I thought that, by entering the C.C.C., I would gain both freedom and the money with which to buy the female clothes that I loved so much. Needless to say, I was never more mistaken in my life. I hated the rough life, the work and the exclusive company of men. I had gained none of the freedom I thought to have and most certainly there was no opportunity to "dress." Here, too, I quickly became the butt of crude and embarrassing jokes.

In October 1940, while on leave from camp, I passed a Navy Recruiting Poster. At once came the idea—a foolish one, it was to prove

—that here was a real opportunity for escape.

My period of Navy service was of short duration. After about ten months I was honorably discharged "as physically undesirable." No further explanation was ever given.

I returned to Reno, Nevada and promptly enrolled in college, but while walking in town one day I happened to see another recruiting poster. This time it was calling for enlistment into the newly formed U.S. Army Paratroops.

My reasons for volunteering for this service were neither heroic nor patriotic. Here, I thought, was an opportunity to prove that I was not homosexual, as some thought, and also that I had the ability to fulfill my social obligations. Also present in my mind was the feeling that, if I could get into the most daredevil branch of service, the enemy would do the job that I had not the courage to do for myself.

As was reported by the newspapers, in the summer of 1943 I married a girl in Charlotte, North Carolina. This was the only true fact ever reported about that marriage. It was never anything more than a marriage of convenience for both of us. I had known her as a member of a horseback riding club that I had joined. One day she told me that she was in love with a soldier of whom her family did not approve and that she wished to get away from home. We agreed to marry—she in the hope of realizing her desire for freedom and I in the hope that by marriage I could divert the thoughts of others away from me.

The newspapers have reported that I fathered two children in this

In 1954, psychiatrists recommended to the American Embassy at Rotterdam that Rees be considered a female.

PSYCHIATRISCHE CLINIEK
DER UNIVERSITEIT LEIDEN
JELGERSMA-CLINIEK
TE OEGSTGEEST
POLICLINIEK : alle werkdagen
behalve Zaterdag
voor volwassenen
en kinderen van 1-3 uur

de   24 Juni   1954

The subsigned psychiatrists have made the statement after personal examination that Robert Rees (known as Temora Rees) is not of the masculine sex and therefore recommend that she may be considered as a female

Prof. Dr. E.A.D.E.Carp,

A.H.Fortanier,

458

marriage. *Medical records will show that I was never capable of fathering anything, even if we had lived together, which we did not, for shortly after the marriage I volunteered and was accepted for active paratroop duty in the European theatre.*

Although newspaper stories later described me as a "war hero," I have never claimed to be one. True, I did receive a number of decorations, one of which was the Bronze Star Medal, but this does not make one a hero. I have always maintained that the main requirement for an act of heroism is to be in the right place at the right time. In April, 1945 I was placed aboard a hospital ship and returned to the United States, where I was hospitalized until my honorable discharge on July 13th, 1945, as a disabled veteran.

Beginning in February, 1946, I returned to my college studies. In the late spring of that year I started consulting psychiatrists about my problem which by this time had such a compelling force that I no longer had any control over it. *At night, in my apartment I would dress and become the woman that I thought I should have been.* It was only in this atmosphere that I could find peace of my mind for my studies.

The first psychiatrist that I was to consult, when told of my problem, only laughed and told me to forget it. I left in anger and the next week mustered up sufficient courage to seek out another psychiatrist. This second man also appeared to have no understanding of my problem. He assumed that I was a homosexual and suggested that I seek women of a commercial vein as a solution. Naturally this suggestion repulsed me and I promptly rejected it.

It was not until the summer of 1947 that I again made any attempt to seek further help. I had become depressed and very restive. Finally, in desperation and forearmed with more knowledge of the problem and past histories of several previous cases, I again contacted a psychiatrist. This man had been a medical officer in the U.S. Navy during the war.

After the first few interviews I felt that I could risk telling this psychiatrist my problem. He neither laughed nor tried to suggest a compromise but was content merely to have me talk of my frustrations and desires. Later, of course, we attempted a number of experiments in the nature of appeasement, always with the hope on his part that I could be directed away from my goal.

I had by this time established contact with a psychiatrist in Germany, who having been one of a team in the effecting of sex transformation with a patient of his country, gave me much valuable information. He also referred me to an endocrinologist in yet another country and suggested that through him I might gain the release that I sought.

This man was most kind. At first he suggested certain experiments with female hormones, requesting that various psychological and biological tests be conducted and that reports be sent to him.

My psychiatrist was willing to

aid me with certain limitations but he did not wholeheartedly agree with the full extent that I expressed the determination to achieve. In due time the tests were assembled and the reports sent off to Europe. This took place in the summer of 1953.

Through the past year, with the knowledge and consent of my psychiatrist, I had assumed the full-time identity of a female. I was a guest in his home and was accepted for what I wished to appear. My psychiatrist had hoped that in this way I would be content and seek no further, though I had told him before starting the experiment that I knew that this would never fully satisfy me.

In November, 1953 I sailed for Holland. I had no promise that my wishes would be granted. I knew that I had yet to submit to further tests and examinations in Holland before I would know if the psychiatrists felt that transformation would be justified or even feasible.

As the reader can clearly see, the road is a long, hard one, full of heartache, disappointments and great expense. Surgical transition is a prolonged and complicated one. It requires two stages, the first of which is castration and penotomy (excision of the penis). After some time has lapsed, plastic surgery is performed to effect the physical appearance of the female genitalia.

This surgery does not create a woman where the patient was once a biological male, nor can the patient ever hope to have children. It merely brings the physical appearance of the patient into harmony with the mental pattern.

Upon my return to this country, I had hoped to escape publicity and start a new life, my past unknown to anyone. Unfortunately, this was not the way matters turned out. With the temptation of large sums of money and contracts offered to me, I must admit that I strayed from the course and was almost lost by my decision to enter show business. After some two years of nightclub appearances I became ill as a result of the fast pace and irregular hours. During this illness I had the opportunity to reexamine the situation and came to realize that I could never find peace and happiness as long as I remained in the public spotlight.

Today I am told I am a well-adjusted person serving society in a useful and worthwhile manner. I am quite happy and have a deep feeling of gratitude and indebtedness to the doctors who have made all of this possible.

Considering the living proof of my present adjustment, as contrasted to the maladjusted and vengeful person I once was, I feel the medical world has every justification in extending aid of this or similar nature to other cases warranting therapy similar to mine.

DEMI-VIRGINITY — By Tina

The *demi-virgin* is an adventure-seeking girl who refuses sexual congress but allows intimate caresses purely for material gain. She assumes simultaneously an air of chaste virginity and exotic sexuality. This is surrealistically illustrated by our artist. In the center of the flower is seen the face of a beautiful girl (representing the demi-virgin). The stalk of the flower terminates into the scaly body and tail of a reptile (symbolic of the *true* nature of the demi-virgin). Extending from the body are arm-like appendages; two are seen grasping a necklace of pearls and a fur-piece and the others are bedecked with diamonds and jewels so much desired by the demi-virgin).

Nature's Sex Oddities...

The Rhyssa locates its prey, buried in the pine wood. . . .

IN this series of remarkable photographs, the noted German photographer Georg Schützenhofer has succeeded in capturing on film an unusual sex phenomenon, several aspects of which biologists have not yet been able to explain completely.

The photographs show the brown and yellow wasp-like insect known as *Rhyssa* in the process of injecting her egg into the caterpillar of a wood-boring insect deep within the wood of a pine tree. The worm-like larva that develops from these eggs lives as a parasite on the larvae of other insects, using the caterpillar as food for itself.

When first observed in the woods, the Rhyssa is seen flying round and round one particular pine stump. Suddenly it stops, alights on the stump, and immobilizes itself with its rear in the air, its curious position resembling that of a Yogi. Though nothing can be observed by anyone, it has apparently sensed the presence of the caterpillar which it has chosen as its prey, through more than an inch of good wood.

At this point, the Rhyssa begins to plunge its stiff, hairlike ovipositor (a special organ to deposit eggs in position), into the wood. This hollow, needle-like shaft is enclosed in the long sheath at the rear of its body.

Slowly the ovipositor sinks in and the abdomen of the insect bends itself into a painful-looking contortion. Finally, when the point of the shaft has plunged into the living mass of the caterpillar buried within the tree, the insect injects its eggs in a final spasm.

Several things have puzzled biologists. First, how does the insect sense the presence of the larva which is buried out of sight in the pine wood? The possibility of scent has been mentioned and also of vibrations. How-

Above—the Rhyssa begins to plunge its ovipositor into the wood.

Above right—its abdomen bends itself into a painful contortion until . . .

Right—the tiny shaft of the ovipositor reaches the caterpillar and the insect, in a final spasm, injects its eggs.

ever, to many it seems unbelievable that the weak odor of a caterpillar can manifest itself through the solid wood or that the least vibration can be emitted by the placid larva.

Secondly, biologists are amazed at the fact that the insect succeeds in piercing a dense wood with a biological needle that is as fine as a horse hair.

THE HAIR FETISHIST — by Tina

The Hair Fetishist—a sexual deviate who attains erotic gratification in the act of forcibly cutting off women's hair, is
here portrayed by our surrealist artist. The face of the woman
expresses incredulity and horror as she sees her luxurious
tresses being cut by a sadistic hair fetishist (symbolized
by the scissor whose handle shapes the eyes of the deviate.)

The mind of the

FETISHIST

by Edward Podolsky, M.D.

A fetish is something—perhaps the hair, the lips or a feminine garment—which attracts a person of the opposite sex. The fetishist values the fetish abnormally. It sexually arouses the fetishist and enables him to derive much sexual gratification.

r...ult in res...ctive le...on.

Snipper Clips 6th Capital Girl

By the Associated Press.

WASHINGTON, Dec. 30.—Harried police found a sixth young woman today who said a lock of her hair had been swished off by Jack the Snipper.

Last week five girls reported that a young man sheared their locks as they sat in street cars or buses.

FETISHISM is a term coined by Dr. Alfred Binet, a French psychologist, to denote a form of sexual deviation in which the individual forms a sexual attachment to an *object*. In fetishism, sexual gratification can be obtained only by the sight of, contact with or possession of some object which belongs to the body or person of another, usually of

the *opposite* sex. It may be some intimate article of wearing apparel, such as a shoe, a stocking, furs, underclothing, etc, or it may be a part of the body, such as the hair, the hand, the foot, etc.

Origin of Fetishism

Fetishists can obtain sexual gratification only when the chosen fetish and certain specific conditions are present. Like all other sexual deviations fetishism begins in childhood. It is a childish habit. Instead of deriving sexual gratification through normal means, the fetishist chooses some non-sexual object and endows it with sexual significance, usually because in early childhood this object became important to him sexually.

Fetishism has been the subject of study among psychiatrists for a great many years. Dr. Sigmund Freud, who made some of the profoundest studies on sexual life, maintained that fetishism, like most other sexual deviations, is often a part of the sexual life of normal persons. In no person is normal sexual feeling entirely without some abnormal elements. There is a little bit of deviation in all of us. However, this element is so slight that there is nothing to worry about.

As a matter of fact, a slight amount of fetishism plays an important rôle in our sexual life. We fall in love with a certain woman because of some fetish. The man or woman must possess a certain stature (tall, dark and handsome), coloring (blonde, blue eyes, a cream and peaches complexion), voice (a deep resonant voice, a sweet voice,

An artist's drawing showing how the hair fetishist sometimes cuts off a woman's hair. Sexual satisfaction results from such an act, according to these fetishists.

a husky voice), or mannerisms (the way a person walks, or holds his head, or acts in general). *All these are actually fetishes,* but they are normal expressions. These may be associated with early childhood impressions and they are quite within normal limits. A fetishism becomes abnormal when the fetish, instead of the person, becomes the sexual object. That is, when the nonsexual object becomes so important sexually that normal sexual aims are entirely forgotten.

The fetishist is an individual who actually worships a bit of clothing or a part of the body and derives all his sexual satisfaction therefrom. He has no sexual aim toward an individual of the opposite sex. He uses an *object* for his sexual gratification. Self-gratification with the fetish or while viewing it, is his entire sexual life. To the fetishist the sexual partner is often *incidental* to the particular part of the body or body substitute, which is sexually stimulating.

The fetish, while in itself, *nonsexual,* represents to the fetishist, one of the sexual organs. It may represent the penis, the vagina or the womb. The fetishist must feel that he possesses some part of the body or something that represents that part in order to experience any degree of sexual satisfaction. The actual presence of the fetish is a necessary condition for sexual fulfillment.

Rôle of Fetish

The sexual life of the fetishist is of interest. There are cases in which sexual intercourse is possible in the absence of the fetish, but

The female "foot" fetishist obtains sexual satisfaction from kissing a woman's feet. The picture shows an old Gotham (New York
City) homage exacted at one time by imperious society belles
from their admirers before men could enjoy their society.

*such coitus is forced and incomplete
to him* and not very satisfactory. It
is often, if not invariably, accompanied by fetishistic fantasies (imagining the presence or handling
of some fetish while having sexual
intercourse). Under these conditions satisfaction is usually absent,
or at best, only partial. It is inter-

esting to note that among fetishists, self-gratification is practiced
not only by those who cannot obtain a sexual partner, but also by
those who have access to coitus. In
other words, the fetishist usually
prefers self-gratification with or by
means of a fetish rather than normal sexual relations.

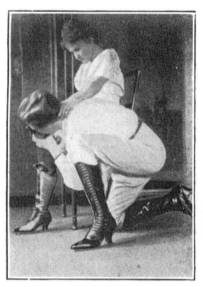

Fetishist kissing the sole of a woman's shoe. This gives sexual satisfaction to a deviate of this type, foolish as it may seem to normal persons.

What sort of individuals are fetishists? Most of them are passive persons who use passive means of obtaining their fetishes. Others are aggressive and sadistic and are much more dangerous. They snip off hair, steal shoes, and even commit bodily assault to obtain their fetish. The most dangerous have been known to commit murder to get possession of their fetishes.

Many fetishists are abnormal mentally and emotionally. The satisfaction of some fetishists depends on a certain ritual which may be weird and harmful. Some of them must experience fantasies which are often bloodthirsty, perhaps leading to assault, mutilation and even murder. There are also fetishists

who are less dangerous. These individuals have criminal tendencies *without the courage* to carry out their impulses. Their method is to symbolize and substitute, rather than to execute the underlying desires.

"Escape from Women" Factor

Like the homosexual, the fetishist is always attempting to *escape* from women. When he cannot do so, he compromises by belittling them. It is an indirect attempt to escape. Succeeding in depreciating his mate, he can then consider her of no importance in his sexual life. The fear of the sexual partner plays an important rôle at all times.

This leads us to the observation that many fetishists among men are *impotent* — and among women *frigid!* Fetishism is an attempt to attain sexual satisfaction by fondling a fetish because normal ways of obtaining sexual gratification are impossible or are not available. The fetish is an attempt to arouse sexual feeling which is lacking because of impotence or frigidity.

Fetishism is widespread in its implications. Thus, coherent fetishism is the attraction which is exercised for many persons far more than is normal by objects and materials which are not donned or thrown over the body as clothing, but are brought into intimate contact with some part of the body. Coherent fetishists are individuals who obtain sexual satisfaction by putting some object into contact with their body. They may be also called *tactile* fetishists because the skin seems to act as the genital organ in their case.

Another usual type of fetishism is that known as *acoustic* fetishism which is the satisfaction obtained by listening to sexual stories. There are many such fetishists, whose normal sexual life is non-existent, but who are always ready to listen to "sexy" stories because of the great satisfaction they derive from them. *Many tellers of off-color stories are oral fetishists.* They are constantly telling sex stories to all who will or even will not listen to them. The telling of these stories is their sole sexual outlet.

Extreme Types Dangerous

Fetishism, in its more extreme types, is a very definite sexual deviation. It is also a criminal activity. Many fetishists commit burglary, theft and assault in order to gain possession of the required article of clothing, and some fetishists find that the garment must be stolen if full satisfaction is to be obtained. The more vicious type is the hair fetishist, who assaults women and cuts off their hair in order to secure his fetish. In such cases there is also a very strong element of sadism.

The murderous fetishist is the most dangerous of all! One such case was that of a man who obtained sexual satisfaction from collecting, making and playing with knives and from the sadistic fantasies in which he at first made imaginary attacks on girls. Later he began to make *actual* attacks and culminated in murdering one of his victims.

Fetishism is a mental and emotional, as well as *sexual* deviation. It requires the careful attention of a psychiatrist who can help the fetishist to gain some degree of insight into his difficulties. Many cases of fetishism can be helped considerably by proper treatment. Deep probing into the subconscious mind will often bring to the surface the reason for this sexual defect. If impotence or frigidity is the cause, these can often be corrected by intensive treatment. All cases of fetishism require treatment, and with the modern psychiatric methods now available, excellent results can be obtained in the majority of them.

A lamp being sold in this country—unless you are a fetishist you will not appreciate the high laced feminine shoe and the black lacing on lamp shade, suggestive of corset lacing.—*Courtesy The Bar Mart, N. Y.*

SHUNAMMITISM

Rejuvenation of old men has been the will-'o-the-wisp since the dawn of humanity. One of the most popular means to regain youth was close physical contact with a young female—but without sexual congress. The idea behind this was that young and vigorous people exude an invisible, yet powerful substance that might rejuvenate the oldster. The present article, written by a scholarly expert on the subject, throws much light on this ancient belief—for which science, so far, has found no answer.

by A. F. Niemoeller

AMONG the oldest and most consistent of man's efforts is that directed toward the achieving of rejuvenation of one sort or another, a recapturing of one's youthtide. Rarely, if ever, is it a returning to a state similar to one's actual youthfulness that is sought, a living over of, say, the years of the late 'teens and early twenties with all the numerous little trials and vexations of those callow days, but *what is usually eagerly desired is a regaining of some tangible degree of the physical and physiological vigor of those years.* A recrudescence of juvenescent vigor may be striven for for any of a variety of reasons—from improved hearing and sight and a heartier digestion to freedom from aches and pains and more limber joints—but the commonest object of such endeavors is by a large margin a return to as much of the sexual vigor of one's earlier years as can be managed.

Just how ancient the search for sexual rejuvenation may be it is impossible to say, for its origins are lost in the mists that cloud the times before recorded history. Egyptian papyri dating from several thousand years before Christ give procedures and formulæ for achieving this purpose, and ancient Greek literature contains references that indicate the attempt at rejuvenation to have been an old and accepted practice of the time. Most people regard Ponce de Leon and his search for the Fountain of Youth as more or less the progenitor in the field of rejuvenescence, but actually he is a relative newcomer.

The means by which it was sought to gain second youthfulness are of a variety limited only by the ingenuity and credulity of man. Scarcely any means, matter, or agency has been overlooked, and the approach had been from all conceivable directions—magical, religious, medical, physical, therapeutic, and just plain hopeful. In the ancient Greek story of the Argonautic expedition after the Golden Fleece, Medea, who made it possible for Jason to gain his objective, marries him and returns to Greece with him. However, she soon becomes rather dissatisfied with Jason as a husband (for he is getting pretty well along in middle age by this time) so she renews her husband's youth by the somewhat extreme expedient of boiling him! According to the classic story this proved quite effective, but it definitely is not recommended here as a method for home treatment. There must have been a trick to it.

Medea also attempted the rejuvenation of her aged father Æetes by boiling magic herbs in a golden kettle and giving him the resultant decoction to drink. But she didn't seem to do so well this time for, according to some reports, the liquor turned out to be too strong and the old man died.

Incidentally, there has been a similar outcome to not a few inconsidered attempts at rejuvenation in modern times. In the fragments of an ancient Greek play from 414 B.C., the *Amphiarius*, by that great old comedy writer Aristophanes, there is a fanciful if incomplete description of the rejuvenation of a feeble old man, part of the treatment consisting of his eating a huge dish of lentils. On the other hand, a physician of the 4th century A.D., Theodorus Priscianus, has left a method of treatment that might be sound yet

"The Shulamite"—famous painting by Alexander Cabanel, the French artist, renowned for his biblical paintings. The picture is that of a Shunammite woman—who yearned and dreamed continually of the man to whom she had pledged herself—but from whom she was shut away. "I charge you, O daughters of Jerusalem, if ye find my beloved, that ye tell him, that I am sick of love."—From Song of Solomon—5, 8.—From the Metropolitan Museum of Art collection.

today: "Let the patient," he says, "be surrounded by beautiful girls or boys; also give him books to read, which stimulate lust and in which love stories are insinuatingly treated."

Men have grown old and hastened the onset of age in trying to find their way back to youth. The whole immense and venerable field of aphrodisiacs is but a specialized attack of the problem. Modern science has brought new resources to bear, from improved medicaments and hormone injections to surgical techniques and the implantation of "goat glands." But of all the lavish variety of agents for rejuvenation that have been known over the centuries, none is more curious and few have a longer or more interesting history than that known as "Shunammitism."

The name of this practice is derived from an incident in the life of King David recorded in the Old Testament, but the procedure is so complacently accepted there that its origin is obviously of a much earlier age. In essence, the technique is based simply in the belief that the bodies of healthy, vigorous young persons, especially virgins, give off exhalations which are assimilable by aged and feeble men in close proximity to them and exercise a fortifying and juvenescent effect upon them. This first recorded case of Shunammitism is to be found in the First Book of Kings, chapter 1, verses 1-4:

"Now king David was old and stricken in years; and they covered him with clothes, but he gat no heat. Wherefore his servants said unto him, 'Let there be sought for my lord the king a young virgin; and let her stand before the king, and let her cherish him, and let her lie in thy bosom, that my lord the king may get heat.'

"So they sought for a fair damsel through all the coasts of Israel, and found Abishag a Shunammite, and brought her to the king. And the damsel was very fair, and cherished the king, and ministered to him: but the king knew her not."

In addition to giving us the origin of the name for the practice [the nationality of the first maid on record to be employed for this purpose], this short passage furnishes us with the salient elements necessary to the success of the procedure: the Shunammite must stay in close physical relationship with the aged one, she must be a virgin, and *there must be no sexual connection between patient and palliative.* Subsequent centuries introduced certain additions or alterations to the ritual, but these fundamental features were always there.

Two questions that arise very naturally are: Is there any truth in this belief? If so, how does it operate? It is, of course, impossible to give any precise and indisputable answer to either, but in response to the first it may fairly be stated that a practice which has had currency for so many thousands of years and is yet here and there receiving some serious consideration, should in all likelihood have some basis in fact, even if not exactly as is commonly supposed. That is to say if somehow, in some manner, it had not produced or given rise to some effect or reaction, the practice would in all reason have been abandoned centuries ago. And when it comes to the question of the implementation of Shunammitism, fact, fancy, and bald guesswork vie with each other on about an equal footing. Superstition and desperate hope are often powerful factors in its success and serve to enhance any real effect that might be obtained — these are the psychological elements that are present in any therapeutic measure employed upon a conscious patient.

Here the ordinary erotic stimuli of the situation—the sight of a beautiful young female, propinquity to and contact with a firm, vigorous body of the opposite sex, the exciting awareness of virginity —are by no means to be ignored— even in an old man—and have on many occasions been known to implant delusions of youth in old persons. But in all probability the most potent single factor is the patient's continued exposure to the *odor foemina* of the girl, the scent naturally present in any healthy, normal female and consisting of a complex of odors: that of the hair and scalp, the armpits, the breath, the genitals, and the skin, plus some minor contributors. The power and importance of the sense of smell in sexual stimulation and selection is too well authenticated to be susceptible of question (just note how a dog leads with his nose when courting a bitch).

The young woman's natural body odor is probably the most vital medication the Shunammite brings to her task. And finally, who knows but that the bodies of healthy young virgins *may* actually give off some as yet unrecognized emanation that exerts a revivifying and rejuvenating effect upon a feeble man who is exposed to it?

Shunammitism has had a long and curious history intriguing to scholar, antiquarian, folk-lorist, and sexologist alike, but here we can touch upon only a few of its most interesting and outstanding facets.

One of the most remarkable incidents connected with Shunam-mitism occurred more than five centuries ago when a certain Gommarus, an antiquarian from Bologna, accidentally stumbled across a marble votive tablet bearing the following inscription:

ÆSCULAPIO. ET. SANITATI.
L. Clodius Hermippus.
Qui. Vivit. Annos. CXV. Dies V.
Puellarum. Anhilitu.
Quod. Etiam. Post. Mortem.
Eius.
Non Parum. Mirantur. Physici.
Jam. Posteri. Sic. Vitam. Ducite.

Which may be translated as:

To Æsculapius and Sanitas, this tablet is erected by L. Clodius Hermippus, who lived 115 years and 5 days with the aid of exhalations of young girls; which circumstance causes physicians no little wonder even after his death. You, descendants, lead your life in the same way.

This tablet has given rise to an alternate adjective for Shunam-mitism, namely *Hermippian,* drawn from the name of the man for whom the stone testifies Shunam-mitism had done so much. It also furnishes title and subject matter for the only full-length scholarly (or at least pseudo-scholarly) volume on the subject: *Der wiederlebende Hermippus* (The Reborn Hermippus) [this is only the opening of the tremendous full title which runs a long paragraph], which appeared in 1783 and was written by a German doctor, Johann Heinrich Cohausen. The book is really a satire on Shunam-mitism, but so finely is the satire veiled that there have been some who took the work seriously. The fact that Cohausen himself did not place too much stock in the whole matter is evidenced by his pointing out that the Hermippian tablet was not erected by Hermippus himself, but by others in his memory after his death, which gave him cause to suspect that the whole thing might have been an ancient hoax.

Cohausen's book is, in the main, a clever and most amusing account of this legendary Hermippus and his life among his Shunammites. According to him, Hermippus went even farther than King David in the matter of their youth and surrounded himself with girl children, still very small and yet with breasts undeveloped, who had not yet outgrown their dolls. This permitted him to dally quite innocently and chastely in the beneficial presence of young virgin bodies for, as the book puts it: "Playing with these girls will not arouse lust, induce gloom, interfere with sleep; nor will those melancholy thoughts be induced which generally follow and plague the spirit of an old man who loves." In order to safeguard the chasteness of this association Hermippus found it necessary periodically to change his company of tiny virgins as they began to emerge from childhood's estate, possibly about every five years or so. The elaborate details of Hermippus' daily life in the midst of his immature "harem" is interesting in the extreme, and it is a pity that Cohausen's book is not available in English.

There have been many practitioners of Shunammitism since the time of Hermippus, some of them by no means obscure men. Francis Bacon tells us that when Frederick Barbarossa grew old he made a practice of holding young boys close to his stomach and hips, and the Swabian historian Martin Crusius declares that when Emperor Rudolph of Hapsburg was taken with a fever he urged his nobles to bring their wives and daughters to him, whereupon he would kiss them, maintaining that he knew of no more excellent method of regaining health than when he drew to himself the sweet souls of virgins and the pleasant spirits of young girls. And in this connection there is often cited the well-known case of Thomas Parr who lived for over a century and a half (1483-1635) and had married many young women, to which fact Shunammite enthusiasts attribute his longevity. Possibly one of the most famous of the more recent addicts of Shunammitism is the French author and rake the Abbé Claude Henri Fusée de Voisenon (1708-1775) who, after a long and busy life of dissoluteness and indiscretion, settled down in his old age and took into his home a Miss Huchon whom he employed as a Shunammite and with whom he had no carnal commerce, much to the amazement of the French of the time.

In 18th century France Shunammitism grew almost to the proportions of a vogue and was utilized more often as a refinement of debauchery than as a *modus* for rejuvenation. There were even dealers who made a commercial enterprise of hiring out Shunammites to

474

old men, or presumably to any man who had the price. The most renowned of such merchants was a Madame H. Janus whose celebrity is due largely to the depiction of her activities by Rétif de la Bretonne in his book *Le Palais-Royal.*

Madame Janus had about forty girls in her service (drawn mainly from the rural portions of the country rather than from Paris, where she operated) and she conducted her business in a methodical, efficient, and strict manner. Her girls were kept in a remote and secluded establishment where they received special training, received a special nourishing diet, and had to take daily exercises to keep themselves in perfect health. Her manner of rendering service was also most businesslike and followed a set procedure. She would go along with the girl on her first visit to a new client and take care of certain preparations. She would give the old man an aromatic bath, massage and dry him thoroughly, fasten a close-fitting "bridle" to him—a sort of male chastity belt— [an example of the realistic caution so typical of the French] and then put him into bed between two Shunammites so that his skin would be in contact with theirs.

Madame Janus would attempt to persuade her customer that a single exposure was of little avail; that *what he needed was a course of treatments.* However, no girl could be utilized for more than eight nights consecutively—at the end of this period the first pair was replaced by another, the first then undergoing a recuperative period of two weeks to restore their forces. Mme. Janus held that a cure could not be expected without the application of at least three pairs of Shunammites. As her charge per night per girl was a *louis d'or* [a 20-franc piece, worth then between $4 and $5] it will be seen that the complete "cure" would cost the old man a tidy sum—something over $200. Shrewd Madame Janus took no chances of any sort. As her essential stock in trade was the virginity of her girls, she took every precaution to insure it. Not only was the patient solemnly warned that any attempt to test the extent to which he had regained his virility would do serious injury to his health, but he was also required to post a considerable deposit which he would forfeit if he caused either of the girls to become unchaste.

On the other hand, Madame Janus also had regulations for the protection of her clients. Since it was believed that a girl could not render effective Shunammite service for more than three years after the onset of puberty, and that any girl who was put to daily use would "burn out" in one year, she watched her girls' schedules and ages and dismissed them after they had outworn their usefulness. As it was also believed that a Shunammite team was more potent if one was a blonde and the other a brunette, the Madame took care that her little purveyors of youthfulness were properly matched when she rented them out.

Modern medical authorities would, of course, smile indulgently at anyone who inquired of them the value of Shunammitism, but some of the greatest scientific minds of previous centuries accorded it grave acceptance. The Italian Renaissance physician, Marsilius Ficinus, devoted considerable writing to the subject and concluded that if the soulless exhalations of plants and flowers can give us so much pleasure, how much more healing and vitalizing to an old man must be the odor arising from a vigorous, living young girl. Francis Bacon was of much the same viewpoint, which in his *Silva Silvarum* he put into these words: "The spirits of young people can, when they enter an older body, restore life to it, or at least keep it in good health for a long time thereafter. It has been observed that old men who spend much time in the company of youths live long, for their spirits emerge strengthened from such contacts. Thus the ancient rhetoricians and sophists were always to be found among youthful bearers, as witness Gorgias, Pythagoras and Isocrates, and grammarians like Orbilius, among others, who reached the century mark." According to Bacon's notion, the effectiveness of a Shunammite would be increased by rubbing her body with myrrh and other aromatic substances because this would increase the warmth arising from her body.

Nor must we be satisfied with mere abstract philosophical conclusions. The old 16th-century physicians Gapivaccio and Forestus have left us case histories of their practical experience and success (they say) with Shunammitism in curing feeble old men and prolonging

their life, as likewise was done by the Dutch physician Bœrhaave in the next century. But by the 18th century the more skeptical attitude of the objective scientist was beginning to creep in and Cohausen, despite his lengthy treatise on the subject, voices his doubt of the efficacy of the practice in these very lucid and logical terms: "A nubile (marriageable) virgin cannot serve to strengthen an old man by her nocturnal presence. She can, it is true, fan the extinguished flames of the old man, but this will more often consume than strengthen him. Gray and withered senility is not always free from the friction of passion. King David's virgin may have remained such in the royal bed, but in general, one cannot be too trustful in such matters. Oldsters often rebound."

So there we have it. After dozens of centuries of old men persuading themselves that sleeping with young virgins was giving them a real lift, modern science comes along and declares flatly there is nothing to it. To one thing, I feel certain, we will all agree: regardless of the effectiveness of Shunammitism, it must have been gratifying, if only in a purely psychological manner. Sometimes it appears that the progress science forces upon us leaves a suggestion of bitterness in its aftertaste, and it seems more than slightly likely that if we could look forward to an old age attended by a physician who held at least an open mind on the matter of Shunammitism, many of us would approach his dotage in a far more optimistic frame of mind.

SEXUAL VAMPIRISM

by Otto Burma

HUMAN vampirism is as old as man himself. Very often it is mistaken and misconstrued. Vampirism is rather rare, but when it comes to the attention of the public, it is always looked upon with horror—and rightly so.

To understand the mechanics and the background of this deviation, we should realize that practically all of our actions, instincts, and behaviorisms go back to our animal ancestors, from whom we have inherited most traits. Many of these traits have become erased in modern man, but once in a while they do crop up. We know them under the name of atavist (throwback). For instance, every once in a while a child is born with a tail. This is a physical throwback.

Vampirism is a form of psychical throwback, and for a better understanding of this rather unusual deviation, it behooves us to know all about it, so that when it crops up we may know how to deal with it. Modern medical science has achieved good results with psychiatric treatment in a number of vampirism cases.

DR. CRAVEN, assistant to the famous sexologist, Wilhelm Stekel, has reported the case of a beautiful woman who preferred aspirating of blood, particularly from the cavity of the collar bone, to normal sexual intercourse.[1] The patient, Mme. Z., fits the rôle of the vampire; she is snakelike, with black reptilian eyes and her movements are smooth and graceful. She describes herself as *"imprisoned in a black cave inhabited only by slimy creatures."* She is a professional dancer and singer, daughter of an Indian mother and a Portuguese - French father.

Her thoughts and daydreams mainly concern the subject of blood. She thinks and feels in terms of blood metaphors. To her, blood is the symbol of love, hate, anger, and passion. She likes to ingest blood by suction but she is afraid to do this lest she cause pain to others, so she contents herself with fantasy.

During intercourse she thinks she is going to die and lies motionless like a corpse. The penis seems to her like a dagger and the act as though she were being stabbed. Usually she likes being treated somewhat roughly before intercourse for this induces intense sexual excitement in her. Hers is an unusual case of what Havelock Ellis has called *sado-masochism* (the desire to hurt and be hurt during sexual relations).

Case Report by Krafft-Ebing

Dr. Krafft - Ebing reports the case of a married man who came to him covered with numerous scars on his arms.[2] The patient said that when he wished to have sexual relations with his wife he

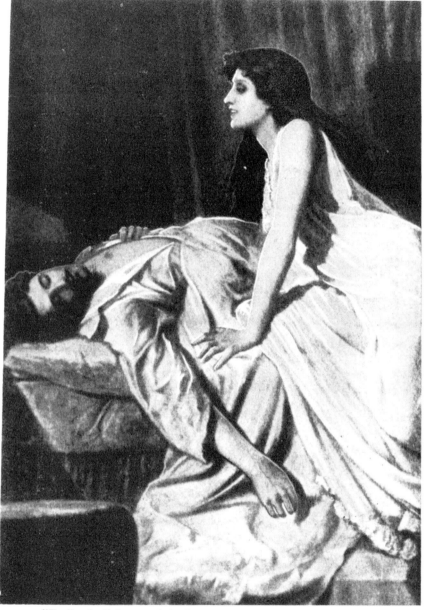

"The Vampire," famous painting by Sir Philip Burne-Jones, portrays in a striking manner the rather rare case where an individual derives sexual gratification by aspirating (extracting) the blood of her victim. Several well-known sexologists, Dr. Wilhelm Stekel and others, have recorded instances of human vampires who prefer to extract the blood of their partners instead of performing coitus in the usual manner. Some individuals satisfy their thirst for blood by merely watching a sanguinary fight between humans or animals.

had to make a cut in his arm. Then she would suck the wound and become strongly excited sexually.

Only a few months ago, a twenty-seven-year-old woman was arrested in the Philippine Islands on the charge of attacking several people, biting them and drawing their blood. The Mayor of the town said the girl had confessed her guilt of these crimes. She claimed to have acquired the habit of blood-imbibing from her husband, and now the urge comes on her at regular intervals and is irresistible. She acted like a mad woman when first taken to prison, screaming and begging for human blood. Finally a guard took pity on her and after pricking his arm allowed her to draw blood from the wound. After satisfying her urge she became normal. Psychiatrists are studying her in order to determine the psychological factors behind her abnormal craving for blood.

A Lesbian Vampire

Doctors London and Caprio describe the case of a lesbian (woman whose sexual love is for another woman) who discovered that she became sexually excited by biting her girl-friend on the neck and shoulders.[3] She liked to bite and aspirate the skin until it became red. On one occasion her girl friend cut herself while opening a can of vegetables. She went over and extracted the blood from the bleeding finger, telling her friend that saliva was an antiseptic and would heal the wound. She admitted that she felt a strong sexual sensation as she tasted the blood of her "lover."

A young married woman of good position related her vampiristic desires to Havelock Ellis.[4] She described the intense excitement she derived from watching dog-fights. If much blood was shed during the fight her excitement would become so great that she would have a climax. Clean cuts and wounds greatly attract her and she has frequently cut or scratched herself in order to see the blood and derives satisfaction by aspirating the wound. If while she is doing this she imagines that it is some attractive man's blood that she is imbibing she immediately has a climax. She likes to think that the man wished to rape her and that she fought him in order that he more greatly value her sexual favors.

During sexual intercourse she has frequently bitten her husband until the blood came and then aspirated the bite. She becomes frenzied with excitement during intercourse and is insensible to everything except the satisfaction derived from her vampiristic habit.

In 1867 James Brown, a Portuguese sailor, who had shipped out of Boston on a trawler bound for the Labrador fishing grounds, was seen bending over the dead body of one of the other crew members. Brown had absorbed the blood from the man's body. The corpse of another seaman was found near by, every ounce of its blood extracted. Sailor Brown was sent to prison where he murdered two other men in similar fashion, whereupon he was committed to the National Asylum in Washington. There he died twenty-five years later.

One of the most gruesome murderers in British history was John George Haigh who was sentenced to death only a few years ago. He killed and ingested the blood of nine persons, one of whom was a 69-year-old widow. In 1929 Peter Kurten murdered nine persons in Dusseldorf, Germany, all but one being female. At his trial he made no defense and described himself as a *vampire*. In 1910 the bloodless corpse of a child was found near the town of Galazanna, Portugal. A man named Salvarrey was arrested and confessed that he was a vampire.

Sexual Motive of Vampire

In all these cases one suspects the *sexual* motives of the criminal. Their cruel sadistic lusts could not be content with fantasy and eventually they broke through the bounds of restraint and were responsible for the horrible and gruesome crime, *vampirism*.

The most notorious of all sexual vampires was Countess Elizabeth Bathory who was placed in solitary confinement in her own château for her crimes. She lived during the sixteenth century in Hungary and is believed to have murdered as many as three hundred women. She was a lesbian who began by aspirating blood and later went so far as to bathe in it.

An otherwise normal girl who possessed an uncontrollable craving for blood is reported by William Seabrook.[5] Seabrook met this girl at a party where he noticed that she became pale when one

of the members of the party cut himself and bled. Later while swimming with her, Seabrook cut himself and she suddenly leaned over him and began to draw blood from the wound. She confessed to Seabrook that on two previous occasions she had a similar experience with girl room-mates, hating herself for it afterwards. Superstition-ridden, the girl believed she was a victim of a bloodsucking ghost who had passed this curse on to her. Seabrook wisely advised her to see a psychiatrist, which she did. She was eventually cured of this abnormal craving.

Biting, scratching, squeezing, and aspirating the skin during the sexual act are semi-sadistic phenomena which are so universal that they cannot be called abnormal, *unless they result in real injury.* For most persons these actions are merely *by-products* of normal courtship.

With some persons, however, especially women, these actions are consciously associated with the desire, even if more or less restrained, to draw blood. Clearly this deviation occurs only in abnormal persons.

It is only when the shedding of blood becomes a *goal in itself* and is preferred to other types of sexual release that it becomes a definite and dangerous abnormality.

References

1—Sexual Anomalies. By Magnus Hirschfeld. Emerson Books, Inc.
2—Psychopathia Sexualis. By Richard von Krafft-Ebing. Pioneer Publications, Inc.
3—Sexual Deviations. By Louis S. London and Frank S. Caprio. The Linacre Press, Inc.
4—Studies in the Psychology of Sex. By Havelock Ellis. Random House.
5—Witchcraft: Its Power in the World Today. By William Seabrook. Harcourt, Brace and Co.